COMMUNICATING INTERPERSONAL CONFLICT IN CLOSE RELATIONSHIPS

Communicating Interpersonal Conflict in Close Relationships: Contexts, Challenges, and Opportunities provides a state-of-the-art review of research on conflict in close personal relationships. This volume brings together both seasoned and new voices in communication research to address the challenges in evaluating conflict. Contributors review the current state of research on themes related to power, serial arguments, interpersonal and family dynamics, physiological processes, and mechanisms of forgiveness by presenting theoretical reviews, original unpublished data-driven research, and discussions about the methodological challenges and opportunities in studying interpersonal conflict.

An essential resource for graduate students and faculty interested in interpersonal conflict in close relationships between romantic partners, families, or friends, this volume is intended for advanced coursework and individual study in communication, social psychology, and close relationship scholarship.

Jennifer A. Samp is Professor of Communication Studies at the University of Georgia, USA.

COMMUNICATING INTERPERSONAL CONFLICT IN CLOSE RELATIONSHIPS

Contexts, Challenges, and Opportunities

Edited by Jennifer A. Samp

NEW YORK AND LONDON

First published 2017
by Routledge
711 Third Avenue, New York, NY 10017

and by Routledge
2 Park Square, Milton Park, Abingdon, Oxon, OX14 4RN

Routledge is an imprint of the Taylor & Francis Group, an informa business

© 2017 Taylor & Francis

The right of Jennifer A. Samp to be identified as author of this work has been asserted by him/her in accordance with sections 77 and 78 of the Copyright, Designs and Patents Act 1988.

All rights reserved. No part of this book may be reprinted or reproduced or utilised in any form or by any electronic, mechanical, or other means, now known or hereafter invented, including photocopying and recording, or in any information storage or retrieval system, without permission in writing from the publishers.

Trademark notice: Product or corporate names may be trademarks or registered trademarks, and are used only for identification and explanation without intent to infringe.

British Library Cataloguing in Publication Data
A catalogue record for this book is available from the British Library

Library of Congress Cataloging in Publication Data
Names: Samp, Jennifer A., editor.
Title: Communicating interpersonal conflict in close relationships : contexts, challenges, and opportunities / edited by Jennifer A. Samp.
Description: New York, NY : Routledge, 2016.
Identifiers: LCCN 2015049236 (print) | LCCN 2016005762 (ebook) | ISBN 9781138774896 (hardback) | ISBN 9781138774902 (pbk.) | ISBN 9781315774237 (ebook)
Subjects: LCSH: Interpersonal conflict. | Interpersonal relations. | Interpersonal communication.
Classification: LCC BF637.I48 .C626 2016 (print) | LCC BF637.I48 (ebook) | DDC 158.2--dc23

ISBN: 978-1-138-77489-6 (hbk)
ISBN: 978-1-138-77490-2 (pbk)
ISBN: 978-1-315-77423-7 (ebk)

Typeset in Bembo
by Integra Software Service Pvt. Ltd.

Printed and bound in the United States of America by Publishers Graphics, LLC on sustainably sourced paper.

CONTENTS

Editor Biography   viii
Contributors   ix

Introduction   1
Jennifer A. Samp

SECTION 1
Influences on Conflict Processes in Close Relationships   9

1. Cognitive and Physiological Systems Linking Childhood Exposure to Family Verbal Aggression and Reactions to Conflict in Adulthood   11
   Lindsey Susan Aloia and Denise Haunani Solomon

2. There Is Nothing As Calming As a Good Theory: How a Soulmate Theory Helps Individuals Experience Less Demand/Withdraw and Stress   28
   Rachel M. Reznik, Michael E. Roloff, and Courtney Waite Miller

3. Conflicts with Heterosexual Partners about Sexual Discrepancies: Conflict Avoidance, De-escalation Strategies, Facilitators to Conversation   40
   Moon Sook Son, Lynne M. Webb, and Patricia Amason

4. The Connections between Communication Technologies and Relational Conflict: A Multiple Goals and Communication Interdependence Perspective   57
   John P. Caughlin, Erin D. Basinger, and Liesel L. Sharabi

SECTION 2
Power and Conflict in Close Relationships   73

5 Power in Close Relationships: A Dyadic Power Theory
   Perspective   75
   Norah E. Dunbar, Brianna L. Lane, and Gordon Abra

6 Complaint Expression in Close Relationships: A Dependence
   Power Perspective   93
   Timothy R. Worley

SECTION 3
Conflict as an Ongoing Process   109

7 Serial Arguments in Interpersonal Relationships: Relational
   Dynamics and Interdependence   111
   Amy Janan Johnson and Ioana A. Cionea

8 Romantic Serial Argument Perceived Resolvability, Goals,
   Rumination, and Conflict Strategy Usage: A Preliminary
   Longitudinal Study   128
   *Jennifer L. Bevan, Megan B. Cummings, Makenna L. Engert, and
   Lisa Sparks*

9 Worth Fighting For: The Correlates, Context, and
   Consequences of Avoiding Versus Enacting Domestic Labor
   Conflict   144
   Kendra Knight and Jess K. Alberts

SECTION 4
Conflict in Families   163

10 Demand and Withdraw Behavior and Emotion in
   Mother–Adolescent Conflict   165
   *Christin E. Huggins, Melissa Sturge-Apple, and
   Patrick T. Davies*

11 The Role of Perception in Interparental Conflict   185
   *Tamara D. Afifi, Shardé Davis, Anne F. Merrill, and
   Samantha Coveleski*

12 Family Conflict is Detrimental to Physical and Mental Health 207
   Chris Segrin and Jeanne Flora

SECTION 5
Forgiveness as Part of Interpersonal Conflict　　225

13　Forgiveness Following Conflict: What It Is, Why It Happens, and How It's Done　　227
Andy J. Merolla

14　Expressing and Suppressing Conditional Forgiveness in Serious Romantic Relationships　　250
Dayna N. Kloeber and Vincent R. Waldron

Index　　*267*

EDITOR BIOGRAPHY

Jennifer A. Samp, Ph.D., is Professor in the Department of Communication Studies at the University of Georgia. Using survey, real-time, and laboratory-based observational methods, her work illuminates how and why individuals do not always respond the same way when managing relational problems and conflicts with close friends, romantic partners and family members. She is a Fellow of the University of Georgia Owens Institute for Behavioral Research, a Faculty Affiliate of the University of Georgia Center for Risk Communication, and a Faculty Affiliate of the Emory University Center for Injury Control. Her research has been supported by grants from the National Institutes of Health, UGA Research Foundation, UGA Owens Institute for Behavioral Research, and the Arthur W. Page Center.

CONTRIBUTORS

Gordon Abra, Ph.D., is a Lecturer in Sociology and Communication at the University of California Santa Barbara. He has co-authored articles on social power, and is currently looking at the way in which power is distributed in dyads as well as the effects of power distribution across different relational domains. He teaches courses in the sociology of crime and law, social psychology, and social scientific research methods.

Tamara D. Afifi, Ph.D., is a Professor in the Department of Communication Studies at the University of California, Santa Barbara. Her research focuses on communication patterns that foster risk and resiliency in families and other interpersonal relationships, with particular emphasis on, first, information regulation (privacy, secrets, disclosures, avoidance, stress contagion); and, second, on how people communicate when they are stressed and how these communication patterns harm and/or help personal and relational health. Her research examines how environmental factors (e.g., divorce, refugee camps, natural disasters, balancing work and family, chronic illness, obesity, daily stress, the Great Recession) interact with family members' communication patterns (e.g., conflict, stressful disclosures, social support, avoidance, verbal rumination, communal coping) to affect stress, adaptation, growth, and physical/mental/relational health. Professor Afifi has received numerous research awards, including the Young Scholar Award from the International Communication Association in 2006 and the Brommel Award for a distinguished career of research in family communication from the National Communication Association in 2011. She is also editor elect of *Communication Monographs*.

Jess K. Alberts, Ph.D., is President's Professor and Director of the Conflict Transformation Project for the Hugh Downs School of Human Communication at Arizona State University (Tempe). Her research interests focus on conflict in personal and professional relationships. Her current work examines marital conflict and the division of domestic labor, married couples' conflict and daily interaction, workplace bullying, community mediation and work/life balance.

Lindsey Susan Aloia, Ph.D., is an Assistant Professor of Communication at the University of Arkansas. Her research focuses on illuminating the causes and consequences of verbal aggression in interpersonal associations. Specifically, Lindsey aims to understand how qualities of interpersonal interactions and the interactants influence the use of and reactions to verbally aggressive experiences. Her work considers psychological and physiological reactions to verbal aggression, to elucidate the personal, relational, and health implications of aggressive communication.

Patricia Amason, Ph.D., is Associate Professor and Associate Chair in the Department of Communication at the University of Arkansas-Fayetteville. Her current research focuses on the role communication plays in excellent healthcare delivery. Professor Amason's research has been published in *Communication Yearbook 10*, *Communication Studies*, *Journal of Applied Communication Research*, *Health Communication*, and the *Journal of Thought*.

Erin D. Basinger, M.A., is a doctoral student in the Department of Communication at the University of Illinois, Urbana-Champaign. She studies interpersonal and family communication, focusing specifically on how people cope with stressors alongside their family members and other relational partners.

Jennifer L. Bevan, Ph.D., is Professor and Director of the Health and Strategic Communication M.S. program in the School of Communication at Chapman University in Orange, California. Dr. Bevan's publications include approximately 45 peer-reviewed scholarly articles and book chapters. She was recognized by a November 2009 article in Communication Research Reports as one of the most prolific scholars in the field of communication studies and has won the Interpersonal Communication Division Dissertation Award from the International Communication Association and the Communication and Social Cognition Division Book Award and Gerald R. Miller Outstanding Interpersonal Communication Division Book Award from the National Communication Association.

John P. Caughlin, Ph.D., is Acting Head and Professor of Communication at the University of Illinois at Urbana-Champaign. His research focuses on effective interpersonal communication in relationship, family, and health contexts. His awards include the Brommel Award for contributions to family communication, the Miller Early Career Achievement Award, and the Arnold Beckman Research Award.

Ioana A. Cionea, Ph.D., is an Assistant Professor in the Department of Communication at the University of Oklahoma. Her research brings together elements of interpersonal communication and intercultural communication with a specific emphasis on the way in which people from different cultures argue and the effects of such behaviors on their interpersonal relationships. Her research has been presented at various national and international conferences and published in venues such as the *International Journal of Intercultural Relations, Journal of Argumentation in Context*, and *Communication Yearbook*.

Samantha Coveleski, M.A., is a graduate student at the University of California, Santa Barbara where she is currently working on her dissertation regarding social support and chronic pain. Her research focuses on interpersonal coping and support processes in health contexts—specifically, the challenge of persistent, permanent stressors. Samantha received her M.A. in Communication from Ohio State University where her thesis extended support message construction to include the reframing of responsibility.

Megan B. Cummings, B.A., received her Bachelor of Arts in Communication Studies from Chapman University in May 2014. She intends to study health and interpersonal communication at the postgraduate level with the hopes of continuing her research and becoming a professor in the field of Communication Studies. She currently resides in Thousand Oaks, California, where she works as a marketing assistant.

Patrick T. Davies, Ph.D., is a Professor of Developmental Psychology at the University of Rochester. His research interests include marital conflict, family discord, parental adjustment, child emotion regulation and coping with family stress, child psychosocial maladjustment, and competence.

Shardé Davis, M.A., Ph.D., is Assistant Professor at the University of Connecticut. She is an alumna of the University of California, Santa Barbara where she earned a B.A. in Communication and Feminist Studies in 2010 and a M.A. in Communication in 2012. Her interdisciplinary research program uses theories and approaches from Communication, Feminist Studies and Ethnic Studies to investigate how ethnicity and gender shape relational dynamics and communication processes. Her research focuses on the social support process among Black and White women friend circles to examine the ways in which Black American women uniquely provide support that bolsters their strong Black womanhood.

Norah E. Dunbar, Ph.D., is a Professor of Communication at the University of California, Santa Barbara. Her expertise is in nonverbal and interpersonal communication, with special emphasis on dominance and power relationships, interpersonal synchrony, and interpersonal deception. She has published over 35 journal articles and book chapters including those in *Journal of Computer-Mediated Communication, Journal of Nonverbal Behavior,* and *Communication Research.* She has been awarded over U.S. $6 million in external grants and contracts from sources such as the Intelligence Advanced Research Projects Activity, the National Science Foundation, the Central Intelligence Agency, and the Center for Identification Technology Research.

Makenna L. Engert, B.A., is a recent graduate from Chapman University, earning a Bachelor of Arts in Communication Studies with departmental honors, and a minor in Public Relations.

Jeanne Flora, Ph.D., is Associate Professor of Communication Studies at New Mexico State University. Her research and teaching interests include interpersonal and family relationships, with a focus on relationship development and maintenance. Her research can be found in journals such as *Journal of Social and Personal Relationships, Journal of Family Psychology, Journal of Family Communication,* and *Human Communication Research.* She is co-author (with Chris Segrin) of the book *Family Communication,* which examines cutting-edge research as well as classic theories in family interaction.

Christin E. Huggins, Ph.D., is a Lecturer at the University of Georgia where her research focuses on how individuals strategically manage problematic discussions with close others. Her work on romantic dating relationships has examined how one's communicative goals for a conflict interaction motivate nonverbal expression of emotions, both positive and negative. Huggins has examined how parents communicatively manage conflicts across the marital and parent–child subsystems of the family, demonstrating that conflict strategies and emotions expressed toward one's romantic partner in a marital conflict can be transferred to conflict interactions with one's adolescent child. Her work has been published in *Communication Studies, Health Communication,* and *Human Communication Research.*

Amy Janan Johnson, Ph.D., is a Professor in the Department of Communication at the University of Oklahoma. Under the broad umbrella of interpersonal and relational communication, Dr. Johnson's research examines interpersonal argument and conflict, communication in long-distance relationships and friendships, and communication in stepfamilies. Her research has been published in such venues as *Communication Monographs, Communication Yearbook, Journal of Social and Personal Relationships,* and *Argumentation and Advocacy.*

Dayna N. Kloeber, M.A., teaches conflict and negotiation and storytelling as a Communication Studies Faculty Associate at Arizona State University. Most of her work has investigated the use of conditional forgiveness in serious romantic relationships. She also has numerous other publications in both the family communication context and forgiveness in workplace relationships. With ASU and *Family Communication Consortium* colleagues Vince Waldron and Doug Kelley, she is also currently engaged in *The Forgiveness Tree Project*, a new ASU initiative aimed at conductive community forgiveness education.

Kendra Knight, Ph.D., is an Assistant Professor in the College of Communication at DePaul University (Chicago, Illinois). Her primary research specializations include interpersonal communication in the management of the work/life interface (e.g., division of domestic labor), and relational communication in non-committed sexual relationships (e.g., hookups, friends with benefits).

Brianna L. Lane, Ph.D., is an Assistant Professor in the Department of Communication at Christopher Newport University. Her research focuses on relational maintenance within mediated contexts, specifically how evaluations and impressions of individuals' online identity claims are formed.

Andy J. Merolla, Ph.D., is an Assistant Professor in the Department of Communication at the University of California, Santa Barbara. He researches how communication processes shape interpersonal relationships, including the topics of relationship maintenance, conflict management, and forgiveness.

Anne F. Merrill, Ph.D., works for Citrix Corporation in Goleta, California. Anne received her Ph.D. (2014) and M.A. (2011) from the Department of Communication at the University of California, Santa Barbara. Her research focuses on processes such as information regulation (i.e., topic avoidance, disclosure, secrecy, and privacy), conflict, uncertainty, stress, and coping within close relationships, such as romantic relationships and families.

Courtney Waite Miller, Ph.D., is a Professor of Communication Studies at Elmhurst College. Her research interest is interpersonal conflict, specifically conflicts that are difficult to resolve. She has published in journals such as *Communication Yearbook*, *International Journal of Conflict Management*, and the *Western Journal of Communication*.

Rachel M. Reznik, Ph.D., is Professor of Communication Studies at Elmhurst College. She researches interpersonal processes with an emphasis on how ongoing relational conflict affects well-being. Her work has been published in *Human Communication Research*, the *Journal of Social and Personal Relationships*, *Argumentation and Advocacy*, *Communication Studies*, *Communication Reports*, the *Review of Communication*, and the *Western Journal of Communication*.

Michael E. Roloff, Ph.D., is Professor at Northwestern University. He is past chair of the Interpersonal Communication Division of the National Communication

Association. He is a Fellow of the International Communication Association and a Distinguished Scholar of the National Communication Association. His research is broadly focused on interpersonal influence with a specific emphasis on conflict management and negotiation.

Chris Segrin, Ph.D., is Steve and Nancy Lynn Professor of Communication and Head of the Department of Communication at the University of Arizona. His research focuses on family and other interpersonal relationships and their association with mental and physical health problems such as depression, anxiety, and quality of life during cancer diagnosis and treatment. This research can be found in journals such as *Human Communication Research, Communication Monographs, Journal of Abnormal Psychology*, and *Health Psychology*. He is the author of *Interpersonal Processes in Psychological Problems*, and is co-author (with Jeanne Flora) of the book *Family Communication*, which examines cutting-edge research as well as classic theories in family interaction.

Liesel L. Sharabi, M.A., is a Ph.D. student in the Department of Communication at the University of Illinois at Urbana-Champaign. Her research lies at the intersection of interpersonal and computer-mediated communication. She is especially interested in how communication technologies operate in romantic relationships.

Denise Haunani Solomon, Ph.D., is Liberal Arts Research Professor of Communication Arts and Sciences at Penn State University. Her research focuses on communication experiences in personal relationships, such as support and conflict, that promote or erode well-being. She and her colleagues have developed the Relational Turbulence Model to describe how transitions in relationships complicate emotions, cognitions, and communication. In particular, her work examines how transitions in romantic relationships promote relationship qualities that polarize reactions to both ordinary and extraordinary experiences.

Moon Sook Son, M.A., received her Master's degree from the University of Arkansas-Fayetteville.

Melissa Sturge-Apple, Ph.D., is Associate Professor of Developmental Psychology at the University of Rochester. Her research interests include parenting, inter-parental conflict, and children's socio-emotional adjustment; ethological and family systems theories; psychophysiology; quantitative methods.

Lisa Sparks, Ph.D., is Foster and Mary McGaw Endowed Professor in Behavioral Sciences at Chapman University in Orange, California, where she serves as Dean of the School of Communication with a Joint Faculty Appointment in the School of Pharmacy (CUSP). Dr. Sparks also serves as Full Member of the Chao

Family/NCI Designated Comprehensive Cancer Center at the University of California, Irvine in the School of Medicine, Division of Population Sciences, and Adjunct Professor in the Department of Population Health and Disease Prevention Program in Public Health. Dr. Sparks's published work spans more than 100 research articles and scholarly book chapters, and she is the author and editor of more than ten books in the areas of communication, health, and aging.

Vincent R. Waldron, Ph.D., is Professor of Communication Studies at Arizona State University. He serves as faculty coordinator of the *Family Communication Consortium*, a university-wide effort by faculty and students to strengthen families though research, teaching and service. He is the author of numerous articles and four books, including *Communicating Forgiveness* (Sage, 2008), *Marriage at Midlife* (Springer, 2009), both with Douglas Kelley, and *Communicating Emotion at Work* (Polity, 2012). He is currently co-editing a volume entitled *Good Relationships: Moral Communication across the Lifespan* (Peter Lang, forthcoming).

Lynne M. Webb, Ph.D., is Professor of Communication Arts, Florida International University. Her research examines interpersonal communication in a variety of forms, venues, and relationships, often from a feminist perspective. Dr. Webb has co-edited three scholarly readers and published over 80 essays, including multiple theories, research reports, methodological pieces, and pedagogical essays. Her work has appeared in numerous national and international journals including the *Journal of Family Communication, Journal of Applied Communication, Health Communication, Computers in Human Behavior*, and the *International Journal of Social Research and Methodology*, as well as in prestigious edited volumes including the *Handbook of Family Communication* (Sage, 2014) and *Advancing Research Methods with New Technologies* (IGI Global, 2013). Dr. Webb is a past president of the Southern States Communication Association and received a Presidential Citation for her Service to the National Communication Association.

Timothy R. Worley, Ph.D., is Assistant Professor in the Department of Organizational Communication at Murray State University. His research focuses on the ways in which partners in close relationships communicate about relational challenges, such as complaints, ongoing arguments, and jealousy. In particular, he examines the contribution of relational power and multiple goals to communication challenges in these contexts. His work has been featured on several top paper panels at national and regional conferences, and appears in journals such as *Communication Research, Communication Studies*, and *Western Journal of Communication*. Tim's teaching interests include interpersonal communication, conflict management, and social science research methods.

INTRODUCTION

Interpersonal conflict is an inherent but often dreaded part of close relationships. While everyone is familiar with conflict, how we perceive, manage, and communicate about conflict varies from person to person. Our current relationships are often sources of conflict. However, the ways in which we experience conflict are also influenced by our expectations, our personal histories, what we see in the media, and even by different cultures of conflict. Some of those cultures are shaped by religious, ethnic, regional, or national norms. Some of them are shaped by popular literature about conflict, such as those featured in "self-help" books and various online sites. From these sources, these experiences, and other factors, the thought of conflict conjures up an array of different feelings, some positive and some negative. For example, when asked to provide a metaphor for conflict, some focus on conflict as negative and problematic, likening it to "a war", "a battle," "unhealthy," "a struggle," "an explosion," "abusive," or a "circus" (McCorkle & Mills, 1992). Others view conflict as a positive environment for growth, creativity, and renewal; they describe conflict as "a dance," "a quilt," or "a tide" (Wilmot & Hocker, 2014).

I prefer to think of conflict as "a tide." Like a tide, conflict is "repetitive, powerful, and inescapable" (Wilmot & Hocker, 2014). Indeed, the ebb and flow of a tide shows reliable patterns. Experts can predict the timing of high and low tides with incredible accuracy. However, though we can observe patterns, the specific waves are nearly impossible to predict, and the waters will change from one moment to the next. Moreover, the timing and range of a tide in a given locale is influenced but not infallibly determined by the sun, the moon, and the shape of a coastline. Similarly, communication scholars can offer predictions and explanations about how, for instance, couples might argue. But their theories can be more or less precise and do better or worse at explaining or predicting particular conflicts. As I remind my students, one of the wonderful aspects of studying human behavior is that we are not always predictable. We do not always act in a consistent pattern, just like the waters in tides. And this is why sharpening our understanding of the perceptions, behaviors, and outcomes related to interpersonal conflict in close relationships is an important and ongoing discussion.

People have a growing appreciation of the significance of conflict in their lives and those of others. Lay literature reflects this interest. It is then no surprise that communication scholars echo this persistent interest in conflict (Roloff, 2014). Such scholars contribute to a growing literature that studies conflict in a variety of close relationship contexts such as romantic pairings and families. Even with this growing literature, much is still to be learned regarding how individuals talk about and navigate conflict with friends, partners, and family members. As well, we are just at the beginning of understanding how individuals transform conflict from a negative circumstance to one of forgiveness and relational growth. This anthology contributes to this growing literature. It will be a resource to scholars and students in the communication discipline. It features original essays by leading theorists who draw upon their research expertise to provide new and original contributions on interpersonal conflict processes between romantic partners, families, and/or friends. Some of the contributors are well established in the communication discipline; others are well on their way in establishing a solid research trajectory on conflict.

This volume focuses on the conflict dynamics of close relationships for a reason. Friend, dating, partnered, or married relationships are often marked by more commitment, emotional intensity, and investment than other relationships, such as acquaintances or co-workers. As readers will see in the various chapters, the nuances of close relationships generate differential impacts upon perceptions of, responses to, and the outcomes associated with conflict. The authors take either or both of two approaches in their essays. Some offer original discussions of a particular data set (a "spotlight study"); others draw on their recent research to highlight an important aspect of the conflict process. Of special note is how the authors reflect on the methodological challenges of studying conflict in close relationships. These recurrent themes lend the volume a unique appeal. While there is a growing number of book chapters and journal articles about conflict processes, the format of such research sometimes constrains authors from reflecting on some of the challenges and opportunities in studying their passion. Readers will also notice that many of the authors in this volume cite authors featured in other chapters. Such cross-citing and cross conversations are an important part of us better understanding communication and conflict processes as a scholarly community. And such cross-citing and acknowledgment shows what great academic citizens are featured in this volume, who are all working to continue scholarly conversations on conflict.

This book is divided into five sections. Although the chapters are divided into thematic sections, readers will find many overlaps in ideas, concepts, and measurements across the discussions and reported studies. For example, many of the chapters show a recurring theme that conflict is defined and informed by relational perceptions, interdependence, and histories. Another theme is that conflict often reoccurs and is cyclical in close relationships. And of course, all of the chapters provide more evidence for studying conflict from a communication perspective. Section 1, entitled "Influences on Conflict Processes in Close Relationships," focuses on some of the important physiological and psychological influences on interpersonal conflict. These chapters all highlight important influences on conflict processes. In Chapter 1, Lindsey Aloia and Denise Solomon highlight the communication of conflict via aggression. One of the important contributions of this chapter is how the authors study the influence of exposure to verbal aggression on responses to aggression later in life. Such findings are particularly relevant for persons such as those who experienced frequent and severe verbal aggression as a child: they were less responsive to conflict in adulthood. In Chapter 2, Rachel Reznik, Michael Roloff, and Courtney Miller highlight the impact of positive thoughts about relationships, specifically focused on the idea of "soul mates," and how such an implicit relationship theory may impact stress about a conflict. In particular, this chapter highlights how endorsing the idea of a "soul mate" is associated with less stress about a conflict by the initiator of the conflict. Moon Sook Son, Lynne Webb, and Trish Amason's focus in Chapter 3 is on how perceptions of sexual desires and activities may differ among couples, and how such differences may result in conflict. In particular, Son and colleagues' research suggests that even when people perceive that there may be a sexual conflict, they often avoid or downplay discussion. The results synthesized in this chapter highlight that interpersonal conflict research has important implications in better understanding health-related decisions. This section concludes with Chapter 4, where John Caughlin, Erin Basinger, and Liesel Sharabi present a study focused on the influence of technologically mediated communication on the experience of conflict. This is a timely chapter because as the authors note, the rise in smart phones and social media changes the sphere of understanding for how people manage their close relationships. In particular, their work flags the evolving opportunities relational partners face in achieving relational goals and strategically managing conflict in different environments.

Section 2, entitled "Power and Conflict in Close Relationships," highlights two different perspectives on how power affects conflict in close relationships. How power is defined within an individual's perceptions or between conversational partners and how such power-defined influences structure communication during conflict is a very important issue that demands more research in the communication discipline. In Chapter 5, Norah Dunbar, Brianna Lane, and Gordon Abra focus on the substantial research on Dyadic Power Theory. Largely focused on the relationship between individuals' perceptions of power relative to another and observed displays of dominance behaviors including gestures, facial expressions, and touch, this chapter highlights the compelling pattern that power and control attempts are curvilinear, yet asymmetrical. Equal power dyads demonstrate the most dominance, followed by those in high power positions and then low power positions. Chapter 6 focuses on a different power dynamic related to conflict in close relationships: dependence power. Dependence is based on an individual's judgment about his or her commitment and alternatives, such that individuals who are relatively uncommitted, have good alternatives to their current romantic relationship, and have partners who are highly committed, gain relational power over their more dependent partners (Cloven & Roloff, 1993). In his chapter, Timothy Worley extends prior research to examine how perceptions of dependence power from both individuals in a romantic dyad affect the likelihood of avoiding complaints about a relationship. Worley's research found differences in the impact of dependence power for males and females, such that the more powerful they perceived themselves to be, the more they voiced complaints, whereas the more powerful males perceived themselves to be, the *less* they voiced complaints to their partners.

Section 3, titled "Conflict as an Ongoing Process," focuses on some recent research on serial arguments. As the authors of the two chapters defining this section note, most conflict in close relationships is intractable. Therefore, conflicts on the same, or similar topic may occur repeatedly among friends, married couples, or families (Roloff & Johnson, 2002). The two chapters in this section focus on different dimensions related to serial arguments. In Chapter 7, Amy Johnson and Ioana Cionea focus on the importance of perceived interdependence of partners, as well as the role that individuals take in an interaction – for instance, if one person brings up the issue, or if both interactants bring up the topic. Importantly, the dynamic in which both partners introduce or acknowledge an issue is related to less stress about a conflict. In Chapter 8, Jennifer Bevan, Megan Cummings, Makenna Engert, and Lisa Sparks focus on the conflict styles utilized during serial conflicts and perceptions of resolvability. In examining reports of resolvability generally across a two-month period, more positive conflict strategies during a discussion about a serial argument were linked to perceived resolvability weeks later. Although not focused specifically on serial arguments, in Chapter 9, Kendra Knight and Jess Alberts tackle an instance of recurring conflict by focusing on how couples negotiate "domestic labor." Even something as mundane as taking out the garbage can become a flashpoint for conflict. While such domestic labor may seem trivial to outsiders, the tasks individuals perform in shared environments are often quite important to intimates. Here, Knight and Alberts focus on married couples and observe that individuals avoid conflict about household labor out of a belief that addressing the issue will not lead to a positive change. Interestingly, individuals reported that they would rather perform the household task than engage in discussion about it. These results are intriguing beyond the marital relationship; as many communication educators can attest, students frequently report that the number one source of conflict with their roommate(s) is about keeping the shared space clean.

Section 4, entitled "Conflict in Families," addresses conflict dynamics relevant to family contexts. This section showcases the important but arduous work involved in collecting conversational data from multiple family members. In Chapter 10, Christin Huggins, Melissa Sturge-Apple and Patrick Davies explore the display emotions and demand-withdraw during interactions between a mother and her adolescent child about a recent conflict. Extending the work of Caughlin and Malis (2004) on demand-withdraw processes, Huggins and colleagues' research highlights that a mother's withdraw behavior during conflict is associated with her adolescent child's report of negative emotions. As well, a mother's withdraw behavior when her adolescent is engaged in demand behavior was associated with the experience of negative emotions and her perception that the conflict was likely to be unresolved. Tamara Afifi, Shardé Davis, Anne Merrill, and Sam Coveleski's research reported in Chapter 11 provides an in-depth analysis of conversations between a child and parent about a stressful topic. Using a video-recall protocol of the discussions, Afifi and colleagues found that children often feel "caught" between their parents when discussing conflicts. Such a feeling about "who to side with" creates additional stress for a child dealing with parental conflict. Supporting Afifi's (2003) research on coping with difficult conversations in families, this chapter highlights that sometimes children believe the best option by which to manage their parents' conflicts is to avoid discussion of the issue. Of course, avoidance may serve many positive functions, including allowing a separation from discussing a stressful issue, or giving a person some time to think about how to manage the situation. Yet, as many of the chapters in this volume suggest, avoidance can also hinder conflict management and resolution. And an unresolved conflict can have implications for communicators' physical and mental health. Relatedly, Chapter 12 focuses on the implications of family conflict on physiology, psychology, and behaviors. Chris Segrin and Jeanne Flora point out that the experience of conflict within a marriage or a family is linked to chronic physiological arousal and sensitivity to stress, as well as greater irritability, aggression, anger, and depression, among both parents and children. Their chapter highlights the serious public health implications of not managing conflict in a manner that can promote greater self-understanding and relational growth.

Section 5 spotlights "Forgiveness as Part of Interpersonal Conflict." As conflict, aggression and violence can leave long-lasting scars and render people feeling forever helpless or wounded, an understanding of their processes, dynamics, and outcomes deserves increased attention by conflict researchers. Yet, forgiveness is an understudied area in the field of interpersonal conflict. These chapters help to conclude the volume on an optimistic note by highlighting the growth that can be achieved after experiencing interpersonal conflict. In Chapter 13, Andy Merolla argues that the process of forgiveness involves emotion, motivation, and interaction between victims and offenders of conflicts. In considering several of his studies on forgiveness, Merolla argues that forgiveness is in many respects an opportunity for communicators to negotiate the meaning of their experiences together. Merolla thus notes some of the reconciliatory and healing functions of communication. By focusing on forgiveness as a speech act, Merolla highlights that forgiveness is not a one-off process, but rather one that it is mutually determined through communication and a recognition of partners' past, present, and future behavior and responsibilities to one another. Dayna Kloeber and Vincent Waldron explore the notion of "conditional forgiveness" in Chapter 14. One of the fascinating outcomes of their research is the idea of explicit versus implicit conditional forgiveness and that explicit conditional forgiveness is more likely to result in reconciliation in the face of serious relationship problems. This chapter nicely highlights the importance of communication in relationship functioning and recovery.

This edited volume was inspired by my ever-growing interest to achieve a better understanding of the nuances of conflict in friendships, dating relationships, and marriage, as well as the many insightful questions and conversations that emerged during my undergraduate and graduate courses on close relationships and interpersonal conflict. I am truly honored that the scholars who contributed to each chapter are part of this volume. This collection would have never occurred without the support and enthusiasm of Linda Bathgate and Ross Wagenhofer at Taylor & Francis/Routledge. I am also grateful to Denise Solomon, Tina Harris, Jennifer Monahan, and Jerry Hale, who have always provided unwavering support and encouragement. And perhaps most importantly, there are three people who are my cheerleaders and primary sources of motivation. Andrew took a big gamble marrying someone who continually thinks about relational dynamics. Spencer and Marshall never fail to remind me about the importance of communication, negotiation, and humor. All three of you teach me something new every day. As conflict is a phenomenon that occurs in all of our lives, it is my hope that the excellent contributions in this volume inspire future dialogue, research, and a better understanding of how communication unfolds and is perceived before, during, and after conflict.

–Jennifer A. Samp

References

Afifi, T. D. (2003). "Feeling caught" in stepfamilies: Managing boundary turbulence through Appropriate communication privacy rules. *Journal of Social and Personal Relationships, 20*, 729–755, doi: 10.1177/0265407503206002.

Caughlin, J. P., & Malis, R. S. (2004). Demand/withdraw communication between parents and adolescents as a correlate of relational satisfaction. *Communication Reports, 17*, 59–71, doi: 10.1080/08934210409389376.

Cloven, D. H., & Roloff, M. E. (1993). The chilling effect of aggressive potential on the expression of complaints in intimate relationships. *Communication Monographs, 60*, 199–219. doi:10.1080/03637759309376309.

McCorkle, S., & Mills, J. L. (1992). Rowboat in a hurricane: Metaphors of interpersonal conflict management. *Communication Reports, 5(2)*, 57–66, doi: 10.1080/08934219209367547.

Roloff, M. E. (2014). Conflict and communication: A roadmap through the literature. In N. A. Burrell, M. Allen, B. M. Gayle, & R. W. Presiss (Eds.). *Managing interpersonal conflict: Advances through meta-analysis*, (pp42–58). New York: Routledge.

Roloff, M. E., & Johnson, K. L. (2002). Serial arguing over the relational life course: Antecedents and consequences. In A. L. Vangelisti, H. T. Reis, & M. A. Fitzpatrick (Eds.) Stability and change in relationships (pp107–128). New York: Cambridge University Press.

Wilmot, W., & Hocker, J. (2014). *Interpersonal conflict* (9th ed.). New York: McGraw-Hill.

SECTION 1
Influences on Conflict Processes in Close Relationships

1

COGNITIVE AND PHYSIOLOGICAL SYSTEMS LINKING CHILDHOOD EXPOSURE TO FAMILY VERBAL AGGRESSION AND REACTIONS TO CONFLICT IN ADULTHOOD

Lindsey Susan Aloia and Denise Haunani Solomon

Verbal aggression is defined as a communication behavior in which a person purposefully uses language to attack the self-concept of another person (Infante, 1987; Renfrew, 1997; Straus, 1979). Verbally aggressive communication is destructive and consequential for recipients of any age (Stemmler & Meinhardt, 1990); however, exposure to verbal aggression, including witnessing or receiving aggressive messages, is especially harmful during formative childhood years. For example, researchers have found that prolonged exposure to interparental conflict during childhood creates a predisposition toward psychological and marital difficulties in later life (Adam et al, 1982; Amato & Keith, 1991). In addition, adult impairments, such as a limited capacity for empathy, the inability to make accurate attributions for thoughts and feelings, and poor social judgment, appear to be adult symptoms of witnessing and/or receiving verbally aggressive messages during childhood (Ornduff et al, 2001). These findings suggest that efforts to understand the effects of childhood exposure to family verbal aggression can shed light on how people experience and manage conflict within adult romantic relationships.

Perhaps not surprisingly, theory and research linking experiences of verbal aggression in childhood to experiences in adulthood have focused primarily on factors that promote a tendency to communicate aggressively. For example, social learning theory proposes that children develop models of interpersonal relationships by learning from and imitating the behaviors of influential individuals (Bandura, 1977). In other words, children's exposure to family conflict provides them with scripts that specify when, why, and how to use verbal aggression within situations they may encounter as adults (Zimet & Jacob, 2001). Similarly, the argumentative skills deficiency model highlights how verbal aggression results when children fail to learn verbal skills that can diffuse negatively escalating interactions (Infante et al, 1989). This theory suggests that when children witness escalating exchanges characterized by aggressive communication, rather than reasoned argument, they learn inappropriate responses to disagreement that they use throughout their lives (Infante et al, 1990).

Whereas the link between childhood experiences and the tendency to enact verbal aggression is well established, theory and research explaining people's reactions to verbally aggressive communication is in a more formative stage. In a sense, social learning and skills deficit accounts for being aggressive can also explain people's reactions as targets of verbal aggression: scripts for conflict and a person's repertoire of communication skills inform the meanings that an individual attaches to aggression, the threats associated with verbal assault, and reactions to conflict. Whereas these perspectives highlight cognitions in the form of knowledge and skills, we see benefits in considering somewhat more automatic cognitive and physiological processes that are attuned to aggressive behavior. In this chapter, therefore, we turn our attention to cognitive and physiological processes through which childhood experiences influence people's responses in the face of a romantic partner's verbal aggression.

Our thinking highlights how experiences in early life calibrate adult reactions to the occurrence of aggression in interpersonal interactions. In general, we suggest that individuals who experienced frequent and severe verbal aggression during childhood have decreased responsivity to episodes of conflict in adulthood compared to people who do not report recurrent conflict exposure in childhood. Through the calibration of cognitive processes, people's childhood experiences of conflict influence how they attend to, make sense of, and respond to aggression in adulthood (Crick & Dodge, 1994). Through the calibration of physiological processes, people who were exposed to persistent aggression during formative years may exhibit attenuated arousal in response to conflict stimuli. In the sections that follow, we begin with an explication of verbal aggression. We then define desensitization and clarify how it encompasses the cognitive and physiological recalibration that occurs as a result of childhood exposure to family verbal aggression. Next, we report data from two studies that illustrate how childhood exposure to family conflict interfaces with cognitive and physiological systems to shape adults' reactions to verbal aggression from a romantic partner. We conclude this chapter by identifying directions for future research.

Explicating Verbal Aggression

Verbal aggression is defined as a communication behavior in which an individual explicitly uses language to attack the self-concept of another individual (Infante, 1987; Renfrew, 1997; Straus, 1979). As made clear by this definition, verbal aggression is considered a type of verbal communication. This is not to say that nonverbal behavior is irrelevant; rather, nonverbal aggressive behavior is considered to be an intensifier of the verbal behavior, which is the primary channel for conveying aggressive content. Nonverbal behavior, such as posture, touching, facial expression, eye contact, and vocal cues, can exacerbate the effects of the verbal communication. More specifically, expressive displays of emotion in the face or voice can intensify the meaning assigned to the symbols exchanged. Language is, however, at the core of verbal aggression because it encompasses the symbols that stimulate meaning.

Verbal aggression is also classified as a behavior. A behavior refers to an observable action of an individual in relation to a stimulus. The stimulus may be internal or external, conscious or subconscious, overt or covert, voluntary or involuntary. A behavior can be observed by others and, with an appropriate definition, two or more observers can agree as to whether the behavior did or did not occur. Behavior is, as such, classified as an objective piece of information. By restricting verbal aggression to an observable behavior, internal conditions such as aggressive feelings, attitudes, or thoughts are de-emphasized.

Verbal aggression is also considered to be directed. Directed behavior is oriented toward an end goal that is intended to be accomplished. Directed behavior can also be considered deliberate or intentional. For a person's behavior to be considered verbally aggressive, the behavior must be perceived as being carried out with the intention to inflict negative consequences on the targeted individual. This specification excludes behaviors that result in unintended harm or damage by accident, through negligence, or as a result of incompetence.

Lastly, this definition of verbal aggression stipulates that the individual directly attacks another individual's self-concept. In very broad terms, an individual's self-concept refers to the person's perception of himself or herself. These perceptions are formed through personal experience with the environment. In addition, people's self-concept is important and useful in explaining and predicting actions. Self-perception is thought to influence the way an individual behaves, and this behavior in turn influences the way the individual perceives himself or herself.

In sum, verbal aggression is defined as the use of the language symbol system in ways that are perceived to be aimed at negatively influencing an individual's self-concept. This definition is parsimonious, but it embraces the inherent complexity of the communication phenomena. In addition, this definition does not specify a particular victim or perpetrator. As a result, verbal aggression can be detrimental to the receiver in a variety of contexts. The following sections discuss desensitization to conflict due to childhood exposure to verbal aggression.

Desensitization to Conflict

Desensitization is defined as the attenuation or elimination of cognitive, emotional, physiological, and, ultimately, behavioral responses to a stimulus (Rule & Ferguson, 1986). Desensitization can be manipulated directly and purposefully. For example, desensitization is a technique used in behavioral therapy to decrease or eliminate certain emotional responses through exposure to anxiety-inducing stimuli (Wolpe, 1973). This process has documented effectiveness in changing children psychologically and behaviorally (Weersing & Weisz, 2002). In addition, desensitization has been described as an influential process in understanding the psychological impact of witnessing chronic violence. In particular, children who have experienced severe and chronic physical aggression have described violence as a way of life, and they report that they no longer feel overwhelmed or upset by violence (Guterman & Cameron, 1997).

Cognitive processes that link childhood experiences of verbal aggression to reactions to conflict in adulthood include the operation of more or less conscious schemas that attune people to the occurrence and meaning of aggressive interactions. Schemas are mental structures that frame an individual's perception of stimuli. Schemas define expected features of a phenomenon, which are developed over time from past experiences with similar phenomena. Schemas also prime attention and information processing in ways that exert a nonconscious effect on experiences with a phenomenon. Hence, schemas enable people to encode cues efficiently and accurately, and the heuristic rules that people cultivate influence the meanings that they derive from those cues. We suggest that witnessing or receiving sustained verbal aggression during formative years causes individuals to create biased mental frames about the experience of conflict, such that the conflict is perceived as typical or expected. In other words, schemas are recalibrated to normalize the experience of verbal aggression and, in turn, reactions to aggression are dampened.

Physiological aspects of desensitization are embodied by the body's stress response and the production of adrenal steroids and stress hormones that promote defense against stressful stimuli. Under normal, non-stressful conditions, the hypothalamic-pituitary-adrenal (HPA) axis, one of the body's primary stress response systems, produces the stress hormone cortisol in a diurnal pattern of activation, releasing the greatest concentration of cortisol during the morning, dramatically reducing the production during the afternoon, and slowly decreasing the production of cortisol during the evening. During times of stress, however, the HPA system is taxed to release additional cortisol to mobilize energy against the stimulus. In cases of regular and repeated exposure to family conflict, the demands on the HPA axis are sustained. Unfortunately, the HPA axis cannot operate effectively under constant stress. As a result, children who continue to tax the HPA axis due to high levels of family conflict are forced to recalibrate their stress response systems, such that the normal physiological responses to conflict cues are attenuated.

Two Spotlight Studies on Exposure to Aggression

Cognitive and physiological recalibrations, in the form of desensitization to conflict cues, are adaptive responses to frequent and severe experiences of childhood verbal aggression. In effect, the recalibration of cognitive and physiological processes spares individuals from the immediate distress of a conflict interaction by numbing their responses. Hence, desensitization should be manifest in both automatic aspects of cognitive and physiological functions and in people's subjective experience of conflict. To test this reasoning, we report data from two studies. The first study examines associations between childhood exposure to family aggression and evaluations of verbally aggressive acts in romantic relationships, and it features motivational systems as a cognitive process relevant to this association. The second study we report investigates the physiological stress response as both a manifestation of desensitization and a process that affects subjective experiences of conflict with a romantic partner.

Study 1: Childhood Exposure to Aggression and the Behavioral Inhibition System

Thus far, our description of cognitive processes that link childhood experiences of verbal aggression to reactions to conflict in adulthood has rested generally on the notion of schemas. In this study, we considered a more specific cognitive process likely to reflect desensitization. In particular, we suggest that exposure to family aggression in childhood may influence the extent to which children come to attend to and be influenced by the threat of punishment. In the paragraphs that follow, we define motivational systems and explain how they may contribute to an association between childhood exposure to aggression and adult experiences of conflict. We then report results from a study that tested our thinking.

Gray (1987) postulated two motivational systems that predict an individual's response to social cues in an environment: the behavioral inhibition system (BIS), which attends to signals of punishment and non-reward; and the behavioral activation system (BAS), which emphasizes cues of reward, non-punishment, and escape from punishment. Gray (1987) argued that the BIS controls the experience of anxiety in response to anxiety-relevant cues and inhibits behavior that may lead to negative or painful outcomes. Accordingly, measures of the BIS have been found to correlate highly with indicators of trait anxiety, negative reactivity, negative temperament, negative affect, harm avoidance, and reward dependence (Carver & White, 1994). In addition, individuals high in BIS sensitivity react with greater nervousness when punishment is anticipated. Gray and McNaughton (2000) established that over activity of the BIS results in anxious personality traits that predispose individuals to certain anxiety disorders. Conversely, Beauchaine et al (2001) found decreased activity in the BIS to be related to the development of conduct disorders.

Because BIS functioning attunes people to negative threats in the environment, it constitutes a cognitive system that may participate in desensitization to conflict as a function of childhood experiences. In particular, we offer three hypotheses, the first of which captures the general effect of desensitization that undergirds our perspective. We hypothesize that reported exposure to family verbal aggression in childhood is negatively associated with the perceived acceptability of verbal aggression in adult romantic relationships. Our second hypothesis reflects our expectation that BIS functioning is calibrated by childhood experiences; in particular, we suggest that heightened exposure to family verbal aggression in childhood dampens the sensitivity of the motivational system to conflict cues. Specifically, we posit that reported exposure to family verbal aggression in childhood is negatively associated with the strength of the BIS in adulthood. Finally, to test whether BIS functioning links childhood experiences to adults' assessments of verbal aggression, our third hypothesis advances a negative association between reported exposure to family verbal aggression in childhood and the perceived acceptability of verbal aggression in adult romantic relationships is mediated by the strength of the BIS in adulthood.

To test our hypotheses, we conducted new analyses of data from a study reported in a previous manuscript (Aloia & Solomon, 2013). In that study, 87 participants were recruited by students enrolled in a first-year seminar taught by the second author. Participants were emailed a URL that directed them to an online survey. Of particular relevance to this report, the survey collected responses to measures of a history of family verbal aggression (Straus et al, 1996), strength of motivation systems (Carver & White, 1994), and the perceived acceptability of verbal aggression in romantic relationships (Straus et al, 1996).

To measure exposure to family verbal aggression, we asked participants to indicate the frequency of behaviors identified in the Revised Conflict Tactics Scale (CTS2, Straus et al, 1996; 1 = *This has never happened*; 2 = *About once a year*; 3 = *About twice a year*; 4 = *3–5 times a year*; 5 = *6–10 times a year*; 6 = *11–20 times a year*; 7 = *20–50 times a year*; 8 = *More than once a week*) during the years corresponding with third, fourth, fifth, and sixth grade. We used the CTS2 because it offers concrete and validated instances of verbal aggression to anchor respondents' recollections, and we focused on middle childhood based on evidence that this period of life is both formative and available for retrospective reporting (Schwab-Stone et al, 1999). Descriptive statistics suggest that our measure of reported exposure to family verbal aggression during childhood was reliable ($M = 3.21$, $SD = 1.75$, $\alpha = .89$); however, the mean score for childhood family verbal aggression suggests that the participants experienced only low to moderate levels of aggression.

Our measure of BIS strength was drawn from Carver and White's (1994) widely used self-report instrument. Responses to items (e.g., "If I think something unpleasant is going to happen, I usually get pretty 'worked up'") are recorded on a 5-point scale (1 = Strongly disagree, 5 = Strongly agree), such that higher values correspond with a stronger BIS. In this sample, the mean score for the composite scale was 3.96 ($SD = 1.26$, $\alpha = .76$).

Finally, we assessed reactions to verbal aggression by asking participants to rate the perceived acceptability of behaviors included in the CTS2 when they occur in the context of a romantic relationship. Whereas the CTS2 typically asks respondents to record the frequency of past experiences, our hypotheses were focused on the extent to which people evaluated behaviors as normative or allowable within their romantic relationships. Thus, our measure focused on the subjective evaluations of the occurrence of these behaviors, rather than their incidence *per se*. In the scale we used, a score of 1 corresponded with the perception that the behavior was not appropriate and a score of 6 reflected acceptance for the behavior. Descriptive statistics suggest that participants found the acts of verbal aggression included in the CTS2 (e.g., "Insult or swear at a romantic partner") minimally acceptable ($M = 1.81$, $SD = 0.96$, $\alpha = .83$).

The central claim underlying our perspective, and embodied in H1, is that childhood experiences of family conflict are linked to perceptions of the acceptability of verbal aggression in adult romantic relationships. Consistent with the hypothesis, we observed a positive and significant correlation between these variables, $r = .47$, $p < .01$. H2 reflected the assumption that childhood experiences of family verbal aggression are associated with the calibration of cognitive systems. In line with our thinking, we observed that people who reported greater exposure to family verbal aggression during childhood had lower scores on the measure of BIS strength, $r = -.20$, $p < .05$.

The patterns in the data relevant to H1 and H2 were consistent with the mediating role ascribed to the BIS in our third hypothesis. To complete the test of mediation, we conducted a regression analysis to observe the partial correlation between reported exposure to family verbal aggression in childhood and the perceived acceptability of verbal aggression in adult romantic relationships when the BIS was co-varied. With the BIS in the regression model, the association between reported exposure to family verbal aggression in childhood and the perceived acceptability of verbal aggression in romantic relationships was not significant, $\beta = .09$, *ns*. Notably, the coefficient for the BIS was, $\beta = -.23$, $p < .001$. These results suggest that, relative to family history of aggression, BIS is the proximate predictor of perceived acceptability of verbal aggression in adult romantic relationships.

In total, the results of these analyses are largely consistent with our reasoning. Not only did we find that reported exposure to family verbal aggression was associated with the perceived acceptability of verbal aggression in adult romantic relationships, but our results point to the strength of the BIS as a cognitive mechanism contributing to this effect. In general, these results suggest that childhood exposure to family verbal aggression dampens the sensitivity of the BIS, and thereby attenuates reactions to conflicts that occur in adult relationships. We turn next to a study in which we explored physiological manifestations of desensitization to conflict.

Study 2: Childhood Exposure to Aggression and the Stress Response System

As detailed previously in this chapter, children's experience of stress caused by exposure to verbally aggressive messages within their family can undermine the development of a regulated stress response system. In particular, we argued that the continued strain on the HPA axis due to high levels of family conflict forces the system to adjust and recalibrate. As a result of this recalibration, the normal physiological responses to conflict cues are desensitized, and individuals experience verbal aggression as less adverse and normative.

Our reasoning leads us to three hypotheses that parallel the predictions tested in Study 1. The first hypothesis reflects our basic assumption that individuals who experience family verbal aggression in childhood evaluate conflict as less negative in adulthood. Specifically, we posit that reported exposure to family verbal aggression in childhood is negatively associated with the perceived negativity of conflicts in adulthood. Our second hypothesis highlights calibration of the physiological stress response system as a consequence of exposure to family verbal aggression in childhood and posits that reported exposure to family verbal aggression in childhood is negatively associated with physiological reactivity to conflict in adulthood as indexed by increases in cortisol production. Finally, we suggest that the physiological stress response provides a link between childhood exposure to verbal aggression and the subjective experience of adult conflicts. Accordingly, we hypothesize that the negative association between reported exposure to family verbal aggression in childhood and the perceived negativity of conflicts in adulthood is mediated by physiological reactivity to conflict in adulthood as indexed by increases in cortisol production.

To test these predictions, we used data from a dyadic interaction study conducted as part of the first author's doctoral dissertation (Aloia, 2013). In that study, 100 college students were recruited from a general education communication course to participate in the study in fulfillment of a course research participation requirement. All participants were asked to bring a current romantic partner with them to the study session, and partners were compensated $10 for participating in the study. Upon arriving to the lab, partners were separated and administered informed consent forms. Participants then provided a saliva sample using oral swabs; all samples were immediately frozen after collection. Next, participants were asked to identify and describe the three most stressful areas of conflict in their relationship. Finally, participants completed an online questionnaire which collected demographic information, activity and food consumption prior to arriving at the lab, and information about childhood experiences of conflict.

As in Study 1, we measured childhood exposure to family verbal aggression by asking participants to focus on experiences in middle childhood (corresponding with third through sixth grade). For this study, we augmented the Revised Conflict Tactics Scale by including items from the Verbal Aggressiveness Scale (Infante & Wigley, 1986) and the Aggression Questionnaire (Buss & Perry, 1992). In particular, we selected items from these scales that focused on the use of aggressive language, and we omitted items from the contributing scales that discussed physical assault, sexual coercion, or injury, as well as those describing pro-social and benevolent actions. We also privileged items that classified verbal aggression as a behavior, and we excluded items that described a communication trait or aggressive feelings, attitudes, or thoughts. This elaborated measure was intended to provide a more complete assessment of childhood experiences relative to the measure used in Study 1 ($M = 3.25$, $SD = 1.16$, $\alpha = .94$).

After completing the self-report measures, partners were reunited for an interaction. We instructed the dyad to discuss whichever area of conflict was the most distressing topic reported by either partner. The couple was left alone in the lab to discuss that issue of conflict for 10 minutes, at which point we re-entered the lab and separated the participants. Following their interaction, participants sat quietly for 15 minutes and then provided a second saliva sample. Participants relaxed for 5 additional minutes before we collected a third saliva sample. Next, participants completed a post-interaction questionnaire in which we included five items indexing evaluations of the interaction (e.g., "How aggressive was this conversation?" "How negative was this conversation?"). Responses were recorded on a 5-point scale (1 = Not at all, 5 = Very), and we aggregated scores to form a measure of perceived conflict negativity ($M = 2.61$, $SD = 1.08$, $\alpha = .89$). As a final step in the procedures, the couple was reunited and debriefed on their participation in the research study.

Our procedures generated three measures of cortisol: baseline, 15 minutes after the interaction, and 20 minutes after the interaction. Two calculations were computed to operationalize cortisol reactivity. The first measure of change was area under the curve with respect to increase (AUC_I). This measure assessed the overall intensity of cortisol change over time and measured sensitivity (Pruessner et al, 2003). The second measure of change was area under the curve with respect to the ground (AUC_G). This measure addressed whether changes in cortisol are a result of over time hormonal output.

Data from partners were linked by joint participation in the conflict interaction, so we used structural equation modeling techniques to evaluate an actor-partner-interdependence model that accounted for covariation in data from partners. We used participant sex as the grouping variable, which also allowed us to estimate separate coefficients for male and female partners. In the model, the paths that represented the partner influence were non-significant. Accordingly, the model was re-run with these paths removed. Figure 1.1 shows the model with all the paths encompassed by our three hypotheses; tests of H1 and H2 used models in which only the relevant independent and dependent variables were included.

Our first hypothesis articulated the assumption that a history of family verbal aggression is linked to evaluations of conflict in adulthood. Consistent with H1, we observed a significant and negative association between a history of family verbal aggression and the perceived negativity of the conflict interaction for male ($\beta = -.31$, $p < .01$) and female ($\beta = -.25$, $p < .05$) participants.

H2 predicted an association between childhood exposure to family verbal aggression and physiological reactivity to conflict in adulthood as indexed by our two measures of cortisol reactivity. In line with our thinking, we observed that

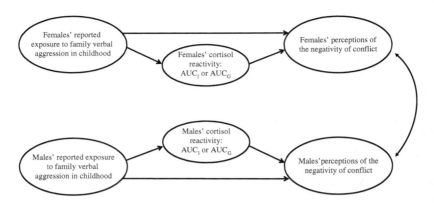

FIGURE 1.1 Family verbal aggression in childhood as a predictor of negativity of conflict mediated by physiological reactivity

females who were exposed to family verbal aggression during childhood were physiologically less reactive to experiences of conflict with romantic partners as measured by AUC_I, $\beta = -.27$, $p < .01$ and AUC_G, $\beta = -.28$, $p < .01$. Contrary to H2, the negative associations between childhood experiences of verbal aggression and cortisol reactivity were not significant for males, AUC_I: $\beta = -.13$, ns; AUC_G: $\beta = -.06$, ns.

Our final hypothesis addressed the extent to which cortisol reactivity mediates the association between childhood exposure to family verbal aggression and assessments of the negativity of the conflict interaction. Because H2 was not supported for males, our substantive test of mediation was limited to female participants; however, our use of an APIM model to account for dependence in the data required that we assess these patterns for both males and females. The model was first run with AUC_I as the mediating variable. The standardized path coefficients showed that reported exposure to family verbal aggression in childhood was significantly and negatively associated with AUC_I for females, $\beta = -.32$, $p < .001$, but not for males, $\beta = -.07$, ns. In addition, AUC_I was significantly and positively associated with perceived negativity of conflicts in adulthood for females, $\beta = .30$, $p < .01$, and males, $\beta = .27$, $p < .01$. Within this full model (see Figure 1.1), reported exposure to family verbal aggression in childhood was not significantly associated with perceived negativity of conflicts in adulthood for female participants, $\beta = -.12$, ns, but was significantly and negatively associated for male participants, $\beta = -.28$, $p < .001$.

The model was then rerun with AUC_G as the mediating variable. As was the case in the analysis of AUC_I and the test of H1, reported exposure to family verbal aggression in childhood was significantly and negatively associated with AUC_G for females, $\beta = -.27$, $p < .01$, but not for males, $\beta = -.14$, ns. AUC_G was significantly and positively associated with perceived negativity of conflicts in adulthood for females, $\beta = .29$, $p < .01$, and males, $\beta = .25$, $p < .01$. Once again, analysis of the full model (see Figure 1.1) showed that reported exposure to family verbal aggression in childhood was not significantly associated with perceived negativity of conflicts in adulthood for female participants, $\beta = -.08$, *ns*, but was significantly and negatively associated for male participants, $\beta = -.29$, $p < .001$.

In total, we found the predicted association between family history and perceptions of conflict negativity for both males and females, but the hypothesized role of physiological reactions was documented only among females. For male participants, childhood exposure to family verbal aggression and physiological stress responses both predicted perceptions of conflict negativity, but increases in cortisol did not mediate the effect of family history on perceptions of conflict. For females, the results were wholly consistent with our predictions: childhood exposure was negatively associated with perceptions of conflict negativity, and this association was mediated a dampened physiological response among women who were exposed to heightened family aggression in childhood.

Discussion

We opened this chapter by defining verbal aggression as communication behavior that attacks the recipient's self-concept and, in turn, may produce negative personal and relational consequences. Indeed, the research we reviewed suggests that childhood exposure to verbal aggression can have lasting effects on people's ability to form healthy and well-functioning relationships in adulthood (Adam et al, 1982; Amato & Keith, 1991; Ornduff et al, 2001). Whereas ample work has linked childhood experiences to the tendency to enact aggression, we focused instead on how formative experiences within the family might calibrate people's reactions to verbally aggressive messages. The results of the two studies we reported provide initial evidence that exposure to family verbal aggression affects cognitive and physiological systems in ways that leave people less sensitive to negative conflict behaviors. As we reflect on the implications of our findings, we offer three core theoretical questions and three methodological concerns to guide future research.

Learning or Recalibration?

The theoretical frameworks offered to explain why childhood experiences with aggression influence conflict management in adulthood typically highlight the ways in which people learn how to manage conflict. Social learning theory, for example, describes how significant individuals, such as parents, serve as models who illustrate how to handle conflict in close relationships (e.g., Zimet & Jacob, 2001). From experiences participating in or witnessing conflict, children are assumed to internalize norms for conflict behavior and to learn skills for navigating disagreements. When family conflicts are fraught with verbal aggression, children come to see aggression as a tool for addressing problems, and they fail to learn communication behaviors that can attenuate or de-escalate conflict (Infante et al,

1989). Thus, these perspectives emphasize the acquisition of knowledge about conflict as the bridge between childhood and adult experiences.

Our focus on the calibration of reactions to conflict emphasizes cognitive and physiological processes that are somewhat more fundamental in nature. In our view, people's norms for conflict or their repertoire of conflict skills are higher order cognitions, which no doubt shape perceptions and reactions within specific conflict episodes. But before these cognitions are salient, more automatic cognitive and physiological processes attune people to noxious stimuli in their environment. It is the impact of childhood experiences on the sensitivity of those instruments that is central to our perspective. Put simply, we suggest that excessive exposure to verbal aggression during formative years within the family environment blunts the sensitivity of the cognitive and physiological systems that monitor the environment for threats.

Notably, these two points of view are not incompatible. When the behavioral inhibition and physiological stress response systems alert a person to a threat, higher order cognitions can be utilized to direct resources, guide strategic behavior, and evaluate alternative responses. By focusing on how childhood experiences calibrate the sensitivity of these warning systems, we privilege the more automatic processes that determine whether a threat is perceived and, in turn, acted upon. We have positioned the BIS and the physiological stress response as processes that guide people's reactions to challenging social situations, and we see them as an alternative and complementary route by which childhood experiences shape adult responses to interpersonal conflicts.

It bears mentioning that our characterization of the behavioral inhibition system as a product of experiences in middle childhood runs counter to prevailing conceptions of motivational systems. In general, motivational systems are assumed to be enduring and consistent (Gray, 1987). Although behavioral inhibition and behavioral activation systems can be activated by cues in the environment that make threats or rewards salient (Yan & Dillard, 2010), the strength of people's BIS and BAS are typically characterized as dispositional and stable qualities (Gray, 1987). Our findings lead us to wonder if BIS and BAS are genetically based dispositions that are expressed to greater and lesser degrees depending on personal experiences and cues in the environment (cf. Cicchetti, 2007). Although speculative in the absence of more definitive data, the results of Study 1 suggest that experiences in middle childhood influence the strength of the behavioral inhibition system in adulthood.

Desensitization or Measurement Bias?

Our perspective is built upon studies of how children living amidst ongoing and extreme violence come to accept aggression as a way of life (Guterman & Cameron, 1997). We recognize, however, that the participants in our two studies probably did not have childhood experiences characterized by ongoing physical violence and the threats to safety that have been the focus of other work on desensitization (e.g., Garbarino, 1995). Indeed, our samples reported only modest to moderate levels of family verbal aggression during their middle childhood years. Is it appropriate, then, to call the patterns we observed "desensitization"?

The level of childhood exposure to family verbal aggression reported by our research participants, while low, was sufficient to produce effects consistent with our hypotheses. Specifically, Study 1 documented a positive association between reported family history of verbal aggression and evaluations of the appropriateness of verbally aggressive acts in adult romantic relationships. That study also showed the expected negative association between childhood exposure to aggression and the strength of the BIS. In Study 2, we observed a negative association between reported exposure to family verbal aggression and the perceived negativity of a conflict interaction. In addition, a history of family verbal aggression corresponded with an attenuated physiological stress reaction to the conflict episode for females in Study 2, but not for males. With the exception of the nonsignificant association between childhood exposure to verbal aggression and cortisol reactivity for males in Study 2, these patterns are consistent with desensitization processes.

Although the data are accommodating to our argument, our reliance on retrospective accounts of childhood exposure to family verbal aggression poses a nontrivial threat to internal validity. Because recollections may be influenced by the very phenomena we seek to measure (i.e., family history may bias perceptions of conflict in ways that distort reports of family history), we cannot definitively attribute our findings to desensitization. We sought to strengthen our measure by anchoring it with measures of verbal aggression that are widely used and validated. In addition, we focused participants on experiences during middle childhood, in light of evidence that this period of life can be described accurately. Interestingly, if a family history of verbal aggression blunts perceptions of conflict negativity, we might expect people who experienced heighten family aggression to underestimate, rather than overestimate, family verbal aggression, which in turn should have attenuated the associations we observed in our data. Nonetheless, we recognize that our ability to draw strong conclusions from cross-sectional, self-report data is compromised.

Action or Reaction?

In articulating the focus of our investigation, we clarified our intention to emphasize people's reactions to verbal aggression or conflict, rather than their tendency to behave aggressively. This agenda led us to examine cognitive and physiological processes that index the negativity of conflict. Within Study 1, we assessed the endorsement of verbally aggressive message strategies; within Study 2, we measured evaluations of the negativity of laboratory-staged conflict interactions. Our measure of cortisol reactivity in Study 2 comprises another index of reactions to the conflict episodes. Within these operationalizations, however, we cannot cleanly distinguish between effects that are reactions to a communication partner and effects that reflect reactions to conflict interactions in which our respondents are also participants.

Upon reflection, our efforts to parse reactions to conflict from verbally aggressive actions impose a false dichotomy on the phenomenon of verbal aggression during conflict interactions. As conflicts unfold, people's behavior constitutes both their actions and their reactions to the dyadic exchange. When people are desensitized to conflict, for example, they experience less stress in reaction to their partner's negative behavior and they also experience less stress in reaction to their own negative behavior. In other words, becoming insulated from the negative consequences of verbal aggression can make it easier for people to envision the use of aggressive language and to enact their own aggressive behavior (Huesmann, 1998). For example, Singer et al (1998) found that exposure to community violence and heavy television viewing predicted violent behavior among youth in grades 3 through 8. In light of the research attention devoted to understanding the genesis of aggressive action, we see utility in studying the role of reactions to verbal aggression, alongside tendencies to behave aggressively. More generally, then, we endorse a dyadic view of conflict interactions that recognizes how both partners contribute to the incidence and experience of verbal aggression.

Methodological Challenges

Our research also invites further consideration of three methodological concerns. One methodological issue focuses on the conceptualization and operationalization of problematic exposure to childhood aggression. Previous research suggests that exposure to family verbal aggression, including witnessing or receiving aggressive messages, is detrimental to children contemporaneously and generates adult deficiencies. Exposure to conflict, however, can teach children constructive conflict management skills necessary for successful adult relationships. It is unclear, then, where we draw the line between normative childhood exposure to conflict and problematic experiences with aggression. In turn, how to operationalize childhood experiences in ways that capture these different aspects of exposure to conflict remains an unresolved question.

A related methodological challenge is elucidating the (mal)adaptive nature of desensitization. As previously reviewed, desensitization is the eradication of cognitive, psychological, physiological, and behavioral responses to a stimulus following repeated exposure (Rule & Ferguson, 1986). For children who have experienced high levels of family conflict, verbal aggression is perceived as less adverse, increasing their own verbal aggression and tolerance for other's verbal aggression. Although this desensitization to conflict may be maladaptive, increasing people's propensity to engage in violence, it also spares children from the immediate distress of aggression. Developing uncaring attitudes toward conflict protects children from the cognitive, psychological, and physiological effects of violence. As a result, desensitization can be adaptive and considered a form of coping. To the extent that desensitization shares conceptual space with the notion of resilience, devising methods that distinguish these processes is warranted.

Finally, researchers studying verbal aggression face heightened concerns about ethical conduct when investigating conflict in an academic setting. Engaging in ethical research requires maximizing the benefits of the research study and providing practical guarantees that the study population will profit in some way from the research being conducted. This can be challenging for researchers studying the experience and effects of conflict. If conflict is induced in the laboratory, cognitive, emotional, and physiological distress may be fabricated. In addition, asking an individual to reflect on previous experiences with aggression can cause anguish and potentially increase the level of trauma associated with the event. Accordingly, researchers studying conflict have an ethical responsibility to the participants to be sensitive to the induced or reflective conflict experience.

Conclusion

This chapter offers desensitization as a framework for understanding how childhood exposure to verbal aggression is manifest in people's reactions to conflict in adult romantic relationships. In Study 1, we used a self-report methodology and featured the behavioral inhibition system as a cognitive mechanism subject to desensitization effects and relevant to evaluations of verbally aggressive messages. In Study 2, we conducted a laboratory-based dyadic interaction study to observe the association between childhood experiences and physiological reactions to a conflict discussion. While both studies are subject to limitations, the findings are largely consistent with the perspective we advanced.

References

Adam, K. S., Bouckoms, A., & Streiner, D. (1982). Parental loss and family stability in attempted suicide. *Psychiatry*, *39(9)*, 1081–1085, doi: 1982.04290090065013.

Aloia, L. S. (2013). *Childhood exposure to verbal aggression and desensitization to conflict in young adulthood*. PhD thesis, Pennsylvania State University, University Park, doi: 10.1177/027112149801800102.

Aloia, L. S., & Solomon, D. H. (2013). Perceptions of verbal aggression in romantic relationships: The role of family history and motivational systems. *Western Journal of Communication*, *77(4)*, 411–423, doi: 10.1080/10570314.2013.776098.

Amato, P. R., & Keith, B. (1991). Parental divorce and the well-being of children: A meta-analysis. *Psychological Bulletin*, *110*, 26–46, doi: 10.1037/0033–2909.110.1.26.

Bandura, A. (1977). *Social learning theory*. Englewood Cliffs, NJ: Prentice-Hall.

Beauchaine, T. P., Katkin, E. S., Strassberg, Z., & Snarr, J. (2001). Disinhibitory psychopathology in male adolescents: Discriminating conduct disorder from attention-deficit/hyperactivity disorder through concurrent assessment of multiple autonomic states. *Journal of Abnormal Psychology*, *110*, 610–624, doi: 10.1037/0021–843x.110.4.610.

Buss, A. H., & Perry, M. (1992). The aggression questionnaire. *Journal of Personality and Social Psychology, 63,* 452–459, doi: 10.1037/0022–3514.63.3.452.

Carver, C. S., & White, T. L. (1994). Behavioral inhibition, behavioral activation, and affective responses to impending reward and punishment: The BIS/BAS scales. *Journal of Personality and Social Psychology, 67,* 319–333, doi: 10.1037/0022–3514.67.2.319.

Cicchetti, D. (2007). Gene-environment interaction. *Development and Psychopathology, 19,* 957–959, doi: 10.1017/s0954579407000466.

Crick, N. R., & Dodge, K. A. (1994). A review and reformulation of social information-processing mechanisms in children's social adjustment. *Psychological Bulletin, 115(1),* 74–101, doi: 10.1037/0033–2909.115.1.74.

Garbarino, J. (1995). *Raising children in a socially toxic environment.* San Francisco, CA: Jossey-Bass.

Gray, J. A. (1987). *The psychology of fear and stress.* Cambridge, England: Cambridge University Press.

Gray, J. A., & McNaughton, N. (2000). *The neuropsychology of anxiety: An enquiry into the functions of the septo-hippocampal system.* Oxford, England: Oxford University Press.

Guterman, N. B., & Cameron, M. (1997). Assessing the impact of community violence on children and youths. *Social Work, 42,* 495–505, doi: 10.1093/sw/42.5.495.

Huesmann, L. R. (1998). The role of social information processing and cognitive schema in the acquisition and maintenance of habitual aggressive behavior. In R. G. Green and E. Donnerstein (Eds.), *Human aggression: Theories, research, and implications for social policy* (pp73–109). New York, NY: Academic Press, doi: 10.1016/b978–012278805–5/50005–5.

Infante, D. A. (1987). Aggressiveness. In J. C. McCroskey and J. A. Daly (Eds.), *Personality and interpersonal communication* (pp157–192). Newbury Park, CA: Sage.

Infante, D. A., & Wigley, C. J. (1986). Verbal aggressiveness: An interpersonal model and measure. *Communication Monographs, 53,* 61–69, doi: 10.1080/03637758609376126.

Infante, D. A., Chandler, T. A., & Rudd, J. E. (1989). Test of an argumentative skill deficiency model of interspousal violence. *Communication Monographs, 56,* 163–177, doi: 10.1080/03637758909390257.

Infante, D. A., Chandler, T. A., Rudd, J. E., & Shannon, E. A. (1990). Verbal aggression in violent and nonviolent marital disputes. *Communication Quarterly, 38,* 361–371, doi: 10.1080/01463379009369773.

Ornduff, S. R., Kelsey, R. M., & O'Leary, K. D. (2001). Childhood physical abuse, personality, and adult relationship violence: A model of vulnerability to victimization. *American Journal of Orthopsychiatry, 71(3),* 322–331, doi: 10.1037//0002–009432.71.3.322.

Pruessner, J. C., Kirschbaum, C., Meinlschmid, G., & Hellhammer, D. H. (2003). Two formulas for computation of the area under the curve represent measures of total hormone concentration versus time-dependent change. *Psychoneuroendocrinology, 29,* 916–931, doi:10.1016/s0306–4530(02)00108–00107.

Renfrew, J. W. (1997). *Aggression and its causes: A biopsychosocial approach.* New York, NY: Oxford University Press.

Rule, B. K., & Ferguson, T. J. (1986). The effects of media violence on attitudes, emotions, and cognitions. *Journal of Social Issues, 42,* 29–50, doi: 10.1111/j.1540–4560.1986.tb00241.x.

Schwab-Stone, M., Chen, C., Greenberger, E., Silver, D., Lichtman, J., & Voyce, C. (1999). No safe haven II: The effects of violence exposure on urban youth. *Journal of the American Academy of Child and Adolescent Psychiatry, 38,* 359–367, doi: 10.1097/00004583–199904000–00007.

Singer, M. I., Slovak, K., Freierson, T., & York, P. (1998). Viewing preferences, symptoms of psychological trauma, and violent behaviors among children who watch television. *Journal of the American Academy of Child and Adolescent Psychiatry, 37,* 1042–1048, doi: 10.1097/00004583-199810000-00014.

Stemmler, G., & Meinhardt, E. (1990). Personality, situation and physiological arousability. *Personality and Individual Differences, 11*(3), 293–308, doi: 10.1016/0191-8869(90)90243-k.

Straus, M. A. (1979). Measuring intrafamily conflict and violence: The conflict tactics scales. *Journal of Marriage and the Family, 41,* 75–88, doi: 10.2307/351733.

Straus, M. A., Hamby, S. L., Boney-McCoy, S., & Sugarman, D. B. (1996). The revised conflict tactics scale (CTS2): Development and preliminary psychometric data. *Journal of Family Issues, 17*(3), 283–316, doi: 10.1177/019251396017003001.

Weersing, V. R., & Weisz, J. R. (2002). Mechanisms of action in youth psychotherapy. *Journal of Child Psychology and Psychiatry, 43,* 3–29, doi: 10.1111/1469-7610.00002.

Wolpe, J. (1973). *The practice of behavior therapy.* New York, NY: Pergamon Press.

Yan, C., & Dillard, J. P. (2010). Emotion inductions cause changes in activation levels of the behavioural inhibition and approach systems. *Personality and Individual Differences, 48,* 676–680, doi: 10.1016/j.paid.2009.12.002.

Zimet, D. M., & Jacob, T. (2001). Influences of marital conflict on child adjustment: Review of theory and research. *Clinical Child and Family Psychology Review, 4*(4), 319–335, doi: 10.1023/a:1013595304718.

2

THERE IS NOTHING AS CALMING AS A GOOD THEORY

How a Soulmate Theory Helps Individuals Experience Less Demand/Withdraw and Stress

Rachel M. Reznik, Michael E. Roloff, and Courtney Waite Miller

When interpersonal conflicts cannot be resolved they may be repeated. Frequently during serial arguments individuals become locked in repetitive patterns of communication that are deleterious for one's relationship and well-being (Roloff, 2009) such as the demand/withdraw pattern (Johnson & Roloff, 1998). However, believing one's serial argument can and eventually will be resolved is negatively related to individuals' experiencing stress and other mental and physical health problems (Malis & Roloff, 2006a, 2006b). Individuals holding positive relational beliefs are optimistic about their relationships and may be protected against maladaptive sequences. The present research investigates if endorsing positive beliefs about relationships reduces the likelihood of demand/withdraw and thus buffers against the negative impact of serial arguing.

Explicating Demand/Withdraw in Serial Arguments

Demand/withdraw is a destructive pattern and occurs when one partner seeks change in the other partner's behavior or their relationship (Schrodt et al, 2014). Demand/withdraw consists of one partner complaining, nagging, or criticizing while the other partner withdraws or tries to avoid the issue (Eldridge & Christensen, 2002). Demand/withdraw patterns are linked to using more negative conflict tactics, expressing higher levels of negativity, and aggressive and unresolved conflicts (Papp et al, 2009).

Individuals report that they either initiate a serial argument (initiator) or their partner initiates the argument (resistor) and these roles are related to demand/withdraw (Johnson & Roloff, 2000). Initiators typically report that they confront their partners because they are upset and feel a sense of urgency regarding the topic of confrontation. Thus, when individuals reported taking an initiator role, they also reported that they engaged in more demanding behavior while their partners tended to withdraw from the interaction. Also, resistors report that their partners were more demanding while they were likely to withdraw (Johnson & Roloff, 2000). This is consistent with other demand/withdraw research. In a study of spouses, being an initiator was consistently related to demanding behavior (Papp et al, 2009). Also, discussing an individual's issue was related to the couple demonstrating more self-demand/partner-withdraw (SD/PW) and discussing a partner's issue was related to the couple enacting more partner-demand/self-withdraw (PD/SW; McGinn et al, 2009).

Having goals of hurting one's partner and negative expressiveness were positively related to SD/PW (Hample et al, 2012). Thus, initiators may be prone to abrasive confrontations that emotionally flood their partners who react by withdrawing, ultimately prolonging the argument beyond the initial episode (Reznik & Roloff, 2011). When individuals fail to achieve their goals in a serial argument, they may become frustrated and mull about the argument, which in turn motivates them to continue pursuing the argument (Carr et al, 2012). This can lead to negative outcomes.

Indeed, demand/withdraw is detrimental for one's health. Both SD/PW and PD/SW in serial arguments are stressful and related to thought avoidance and disruption in daily activities due to physical health problems (Malis & Roloff, 2006a). However, only SD/PW was predictive of individuals feeling hyper-aroused and reporting intrusive thoughts about the episode (Malis & Roloff, 2006a). Also, individuals reporting SD/PW indicate that their arguments are less resolvable (Malis & Roloff, 2006a). When an initiator's partner withdraws the initiator may perceive that their feelings and needs are being ignored (Reznik & Roloff, 2011). Thus, initiators leave the episode angrier than when they entered it (Reznik & Roloff, 2011) and report being aroused after the episode because they are not able to effectively change their partners' behaviors or attitudes and the issue remains a problem in the relationship. Kiecolt-Glaser et al. (1996) found that later in the day after a conflict, wives whose husbands withdrew in response to their complaints had elevated levels of stress hormones, while their husbands did not experience these increased levels of hormones. Demanding behaviors increases one's emotional arousal, and demanders demonstrated more arousal than withdrawers (Baucom, et al, 2011).

Resistors report more PD/SW and this impacts the resistor's health. Gottman (1993) suggests that individuals withdraw in response to being physiologically aroused or flooded. Taking an avoider role during confrontational discussions led to increased systolic blood pressure reactivity (Denton et al, 2001). This withdrawal starts the process of distancing and isolation leading to emotional separation and, potentially, divorce (Gottman, 1993). Cardiac patients tend to avoid relationship problems and indicate that their partners are more initiating (Denton et al, 2009). Hence, individuals who avoid the D/W pattern may be able to engage in conflict episodes without experiencing stress. One factor that may help individuals avoid this destructive pattern is their implicit theory of relationships.

Implicit Theories of Relationships

Implicit theories of relationships constitute the beliefs that individuals hold as to the factors that make for a good relationship (Knee et al, 2003). A soulmate theory posits that relationships are either meant to be or not meant to be (Franiuk et al, 2002). Endorsing a soulmate theory promotes passion about the relationship and partner idealization, which are strong predictors of relationship satisfaction (Hendrick et al, 1988; Murray et al, 1996).

The degree to which individuals endorse a soulmate theory may influence how they respond when engaged in serial arguing. Even individuals in satisfying relationship engage in behaviors that their partners find problematic and disagreements may not be resolved in a single episode. Individuals who endorse beliefs similar to a soulmate theory believe they are destined to be with their partners and this may supplant any negative meanings arising from the conflicts (Knee et al, 2004). Moreover, Murray et al (1996) proposed that individuals who idealize their partners do not place as much importance on conflicts in their relationships as people who did not idealize their partners. After all, the partner is perfect in most other regards. Endorsing a soulmate theory may inhibit individuals in long-term relationships from engaging in angry confrontations.

As noted earlier, individuals engaging in serial arguments frequently adopt initiator and resistor roles. Initiators prompt conflict episodes often with the goal of prompting change. They may demand that their partners change, which can cause the partners to experience emotional flooding. The partners resist by withdrawing. Partner withdrawal can be stressful for both initiators who feel disconfirmed and resistors who feel attacked. However, initiators who endorse soulmate theories may be able to avoid D/W and a stressful argument. Individuals who are high in destiny theory (akin to soulmate theory) disengage from their partners after a negative event occurs (Knee & Canevello, 2006) and likely do not confront them. Although they want their partners to change, their positive view of the relationship may reduce the likelihood that they will be demanding, which decreases the likelihood that their partners will become emotionally flooded and withdraw. This, in turn, allows initiators to avoid the stress resulting from a partner who withdraws. Hence, we predict the following:

H1: The degree to which initiators endorse a soulmate theory will be negatively related to their self-reported post episodic stress and this relationship is mediated by the degree to which they report SD/PW occurred during the argument.

H2: The degree to which initiators endorse a soulmate theory will be negatively related to their partner's reported post episodic stress and this relationship will be mediated by the degree to which initiators report SD/PW occurred during the argument.

The benefits of endorsing a soulmate theory may also accrue for resistors. Because soulmate resistors engage in idealization, they may react to their partner's demands by remaining calm and engaged during the conflict rather than withdrawing. Although being the target of demands may be unpleasant, individuals who believe relationship partners are destined to be together may be able to deny their importance (e.g., Knee & Canevello, 2006). By not withdrawing, their partners who initiated the confrontation may feel less disconfirmed and stressed during the encounter. Hence, we predict the following:

H3: The degree to which resistors endorse a soulmate theory will be negatively related to their self-reported post episodic stress and this relationship is mediated by the degree to which they report PD/SW occurred during the argument.

H4: The degree to which resistors endorse a soulmate theory will be negatively related to their partner's self-reported post episodic stress and this relationship will be mediated by the degree to which resistors reports of PD/SW occurred during the interaction.

A Spotlight Study on Soulmate Theory and Conflict

Participants and Procedures

Fifty-three couples were recruited via network sampling and completed a series of measures. Eight couples were removed from the analyses, as they did not agree on the roles taken during the most recent serial argument episode. We were left with a sample of 45 couples (45 = male, 45 = female).[1] The mean length of the relationship was 131.25 months (SD = 138.62) or about 11 years. Thirty-seven (81.1%) couples were married, 7 (15.6%) couples were engaged and 1 (3.3%) couple was dating. Forty-four (97.8%) of the couples lived together while one (2.2%) lived apart. The participants' mean age was 34.36 years (SD = 12.35). Participants read a definition of serial arguing. They were then asked to individually identify topics that they serially argue about. One of the authors selected a topic that both members identified as being the most important argument. Next, couples were told which topic they would focus on, and they completed measures described below. Participants were then paid $15 each and debriefed.

Measures

Relationship theories. Franiuk et al' s (2002) Relationship Theory Scale was used to assess soulmate theory (11 items; 1 to 7 scale; higher numbers equals a greater soulmate belief).

Demand/withdraw. We used three items based on Christensen's Communication Pattern Questionnaire (Christensen and Heavey, 1993) to assess initiator's SD/PW and three items to assess resistor's PD/SW (1 = *very little*, 7 = *very much*).

TABLE 2.1 Correlations among Variables of Interest and Descriptive Statistics

Variables	1	2	3	4	5	6	M	SD	α
1. I Soulmate	–	–.39**	–.55***	.17	–.00	–.06	4.31	0.95	.83
2. I SD/PW		–	–.50***	–.07	.20	.01	3.51	1.76	.78
3. I Stress			–	–.20	.04	.10	2.59	0.54	.86
4. R Soulmate				–	–.02	–.30*	4.66	0.91	.91
5. R PD/SW					–	.04	3.86	1.71	.80
6. R Stress						–	2.31	0.50	.86

Note. I = Initiator. R = Resistor. SD/PW = self-demand/partner-withdraw. PD/SW = partner demand/self-withdraw. * p <.05. ** p <.01. *** p <.001.

Stress. We adapted the Perceived Stress Scale (Cohen et al, 1983) to assess the degree to which situations in a person's life are stressful following their most recent argumentative episode (14 items; 1 = *never*, 5 = *very often*). See Table 2.1 for descriptive statistics of the measures.

Results

Preliminary Analysis

We tested whether initiators and resistors agreed when the most recent episode occurred. Participants reported how many months ago their most recent episode took place. Initiators did not significantly, $t(43) = -.69$, $r^2 = .065$, $p = .50$, differ in their reports of when the most recent episode occurred ($M = 1.56$, $SD = 1.79$) from resistors ($M = 1.36$, $SD = 1.47$).

Our predictions are based on the assumption that initiators will report more SD/PW and resistors will report more PD/SW. We conducted paired t-tests to test these assumptions. Initiators were significantly, $t(44) = 6.27$, $r^2 = .034$, $p < .001$, more likely to report that they demanded and their partners withdrew ($M = 3.51$, $SD = 1.76$) than did those who reported they resisted ($M = 1.81$, $SD = .89$). Conversely, resistors were significantly, $t(44) = 6.11$, $r^2 = .001$, $p < .001$, more likely to report that they withdrew and their partners demanded ($M = 3.86$, $SD = 1.71$) than did those who reported they initiated the most recent episode ($M = 2.09$, $SD = .99$). We also examined the bivariate associations among the variables (see Table 2.1).[2]

Primary Analysis

To test our hypotheses we used MPlus (Muthen & Muthen, 2007) to calculate a structural equation model using the dyad as the unit of analysis. We report the unstandardized regression coefficients from actor-partner interdependence model

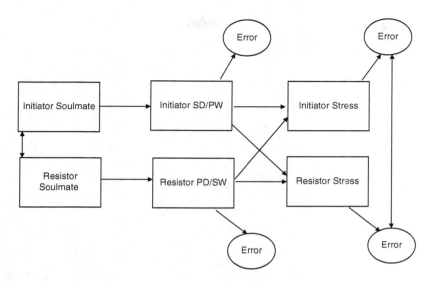

FIGURE 2.1 Conceptual Actor-Partner Interdependence model of dyadic perception effects between relationship theory, demand/withdraw, and stress
Note: SD/PW = self-demand/partner-withdraw. PD/SW = partner demand/self-withdraw. Error terms for initiator SD/PW and resistor PD/SW were allowed to correlate
Source: Kenny et al (2006)

(APIM) using distinguishable dyads (Kenny et al, 2006). Actor effects refer to the relationship between individuals' relationship theory and their stress as mediated by their perception of how frequently the demand/withdraw pattern occurred. Partner effects refer to the relationship between individuals' relationship theory and their partner's stress as mediated by the individuals' perception of how frequently they experienced the demand/withdraw pattern (see Figure 2.1). Table 2.2 contains the results.

Hypothesis 1. The first hypothesis predicted that the degree to which initiators endorse a soulmate theory would be negatively related to the degree to which they experienced post-episodic stress and this relationship would be mediated by the degree to which they reported SD/PW during the disagreement. We found significant direct relationships between initiator endorsement of a soulmate theory and their perceptions of SD/PW and between reports of SD/PW and their self-reported stress. As predicted, the confidence intervals associated with indirect path from initiator soulmate endorsement to stress through SD/PW did not include 0 and the coefficient was positive. The direct relationship between the initiator's endorsement of soulmate theory and self-reported stress was also statistically significant.

Hypothesis 2. The second hypothesis predicted that the degree to which initiators endorse a soulmate theory would be negatively related to their partner's

TABLE 2.2 Results of the tests of the indirect paths from argument role to stress through demand/withdraw.

Model Path Estimates	Coeff	SE
Initiator Soulmate with Resistor Soulmate	.143	.128
Initiator SD/PW with Resistor PD/SW	.592	.412
Initiator Soulmate → Initiator SD/PW	-.732**	.249
Initiator Soulmate → Initiator Stress	-.233***	.072
Initiator SD/PW → Initiator Stress	.106**	.040
Initiator SD/PW → Resistor Stress	-.004	.041
Resistor Soulmate → Resistor PD/SW	-.039	.273
Resistor Soulmate → Resistor Stress	.012	.042
Resistor PD/SW → Resistor Stress	-.158*	.079
Resistor PD/SW → Initiator Stress	-.010	.038

Indirect Paths (bootstrap percentile biased corrected 95% confidence intervals and standard errors)

	Coeff	BootSE	LL95%CI	UL95%CI
Initator Soulmate → Initiator SD/PW → Initiator Stress[a]	-.078	.039	-.154	-.001
Resistor Soulmate → Resistor PD/SW → Resistor Stress[a]	.000	.004	-.008	.007
Initiator Soulmate → Initiator SD/PW → Resistor Stress[b]	.003	.030	-.056	.062
Resistor Soulmate → Resistor PD/SW → Initiator Stress[b]	.000	.030	-.006	.006

Note: $N = 45$.
All coefficients are unstandardized. SE = standard error. Number of bootstrap samples = 5000. SD/PW = self-demand/partner-withdraw. PD/SW = partner-demand/self-withdraw.
[a] Actor effects.
[b] Partner effects.
*$p < .05$. **$p < .01$. ***$p<.001$.

reported post-episodic stress and this relationship will be mediated by the degree to which initiators report SD/PW occurred during the argument. The relationship was not statistically significant.

Hypothesis 3. The third hypothesis predicted that the degree to which resistors endorse a soulmate theory will be negatively related to their self-reported post-episodic stress and this relationship is mediated by the degree to which they report PD/SW occurred during the argument. We found no support for the indirect path from resistor endorsement of soulmate theory to their stress through PD/SW. In part this reflects the small relationship between partner soulmate theory endorsement and PD/SW. However, a statistically significant direct relationship existed between the degree to which resistor's reported PD/SW and the degree of stress they reported experiencing during the argument.

Hypothesis 4. The fourth hypothesis predicted that the degree to which resistors endorse a soulmate theory would be negatively related to their partner's self-reported post-episodic stress and this relationship would be mediated by the degree to which resistors reported that PD/SW occurred during the argument. There is no support for this indirect relationship or either of the bivariate relationships of which it is composed.

Discussion

This study examined the dyadic perceptions of relationship theory, role, and demand/withdraw patterns on self-reported stress. We only found significant actor effects for initiators and resistors. Initiators who were more likely to endorse a soulmate theory were less likely to report SD/PW and therefore experienced less stress following their most recent serial arguing episode. If resistors were likely to report holding a soulmate theory, they were also less likely to experience stress following an episode of their serial argument. For both initiators and resistors, soulmate theory reduces stress, but for initiators, part of the reduction is due to avoiding SD/PW. The impact of bad experiences is stronger than the positive impact of good experiences (Baumeister et al, 2001). Thus, having a soulmate theory is important because it helps individuals put a positive frame on relationship problems, which allows people who want to confront their partners to avoid maladaptive sequences.

Our findings are consistent with prior research on positive illusions. A small to medium relationship threat for happy soulmate theorists prompts them to think about their partners in a more positive way and "it may provide the impetus for externalizing these thoughts into positive, affectionate behaviors that bring couples closer together and provide a foundation for future relationship success" (Franiuk et al, 2004, p1505). We believe that a serial argument might serve as this type of stimulus for soulmate theorists.

Surprisingly, having a soulmate theory did not lead to a reduction in reports of PD/SW for resistors. Resistors do typically report in engaging in more PD/SW (Johnson & Roloff, 2000) and holding a soulmate theory does lead one to want to respond passively to conflict. Franiuk et al (2002) hypothesizes that to maintain satisfaction when a problem in the relationship does occur, a soulmate theorist may ignore the problem or swiftly try to alleviate it as this may be best for individuals who believe that putting a lot of effort into solving relational difficulties could be a sign of severe trouble. For example, individuals who hold a soulmate theory may avoid extended disagreement by apologizing, supporting, or affirming their partners rather than withdrawing. Such actions may placate themselves and their partners. As a result, they do not threaten the relationship and avoid a stressful encounter.

The absence of crossover effects on stress could reflect the fact that initiators and resistors had different perceptions of what occurred during the encounter and that their stress levels were not the same. The correlation between the initiator's perception of SD/PW and the partner's report of PD/SW was positive but modest in size and not statistically significant, as was the correlation between their self-reported stress. Consequently, it is not surprising that their personal experience of stress was not related to how each perceived the communication occurring during the encounter.

Limitations and Future Directions

This study has methodological limitations. First, it is possible that partners did not fully agree on the amount of SD/PW and PD/SW occurring in the most recent episode. Participants may have recalled different parts of the episode. Episodes are scripted and predictable (Johnson & Roloff, 1998), but the content might change as a conflict escalates or cools off. Second, although self-report is useful, it is potentially biased (Roloff & Johnson, 2002). Participants could have experienced social desirability concerns or a recollection bias. This bias might be enhanced if the participants hold a positive illusion regarding their relationships.

Despite these limitations, we believe this research suggests several avenues for future investigation. First, scholars are beginning to look at demand/withdraw from a multiple goals perspective (Caughlin & Scott, 2010), and implicit theories of relationships influence goals (Knee et al, 2003). Future research could examine how a soulmate belief might promote goals that influence demand/withdraw behavior. Viewing partners in an idealistic way would seem to reduce the likelihood that one would confront partners with the goals of changing them in a radical way, expressing negativity about their actions, or hurting them. Indeed, one might form a goal of wanting to express positive emotions (e.g., caring) by recommending changes. These goals could lower the likelihood of a harsh initial start-up and increase the likelihood of constructive communication, both of which should attenuate the likelihood of demand/withdraw and reduce stress.

Second, implicit theories could also influence coping strategies. A soulmate theorist might cope with relational difficulties passively (Franiuk et al, 2002). This might lower one's stress as the individual is not dwelling on the relational difficulty. When individuals who coped with their serial arguments by selectively ignoring problems, including telling oneself that the conflict is not that important, they experienced fewer health problems (Malis & Roloff, 2006b).

The serial arguing literature has documented the importance of being optimistic with regard to resolving one's conflict. Our research shows that holding an optimistic view of one's relationship and relational partner also helps one deal with stress associated with the demand/withdraw pattern occurring during an episode of serial arguing.

Notes

1 Others have used similar sample sizes when conducting this type of analysis (see Caughlin & Malis, 2004).
2 An exploratory analysis was conducted to uncover variables that might be correlated with our variables and could create artefactual relationships. We examined the length of the serial argument, episode frequency, length of the relationship, and how long ago the most recent episode occurred. None of these correlations were significant so we did not control for these variables in our analyses.

References

Baumeister, R. F., Bratslavsky, E., Finkenauer, C., & Vohs, K. D. (2001). Bad is stronger than good. *Review of General Psychology, 5*, 323–370, doi: 10.1037/1089–2680.5.4.323.

Baucom, B. R., Atkins, D. C., Eldridge, K., McFarland, P., Sevier, M., & Christensen, A. (2011). The language of demand/withdraw: Verbal and vocal expression in dyadic interactions. *Journal of Family Psychology, 25*, 570–580, doi: 10.1037/a0024064.

Bevan, J. L. (2010). Serial argument goals and conflict strategies: A comparison between romantic partners and family members. *Communication Reports, 23*, 52–64, doi: 10.1080/08934211003598734.

Carr, K., Schrodt, P., & Ledbetter, A. M. (2012). Rumination, conflict intensity, and perceived resolvability as predictors of motivation and likelihood of continuing serial arguments. *Western Journal of Communication, 76*, 480–502, doi: 10.1080/10570314.2012.689086.

Caughlin, J. P., & Malis, R. S. (2004). Demand/withdraw communication between parents and adolescents: Connections with self-esteem and substance abuse. *Journal of Social and Personal Relationships, 21*, 125–148, doi: 10.1177/0265407504039843.

Caughlin, J. P., & Scott, A. M. (2010). Toward a communication theory of the demand/withdraw pattern of interaction in interpersonal relationships. In S. W. Smith & S. R. Wilson (Eds.) *New directions in interpersonal communication research* (pp180–200). Thousand Oaks, CA: Sage Publications.

Christensen, A., & Heavey, C. L. (1993). Gender differences in marital conflict: The demand/withdraw interaction pattern. In S. Oskamp & M. Costanzo (Eds.), *Gender issues in contemporary society* (pp113–141). Newbury Park, CA: Sage.

Cohen, S., Kamarck, T., & Marmelstein, R. (1983). A global measure of perceived stress. *Journal of Health and Social Behavior, 24*, 385–396.

Denton, W. H., Burleson, B. R., & Brubraker, P. H. (2009). Avoidance may be bad for the heart: A comparison of dyadic initiator tendency in cardiac rehabilitation patients and matched controls. *Behavioral Medicine, 35*, 135–142, doi: 10.1080/08964280903334535.

Denton, W. H., Burleson, B. R., Hobbs, B. V., Von Stein, M., & Rodriguez, C. P. (2001). Cardiovascular reactivity and initiate/avoid patterns of marital communication: A test of Gottman's psychophysiologic model of marital interaction. *Journal of Behavioral Medicine, 24*, 401–421, doi: 0160–017715/01/1000–0401.

Eldridge, K. A., & Christensen, A. (2002). Demand-withdraw communication during couple conflict: A review and analysis. In P. Noller & J. A. Feeney (Eds.) *Understanding marriage: Developments in the study of couple interaction* (pp289–322). Cambridge, UK: Cambridge University Press.

Franiuk, R., Cohen, D., & Pomerantz, E. M. (2002). Implicit theories of relationships: Implications for relationship satisfaction and longevity. *Personal Relationships, 9*, 345–367, doi: 10.1111/1475–6811.09401.

Franiuk, R., Pomerantz, E. M., & Cohen, D. (2004). The causal role of theories of relationships: Consequences for satisfaction and cognitive strategies. *Personality and Social Psychology Bulletin, 30*, 1494–1507, doi: 10.1177/0146167204264894.

Gottman, J. M., (1993). A theory of marital dissolution and stability. *Journal of Family Psychology, 7*, 57–75, doi: 10.1037/0893-3200.7.1.57.

Hample, D., Richards, A. S., & Na, L. (2012). A test of the conflict linkage model in the context of serial arguments. *Western Journal of Communication, 76*, 459–479, doi: 10.1080/10570314.2012.703361.

Hendrick, S. S., Hendrick, C., & Adler, N. (1988). Romantic relationships: Love, satisfaction, and staying together. *Journal of Personality and Social Psychology, 54*, 980–988, doi: 10.1037/0022-3514.54.6.980.

Johnson, K. L., & Roloff, M. E. (1998). Serial arguing and relational quality: Determinants and consequences of perceived resolvability. *Communication Research, 25*, 327–343, doi: 10.1177/009365098025003004.

Johnson, K. L., & Roloff, M. E. (2000). The influence of argumentative role (initiator vs. resistor) on perceptions of serial argument resolvability and relational harm. *Argumentation, 14*, 1–15, doi: 10.1023/A:1007837310258.

Kenny, D. A., Kashy, D. A., & Cook, W. L. (2006). *Dyadic Data Analysis*. New York, NY: Guilford.

Kiecolt-Glaser, J. K., Newton, T., Cacioppo, J. T., MacCallum, R. C., Glaser, R., & Malarkey, W. B. (1996). Marital conflict and endocrine function: Are men really more physiologically affected than women? *Journal of Counseling and Clinical Psychology, 64*, 324–332, doi: 10.1037/0022-006X.64.2.324.

Knee, C. R., & Canevello, A., (2006). Implicit theories of relationships and coping in romantic relationships. In K. D. Vohs & E. J. Finkel (Eds.) *Self and relationships: Connecting intrapersonal and interpersonal processes* (pp160–176). New York, NY: Guilford.

Knee, C. R., Patrick, H., & Lonsbary, C. (2003). Implicit theories of relationships: Orientations toward evaluation and cultivation. *Personality and Social Psychology Review, 7*, 41–55, doi: 10.1207/S15327957PSPR0701_3.

Knee, C. R., Patrick, H., Vietor, N. A., & Neighbors, C. (2004). Implicit theories of relationships: Moderators of the link between conflict and commitment. *Personality and Social Psychology Bulletin, 30*, 617–628, doi: 10.1177/01461617203262853.

Malis, R. S., & Roloff, M. E. (2006a). Demand/withdraw patterns in serial arguing: Implications for well-being. *Human Communication Research, 32*, 198–216, doi: 10.1111/j.1468-2958.2006.00009.x.

Malis, R. S., & Roloff, M. E. (2006b). Features of serial arguing and coping strategies: Links with stress and well-being. In R. M. Dailey, & B. A. Le Poire (Eds.) *Applied interpersonal communication matters: Family, health, and community relations* (pp39–65). New York, NY: Peter Lang.

McGinn, M. M., McFarland, P. T., & Christensen, A. (2009). Antecedents and consequences of demand/withdraw. *Journal of Family Psychology, 23*, 749–757, doi: 10.1037/a0016185.

Murray, S. L., Holmes, J. G. & Griffin, D. W. (1996). The self-fulfilling nature of positive illusions in romantic relationships: Love is not blind, but prescient. *Journal of Personality and Social Psychology, 71*, 1155–1180, doi: 10.1037/0022-3514.71.6.1155.

Muthen, L. K., & Muthen, B. O. (2007). *Mplus user's guide* (5th ed.). Los Angeles, CA: Muthen & Muthen.

Papp, L. M., Kouros, C. D., & Cummings, E. M. (2009). Demand-withdraw patterns in marital conflict in the home. *Personal Relationships, 16*, 285–300, doi: 10.1111/j.1475-6811.2009.01223.x.

Reznik, R. M., & Roloff, M. E. (2011). Getting off to a bad start: The relationship between communication during an initial episode of a serial argument and argument frequency. *Communication Studies, 62*, 291–306, doi: 10.1080/10510974.2011.555491.

Roloff, M. E. (2009). Links between conflict management research and practice. *Journal of Applied Communication Research, 37*, 339–348, doi: 10.1080/00909880903233200.

Roloff, M. E., & Johnson, K. L. (2002). Serial arguing over the relational life course: Antecedents and consequences. In A. L. Vangelisti, H. T. Reis, & M. A. Fitzpatrick (Eds.) *Stability and change in relationships. Advances in personal relationships* (pp107–128). New York: Cambridge University Press.

Schrodt, P., Witt, P. L., & Shimkowski, J. R. (2014). A meta-analytical review of the demand/withdraw pattern of interaction and its associations with individual, relational, and communicative outcomes. *Communication Monographs, 81*, 28–58, doi: 10.1080/03637751.2013.813632.

3

CONFLICTS WITH HETEROSEXUAL PARTNERS ABOUT SEXUAL DISCREPANCIES

Conflict Avoidance, De-escalation Strategies, Facilitators to Conversation

Moon Sook Son, Lynne M. Webb, and Patricia Amason

Sexual discrepancies can be defined as partners' differences in sexual desire, attitudes, and preferred activities (Cupach & Metts, 1995; Davies et al, 1999; Sprecher & Cate, 2004). Many romantic partners encounter sexual discrepancies (Sprecher & Cate, 2004) such as one person's desire for more types of sexual behaviors than the partner (Hatfield et al, 1988). The small body of research on sexual discrepancies examines primarily the association between sexual discrepancies and relationship quality (e.g., sexual satisfaction and relationship satisfaction; Cupach & Metts, 1995; Davies et al, 1999; Purnine & Carey, 1997). The purpose of our study was to extend this line of research to examine, from the perspective of the female partners, the communication between heterosexual partners as they address sexual discrepancies – specifically, how partners avoid and manage conflicts surrounding sexual discrepancies.

Cupach and Metts (1995) posited that sexual partners are likely to frame sexual discrepancies as "relationship problems" (e.g., Why does my partner not want/desire me?). Furthermore, Sprecher and Cate (2004, p248) noted that "when discrepancies exist between partners, there is either increased conflict or the potential for conflict". Conflicts can arise concerning any aspect of sexual activities, including how sexual desire is initiated, how sexual initiations are accepted or rejected, as well as the partners' communication about sexual likes and dislikes (Byers & Lewis, 1988; Morokoff et al, 1997; Tschann, & Adler, 1997). Despite this commonly agreed-upon assumption of a potential causal relationship between sexual discrepancies and sexual conflicts, no previously published studies document conflicts about sexual discrepancies or the possible mediating role of effective communication in ameliorating such conflicts. Perhaps sexual discrepancies do not necessarily become sexual conflicts if couples talk about discrepancies in a constructive way. Our study investigated female partners' reports of communication with their heterosexual partners about sexual discrepancies and the potential ameliorating effects of communication in preventing or diffusing conflicts about sexual discrepancies.

Explicating Sexual Communication as Related to Conflict

Greene and Faulkner defined "sexual communication as the discussion of safer sex, sexual health (e.g., sexual history, STIs), sexual pleasure, and sexual limits" (2005, p239). It is commonly accepted that sexual communication is important in close, romantic relationships as sexual communication permits mutual partner education about sexual desires, needs, and preferences (Duck et al, 1991; Gordon & Snyder, 1986). However, most research on sexual communication was developed in the clinical therapy field because, as Yela (2000) documented, absence of open communication can lead to sexual problems, and open communication is necessary to address sexual problems. Accordingly, many studies outside of the communication field focus on the influence of both the quantity and the quality of sexual communication to minimize sexual dysfunction as well as to enhance sexual and relationship satisfaction.

Importance of Sexual Communication

La France (2010) reported that participants who were sensitive to their partners' sexual interests as well as their own were more willing to engage in dialogue with one another about their sexual desires. Indeed, the more receptive and expressive the sexual communication, the greater the satisfaction with the sexual communication (MacNeil & Byers, 2005), sexual satisfaction (Montesi et al, 2011), and the subsequent relationship adjustments (Benmen & Vogel, 1985). Two studies (Byers & Demmons, 1999; Timm & Keilly, 2011) document that the more couples talked about sex, the greater their satisfaction with both sexual and nonsexual aspects of their relationships.

Although scholars from a variety of disciplines examine sexual communication, communication scholars have published very few studies on the subject. Although few in number, the body of communication scholarship on sexual communication is wide in scope, addressing such topics as negotiation of safer-sex practices (e.g., Broaddus & Dickson-Gomez, 2013), communicating sexual consent (e.g., Lim & Roloff, 1999), discourse among friends-with-benefits (e.g., Goodboy & Myers, 2008), as well as examining the discourse between intimate partners about their sexual behavior (e.g., Miller-Ott & Linder, 2014). Given their relevance to the present study, the latter set of studies is reviewed in more detail below.

Communication Between Sexual Partners

Early communication research documents the importance of effective communication in ongoing sexual relationships. For example, Wheeless et al (1984) reported that sexual communication satisfaction in sexually intimate relationships increased through relationship escalation stages and decreased through de-escalation stages. Yelsma (1986) documented that younger married and cohabiting couples communicated more about sex, and therefore were more sexually satisfied than older married couples. Two research reviews (MacNeil & Byers, 2005; Mark & Jozkowski, 2013) link sexual satisfaction in heterosexual romantic relationships, relationship satisfaction, and the presence or absence of relational conflict. Thus, communication quality is consistently described as a necessary component in satisfying sexual relationships (Frith, 2013).

Conversely, Cupach and Comstock (1990) found that sexual satisfaction and relationship adjustment were not directly related, but mediated by sexual communication satisfaction – suggesting that sexual communication satisfaction may affect relationship satisfaction, which in turn influences sexual satisfaction. More recently, Greene and Faulkner (2005) reported that individuals with less traditional attitudes toward gender roles and sexuality discussed more sexual issues and disclosed more sexual information to their partners. The study found that couples with more dyadic sexual communication and sexual assertiveness reported increased relational satisfaction.

Conflicts with Sexual Partners

Sexual discrepancies and the potential conflict surrounding them are a well-documented phenomenon in the therapeutic literature (e.g., Mark & Murray, 2012; Willoughby et al, 2014). Nonetheless, few scholars have examined the communication behavior in conflicts surrounding discrepancies. Cupach and Metts (1995) were the first scholars to publish research on the communication surrounding sexual conflicts in ongoing heterosexual relationships; they documented that sexual communication satisfaction about couples' discrepancies (and similarities) in their sexual attitudes mediated the association between sexual satisfaction and relationship satisfaction. Although their focus was on attitudes rather than behaviors, these researchers suggested that the manner in which couples interact and communicate about their differences in sexual attitudes should be explored further – thus providing a warrant for our study.

As evidenced in the previous research reviewed above, many scholars highlight the importance of the quantity and quality of sexual communication in committed heterosexual relationships. However, the previously published research provides little information about how couples specifically communicate with one another about sexual discrepancies.

A Spotlight Study on Sexual Discrepancies and Conflict

Purpose and Research Questions

The purpose of this study was to conduct an exploratory investigation of the specific content and processes of U. S. heterosexual partners' communication about sexual discrepancies, from the perspective of the female partners, hereafter simply called "women." We explored the potential ameliorating effects of communication in preventing, escalating, and diffusing, conflicts regarding sexual discrepancies. We posed three research questions:

Research question 1 (RQ1): Which reported sexual discrepancies, if any, do women report discussing versus not discussing with their sexual partners?
Research question 2 (RQ2): When sexual discrepancies are discussed, how do the women perceive and characterize these conversations?
Research question 3 (RQ3): What communication strategies do women report using in these conversations about sexual discrepancies that escalate or deescalate conflicts?

Method

Participants

Focus on Women

The sample was limited to women who self-reported as engaging in a sexual relationship with a heterosexual partner within the last 6 months prior to the interview, not including casual sex. Multiple studies have documented women's (versus men's) sensitivity to the quality of sexual communication (e.g., Buss, 1989; Byers, 2001; Greene & Faulkner, 2005; Purnine & Carey, 1997; Wheeless & Parsons, 1995). Given their documented differences, it seemed appropriate to analyze women's versus men's perceptions of sexual communication separately, as has become common practice in investigations of sex talk (e.g., Amason et al, 2012). We began our investigation by interviewing women because, given their sensitivity, we believed that women (versus men) might provide more specific and detailed accounts of their sexual conversations.

Size

Thirty U. S. women volunteered to serve as participants in face-to-face, in-depth interviews. Our sample size was consistent with sample sizes of other interview studies of communication about sexual matters, such as Broaddus and Dickson-Gomez (2013; $N = 20$), Miller-Ott & Linder (2014; $N = 22$), Noland (2006; $N = 52$), and Sieg (2007; $N = 22$).

Recruiting

The convenience sample was recruited via the university office for non-traditional students as well as students enrolled in the basic communication course and multiple upper-division classes in interpersonal communication at a flagship, public university in the southeastern U.S. The students enrolled in communication courses received extra credit for participating or recruiting participants. We "snow-balled" the initial sample to include friends and family of previous participants. All participants were unknown to the interviewer prior to data collection.

Sample Description

Participants' ages ranged from 18 to 42 years ($M = 26.10$, $SD = 5.49$). The sample included European Americans ($N = 25$), African Americans ($N = 4$), and Hispanic Americans ($N = 1$). The majority (53.3%, $N = 16$) of the participants had a high school diploma, and were completing undergraduate work; 12 participants (40%) had a bachelor's or two-year college degree; 2 participants had a master's degree. The majority of participants were undergraduate students ($N = 16$) and graduate students ($N = 2$). Other participants' occupations included artist, bank teller, buyer/sales associate, dance teacher, epidemiologist, executive assistant, food server, house sitter, sales manager, nurse, and photographer.

The sample was limited to women who self-reported as engaging in a sexual relationship with a heterosexual partner within the last 6 months prior to the interview, not including casual sex. The majority of the participants ($N = 13$) reported being in a serious relationship; eight participants reported currently cohabituating with a sexual partner. Six participants were married. The participants reported an average length of relationship with their current romantic partner of 2 years and 3.60 months ($SD = 2$ years and 8.99 months).

Participants' Reported Sexual Discrepancies

Consistent with previous research findings (Sieg, 2007), each participant identified one or more sexual inconsistency. The participants reported a total of 16 types of sexual discrepancies across the sample, as listed in Table 3.1. Many specifically identified discrepancies were consistent with previous research on the subject (e.g., Mark & Murray, 2012; Miller & Byers, 2004; Santittila et al, 2008; Willoughby et al, 2014). Thus, we recruited an incident-rich sample for our interviews.

Instruments

We devised an open-ended interview protocol to address our research questions.[1] To assess efficacy, we pretested the interview protocol and procedures with five participants recruited from the research population. Based on the pretest participants' responses, we modified the protocol in minor ways. The revised interview protocol was employed with each interviewee to minimize the introduction of researcher bias. However, the interviewer employed probing questions, as needed, to facilitate specific answers. After her interview, each P completed a

TABLE 3.1 Discrepancies Participants Reported Discussing with their Heterosexual Partners

Discrepancy	n Perceived	n Discussed	Type of Discussion		
			n Surface	n Detailed	n Full
Preferred position	12	15	6	7	2
Foreplay	14	8		7	1
Higher sexual desire	9	7	2	5	
Oral sex	12	16	5	1	
Anal sex	9	6	1	5	
Preferred timing of having sex	9	6	3	2	1
Sex as psychological connection versus physical connection	12	4	1	3	
His quick sex	11	3		3	
Desire for more experimentation	7	3	1	2	

Note: n = number of participants. Seven of the 30 participants in the sample reported never or never seriously discussing sexual discrepancies with their partner.

short demographic questionnaire that provided the information used to describe the sample.

Procedure

After participants expressed an interest in participating, the interviewer (a female in her late 20s with two years of graduate training in communication) contacted the participants via email or telephone (depending on the participants' preference) and scheduled a mutually convenient time and place for the interview. About 48 hours prior to the interview, participants received a confirmation email with three attachments (i.e., an informed consent form, the demographic questionnaire, and the interview protocol to allow participants to review and think about their answers before the interview). The interviewer began by introducing herself and engaged in small talk (e.g., weather, lunch, major) to welcome participants and help them feel comfortable. Then, participants were asked to read and sign the consent form. After a brief explanation of the study, the interviewer assured the participants that the contents of the interview would remain confidential. Next, she asked and received permission to tape record the interview for later transcription. After answering the interview questions, participants completed the short, demographics questionnaire. The next day, participants received an email expressing appreciation for their participation and offering them the option of receiving a summary of the research findings.

Analysis

The interviewer transcribed the audio-tapes, producing 529 single-spaced pages (17,431 lines) of research data. Given the exploratory nature of the study and the lack of extant categories to impose on the data, the interviewer conducted thematic analysis using the grounded theory approach developed by Glaser and Strauss (1967), and later applied extensively in family communication research (LaRossa, 2005; Strauss & Corbin, 1998). Specifically, she employed Owen's (1984) three criteria for identifying themes: repetition (relatively the same language to describe a phenomenon), recurrence (differing language but similar meanings for a phenomenon), and forcefulness (ideas strongly stressed verbally or nonverbally by at least three informants).

Similar to any analytic inductive technique based on grounded theory, the interviewer functioned as a textual critic interpreting language. "Thus, reliability is not established by intercoder agreement. Instead, integrity of the analysis is established through a constant comparison process" (Krusiewicz & Wood, 2001, p791). Using a continuous comparison process, insights from later responses influenced themes and, when appropriate, prompted the reinterpretations of previously reviewed responses and/or recorded themes (Charmaz, 1983). The analysis involved seven steps to discover, verify, and re-verify themes:

1. The interviewer read each transcript underlining phrases that answered the research questions and noted emerging themes.
2. Next, she color-coded phrases, using a different colored highlighter for each research question; parts of the transcript applied to more than one of the research questions.
3. During the third reading, the interviewer specifically looked for emerging themes from color-coded answers for RQ1, creating a list of tentative RQ1 themes and noted how many times each theme was mentioned by each participant. In a separate document, she noted each instance of each theme by interview number, page number, and line number.
4, 5, and 6 Then, the interviewer repeated step 3 for RQ2 and then for RQ3.
7. The interviewer again read the transcript in its entirety to ensure that the identified themes were present, that no additional themes existed, and that each instance of dialogue related to each theme was recorded. Thus, the interviewer analyzed the data set 19 times. Finally, the interviewer carefully selected the wording of each theme to represent the participants' ideas and to closely resemble their actual words.

Results

RQ1, 2, and 3 queried how participants reported discussing sexual discrepancies with their sexual partners and managing any resulting conflicts. Seven participants reported they did not discuss sexual discrepancies, saying they did not experience a need to discuss discrepancies with their partner because there were not many discrepancies or the discrepancies did not cause any problems in the relationship. Two participants stated "There is no need to verbally discuss it; instead I try to learn to like discrepancies" or "I let him get to know my body naturally."

However, the majority of the participants ($n = 23$) reported discussing one or more discrepancies with their partners. The analysis revealed nine discrepancies that the participants reported verbally discussing at least once with their partners, as listed in Table 3.1. Participants reported discussing some discrepancies repeatedly (i.e., preferred position, oral sex); others were rarely discussed (i.e., his quick sex, sex as a psychological versus physical connection).

Furthermore, the discussions themselves varied in depth: Participants reported three types of discussion with their partners about discrepancies: *surface discussion* (one or two sentences providing only a few details), *detailed discussion* (multiple details and/or rationale provided), and *full discussion* (revealed ideas and feelings fully). Few participants reported full discussion of discrepancies; Table 3.1 displays the relevant results.

Twelve participants (40%) reported experiencing conflicts with their partners during conversations about sexual discrepancies. The analyses of participants' descriptions of discourse that *escalated conflicts* revealed five themes:

1. I respond with negative emotion ($n = 6$; e.g., "Like sometimes there's just no way to satisfy him and sometimes I get frustrated over that. And whenever I show him that I am frustrated, usually he feels that I'm mad at him.").
2. My partner does not pick up on subtle hints ($n = 4$; e.g., "I gave him lots of hints. I think he must have known why I am upset by then. He just kept asking 'what is wrong?'").
3. I must repeat my requests ($n = 4$; e.g., "I went through this whole list of things that I liked that he does. He worked on it for a while and then it's kind of go out the door, so we had to revisit it. But it has been long time together. It's kind of tiring.").
4. My partner avoids conversation ($n = 3$; e.g., "He just didn't seem to talk about it and that completely shuts me off too.").
5. My partner does not accommodate my requests ($n = 3$; e.g., "He was not really as accommodating and made a lot of excuses.").

Our participants also described communication strategies they employed to *diffuse and deescalate potential conflicts* surrounding sexual discrepancies. The analysis of these reports revealed eleven themes or strategies. Table 3.2 displays the relevant data.

TABLE 3.2 Results of the tests of the indirect paths from argument role to stress through demand/withdraw

Deescalation strategy	n	Illustrative quotation from participants' reports
Avoidance	12	"Just don't talk about it."
		"Try to keep things inside and just faking."
Timing	10	"I bring it up when guys were vulnerable, like right before having sex. They don't have time to get mad or defensive."
		"Wait for right moment, talk about the issue later like next morning."
Word choice	7	"I try to choose the nicest and softest way possible while talking about what he could have done better for me."
		"Usually give it a minute to think about how to word my request."
Express feelings	7	"The best is just let him know how I feel about that."
		"I feel like this" instead of "you make me feel like this": talking from "I" standpoint.
Positive feedback	6	"Tell him what he was doing well first and then tell him what I would like better afterwards."
		"I kind of butter it up first. He needs a cushion."
Open/honest	6	"Be clear about what I want up-front so that he wouldn't misunderstand. It removes any unnecessary possibility of misunderstandings."
		"Just be open and honest about it [sexual discrepancy]. Then he will understand."
Collaborating	5	"Let's just talk about it and find out what we can do better together so both of us enjoy it more."
		"Suggest to him 'Let's work on it together to meet in the middle on this.' You should emphasize that efforts should be made by both of you, not just him."
No blaming	4	"Avoid sounding like you are blaming each other."
		"Don't blame someone. Don't be mean about it. Explain."
Physical excuse	4	"Saying 'Oh my shoulder hurts.'"
		"When I don't want to have sex, I just use 'I am tired strategy' or 'pass out strategy'."
Soothe his ego	3	"Tried to soothe his ego and let him know clearly there are other reasons [that she didn't enjoy sex], not because of him."
Accommodating	3	"Tried to do whatever he wants to make him feel good. I don't mind doing it for him."

Note: The numbers in the second column indicate how many participants reported each strategy.

Discussion

Interpretation of the Results

Discussed Sexual Discrepancies

Our participants reported *not* discussing discrepancies as frequently as they occur. Furthermore, participants reported discussing some discrepancies very rarely (i.e., initiating sex, his quick sex, sexual expressiveness, previous sexual experience, self-consciousness about body, and sex as psychological connection versus physical connection).

No discussion and rarely discussing disagreements function as classic avoidance strategies. Although previous researchers have documented the tendency for relational partners to initially avoid discussing sexual histories (e.g., Amason et al, 2012; Anderson et al, 2011), the finding that established sexual partners routinely avoid discussing sexual discrepancies is new. Perhaps participants lacked the self-esteem to raise such sensitive issues (Oattas & Offman, 2007) or viewed the issues as not important enough to discuss and preferred to accommodate their partners' requests (Moore et al, 2013). Perhaps participants believed that talking was useless, as behaviors concerning these matters would not change. Finally, participants may have avoided discussion to avert potential damage to their relationships. Conversely, this sample of women in their 20s may lack the conflict management skills to raise delicate issues of disagreement.

Sexual Conflicts and Communication Strategies

In contrast to the assumption of a direct link between sexual discrepancies and sexual conflicts made by Sprecher and Cate (2004), 65 percent of our participants reported not experiencing sexual conflicts during communication about sexual discrepancies. A number of explanations are available for this result. First, 30 percent of the participants in this study reported that they never or never seriously discussed their discrepancies. Thus, for these participants, there were limited opportunities for conflicts to arise in conversations about sexual discrepancies. Second, many participants viewed sexual discrepancies as unimportant and not worthy of conflict. Third, during the interviews, many participants reported overall satisfaction with their partners in their sexual relationships despite discrepancies. Such overall satisfaction may "prime" their experiences into positive memories (Wiederman, 2004) and their small conflicts may not appear sufficiently to label them as issues significant enough to lead to conflict. Finally, the participants consciously or subconsciously may tend to report that they did not have very serious conflicts as having sexual conflicts with a partner may be viewed as indicative of an unhappy relationship (Wiederman, 2004).

Triggering Sexual Conflicts

According to the participants' reports of the factors that escalated and de-escalated conflicts, the following conditions may be necessary for sexual discrepancies to develop into sexual conflicts: First, sexual discrepancies must be considered as problematic issues worthy of discussion. Second, sexual discrepancies must be communicated to and discussed with their partners. Third, participants reported ineffective communicative strategies that escalated conflicts during conversations (i.e., straightforward comments, displaying anger or frustration, and blaming the partner). These strategies appear to describe a competitive conflict style that can be "characterized by aggressive and uncooperative behavior–pursuing your own concerns at the expense of another" (Wilmot & Hocker, 2013, p156). Participants reported that such strategies often prompted defensiveness from their partners, and therefore escalated conflicts.

Communication Strategies that Ameliorate Sexual Conflicts

In contrast, many participants reported employing communicative strategies that effectively diffused possible conflicts during conversations (i.e., expressing feelings, positive feedback, soothing his ego). Thus, communication can play an important mediating role between sexual discrepancies and sexual conflicts. Such effective communicative strategies avoided prompting defensiveness and strategically employed a specific array of tactics (i.e., timing, word choice, positive feedback and using physical excuses). The majority of the participants reported an "avoidance" strategy that was "characterized by denial of the conflict, changing and avoiding topics, being noncommittal, and joking rather than dealing with the conflict at hand" (Wilmot & Hocker, 2013, p151). According to Rahim (1986), avoidance is an appropriate response when a conflict is trivial such as a minor preference. Joking and the use of humor were previously identified as strategies to ease an awkward situation in communication about sex (Amason & Webb, 2007; Miller-Ott & Linder, 2014). The participants reported avoidance when they considered issues trivial or when issues required high-risk disclosure (e.g., lack of orgasm). Such disclosures can involve a careful balance between confrontation and avoidance (Roloff & Ifert, 2000).

The participants' avoidance strategies may have proved effective for multiple reasons:

1. Many participants regarded the discrepancies as unimportant issues, and thus the participants did not experience negative consequences as a result of avoiding the conflict (Rahim, 1986).
2. The participants used coping devices together with avoidance. For example, participants may have employed positive activities to balance the negative activities by engaging in frequent mutually enjoyable activities (i.e.,

suggesting alternative positions) or by making positive optimistic comparisons (i.e., our communication is getting better).
3. Many participants reported using avoidance selectively (i.e., for more risky topics) rather than universally.
4. Participants' choice of avoidance strategy was freely made rather than coerced.

Methodological Challenges and Suggestions for Future Research

Because of the sensitive nature of the subject matter, there are several limitations inherent in studying communication about sexual discrepancies (Wiederman, 2004). First, because participation was voluntary, participants who volunteered for the interviews may have been more sexually experienced, more comfortable with sexual topics, and more liberal in their sexual attitude than women who failed to volunteer.

Second, the majority of the participants were relatively young (in their 20s) and single, although most reported being involved in a serious romantic relationship. Women's experience with communication about sexual discrepancies may vary by marital status and may be different from generation and to generation. A future study could assess how demographic differences (e.g., married versus unmarried, younger woman in comparison to older women) may influence women's communication about sexual discrepancies. Our investigation focused on the heterosexual couple's communication about sexual discrepancies from the female partner's perspective. It would be interesting to investigate the same subject from the male partner's perspective and/or among same-sex couples. However, we limited our sample to women of a certain age, marital status, and sexual preference exactly because we believed each population defined by sex, age-range, marital status, and sexual preference may engage in sex talk and conflict differently. Our limited sample thus allows a focused examination of conflict among a defined group of interactants.

Third, because our study employed in-depth interviewing, we collected self-report data – data that may be distorted in a number of ways, including memory lapses, the social desirability response bias (i.e., providing desirable answers and presenting the relationship/partner in a positive light), and priming memories and perceptions (i.e., answers may be influenced by participants' feelings about their partners at the time of the interview). Furthermore, providing the protocol to the participants 48 hours in advance may have influenced the participants' answers by priming their thoughts and experiences and thus further exacerbated the social desirability response bias. Although our data was limited to self-reports, an argument can be made that the participants' beliefs regarding their private interactions, rather than the interactions themselves, are the repository and most accurate representations of the meanings exchanged and the realities perceived (Tridico, 2003). Indeed, we employed data collection and analytic techniques designed to capture private meanings and perceptions.

The limitations reported above may be unavoidable in examinations of intimate, private interactions – especially those involving sex and conflict, two aspects of human interaction that are culturally considered inappropriate for public display and open discussion. Scholars cannot directly observe such interactions without potentially violating the rights of participants and/or altering the interactions they sought to observe. Thus, we rightfully turn to informants who functioned as participant-observers in the communicative acts understudy. Their reports offer "best evidence" of the communicative behaviors that occur in these most intimate of interactions.

Facilitated by modern technologies, new research methods for self-report have appeared on the scene (e.g., Sunner et al, 2013). If we trust that human subjects will remember to record data in a timely way and/or wear their required data recording devises, modern technologies may usher in a new era of data collection. These data collection devises fail to allow for the "follow-up questions" of interviews or focus groups. Additionally, they may require extensive field testing and refinement. Nonetheless, they hold great promise for providing researchers access to otherwise unobservable yet quite important communication behavior.

Conclusions

Despite these limitations, this study contributes to an understanding of conflicts about sexual discrepancies in multiple ways. Our chapter represents the first investigation of women's communication about sexual discrepancies. Accordingly, it provides the first list of sexual discrepancies that women report discussing with their heterosexual partners. Furthermore, among one sample of women describing communication in their heterosexual relationships, our study documents the mediating role of communication between sexual discrepancies and sexual conflicts. Finally, our study suggested tactical strategies to avoid and ameliorate possible conflicts during conversations between heterosexual partners about sexual discrepancies.

Note

1 A copy of the interview protocol is available upon request from the second author at <LynneWebb320@cs.com>.

References

Amason, P., & Webb, L. M. (2007). Interpersonal communication issues in conversations about sexually transmitted diseases. In K. B. Wright (University of Oklahoma) & S. D. Moore (California State University, Fresno), (Eds.), *Applied Health Communication: A Sourcebook* (pp313–340). Cresskill, NJ: Hampton Press.

Amason, P., Webb, L. M., & Agee, P. K. (2012). College students' descriptions of conflicts during safer sex talk: Managing challenging, intimate conversations. In M. U. D'Silva, J.

Hart, & K. L. Walker, (Eds.), *Communicating about HIV/AIDS: Taboo topics and difficult conversations.* Cresskill, NJ: Hampton Press.

Anderson, M., Kunkel, A., & Dennis, M. R. (2011). 'Let's (not) talk about that': Bridging the past sexual experiences taboo to build healthy romantic relationships. *Journal of Sex Research, 48,* 381–391, doi: 10.1080/00224499.2010.482215.

Benmen, J., & Vogel, A. (1985). The relationship between marital quality and interpersonal sexual communication. *Family Therapy, 12,* 45–58. Retrieved from http://psycnet.apa.org/psycinfo/1985-30615-001.

Broaddus, M. R. & Dickson-Gomez, J. (2013). Text messaging for sexual communication and safety among African American young adults. *Qualitative Health Research, 20,* 1344–1353, doi: 10.1177/1049732313505712.

Buss, D. M. (1989). Conflict between sexes: Strategic interference and the evocation of anger and upset. *Journal of Personality and Social Psychology, 56,* 735–747, doi: 10.1037/0022-3514.565.735.

Byers, E. S. (2001). Evidence for the importance of relationship satisfaction for women's sexual functioning. *Women & Therapy, 24,* 23–26, doi: 10.1300/J015v24n01_04.

Byers, E. S. & Demmons, S. (1999). Sexual satisfaction and sexual self-disclosure within dating relationships. *Journal of Sex Research, 36,* 180–189, doi: 10.1080/00224499909551983.

Byers, E. S., & Lewis, K. (1988). Dating couples' disagreements over the desired level of sexual intimacy. *Journal of Sex Research, 24,* 15–29, doi: 10.1080/00224498809551395.

Charmaz, K. (1983). The grounded theory method: An explication and interpretation. In R. Emerson (Ed.), *Contemporary field research* (pp109–126). Boston, MA: Little Brown.

Cupach, W. R., & Comstock, J. (1990). Satisfaction with sexual communication in marriage: Links to sexual satisfaction and dyadic adjustment. *Journal of Social and Personal Relationships, 7,* 179–186, doi: 10.1177/0265407590072002.

Cupach, W. R., & Metts, S. (1995). The role of sexual attitude similarity in romantic heterosexual relationships. *Personal Relationships, 2,* 287–300, doi: 10.1111/j.1475-6811.1995.tb00093.x.

Davies, S., Katz, J., & Jackson, J. L. (1999). Sexual desire discrepancies: Effects on sexual and relationship satisfaction in heterosexual dating couples. *Archives of Sexual Behavior, 28,* 553–567, doi: 10.1023/A.1018721417683.

Duck, S., Starch, D., Starch, A., Rutt, D. J., Hoy, M., & Hurst, H. S. (1991). Some evident truths about conversations in everyday relationships: All communications are not created equal. *Human Communication Research, 18,* 228–267, doi: 10.1111/j.1468-2958.1991.tb00545.x.

Frith, H. (2013). Accounting for orgasmic absence: Exploring heterosexuality using the story completion method. *Psychology and Sexuality, 4,* 310–322, doi: 10.1080/19419899.2012.76x172.

Glaser, B., & Strauss, A. (1967). *Discovery of grounded theory.* Chicago, IL: Aldine.

Goodboy, A. K., & Myers, S. A. (2008). Relational maintenance behaviors of friends with benefits: Investigating equity and relational characteristics. *Human Behavior, 11,* 71–86. Retrieved from www.uab.edu/communicationstudies/humancommunication/11.6.pdf

Gorden, S., & Snyder, C. W. (1986). *Personal issues in human sexuality.* Newton, MA: Allyn & Bacon.

Greene, K., & Faulkner, S. (2005). Gender, belief in the sexual double standard, and sexual talk in heterosexual dating relationships. *Sex Roles, 53,* 239–251, doi: 10.1007/s11199-005-5682-6.

Hatfield, E., Sprecher, W., Pillemer, J. T., Greenberger, D., Wexler, D. (1988). Gender differences in what is desired in the sexual relationship. *Journal of Psychology and Human Sexuality*, *1*(2), 39–53, doi: 10.1300/Jo56v01n02–04.

Krusiewicz, E. S., & Wood, J. T. (2001). "He was our child from the moment we walked in the room": Entrance stories of adoptive parents. *Journal of Social and Personal Relationships*, *18*, 785–803, doi: 10.1177/0265407501186003.

La France, B. H. (2010). Predicting sexual satisfaction in interpersonal relationships. *Southern Communication Journal*, *75*, 195–214, doi: 10.1080/10417940902787939.

LaRossa, R. (2005). Grounded theory methods and qualitative family research. *Journal of Marriage and Family*, *67*, 837–857, doi: 10.1111/j.1741–3737.2005.00179.x.

Lim, G. Y., & Roloff, M. E. (1999). Attributing sexual consent. *Journal of Applied Communication Research*, *27*, 1–23, doi: 10.1080/00909889909365521.

Mark, K. P., & Jozkowski, K. N. (2013). The mediating role of sexual and nonsexual communication between relationship and sexual satisfaction in a sample of college-age heterosexual couples. *Journal of Sex & Marital Therapy*, *39*, 410–427, doi: 10.1080/0092623X.2011.6444652.

Mark, K. P., & Murray, S. H. (2012). Gender differences in desire discrepancy as a predictor of sexual and relationship satisfaction in a college sample of heterosexual romantic relationships. *Journal of Sex & Marital Therapy*, *38*, 198–215, doi: 10.1080/0092623x.2011.606877.

MacNeil, S., & Byers, E. S. (2005). Dyadic assessment of textual self-disclosure and sexual satisfaction in heterosexual dating couples. *Journal of Social and Personal Relationships*, *22*, 169–181, doi: 10.1177/0265407505050942.

Miller, S. A., & Byers, E. S. (2004). Actual and desired duration of foreplay and intercourse: Discordance and misperceptions within heterosexual couples. *Journal of Sex Research*, *41*, 301–309, doi: 10.1080/00224490409552237.

Miller-Ott, A. E., & Linder, A. (2014). Romantic partners' use of facework and humor to communicate about sex. *Qualitative Research Reports in Communication*, *14*, 69–78, doi: 10.1080/17459435.2013.835344.

Montesi, J. L., Fauber, R. L., Gordon, E. A., & Heimberg, R. G. (2011). The specific importance of communicating about sex to couples' sexual and overall relationship satisfaction. *Journal of Social & Personal Relationships*, *28*, 591–609, doi: 10.1177/0.2654075.10386833.

Moore, D., Wigby, S., English, S., Wong, S., Szekely, T., & Harrison, F. (2013). Selflessness is sexy: Reported helping behavior increases desirability of men and women as long-term partners. *BMC Evolutionary Biology*, *13*, 182–190, doi: 10.1186/1471-2148-13-182.

Morokoff, P. J., Quina, K., Harlow, L. L., Whitmire, L., Grimley, D. M., Gibson, P. R., & Burkholder, G. J. (1997). Sexual Acquiesce Scale (SAS) for women: Development and validation. *Journal of Personality and Social Psychology*, *73*, 790–804, doi: 10.1037/0022–3514.73.4.790.

Noland, C. M. (2006). Listening to the sound of silence: Gender roles and communication about sex in Puerto Rico. *Sex Roles*, *55*, 283–294, doi: 10.1007/s11199–006–9083–2.

Oattas, M. K., & Offman, A. (2007). Global self-esteem and sexual self-esteem as predictors of sexual communication in intimate relationships. *Canadian Journal of Human Sexuality*, *16*, 89–10. Retrieved from http://connection.ebscohost.com/c/articles/31123761/global-self-esteem-sexual-self-esteem-as-predictors-sexual-communication-intimate-relationships

Owen, W. F. (1984). Interruptive themes in relational communication. *Quarterly Journal of Speech, 70,* 274–287, doi: 10.1080/00335638409383697.

Purnine, D. M., & Carey, M. P. (1997). Interpersonal communication and sexual adjustment: The roles of understanding and agreement. *Journal of Consulting and Clinical Psychology, 65,* 1013–5025. Retrieved from http://psycnet.apa.org/index.cfm?fa=buy.op tionToBuy&id=1998-00068-012

Rahim, M. E. (1986). Referent role and styles of handling interpersonal conflict. *Journal of Social Psychology, 125(1),* 79–86, doi: 10.1080/00224545.1986.9713573.

Roloff, M. E., & Ifert, D. E. (2000). Conflict management through avoidance: Withholding complaints, suppressing arguments, and declaring topics taboo. In S. Petronio (Ed.), *Balancing the secrets of private disclosures* (pp151–163). Mahwah, NJ: Erlbaum.

Santittila, P., Wager, I., Witting, K., Harlaar, N., Jern, P., Johansson, M. V., & Sandnabba, K. (2008). Discrepancies between sexual desire and sexual activity: Gender differences and associations with relationship satisfaction. *Journal of Sex & Marital Therapy, 34,* 31–44, doi: 10.1080/00926230701620548.

Sieg, E. (2007). "What you want, or what you get?" Young women talking about the gap between desired and lived heterosexual relationships in the 21st century. *Women's Studies International Forum, 30,* 175–186, doi: 10.1016/vusif.2007.01.007.

Sprecher, S., & Cate, R. M. (2004). Sexual satisfaction and sexual expression as predictors of relationship satisfaction and stability. In J. H. Harvey, A. Wenzel, & S. Sprecher (Eds.) *The handbook of sexuality in close relationships* (pp7–30). Mahwah, NJ: Erlbaum.

Strauss, A., & Corbin, J. (1998). *Basics of qualitative research: Techniques and procedures for developing grounded theory.* Thousand Oaks, CA: Sage.

Sunner, L. E., Walls, C., Blood, E. A., Mehta, C. M., & Shrier, L. A. (2013). Feasibility and utility momentary sampling of sex events in young couples. *Journal of Sex Research, 50,* 688–696, doi: 10.1080/00224499.2012.674574.

Timm, T. M. & Keilley, M. K. (2011). The effects of differentiation of self, adult attachment, and sexual communication on sexual and marital satisfaction: A path analysis. *Journal of Sex & Marital Therapy, 37,* 206–223, doi: 10.1080/0092623x.2011.564513.

Tridico, F. (2003). *The social construction of reality.* Sault Saint Marie, ON: Elsemere Press.

Tschann, J. M., & Adler, N. E. (1997). Sexual self-acceptance, communication with partner, and contraceptive use among adolescent females: A longitudinal study. *Journal of Research on Adolescence, 7,* 413–430. Retrieved from http://www.tandfonline.com/doi/abs/10.1207/s15327795jra0704_4#preview

Wheeless, L. R., & Parsons, L. A. (1995). What you feel is what you might get: Exploring communication apprehension and sexual communication satisfaction. *Communication Research Reports, 12,* 39–45, doi: 10.1080/08824099509362037.

Wheeless, L., Wheeless, R., & Baus, R. (1984). Sexual communication, communication satisfaction, and solidarity in the developmental stages of intimate relationships. *Western Journal of Speech Communication, 48,* 217–230, doi: 10.1080/10570318409374158.

Wiederman, M. W. (2004). Methodological issues in studying sexuality in close relationships. In J. H. Harvey, A. Wenzel, S. Sprecher (Eds.) *The handbook of sexuality in close relationships* (pp31–56). Mahwah, NJ: Erlbaum.

Willoughby, B. J., Farero, A. M., & Busby, D. M. (2014). Exploring the effects of sexual desire discrepancy among married couples. *Archives of Sexual Behavior, 43,* 551–562, doi: 10.1007/s10508–013–0181–2.

Wilmot, W. W., & Hocker, J. L. (2013). *Interpersonal conflict,* 9th ed. Boston, MA: McGraw Hill.

Yela, C. (2000). Predictors of and factors related to loving and sexual satisfaction for men and women. *European Review of Applied Psychology, 50,* 235–243. Retrieved from http://psycnet.apa.org/psycinfo/2000-05855-022

Yelsma, P. (1986). Marriage versus cohabitation couples' communication practices and satisfaction. *Journal of Communication, 36,* 94–107, doi: 10.1111/j.1460–2466.1986.tbx1453.x.

4

THE CONNECTIONS BETWEEN COMMUNICATION TECHNOLOGIES AND RELATIONAL CONFLICT

A Multiple Goals and Communication Interdependence Perspective

John P. Caughlin, Erin D. Basinger, and Liesel L. Sharabi

There is a long history of scholarly interest in relational conflict, and the literature on the topic has become enormous (for reviews, see Caughlin et al, 2013; Sillars & Canary, 2013). For most of the time that scholars have studied relational conflict, the main focus has been on individuals' verbal and nonverbal behaviors during face-to-face (FtF) conflict episodes. Despite the recent rise of research on technologically mediated communication (TMC) and especially computer-mediated communication (CMC) within personal relationships (Barnes, 2003; Baym, 2010; Konjin et al, 2008), extremely little research on relational conflict has considered the role that new communication technologies may play in relational conflict. Indeed, many of the common methods for studying relational conflict effectively preclude learning about the potential functions of TMC; for example, typical observational methods direct participants to have a FtF discussion about conflict topics in a laboratory setting that would discourage the use of TMC (e.g., see Caughlin & Scott, 2010).

Although conflict scholars (including the lead author of this chapter) have been slow to consider the role of TMC in relational conflict, there are good reasons to suspect that understanding contemporary relational conflict will require an understanding of TMC in such conflicts. Young adults often use social networking throughout the day (Duggan & Brenner, 2013), and with the rise in smartphones, the potential for using technologies in their communication is nearly constant (Birnholtz et al, 2012). Although CMC can play a role in establishing and maintaining weak tie relationships, young adults now commonly use TMC in established relationships with friends, family, and romantic partners (Ellison et al, 2007; Subrahmanyam & Greenfield, 2008). Given that conflict is common in such relationships, and individuals are using technologies to communicate in those relationships, it seems likely that people use TMC in at least some relational conflicts.

This chapter explores the role that communication technologies may play in relational conflicts. It begins with a discussion of the small amount of research that exists on the use of computers and other communication technologies in conflict. Next, it provides a theoretical overview for conceptualizing the connections between TMC and conflict within ongoing personal relationships. Finally, it summarizes an exploratory study that provides evidence that communication technologies have become salient in some conflicts and has important implications for the CMC literature, the conflict literature, and for our understanding of close relationships.

Explicating the Connection between Technology and Interpersonal Conflict

Despite the pervasiveness of TMC, there has been a relative dearth of research on how communication technologies are implicated in relational conflict (Ishii, 2010). This comes as somewhat of a surprise, especially given the apparent advantages of using mediated channels alone or in combination with FtF communication to facilitate conflict. Asynchronous CMC, for example, affords users greater control over their self-presentation and more time to consider what they want to say and how they want to say it (Walther, 1996). Moreover, the absences of certain nonverbal cues in much TMC, such as eye contact, facial expressions, and tone of voice, may make it easier to focus on the content of conflicts rather than identity issues that can complicate conflict, turning a resolvable issue into one much more fraught with emotion (Fincham & Beach, 1999). It is also possible that using mediated communication could allow people to approach tense or uncomfortable topics that would otherwise be difficult to discuss. For instance, some people may prefer to broach a conflict-inducing topic through instant messaging (IM), where they do not have to see the looks on their partner's face or hear the emotion in his or her voice. Thus, it would seem that the role of technology in conflict should not be overlooked, as it may act as an important supplement to traditional FtF conversation.

The research that does exist in this area has often viewed FtF conflict as either an antecedent or outcome of technology use. As an example of the former, one line of scholarship has looked at how people use technology for managing disagreements that already exist in their relationships. For instance, in an examination of the channels that romantic partners prefer to use for managing conflict, Frisby and Westerman (2010) found that participants with an avoiding or integrating conflict style tended towards FtF communication, whereas those with a dominating style were more likely to engage in conflict through CMC. Just a few of the reasons that couples report for having chosen CMC for conflict management are that it allowed them to plan out their messages and that it gave them more time to get their emotions under control (Perry & Werner-Wilson, 2011). Technology may also be responsible for improving the quality of already conflicted relationships.

This is demonstrated by Kanter, Afifi, and Robbins (2012), who found that young adult children who perceived greater amounts of conflict in the parent–child relationship ended up feeling closer to their parent after he or she "friended" them on Facebook.

Technology can also be used to avoid a pre-existing conflict. With CMC, it is easier for people to abandon a conversation when emotions become too intense or to evade it altogether (Merkle & Richardson, 2000). One needs simply to shut down the computer or turn off the phone to render him or herself unreachable through technology, which is a luxury that is not afforded by FtF contact. Short message service (SMS) is one technology, in particular, that may be appealing as a means of avoiding conflict. Cho and Hung (2011), for example, found that people who were more concerned with conflict avoidance and who perceived SMS as an effective communication channel generally had more positive attitudes towards the technology.

Other research has focused on technology as a source of contention in ongoing relationships. Findings indicate that one of the primary reasons social media users give for deleting online content is that it caused, or had the potential to cause, conflict in their relationships (Child et al, 2012). In romantic relationships, people also report having experienced conflict over their own or their partner's relationship status (or lack thereof) on Facebook (Papp & Danielewicz, 2012). What is more, Duran, Kelly, and Rotaru (2011) observed that cell phone use (e.g., not responding to text messages or phone calls in a timely manner) contributed to conflict in young adults' romantic relationships. Specifically, they found that the state of "perpetual contact" created by cell phones left participants feeling torn between wanting to connect with their partner and still needing to maintain their own independence.

In sum, when compared to the enormous conflict literature in general, there has not been much research on relational conflict and TMC. Still, the studies that do exist suggest that communication technologies may have multifaceted roles in relational conflict, ranging from facilitating effective emotion management, to serving as a way to offer reconciliation, to providing a means for avoiding communication, to being the source of relational conflicts. Even with such a small number of studies on the topic, it appears that communication technologies have become important to understanding at least some relational conflicts. Whereas the existing studies provide compelling evidence of the importance of TMC in relational conflict, their disparate findings suggest the need for more systematic theorizing about this topic.

A Spotlight Study on TMC: Highlighting the Influence of Goals

The current research is grounded in two theoretical perspectives on interpersonal communication. The first perspective is *multiple goals theories* of communication (for overviews, see Caughlin, 2010; Wilson & Feng, 2007). Multiple goals theories is an umbrella term for a number of specific theories that have similar tenets. A core assumption of these theories is the notion that communication is purposeful; that is, when people communicate they seek to achieve goals or "desired end states for which individuals strive" (Berger, 2004, p50). The goals that people pursue can be related to tasks like influencing another person (e.g., Dillard & Knobloch, 2011), but people also pursue goals related to managing their own identities, other people's identities, and their relationships with other people (Clark & Delia, 1979).

The three broad categories of task, identity, and relational goals encompass a wide variety of more specific communication goals, but it is useful to conceptualize goals at this broad level because these types of goals are relevant in many (if not all) interpersonal communication encounters (Clark & Delia, 1979). Various task, identity, and relational goals are salient within many encounters, which implies that individuals often must attend to more than one goal at a time, hence the phrase "multiple goals." In relational conflicts, the various goals of the individuals involved often are not easily achieved simultaneously (Canary, 2003). Such competition among relevant goals can occur within the set of goals of a particular person; for instance, a person wishing to demand that a partner changes somehow may find that the identity goals of seeming like a reasonable and accepting partner can be threatened by pursuing change too forcefully (Canary, 2003; Caughlin & Scott, 2010). Competing goals can also occur across partners; in fact, seemingly incongruent goals between individuals has long been considered one of the defining characteristics of interpersonal conflict (e.g., Lewin, 1948).

Multiple goals theories also presume that communicative goals shape individuals' communication behaviors. Having concern about the other person's goals in conflict, for instance, is associated with foregoing destructive strategies (Canary, 2003). Although the association between goals and conflict behaviors is usually conceptualized in terms of how goals influence message strategies, the logic of multiple goals perspectives would predict that communicative goals would also influence how various communication resources, such as TMC, would be used. Because research on TMC and relational conflict is in its infancy, it is impossible to make systematic predictions about exactly how goals will be associated with TMC usage, but this theoretical perspective does predict that the use of TMC related to conflict is purposeful and influenced by the multiple goals that are pertinent to relational conflict.

The second theoretical base of the current study is the *communication interdependence perspective* (Caughlin & Sharabi, 2013). This theoretical viewpoint extends research on relational interdependence theory (Kelley, et al, 1983) and concerns the connections between FtF communication and TMC. There is growing evidence that many close relationships utilize both traditional in person communication and newer communication modes within the same relationships and that the closeness of the relationship is related positively to both FtF communication and TMC (Baym & Ledbetter, 2009; Baym et al. 2004; Ramirez & Broneck, 2009).

In addition to predicting that the amount of communication via various modes would be related to relational closeness, the communicative interdependence perspective highlights how communication that happens in person can be interconnected with communication that occurs via technological mediation. For instance, some topics in relationships become the focus of serial arguments, which involve repeatedly discussing a particular conflict issue over time (Reznik & Roloff, 2011). The communication interdependence perspective implies that the discourse about the conflict topic might occur by various modes over time, such as instances in which a dyad discusses the same issue at different times in person, over the phone, via text messaging, and via instant messaging.

In addition to highlighting the interconnections between FtF communication and TMC, communicative interdependence posits that it is important to distinguish between connections that *interfere* with versus those that *facilitate* relational communication. Interference between modes means that the communication via one mode makes communication via another more difficult. Instances in which compulsive internet use harms the relationship (and presumably the quality of the FtF communication) would be an obvious example of interference (Kerkhof et al, 2011). Yet there are also times when communication via one mode may facilitate communication via another; for example, communication technologies could allow a pleasant conversation to continue even if the individuals must physically part.

Consistent with the notion that it is important to distinguish interference and facilitation among communication modes, Caughlin and Sharabi (2013) found that integration of communication between FtF and TMC modes (e.g., talking in person about topics they also texted about) was positively associated with relational closeness in college students' romantic relationships, whereas difficulty transitioning a conversation from one mode to another was inversely related to closeness and satisfaction. Also consistent with communication interdependence, individuals who reported that they had topics that they talked about only via TMC (i.e., there was a lack of interconnection across modes) reported lower closeness and satisfaction than did people who reported that they did not have topics they only discussed via technologies. Yet having topics that were discussed only when FtF was positively related to closeness, suggesting that people may reserve some important topics for discussion in person.

Based on both the multiple goals perspective and the communicative interdependence perspective, it seems likely that college students would utilize communication technologies in their relational conflicts. College students use TMC frequently, and there is evidence that the closer their relationships, the more likely they are to use TMC and to have TMC become interconnected with their FtF communication. Although such interconnections seem likely, the extant literature provides only indirect clues about what these interconnections might look like. To begin understanding the role of communication technologies in contemporary relational conflicts, a first step is to create a descriptive base of how TMC is commonly implicated in conflict. To examine this issue, we asked two general research questions: (*RQ1*): How do college students describe using (or not using) TMC during conflict in their close relationships and (*RQ2*): How (if at all) do college students describe avoiding conflict via TMC?

Method

Participants

Students enrolled at the University of Illinois in Urbana-Champaign were invited to participate in a study reflecting on their experiences with communication technologies and relational conflict. The sample was 64 participants ($n = 33$ males, 52.38%; $n = 31$ females, 49.21%) with an average age of 21.03 years ($SD = 1.22$). Approximately half of the sample was European American ($n = 30$, 47.62%), with other participants reporting their ethnicities as African American ($n = 13$, 20.63%), Asian ($n = 13$, 20.63%), or other ($n = 8$, 12.70%). Participants were asked to think about interactions with someone with whom they frequently have conflict. Over half reported on conflicts with a romantic partner ($n = 34$, 53.97%), whereas others reflected on conflicts with friends ($n = 17$, 26.98%), mothers ($n = 7$, 11.11%), roommates ($n = 3$, 4.76%), and siblings ($n = 3$, 4.76%).

Procedures

Participants were recruited either in class or through a flyer posted on a course website and were offered a small amount of extra course credit for participation. Both recruitment methods directed participants to a link to an online survey on a university-based domain. The survey contained questions about participants' use of communication technology for engaging in or avoiding conflict with a close other (e.g., romantic partner, parent, sibling, roommate). To protect participants' identities, a link on the final page of the survey directed them to a separate survey where they entered their name and course information to receive extra credit.

Measures

After reading informed consent, the survey instructions asked participants to "think about someone you are close to and at least sometimes have conflicts with. This person could be a current or past romantic partner or it could be somebody else you are close enough to that you occasionally have disagreements." Then, they responded to five open-ended questions, four of which are pertinent to the current study. First, two questions asked how they and their partner used technology *during* face-to-face conflict ("Do you/your partner ever have times when you use your communication technologies during a face-to-face conflict? If so, please explain how this happens."). For the next two questions, they reflected on how they used technology to avoid face-to-face conflict ("Do you/your partner ever use communication technologies to avoid having face-to-face conflicts? If so, how does this happen?"). Participants also answered demographic questions about themselves and their communication partner.

Results

We analyzed participants' responses to develop categories that captured the experiences that were salient to them. In our analysis, two of the authors read through the data several times to observe commonalities that emerged at least three times in the responses. First, we considered the two questions about participants' own and their partners' use of technology *during* conflict, followed by the questions about use of technology to *avoid* conflict. After categories were developed, two authors used the categories to code participants' responses and obtain frequencies for each category. One response could be assigned multiple codes, and if the participant did not provide enough information to be categorized, the response was not coded. The categories and frequencies are presented in the sections that follow.

Using Communication Technologies during Face-to-Face Conflict

Because the types of information provided in participants' accounts of their own use of communication technologies during face-to-face conflict did not differ discernibly from their reports of others' use, we analyzed those two questions together. Nine categories emerged, and quotes illustrative of each category can be found in Table 4.1. *Habitual use* ($n = 9$) referred to the use of technology being unimpeded by the fact that participants were engaging in a FtF conflict. For example, some participants talked about checking text messages or social media notifications on their phones, even in the midst of a conflict. Second, *affect regulation* ($n = 6$) describes participants' use of technology to manage their emotional responses during face-to-face conflicts. For example, participants attended to their phones to calm down or distract themselves emotionally from the interaction. Third, *referencing* ($n = 10$) involved looking up information, either on the Internet or on their phones, that was related to the conflict; for example, some participants reported showing the other person a text message that instigated the conflict. Fourth, some participants used technology to *avoid attending to the interaction* ($n = 6$). That is, they used their phones or other technologies to mentally separate themselves from the conflict or the other person, engaging in behaviors like inattention to the other person's expressions. Fifth, technologies were used for *interacting with others* ($n = 6$), using technologies to confer with social network members who were not directly involved in the conflict. For some, this included broadcasting information about the conflict on social media websites. Sixth,

TABLE 4.1 Exemplary participant quotes for categories concerning the use of communication technologies during face-to-face conflict

Category Name	Participant Quotes
Habitual use	"one of us may check a text message or take a phone call or check a social media notification if one of our phones goes off" "Only to check time, check texts/notifications"
Affect regulation	"sometimes I use text messages to mentally escape the argument that is happening at hand" "I think we use them to distract ourselves – to distance ourselves – from the tension"
Referencing	"I may reference something we said previously over text and show them." "Yes, I might use my phone or computer to pull something to prove my argument."
Avoiding attending to the interaction	"I played cell phone games to avoid seeing my mother's angry face." "During a face-to-face conflict, I may begin to text just to show that I'm disinterested in what the other person has to say."
Interacting with others	"I will occasionally use communication technologies during face to face conflict. I do this by either contacting others and asking questions or using social media." "Yea my girlfriend will text me when she's mad at me or tweet about me instead of saying it to my face."
Continuing the conflict	"If I feel like I need to pursue the matter and that it might turn into an actual conflict, I'll text him and say we need to meet up." "If a conflict arises but doesn't get resolved in the time when I'm with someone then sometimes technologies are used. Basically if people have other obligations which is often the case."
Privacy	"Yes, there has been instances where my romantic partner and I are in a public place such as the movies and have had a disagreement therefore we would text one another about what problem we had with the other one." "Not usually, but rarely I will text someone that I am having conflict with even if I am right next to them because other people have shown up in the middle of our discussion/conflict."
Engaging in the conflict with technology only	"Yes, I have used texts messages to discuss certain issues. I send a simple message that briefly describes what I have to say. The other person responds similarly." "Yes. My girlfriend and I often bicker via text message since she is at home for the Summer and I am at school."
No	"No, I think it's best to solve problems face to face." "My significant other would get mad if I used other communication technologies if I was talking to them face-to-face."

technologies were used to *continue the conflict* ($n = 6$) that was begun in person. For example, some participants used technology to set up a meeting via text to finish a face-to-face conflict later. Seventh, participants used technologies to preserve their *privacy* ($n = 3$) by texting or using social media because a third party was present. Eighth, when participants *engaged in the conflict with technology only* ($n = 9$), they used their technology (especially texting) to actually conduct the entire conflict.

Finally, some participants said that they do *not* use communication technologies during face-to-face conflicts ($n = 54$). Often, these individuals even suggested that using technology is inappropriate interpersonal behavior. Because this category was by far the most frequently mentioned, it was possible to compare the responses about participants own conflict versus their reports of others. Although they reported that the others ($n = 30$) did not use technologies during FtF conflict more than they said that they did not themselves ($n = 24$), this differences was not significant: sign test = 1.067, $SE = 2.35$, $p = .29$.

Using Communication Technologies to Avoid Face-to-Face Conflicts

Five categories emerged from our analysis of the questions regarding participants' use of communication technology to avoid face-to-face conflict. Example quotes for each category are listed in Table 4.2. First, participants reported using technology as a means of *incremental introduction* ($n = 9$). That is, they used technology to ease into face-to-face conflicts, including establishing a time or place to meet and talk. Second, participants mentioned *being able to generate desired messages* ($n = 8$). Here, they used the asynchronous and editability features of their communication technologies to be able to formulate exactly what they wanted to say. Often, this involved the ability to craft honest and clear messages, but also sometimes referred to controlling the potential for undesired expressions. Third, many suggested that *technology is easier, and face-to-face conflict is more difficult* ($n = 20$). For these participants, face-to-face conflict was more face threatening or uncomfortable, whereas technologies afforded them ease and convenience. Fourth, some participants *used technology to distance* ($n = 12$) or remove themselves from conflict situations or avoid talking during conflict. For example, they attended to their technologies to signal disinterest in the conflict.

Finally, as in the first set of questions, some participants responded emphatically that they and the other person did *not* use communication technologies to avoid conflict ($n = 44$), often suggesting that it was more appropriate to engage in conflicts in person. In comparing the responses about themselves to those about the other person, participants were more likely to report that the other person ($n = 27$) did not use technology to avoid than they were to claim that they did not themselves ($n = 17$). This difference was statistically significant, sign test = 2.12, $SE = 2.121$, $p = .031$).

TABLE 4.2 Exemplary participant quotes for categories concerning the use of communication technologies to avoid face-to-face conflict

Category Name	Examples
Easing into face-to-face (incremental introduction)	"I will address an issue via text message on occasion before bringing it up in person to ease into the issue." "Even if I use technology to manage a conflict earlier, I will always approach the individual face-to-face later on to resolve the conflict."
Being able to generate the desired messages	"Again we use text messages. It helps give us time to think of excuses and comebacks. If you argue face to face, you are forced reply immediately and your nonverbal communication can be judged. If you use text messages you have more time to think of what to say and your nonverbal communication is not judged." "When I'm not sure I have the words to say quickly."
Technology is easier/face-to-face is more difficult	"It is sometimes easier to talk to a person and get all your thoughts out when you do not have to face them right away." "On certain occasions, I have just left a face-to-face situation, and only once I am behind a screen do I feel comfortable enough to initiate conflict or an argument, usually by saying what was on my mind while face-to-face with the other person, but too nervous or upset to actually say aloud."
Using technology to distance	"Sometimes she will go silent and stare at the computer screen or her phone instead while I'm trying to say something to avoid a conflict." "Yes, when seeing a person I might have had a conflict with in person, I would resort to my phone to act as if I am occupied so I do not have to confront the other person."
No	"I have never used communication technologies to avoid having face-to-face conflicts. I don't feel as if the matter will get settled that way."

Discussion

Overall, the results confirm that at least some college students use technologies for managing relational conflicts. Although it was common for participants to state that they or their counterpart did not use TMC in relational conflict, it is worth noting that these were still the minority of responses, and even some of the people who wrote "no" also admitted to occasionally using TMC in conflict. The current study is not well suited to making claims about the overall prevalence of the use of TMC in relational conflict, but it does suggest that it is common for some college students. Given that communication technologies are becoming more prevalent, this study establishes the importance of understanding how conflict management may be influenced by new communication technologies.

One surprising finding was the number of people who reported that it is inappropriate to use any TMC during conflict or to avoid conflict. In one respect, this is consistent with the possibility that even today's technologically sophisticated college students consider FtF discussion to be special or particularly meaningful (Caughlin & Sharabi, 2013). Yet, the fact that participants were less likely to report that they never avoid conflict using technologies than they were to report that the other never used technologies to avoid suggests that the reports may be somewhat biased. A likely explanation is that some individuals who avoid via technologies are able to do so in a way that goes unnoticed. This would suggest that the actual number of others who never avoid using TMC may be lower than implied by the participants' reports.

Relational Goals

The findings presented here provide some evidence that it is useful to consider how using TMC is related to multiple goals in conflict interactions. Consider, for instance, the reports of people easing into FtF communication with technologies and using technologies to have time to generate the kind of messages they want. These strategies appear very purposeful, and they seem aimed at using the asynchronous feature (Walther, 1996) of the technologies to engage in the issue at hand while mitigating other goals. For instance, a participant who cited concerns about being judged was clearly trying to discuss the conflict issue while managing identities at the same time. Such attempts can be understood as using technology to manage multiple goals.

Another interesting strategy from a goals perspective is using texting to show disinterest. There are more overt ways to show disinterest; one could walk away or overtly attest to a lack of interest. Texting to show disinterest is indirect in the sense that it does not commit the person to going on the record stating disinterest; for instance, if the other person claimed, "you are not even listening to me," the person doing the texting can still deny the avoidance (e.g., by saying something like "I heard every word you said"). Caughlin and Scott (2010) argued that indirect avoidance strategies can be a way for people to pursue a goal of not engaging in a conflict without taking the risks associated with overtly refusing to discuss the matter. Based on these data, it seems likely that cell phones and other new communication technologies have provided at least some young adults with a new resource for attempting a similar strategy. Such examples suggest that there is promise in conceptualizing the connections between TMC and relational conflict from a multiple goals perspective.

Communicative Interdependence

As expected from the communicative interdependence perspective, at least some college students appear to be using both TMC and FtF communication in interconnected ways to manage conflict. Although we did not explicitly ask participants to distinguish between interference and facilitation, it is clear from the data that both can occur. A number of participants reported that communication technologies can get in the way of productive conflict management, but others reported that they use it to initiate difficult conversations or give them time to find the right words to manage the conflict better. These data are plainly exploratory, but they do provide clear evidence that researchers interested in studying how technologies are used in conflict must go beyond examining whether they are used but also examine what they are being used for.

Methodological Challenges and Areas for Examining the Influence of Goals and Technology

Most research on relational conflict in general has not considered the role of communication technologies. Given that the use of technologies was salient to some participants and that technology use appeared to be directed toward communicative goals, the exclusion of technology from conflict research appears to be an important oversight. For example, the notion that people would utilize asynchronicity to gather their thoughts for more constructive messages would not be surprising to scholars familiar with the CMC literature (e.g., Walther, 1996), but we are not aware of any relational conflict research that previously has documented the use of communication technologies to manage emotion or aid in crafting messages. Our findings suggest resources for managing conflict that have not been recognized in the conflict literature.

The need to understand how communication technologies are implicated in relational conflict also has methodological implications. The traditional standard study of relational conflict involves controlled laboratory observations (Feeney & Noller, 2012). The most obvious advantage of controlled observations is they allow objective observations of conflict behaviors. Although such studies of relational conflict have yielded tremendous insights, the typical procedures of such studies would eliminate or at least discourage the use of TMC (Caughlin & Basinger, 2016). If we are to understand the role that TMC plays in relational conflict, it will be important to either augment traditional observational studies with other methods that account for the use of TMC or alter the laboratory procedures so that they provide greater opportunity to observe how some people are integrating TMC into conflict management.

Limitations and Future Directions

The current study obviously was exploratory. The goal was to provide a description of some ways in which TMC is implicated in conflict, but the fairly small sample size and small number of references to most of the categories meant that some important questions could not be examined. For instance, it was only feasible to compare the reports about the self and other with respect to the most commonly cited categories, those denying the use of TMC in conflict.

Also, although some participants believed that using TMC during conflict is inherently detrimental, our study does not provide systematic evidence of that hypothesis. As researchers begin to examine this issue, it is important that they attempt to capture the variety of ways in which communication technologies and relational conflict are interconnected, as well as how they both interfere with and facilitate constructive conflict management. There certainly are instances in which using communication technologies exacerbates conflict; for example, if the focus is on internet compulsion (Kerkhof et al, 2011), the effects might be more negative than would be the case for more typical uses of communication technologies. Still, the existence of some negative uses does not preclude the possibility that other uses might be helpful.

Moreover, although we asked participants to report on both people in the relationship, these data only hinted at the interactivity of relational conflict. As Keck and Samp (2007) demonstrated in an observational study of relational conflicts, partners' goals and behaviors are interconnected; for example, certain conflict tactics can elicit different goals in the other person. In examples like the participant who attributed his use of his cell phone during arguments to his mother's angry face, our data hint at such interconnections. Nevertheless, a more systematic examination is warranted, such as a replication of the Keck and Samp study that encouraged participants to utilize their communication technologies as they would in their everyday lives.

Finally, the differing opinions about the use of TMC that emerged spontaneously from the responses suggest that individual differences in preferences and usage may be important. It may be the case, for example, that a person can use asynchronicity to craft an objectively more constructive message than would be possible FtF, but what if that person's partner strongly believes that conflicts can only be properly handled in person? The current data provide tantalizing clues that it may not always be possible to label particular uses of TMC during conflict as either constructive or destructive; instead, whether a particular utilization is successful might depend on differences in attitudes or in how well partners are able to convince each other that various potential uses of TMC are appropriate. In other words, the very meaning of TMC in relational conflict may be partly negotiated.

References

Barnes, S. B. (2003). *Computer-mediated communication: Human-to-human communication across the Internet*. Boston, MA: Allyn and Bacon.

Baym, N. K. (2010). *Personal connections in the digital age*. Cambridge, UK: Polity Press.

Baym, N. K., & Ledbetter, A. (2009). Tunes that bind?: Predicting friendship strength in a music-based social network. *Information, Communication, & Society, 12*, 408–427. doi: 10.1080/13691180802635430

Baym, N. K., Zhang, Y. B., & Lin, M. C. (2004). Social interactions across media: Interpersonal communication on the Internet, telephone, and face-to-face. *New Media & Society, 6,* 299–318. doi: 10.1177/1461444804041438

Berger, C. R. (2004). Communication: A goal-directed, plan-guided process. In D. R. Roskos-Ewoldsen & J. L. Monahan (Eds.), *Communication and social cognition: Theories and methods* (pp47–70). Mahwah, NJ: Erlbaum.

Birnholtz, J., Hancock, J., Smith, M., & Reynolds, L. (2012). Understanding unavailability in a world of constant connection. *Interactions, 19,* 32–35, doi: 10.1145/2334184.2334193

Canary, D. J. (2003). Managing interpersonal conflict: A model of events related to strategic choices. In J. O. Greene & B. R. Burleson (Eds.), *Handbook of communication and social interaction skills* (pp515–549). Mahwah, NJ: Erlbaum.

Caughlin, J. P. (2010). A multiple goals theory of personal relationships: Conceptual integration and program overview. *Journal of Social and Personal Relationships, 27,* 824–848. doi: 10.1177/0265407510373262

Caughlin, J. P., & Basinger, E. D. (2016). Measuring interpersonal communication. In C. R. Berger & M. E. Roloff (General Eds.) & S. R. Wilson, J. P. Dillard, J. P. Caughlin, & D. H. Solomon (Assoc. Eds.), *International encyclopedia of interpersonal communication* (pp. 1–13). New York, NY: Wiley.

Caughlin, J. P., & Scott, A. M. (2010). Toward a communication theory of the demand/withdraw pattern of interaction in interpersonal relationships. In S. Smith & S. R. Wilson (Eds.), *New directions in interpersonal communication* (pp180–200). Thousand Oaks, CA: Sage.

Caughlin, J. P., & Sharabi, L. L. (2013). A communicative interdependence perspective of close relationships: The connections between mediated and unmediated interactions matter. *Journal of Communication, 63,* 873–893. doi: 10.1111/jcom.12046

Caughlin, J. P., Vangelisti, A. L., & Mikucki-Enyart, S. (2013). Conflict in dating and marital relationships. In J. G. Oetzel & S. Ting-Toomey (Eds.), *Sage handbook of conflict communication: Integrating theory, research, and practice* (2nd ed., pp161–186). Thousand Oaks, CA: Sage.

Clark, R. A., & Delia, J. G. (1979). Topoi and rhetorical competence. *Quarterly Journal of Speech, 65,* 187–206. doi: 10.1080/00335637909383470

Child, J. T., Haridakis, P. M., & Petronio, S. (2012). Blogging privacy rule orientations, privacy management, and content deletion practices: The variability of online privacy management activity at different stages of social media use. *Computers in Human Behavior, 28,* 1859–1872. doi: 10.1016/j.chb.2012.05.004

Cho, V., & Hung, H. (2011). The effectiveness of short message service for communication with concerns of privacy protection and conflict avoidance. *Journal of Computer-Mediated Communication, 16,* 250–270. doi: 10.1111/j.1083–6101.2011.01538.x

Dillard, J. P., & Knobloch, L. K. (2011). Interpersonal influence. In M. L. Knapp & J. A. Daly (Eds.), *The Sage handbook of interpersonal communication* (4th ed., pp389–422). Thousand Oaks, CA: Sage.

Duggan, M., & Brenner, J. (2013, February). *The Demographics of Social Media Users – 2012.* Washington, DC: Pew Internet & American Life Project.

Duran, R. L., Kelly, L., & Rotaru, T. (2011). Mobile phones in romantic relationships and the dialectic of autonomy versus connection. *Communication Quarterly, 59,* 19–36. doi: 10.1080/01463373.2011.541336

Ellison, N. B., Steinfield, C., & Lampe, C. (2007). The benefits of Facebook "friends:" Social capital and college students' use of online social network sites. *Journal of Computer-Mediated Communication, 12,* 1143–1168. doi: 10.1111/j.1083–6101.2007.00367.x

Feeney, J. A., & Noller, P. (2012). Perspectives on studying family communication: Multiple methods and multiple sources. In A. L. Vangelisti (Ed.), *Routledge handbook of family communication* (2nd ed., pp29–45). New York, NY: Routledge.

Fincham, F. D., & Beach, S. R. H. (1999). Conflict in marriage: Implications for working with couples. *Annual Review of Psychology, 50*, 47–77. doi: 10.1146/annurev.psych.50.1.47

Frisby, B. N., & Westerman, D. (2010). Rational actors: Channel selection and rational choices in romantic conflict episodes. *Journal of Social and Personal Relationships, 27*, 970–981. doi: 10.1177/0265407510378302

Ishii, K. (2010). Conflict management in online relationships. *Cyberpsychology, Behavior, and Social Networking, 13*, 365–370. doi: 10.1089/cyber.2009.0272

Kanter, M., Afifi, T., & Robbins, S. (2012). The impact of parents "friending" their young adult child on Facebook on perceptions of parental privacy invasion and parent-child relationship quality. *Journal of Communication, 62*, 900–917. doi: 10.1111/j.1460-2466.2012.01669.x

Keck, L. K., & Samp, J. A., (2007). The dynamic nature of goals and message production as revealed in a sequential analysis of conflict interactions. *Human Communication Research, 33*, 27–47. doi: 10.1111/j.1468-2958.2007.00287.x

Kelley, H. H., Berscheid, E., Christensen, A., Harvey, J. H., Huston, T. L., Levinger, G. & Peterson, D. R. (1983). *Close relationships*. New York, NY: Freeman.

Kerkhof, P., Finkenauer, C., & Muusses, L. D. (2011). Relational consequences of compulsive internet use: A longitudinal study among newlyweds. *Human Communication Research, 37*, 147–173. doi: 10.1111/j.1468-2958.2010.01397.x

Konijn, E. A., Utz, S., Tanis, M., & Barnes, S. B. (2008). *Mediated interpersonal communication*. New York, NY: Routledge.

Lewin, K. (1948). The background of conflict in marriage. In G. W. Lewin (Ed.), *Resolving social conflicts* (pp84–102). New York: Harper.

Merkle, E. R., & Richardson, R. A. (2000). Digital dating and virtual relating: Conceptualizing computer mediated romantic relationships. *Family Relations, 49*, 187–192.

Papp, L. M., Danielewicz, J., & Cayemberg, C. (2012). "Are we Facebook official?" Implications of dating partners' Facebook use and profiles for intimate relationship satisfaction. *Cyberpsychology, Behavior, and Social Networking, 15*, 85–90. doi: 10.1089/cyber.2011.0291

Perry, M. S., & Werner-Wilson, R. J. (2011). Couples and computer-mediated communication: A closer look at the affordances and use of the channel. *Family & Consumer Sciences Research Journal, 40*, 120–134. doi: 10.1111/j.1552-3934.2011.02099.x

Ramirez, Jr., A. & Broneck, K. (2009). "IM me": Instant messaging as relational maintenance and everyday communication. *Journal of Social and Personal Relationships, 26*, 291–314. doi: 10.1177/0265407509106719

Reznik, R. M., & Roloff, M. E. (2011). Getting off to a bad start: The relationship between communication during an initial episode of a serial argument and argument frequency. *Communication Studies, 62*, 291–306. doi: 10.1080/10510974.2011.555491

Sillars, A. L., & Canary, D. J. (2013). Family conflict communication and linkages to relational quality. In A. L. Vangelisti (Ed.), *The Routledge handbook of family communication* (2nd ed., pp338–357). New York, NY: Routledge.

Subrahmanyam, K., & Greenfield, P. (2008). Communicating online: Adolescent relationships and the media. *The Future of Children, 18*, 119–146. Retrieved from http://futureofchildren.org/futureofchildren/publications/docs/18_01_06.pdf

Walther, J. B. (1996). Computer-mediated communication: Impersonal, interpersonal, and hyperpersonal interaction. *Communication Research, 23*, 3–43. doi: 10.1177/009365096023001001

Wilson, S. R., & Feng, H. (2007). Interaction goals and message production: Conceptual and methodological developments. In D. R. Roskos-Ewoldsen & J. L. Monahan (Eds.), *Communication and social cognition: Theories and methods* (pp71–95). Mahwah, NJ: Erlbaum.

SECTION 2
Power and Conflict in Close Relationships

5

POWER IN CLOSE RELATIONSHIPS: A DYADIC POWER THEORY PERSPECTIVE

Norah E. Dunbar, Brianna L. Lane, and Gordon Abra

Interpersonal power is an integral part of all human relationships. Relational power dynamics exist irrespective of whether or not they become expressed in conflict but affect such basic relational elements as conflict topic choice, conflict strategy choice, and conflict outcomes. Power relations are therefore a crucial element to understanding the achievement of instrumental, relationship, and identity goals. Dunbar's (2004) Dyadic Power Theory was created with precisely these considerations in mind. Our goal in this chapter is threefold: to examine the evidence collected thus far about the ability of DPT to explain power in dyads; to evaluate the methodological challenges facing DPT researchers; and finally to consider new applications of DPT to dyadic relationships.

Explicating Interpersonal Dyadic Power

In any relationship, partners negotiate outcomes based on the resources at their disposal, such as the structural authority given to them by society at large (Neal & Neal, 2011). Several theoretical perspectives have examined the dynamics of power in dyadic relationships. Among these perspectives are: social exchange theory (Emerson, 1976; Kelley & Thibaut, 1978; Molm, 1997), interdependence theory (Lennon et al, 2013; Rusbult & Arriaga, 1997), normative resource theory (Blood & Wolfe, 1960), the chilling effect (Roloff & Cloven, 1990; Solomon & Samp, 1998), relational control approaches (Ellis, 1979; Rogers & Farace, 1975; Siegel et al, 1992), necessary convergence communication theory (Miller-Day, 2004; Miller-Day & Jackson, 2012), and sex role theories which encompass sociological, psychological, and cognitive-developmental approaches to gender and power (Bem, 1983; Connell, 1985; Ferree, 1990; Hare-Mustin, 1988).

Since the approaches to power have been multidisciplinary and are based on assumptions that come from very different perspectives, the theories of power can bear little resemblance to one another (Cromwell & Olson, 1975). A comprehensive review of these theories is available elsewhere in Berger, 1994. We here present one theory that developed out of a multidisciplinary view of power and incorporates concepts from several theories mentioned above. DPT is an attempt to explain the dynamic interplay of conversational partners as they manage control of an interaction through dominance behaviors (Dunbar, 2004). It asserts that the relational history and structural forces that bestow power upon actors affect communication patterns and behavioral displays. Those communication patterns then predict outcomes such as satisfaction with the relationship, perceptions of who "wins" an argument, whether or not goals are achieved, and even the likelihood of conflict itself.

Building upon past work by Rollins and Bahr (1976), Roloff and Cloven (1990), and others, DPT was first proposed by Dunbar (Dunbar, 2000, 2004) and its propositions have been tested in several empirical studies by Dunbar and colleagues (e.g., Dunbar & Abra, 2010; Dunbar et al, 2008; Dunbar & Burgoon, 2005; Dunbar et al, 2014) and others (Bevan, 2010; Recchia et al, 2010; Smith et al, 2011). It has been applied to work relationships (Lindsey et al, 2011), families (Dunbar, 2004; Dunbar & Johnson, 2015), romantic couples (Dunbar et al, 2008; Dunbar & Burgoon, 2005; Worley & Samp, 2016) and stranger interactions (Dunbar & Abra, 2010; Dunbar et al, 2014) (see Table 5.1 for a complete list of known DPT studies).

Typical studies testing DPT have examined verbal and nonverbal power strategies in the conflict discussions of interaction partners. In some cases, the conversants are given a task and then the power strategies that are employed can be examined as the dyad's problem-solving unfolds. Dunbar and Burgoon (2005) invited couples to their lab and gave them a task, to decide how to spend a fictional gift of $1000. Dunbar and Abra (2010) paired strangers in the lab and asked them to rank order items from the "desert survival task." Dunbar et al (2012a) asked participants to role play that they were co-workers selecting a job applicant from a selection of resumés and to select the best one. In other cases, we asked couples to identify sources of conflict in their relationship and discuss them as they normally would at home (Dunbar et al, 2012b; Dunbar et al, 2008). We have also used survey methods to examine people's own impressions of their power and their communication strategies (Dunbar & Johnson, in press; Lindsey et al, 2011). Regardless of the task or measurement, power strategies are evident in the participants' behaviors and responses and can be used to understand the nature of the relationship between power and communication.

Propositions of the Theory and Empirical Support

DPT was originally proposed by Dunbar (2004) with eight empirically verifiable propositions. These propositions can be organized into the pre-interactional

TABLE 5.1 Summary of Known Studies on DPT in Chronological Order

	Article or Paper	Type of Sample	N	Methodology Used
1	Dunbar (2004)	Theoretical paper	n/a	
2	Dunbar & Burgoon (2005)	Married & cohabiting couples	194	Laboratory observation
3	Dunbar & Allen (2005)	Friends & dating couples	134	Survey
4	Dunbar (2008)	Married & cohabiting couples	94	Laboratory observation
5	Dunbar & Abra (2010)	Strangers	150	Laboratory experiment
6	Bevan (2010)	Family members & romantic partners	266	Survey
7	Lindsey et al. (2011)	Workplace co-workers	214	Survey
8	Dunbar & Mejia (2012)	Married & cohabiting couples	20	Qualitative analysis of Dunbar & Burgoon (2005) dataset
9	Dunbar et al. (2012)	Strangers	150	Secondary analysis of Dunbar & Abra (2010) dataset
10	Smith et al. (2011) (followed by commentary by Dunbar & Abra, 2012)	Married couples	134	Laboratory observation
11	Dunbar (2012)	Married & cohabiting couples	148	Laboratory observation
12	Dunbar et al. (2014)	Strangers	106	Laboratory experiment
13	Dunbar & Johnson (2015)	Varied relationships	164	Survey
14	Worley & Samp (2016)	Romantic couples	350	Survey

factors that affect the relationship, the interactive process that occurs within the conversation, and then the post-interactional implications of that process.

Pre-interactional Factors

The first three propositions of DPT, as presented by Dunbar (2004), examine the pre-interactional factors of authority and resources and predict that increases in relative authority are related to increases in relative resources, increases in relative resources produce an increase in relative power, and that increases in relative authority produce an increase in relative power. Dunbar argued that actors' resource levels relative to their partners and the legitimate authority to use those resources together create a belief about power relative to one's dyadic partner. Relative authority affects relative power in two ways. First, having the ability to control outcomes confers greater influence. For example, in marital interactions, the spouse who earns the larger income may set spending priorities. Secondly, legitimate authority is a cultural sanction of open power use, and should lead to greater use of power. For example, employment in the paid labor force garners a cultural expectation of control over earned income, even though the income is a dyadic resource. Women who work outside the home may use their extra income to reduce their share of the housework by utilizing services such as restaurants and domestic workers (Kamo & Cohen, 1998).

In a test of the first three propositions of DPT, Dunbar (2000) found that having greater economic resources and having greater authority over household responsibilities and family spending increased perceptions of power for both women and men although men and women reported they derived their power from different resources. Consistent with traditional sex roles, women perceived they had more control over household decisions but men reported greater economic, physical, and psychological resources suggesting that women and men still have different realms of influence despite gains made by women in the workplace. Smith et al (2011) argue that, based on DPT, raising a conversational topic implies legitimate authority over that topic and will then make an actor exhibit dominance. However, raising a topic as an issue for discussion is probably a signal of an expected power balance for that topic. The perceived injustice is a result of an unfulfilled expectation. Wives typically do more of the household labor than their husbands even when they work the same number of hours outside the home (Beckwith, 1992). Thus, it is reasonable that presenting the unfair division of household labor as a topic for discussion comes not out of legitimate authority (and thus greater perceived power) as Smith et al suggest, but out of an expectation of equality (Dunbar & Abra, 2012). More work is needed to tease out the first three propositions of the theory to determine if the relationship between legitimate authority, resources, and perceived power are interconnected in the way that DPT suggests.

Interactional Factors

The fourth proposition of DPT describes the nonlinear relationship between our perceived power and our attempt to communicate that power through "control attempts" within our dyadic interactions. Dunbar (2004) proposed, contrary to Rollins and Bahr's (1976) assertion, that the relationship between perceived relative power and control attempts is *curvilinear* rather than linear. Partners who perceive their relative power as extremely high or low will have fewer control attempts, while partners who perceive their relative power differences as small or moderate will have more control attempts. A control attempt is a behavior by one actor intended to change the behavior of another during a social interaction (Dunbar, 2004). Although Dunbar equates control attempts with dominance behaviors, they really can be demonstrated through a wide variety of verbal and nonverbal messages (Dunbar & Burgoon, 2005; Dunbar & Johnson, in press).

Of all the theory's propositions, P4 has received the most attention in a variety of studies, generally focusing on dominance displays within interactions. In tests of DPT, dominance has been coded in interactions through the use of gestures, facial expressions, and touch (Dunbar & Burgoon, 2005; Smith et al, 2011), through ratings made by participants and observers (Dunbar & Abra, 2010; Dunbar et al, 2008), through verbal counts of arguments and linguistic analyses of text (Dunbar & Burgoon, 2005; Dunbar et al, 2014) and through the use of certain argumentative strategies like aggressive humor, affection messages, and social support (Dunbar et al, 2012a; Dunbar et al, 2012b; Dunbar & Johnson, 2015).

The empirical relationship between power and control attempts (specifically dominance behaviors) has been found to be curvilinear, with an unexpected asymmetry. In general, individuals in equal power dyads demonstrate the most dominance followed by those in high power positions and then low power positions (Dunbar & Abra, 2010; Dunbar et al, 2008; Dunbar & Burgoon, 2005; Dunbar et al, 2014). In result after result, with a wide variety of dominance measures, we have found the same asymmetrical "hook" shape emerging in our studies of the relationship between dominance and power (see Figure 5.1).

Typically, those who either are assigned to the low power position in an experimental manipulation or report they are in the lowest position of power in an existing relationship enact the least dominance, by far. Those who are equal in power demonstrate the most dominance. The high-power individuals appear as

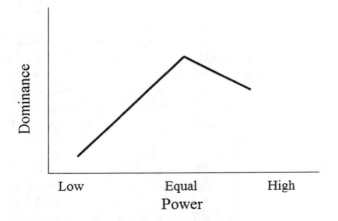

FIGURE 5.1 The observed relationship between power and dominance.

though they are lower in dominance than the equal power individuals, but often, they are not significantly different from that equal-power group. And yet, because of the reoccurrence of that same pattern across studies and with different measures of dominance, we do not believe that the difference between equal and high power individuals is a result of error or chance.

With power dynamics in play, once a control attempt is made the partner may respond with control attempts of his or her own. The degree to which he or she allows the other's control attempts to remain unchallenged will also be related to his/her own perception of power. Dunbar (2004) proposed (in what she labeled proposition 6) that as a partner's perception of his (her) own power relative to that of his (her) partner increases, counter-control attempts will increase as well. This proposition has rarely has been examined in the current DPT literature but an analysis by Dunbar and Mejia (2012) speaks to this. They qualitatively analyzed the interactions of ten couples from the Dunbar and Burgoon (2005) dataset, five of which were couples with the highest self-reported power imbalance and five of which had the most similar power. In their detailed analysis of the couples' conversations, they found that "challenging" or "collaboration" was a type of behavior used by equal power types whereas "marginalization" or "withdrawal" was used more by unequal power types. This suggests that, consistent with proposition 6, those with the greater power equality are also those that engage in more of the counter-control attempts rather than letting their partners' control attempts go unanswered.

Post-interactional Factors

Dunbar's (2004) final three propositions represent the outcomes of the interaction, including the amount of control one gains and the resulting level of satisfaction with both the relationship and the interaction. Although Rollins and Bahr (1976) ended their model with the outcome of a particular interaction, other communication scholars are interested in the outcome of the conflict for the relationship more generally. Dunbar proposed that greater control attempts would lead to more control and counter-control attempts would hinder the control over the outcomes (called P5 and P7, respectively, in the original statement of the theory). Some DPT studies have examined the outcomes of a particular argument such as who "wins" or satisfies more of their demands (Dunbar & Abra, 2010; Dunbar et al, 2008; Recchia et al, 2010), but others have examined sustained effects such as long-term relational satisfaction (Dunbar & Burgoon, 2005; Dunbar & Johnson, 2015).

It is a relatively uncontroversial finding in the close relationships literature that power equality tends to be associated with higher satisfaction (Gray-Little & Burks, 1983; Oyamot et al, 2010). Dunbar (2004) argued (in proposition 8) that relational satisfaction is a key variable that ought to be examined when investigating the impacts power imbalances have on the long-term effects of a relationship. She posited that the relation between perceived relative power and satisfaction is curvilinear such that partners who perceive their relative power as extremely high or low will report lower levels of satisfaction compared to partners who perceive the relative power differences as small or moderate.

While P5 and P7 are concerned with immediate outcomes, P8 is concerned with the long-term effects of power inequality on relational satisfaction. To investigate the immediate outcomes for interactions, Dunbar et al (2008) investigated whether perceptions of power influenced three different interaction outcomes (perceptions of conflict escalation, perceptions of progress on the conflict issue, and "who won" the interaction) and found that perceived power did not have a direct effect on these perceptions of the conflict's outcome. Similarly, Bevan (2010) also found no differences on the types of strategies used in serial arguments and proposes that goal orientation, rather than power alone, predicted the outcome of the serial argument interactions. However, in an experimentally manipulated power relationship, Dunbar and Abra (2010) found that those in the unequal high-power position changed their previous decision the least after interacting with their partner while those in unequal low-power changed their decision the most which suggests power affected control over the decision made after the interaction was over. Few studies have examined the relationship between control and counter-control attempts which would require intensive conversational analysis techniques. Thus, it appears that the "jury is still out" as to whether power or behavioral dominance will have an effect on the outcome of a conflict.

In terms of relationship satisfaction, although previous research has suggested that relational satisfaction is highly correlated with perceptions of power and that inequality is a major determinant of marital dissatisfaction and dissolution (Cahn, 1992; Clements et al, 1997), our work testing DPT's proposition that relational satisfaction is related to power has not found a significant relationship between power and relational satisfaction in a study of married and cohabiting couples (Dunbar, 2000). Relationship satisfaction also did not influence how compliance-gaining messages were reportedly used by the self or the partner in a study of friends or romantic partner conflicts (Dunbar & Allen, 2005). It may be that the homogeneity of our samples influenced these results because the participants overall reported they are highly satisfied, relatively equal in power, and used a limited range of compliance gaining messages in both studies.

We attempted to remedy this shortcoming in the Dunbar and Abra (2010) study in which we also explored the link between power and satisfaction in an experiment between strangers. The results suggest that people in unequal low-power positions are generally less satisfied than people in equal-power positions, and people in unequal high-power positions are also less satisfied than people in equal-power positions (although this difference was not statistically significant). This result is consistent with proposition 8 which suggests that equal power people will be the most satisfied. Equity theory suggests that individuals experience distress when they are in inequitable relationships (when their inputs do not correspond to their outputs) and they attempt to restore equity between the partners. In close relationships, men and women who believe they have been equitably treated feel more content in their relationships and perceive the relationship to be more stable than those in inequitable relationships, even when they benefit from the inequality (Dunbar & Abra, 2010; Sprecher, 2001; Walster & Walster, 1975). There is discomfort experienced when we are placed in a position of power because we are sensitive to the apparent discomfort of our lower-power partners. However, because of the disparate findings reported above, there is more research needed on what the outcomes are for DPT. We now consider important challenges to performing that research.

Methodological Challenges in Testing DPT

The first difficulty rests in people's beliefs about power. Many tests of DPT rely on participants self-reporting power and dominance behaviors. Self-reports of power provide challenges as participants may not be fully aware of their power. In fact, participants who report equal power in their romantic relationships have been found by third-party coders to exhibit characteristics of inequality. Dunbar and Burgoon (2005) suggest that equally balanced relationships are most comfortable so relational partners may convince themselves their relationship is equal when it actually may not be. Or, because U.S. culture emphasizes equality in marriages, couples may be reluctant to report a marriage that departs from this ideal. Alternately, if partners recognize their relationship is unequal, they may compensate through their control attempts to change the power discrepancy (Dunbar & Burgoon, 2005).

Several tests of DPT have found differences in coders' perceptions of dominance compared to that of the participants themselves (Dunbar et al, 2008; Dunbar & Burgoon, 2005). Participants' self-report of power did not influence their perceptions of dominance which indicates that participants may have a different perception of dominance than objective coders. Self-reports provide a methodological challenge in examining what is objectively occurring versus what participants perceive is occurring in an interaction. Participants may not be aware of their or their partner's control attempts. DPT researchers defend the use of self-reports because the mechanism through which power is translated into behavior requires actors to perceive power differentials. Perceived power similarities and differences can be validly measured with self-reports (Dunbar et al, 2008; Dunbar & Burgoon, 2005). However, participants may be unable to separate their perceptions of the current situation from perceptions of their partner generally (Dunbar & Burgoon, 2005). In this case, third-party observers may be more useful because they are unaware of the norms of the couple and can be more objective of the interaction. Research on DPT has shown that participants may not use individual behaviors to evaluate dominance but actually may be making more holistic judgments of the interaction (Dunbar & Burgoon, 2005).

In addition to participants' inability to recognize power differentials and dominance behaviors, self-reports face a cultural challenge: a stigma may be attached to reporting low power in a romantic relationship. As previously stated, participants consistently describe their relationships as equal power, but this could be due to a reluctance to admit one has low power. Participants may not want to admit to a researcher (or to themselves) that they fear potential repercussions and therefore are less likely to report low power in the relationship.

Making this problem even more difficult is the Dunbar and Burgoon (2005) claim that power-discrepant romantic relationships are probably rare and therefore difficult to study in naturally occurring contexts. Relationships that are extremely power discrepant are unlikely to survive marriage or cohabitation.

Further, members of such relationships may not want to be studied. Dunbar and colleagues (Dunbar et al, 2012b) attempted to invite couples to the lab who had clear power discrepancies. Surveys of relationship satisfaction and power were sent to a large sample of participants and those with the largest self-reported power discrepancies and a sample of power-equal couples were invited to participate in a laboratory study where they would discuss an area of conflict on camera for additional compensation. Compared to the equal-power couples, the power-discrepant couples were far more likely to refuse the invitation and were more likely to cancel or no-show the appointment. In the end, the power discrepant sample was only mildly more power-unequal than the equal-power couples. On the self-report measure of power, the low power ($M = 2.9$, $SD = .62$) and high power ($M = 5.1$, $SD = .59$) individuals self-reported they were only 1.1 point (on a 7-point scale) away from the equal power group ($M = 4.00$, $SD = .19$). Thus, getting unequal couples to agree to be studied is more difficult than equal power couples.

Indicators of conflict or power can also be suppressed in a laboratory setting. Caughlin and Scott (2010) claim that a weakness of studies in a laboratory is that couples might not discuss topics in the laboratory that they actually discuss at home. Topics couples discuss in private may be more strongly linked to power. The lack of perceived power differential may be due in part to the inability of researchers to prompt discussion on strongly differentiating topics.

To address the issues of self-reports of power and dominance, there are probably at least two options. One is to study naturally occurring power-discrepant relationships. Some examples are parent–child dyads (Perosa & Perosa, 2001; Recchia et al, 2010) or workplace dyads (de Reuver, 2006; Lindsey et al, 2011; Willemyns et al, 2003) in which occupying a low power position carries less stigma. Researchers can also conduct studies in the laboratory in which power is experimentally manipulated and use trained confederates (Dunbar & Abra, 2010; Hall et al, 2006) providing more control over the interaction. When power is manipulated experimentally, we often use a "layered" approach to ensure that those who are assigned to a high level of power compared to their partner not only "feel" powerful but also actually have power, in terms of controlling outcomes, over their interaction partner (Dunbar & Abra, 2010; Dunbar et al, 2014).

However, in Dunbar and Abra's (2010) laboratory study in which participants and confederates in the high power position could veto their partner's decision, they were surprised to discover that only the experimental confederates actually used this option. Participants in the high power condition rarely used this option and instead tried to convince their partner to acquiesce. This speaks to the methodological challenges of studying power and dominance; individuals in naturally occurring relationships are reluctant to admit low power, but participants in a laboratory experiment may be reluctant to enact behaviors consistent with their position. No DPT studies have determined whether or not these manipulations are isomorphic with the way real couples or dyads determine who is the more powerful among them.

Another methodological challenge to testing DPT is in the structural expectations for power that cannot be changed. The type of relationship, whether it is romantic partner, friend, family member, or coworker can influence dominance behaviors (Dunbar & Johnson, 2015). This could be due to structural expectations (Neal & Neal, 2011). Bevan (2010) found a difference between parent–child, sibling, and romantic partnerships and claims this could be due the inherent characteristics of the relationships such as voluntariness, interdependence, or simply differing expectations. DPT predicts that dyads with discrepant power, such as a supervisor/subordinate relationship, are more likely to use latent power strategies (Dunbar, 2004; Dunbar & Burgoon, 2005). Powerful individuals do not need to use overt control attempts by nature of their position (Lindsey et al, 2011). The predetermined structure of the relationship determines how control attempts are enacted. This provides challenges in testing DPT.

Dunbar et al (2014) attempted to examine this by having participants deceive during a role play. Participants took on the roles of manager and employee in making a hiring decision. Consistent with the findings of a survey of real managers and subordinates (Lindsey et al, 2011), the participants tended to agree that deception by a superior is more acceptable than deception by a subordinate. However, powerless individuals may be reluctant to display dominance for fear of retaliation and so they may resort to deception as a method of minimizing conflict and gaining control. To study the use of power and control attempts in actual workplace situations, especially when involving deception, is a methodological challenge in testing DPT.

Finally, the study of interactions involving participants who lack relational history cannot fully recreate sustained power discrepancies. Experimentally manipulated power differences do not match the timeframe of relational power dynamics, and it would not be surprising to learn that sustained power equality and inequality have effects that are stronger than those produced in the lab. Dunbar and Abra (2010) recognized this, and cautioned that using relationships with a structural power difference and a relational history may produce different results.

Discussion and Suggestions for the Future of DPT

Taking a cue from the methodological limitations discussed above, we believe that DPT can be expanded beyond its current scope. We propose three new directions. The first is the idea that within power-balanced married couples, there are certain domains of influence in which one spouse has relatively higher power. The second is the fact that relationships are embedded within larger power structures that might put limits on the dominance strategies individuals within a given relationship can use. Finally, we suggest that dyadic power dynamics operate similarly with both individual people as actors and with larger social groups (e.g. organizations) as actors.

Expanding DPT to Intra-Dyadic Power Domains

Even within stable and generally power-balanced relationships, there are domain-bounded asymmetries of power. The theoretic and empirical work on DPT thus far has been concerned primarily with the relationship between the general power structure of a relationship and the behavioral expressions of power. Comparisons across dyads have shown the impact of these relational power structures on behavior. In general, DPT has been concerned with reducing dyads to particular "types" (e.g. power balanced vs. unbalanced) and then using that typology to explain and predict power expressions. We propose here that DPT can and should be expanded to consider the dynamic nature of dyads.

Researchers over the past few decades uncovered the unequal power dynamics of traditional marriages, noting that the economic and social resources gained by men in the paid labor force translated into a power advantage for men within the relationship. Other researchers suggested that this masked the ability of women within traditional marriages to create desirable outcomes with respect to particular issues of importance. The tactic of "micromanipulation" (Lipman-Blumen, 1984) allows otherwise low-power actors to negotiate favorable conditions. Our goal is not to validate this tactic, but simply to note its existence and the clever granular parsing of power those actors can tap when broader power conditions are not advantageous.

Within a dyad, power relations shift across contexts. The conception of dyadic power has been that of a monolithic, grand average that creates a particular type of dyad: an unbalanced dyad (power unequal) or a balanced dyad (power equal). While useful for comparing across dyads, this template makes it difficult to explain periodic departures from predicted dyadic behaviors. For example, in a power-unbalanced dyad, there will still likely be situations in which conflict occurs (albeit less often than in power-balanced dyads). Why would we expect to find situations of conflict within power-unbalanced dyads when DPT suggests that low-power actors will mute their disagreements? Relatedly, why would we expect to find conflict-free periods within power-balanced dyads when DPT suggests that equal-power actors will display control attempts? The answer is that although a dyad may *average* to an equal or unequal power structure, the particulars of the dyadic power structure will involve equalities and inequalities across different aspects of the relationship. We call these aspects "relational domains". A relational domain refers to any sphere of activity over which partners may negotiate. This may be a characteristic over which specialized knowledge or competence may be claimed, as in the "specific task competence" of Status Characteristics Theory and Expectation States Theory (c.f. Berger et al, 1972; Ridgeway, 1987; Ridgeway, 1991). Examples of relational domains in romantic relationships include cooking, finance, artistry, and child-rearing.

Each domain contributes toward the "average" power dynamic of the relationship. The degree to which the domain contributes to that power dynamic depends on the importance of that domain to the relationship. Domains valued by both partners (e.g., money) will contribute more to the power dynamic than domains valued by only a single partner (e.g. home decoration). One actor may have great authority over a particular relational domain, and strong task competence that the dyadic partner lacks, but if the resource is not of high value to that partner (e.g., home decoration), then the actor's relative power within the relationship is not increased by much. On the other hand, if the domain is valued highly by both actors (e.g., money), then this increases relative power in the broader sense.

A power-balanced relation represents a situation in which the domains controlled by one partner are collectively of equal import to the domains controlled by the other partner. In this respect, the domains themselves can be thought of as resources in the sense used by Emerson and other power-dependence theorists (e.g., Cook et al, 1993; Emerson, 1962). When the domains collectively are of high value, then the power balance can be high-high, representing a high degree of dependence and strong integration. These dyads are likely to persist. When the resources are collectively of relatively low value, any power balance would be low-low, representing a low degree of mutual dependence and low integration. These dyads are less likely to persist. The number of control attempts is a function of the length of the relationship, so this consideration of dyadic integration leads to a new proposition:

> P9: Control/counter-control attempts will be more frequent in high-high dyads than in low-low dyads.

For the reasons outlined above, we can also predict the topics of conflict that will occur within a relationship:

> P10: Within generally power-balanced relationships, conflict will occur more often in domains over which both partners have high power than in domains in which only one partner has high power.

Consider the case of an auto mechanic married to a computer network engineer. DPT would not expect conflict to arise about vehicle maintenance, nor about the deployment of the household Wi-Fi system. The power inequalities within each of those domains would suppress conflict before it even begins. Within the same relationship, however, we may expect conflict with respect to domains over which both partners claim expertise, such as child discipline.

Empirical investigation of these domain-bounded power dynamics will serve to expand DPT beyond cross-dyad comparisons. On a broader scale, DPT would benefit from a consideration of the role of cultural prescriptions and prohibitions on conflict.

Expanding DPT to Cultural and Structural Power

We recognize that the degree of relational conflict is partially contingent on the cultural acceptability of open conflict and disagreement. In some cultural contexts, conflict itself is considered an inappropriate display. DPT can and should be expanded to integrate our knowledge about cultural differences in conflict and dominance. We expect that this expansion will demonstrate important cross-cultural components, and important intra-cultural components.

For example, there is a notable difference in the display of conflict when comparing Japanese and Italian cultures. It is not true that the power differences exist only in one cultural context, but rather that overt conflict is expected to be suppressed in Japanese culture more than in Italian culture. When the value of overt conflict itself varies, then we need to incorporate this new variable into future DPT analyses. We are suggesting that there may be broad cultural expectations that prevent conflict even when we may expect disagreement between two actors:

> P11: Dyads in cultures that stigmatize open conflict will display less conflict than dyads in cultures that do not stigmatize open conflict.

A study of marital conflict across four cultures found that the role segregation and male dominance of the culture affected the decision-making process in couples (Wagner et al, 1990). For example in Saudi society, women are expected to defer to men on many important issues. We would expect that the degree of cross-sex public and private conflict is lower in Saudi society than in Western societies. It is important to note that we expect DPT to explain this supposed cultural difference by noting that the cultural suppression of male-female conflict does not represent a real difference in the way that power and dominance are related; instead, it represents the cultural imbalance of power between men and women in Saudi society. In fact, DPT would suggest that this power imbalance is fully responsible for the suppression of conflict. By comparison, the relatively high level of male-female conflict in Western societies represents the greater power balance between men and women in Western societies:

P12: Heterosexual couples in strongly patriarchal cultures will have less conflict than couples in less patriarchal cultures.

We expect that these cultural considerations will reveal important cross-cultural differences in dominance and the expression of power, but we also believe that within a given cultural context the basic prediction of DPT will hold: power-equal dyads will display greater conflict than power-unequal dyads.

Expanding DPT to Organizational Actors

Although designed for interpersonal communication, the logic of DPT can be extended to consider inter-organizational communication. Much of the sociological and political science work on power recognizes the similarities between individuals and collectivities as actors. The employer-employee dyad can be thought of as analogous to the colonizer-colony dyad. In both cases, the relatively powerful actor controls highly valued resources (i.e., money and military) while the relatively powerless actor controls easily substitutable resources (i.e., labor and land). As with human dyads, power is based on resource control. Some resources will be similar (e.g., status, money), while other resources may be different, but the power dynamics should play out similarly. In a power-unequal organizational dyad, one organization controls more valuable resources than the other, creating the inequality. This dependence implies an inability of the low-power organization to obtain the resource elsewhere, and hence the low-power organization will fear loss of the resource. This is a weak bargaining position. Under these circumstances, the low-power organization will experience the equivalent of the chilling effect, and will attempt to avoid bargaining, as it is unlikely to result in a favorable outcome. It will also suppress expressions of dissatisfaction to its partner, lest the partner end the relationship. Further, it will proactively ensure the satisfaction of its important partner. Similarly, the relatively high-power organization will find that its problems are proactively addressed by the low-power organization's actions, precluding initiation of conflict.

By contrast, organizations with equal power control equally-valuable resources. Under these conditions, the organizations are free to express dissatisfaction and to attempt to bargain for a favorable outcome. We should therefore see the definitive curvilinear relationship between relative power and control attempts:

P13: Equal-power organizational dyads will display more control attempts than unequal-power organizational dyads.

The parallels between organizational dyads and human dyads can be drawn further, and may stretch to include the items newly included above for human couples (e.g., domain-bounded power). We expect nonetheless that the fundamental idea of DPT – that power dynamics underlie the behavior of dyadic partners – will hold true irrespective of the particular characteristics of each actor.

Conclusion

DPT has received a fair amount of research attention in its short history, drawing in scholars from both within and outside the discipline of communication. We believe this is because of DPT's fundamentally interdisciplinary property: it draws on the knowledge base of several well-established fields. Our goal here was to review and broaden the theory and to summarize the empirical evidence. DPT is gaining momentum but as this review has demonstrated there are important voids to fill in our understanding of the broader implications. We hope that DPT remains worthy of investigation as the evidence accumulates.

References

Beckwith, J. B. (1992). Stereotypes and reality in the division of household labor. *Social Behavior and Personality*, 20(4), 283–288. doi: 10.2224/sbp.1992.20.4.283

Bem, S. L. (1983). Gender schema theory and its implications for child development: Raising gender-aschematic children in a gender-schematic society. *Signs*, 8(4), 598–616. doi: 10.1086/493998

Berger, J., Cohen, B. P., & Zelditch, M. (1972). Status characteristics and social interaction. *American Sociological Review*, 37(3), 241–255. doi: 10.2307/2093465

Bevan, J. L. (2010). Serial Argument Goals and Conflict Strategies: A Comparison between Romantic Partners and Family Members. *Communication Reports*, 23, 52–64. doi: 10.1080/08934211003598734

Blood, R. O., & Wolfe, D. M. (1960). *Husbands and wives*. Glencoe, IL: Free Press.

Cahn, D. D. (1992). *Conflict in intimate relationships*. New York: Guilford.

Clements, M. L., Cordova, A. D., Markman, H. J., & Laurenceau, J. P. (1997). The erosion of marital satisfaction over time and how to prevent it. In R. J. Sternberg & M. Hojjat (Eds.), *Satisfaction in close relationships* (pp335–355). New York: Guilford.

Connell, R. W. (1985). Theorising gender. *Sociology*, 19(2), 260–272. doi: 10.1177/0038038585019002008

Cook, K. S., Molm, L. D., & Yamagishi, T. (1993). Exchange relations and exchange networks: Recent developments in social exchange theory. In J. Berger & M. Jr. Zelditch (Eds.), *Theoretical Research Programs: Studies in the growth of theory* (pp296–322). Stanford, CA: Stanford University Press.

Cromwell, R. E., & Olson, D. H. (1975). Multidisciplinary perspectives of power. In R. E. Cromwell & D. H. Olson (Eds.), *Power in families* (pp15–37). Beverly Hills, CA: Sage.

de Reuver, R. (2006). The influence of organizational power on conflict dynamics. *Personnel Review*, 35(5), 589–603. doi: 10.1108/00483480610682307

Dunbar, N. E. (2000). *Explication and initial test of dyadic power theory*. PhD thesis, University of Arizona, Tucson, AZ.

Dunbar, N. E. (2004). Dyadic Power Theory: Constructing a communication-based theory of relational power. *Journal of Family Communication*, 4(3 & 4), 235–248. doi: 10.1207/s15327698jfc0403&4_8

Dunbar, N. E., & Abra, G. (2010). Observations of dyadic power in interpersonal interaction. *Communication Monographs*, 77(4), 657–684. doi: 10.1080/03637751.2010.520018

Dunbar, N. E., & Abra, G. (2012). Dyadic power theory, touch, and counseling psychology: A response to Smith, Vogel, Madon, and Edwards (2011). *The Counseling Psychologist*, *40*(7), 1085–1093. doi: 10.1177/0011000012456883

Dunbar, N. E., & Allen, T. H. (2005). Power, conflict, and strategic communication: A dyadic view of compliance–gaining during conflict. Paper presented at the National Communication Association Annual Convention, Boston, MA.

Dunbar, N. E., Banas, J. A., Rodriguez, D., Liu, S.-J., & Abra, G. (2012a). Humor use in power–differentiated interactions. *Humor: International Journal of Humor Research*, *24*(4), 469–489. doi: 10.1515/humor-2012-0025

Dunbar, N. E., Bippus, A. M., Allums, A., & King, S. (2012b). The Dark Side of Humor: The Use of Aggressive Humor in Conflicts in Close Relationships. Paper presented at the International Communication Association Annual Meeting, Phoenix, AZ.

Dunbar, N. E., Bippus, A. M., & Young, S. L. (2008). Interpersonal dominance in relational conflict: A view from dyadic power theory. Interpersona, *2*(1), 1–33. doi: 10.5964/ijpr.v2i1.16

Dunbar, N. E., & Burgoon, J. K. (2005). Perceptions of power and interactional dominance in interpersonal relationships. *Journal of Social and Personal Relationships*, *22*, 207–233.

Dunbar, N. E., Jensen, M. L., Bessarabova, E., Burgoon, J. K., Bernard, D. R., Harrison, K. J., & Eckstein, J. M. (2014). Empowered by persuasive deception: The effects of power and deception on interactional dominance, credibility, and decision-making. *Communication Research*, *41*(6), 869–893. doi: 10.1177/0093650212447099

Dunbar, N. E. & Johnson, A. J. (2015). A Test of Dyadic Power Theory: Control Attempts Recalled From Interpersonal Interactions with Romantic Partners, Family Members, and Friends. *Journal of Argumentation in Context*, *4*(1), 42-62. DOI: 10.1075/jaic.4.1.03dun

Dunbar, N. E., & Mejia, R. (2012). A qualitative analysis of power–based entrainment and interactional synchrony in couples. Personal Relationships. doi: DOI: 10.1111/j.1475-6811.2012.01414.x

Ellis, D. G. (1979). Relational control in two group systems. *Communication Monographs*, *46*(3), 153–167. doi: 10.1080/03637757909376003

Emerson, R. M. (1962). Power-dependence relations. *American Sociological Review*, *27*, 31–41. doi: 10.2307/2089716

Emerson, R. M. (1976). Social exchange theory. *Annual review of sociology*, *2*, 335–362. doi: 10.1146/annurev.so.02.080176.002003

Ferree, M. M. (1990). Beyond separate spheres: Feminism and family research. *Journal of Marriage and the Family*, *52*, 866–884. doi: 10.2307/353307

Gray-Little, B., & Burks, N. (1983). Power and satisfaction in marriage: A review and critique. *Psychological Bulletin*, *93*(3), 513–538. doi: 10.1037/0033–2909.93.3.513

Hall, J. A., Rosip, J. C., Smith LeBeau, L., Horgan, T. G., & Carter, J. D. (2006). Attributing the sources of accuracy in unequal–power dyadic communication: Who is better and why? *Journal of Experimental Social Psychology*, *42*, 18–27. doi: 10.1016/j.jesp.2005.01.005

Hare-Mustin, R. T. (1988). Family change and gender differences: Implications for theory and practice. *Family Relations*, *37*, 36–41. doi: 10.2307/584427

Kamo, Y., & Cohen, E. L. (1998). Division of household work between partners: A comparison of Black and White couples. *Journal of Comparative Family Studies*, *29*(1), 131–145.

Kelley, H. H., & Thibaut, J. W. (1978). *Interpersonal relations: A theory of interdependence*. New York: Wiley.

Lennon, C. A., Stewart, A. L., & Ledermann, T. (2013). The role of power in intimate relationships. *Journal of Social and Personal Relationships, 30*(1), 95–114. doi: 10.1177/0265407512452990

Lindsey, L. L. M., Dunbar, N. E., & Russell, J. (2011). Risky business or managed event? Perceptions of power and deception in the workplace. *Journal of Organizational Culture, Communications and Conflict, 15*(1), 55–79.

Lipman-Blumen, J. (1984). *Gender roles and power*. Englewood Cliffs, NJ: Prentice-Hall.

Miller-Day, M. (2004). *Communication among grandmothers, mothers, and adult daughters: A qualitative study of maternal relationships*. Mahwah, NJ: Lawrence Erlbaum.

Miller-Day, M., & Jackson, A. W. (2012). The convergence communication scale: Development and evaluation of an assessment of interpersonal submission. *Journal of Social and Personal Relationships, 29*(8), 1036–1057. doi: 10.1177/0265407512443617

Molm, L. D. (1997). *Coercive Power in Social Exchange*. Cambridge: Cambridge University Press.

Neal, J. W., & Neal, Z. P. (2011). Power as a structural phenomenon. *American Journal of Community Psychology, 48*(3–4), 157–167. doi: 10.1007/s10464-010-9356-3

Oyamot, C. M., Fuglestad, P. T., & Snyder, M. (2010). Balance of power and influence in relationships: The role of self–monitoring. *Journal of Social and Personal Relationships, 27*(1), 23–46. doi: 10.1177/0265407509347302

Perosa, L. M., & Perosa, S. L. (2001). Adolescent perceptions of cohesion, adaptability, and communication: Revisiting the circumplex model. *Family Journal: Counseling and Therapy for Couples and Families, 9*, 407–419. doi: 10.1177/1066480701094008

Recchia, H. E., Ross, H. S., & Vickar, M. (2010). Power and conflict resolution in sibling, parent–child, and spousal negotiations. *Journal of Family Psychology, 24*(5), 605–615. doi: 10.1037/a0020871

Ridgeway, C. L. (1987). Nonverbal behavior, dominance, and the basis of status in task groups. *American Sociological Review, 52*, 683–694. doi: 10.2307/2095603

Ridgeway, C. L. (1991). The social construction of status value: Gender and other nominal characteristics. *Social Forces, 70*(2), 367–386. doi: 10.2307/2580244

Rogers, L. E., & Farace, R. V. (1975). Analysis of relational communication in dyads: New measurement procedures. *Human Communication Research, 1*, 222–239. doi: 10.1111/j.1468-2958.1975.tb00270.x

Rollins, B. C., & Bahr, S. J. (1976). A theory of power relationships in marriage. *Journal of Marriage and the Family, 38*(4), 619–627. doi: 10.2307/350682

Roloff, M. E., & Cloven, D. H. (1990). The chilling effect in interpersonal relationships: The reluctance to speak one's mind. In D. D. Cahn (Ed.), *Intimates in conflict: A communication perspective* (pp49–76). Hillsdale, NJ: Erlbaum.

Rusbult, C. E., & Arriaga, X. B. (1997). Interdependence theory. In S. Duck (Ed.), *Handbook of Personal Relationships* (2nd ed., pp221–250). Chichester: John Wiley & Sons.

Siegel, S. M., Friedlander, M. L., & Heatherington, L. (1992). Nonverbal relational control in family communication. *Journal of Nonverbal Behavior, 16*(2), 117–139. doi: 10.1007/BF00990326

Smith, J. C. S., Vogel, D. L., Madon, S., & Edwards, S. R. (2011). The power of touch: Nonverbal communication within married dyads. *The Counseling Psychologist, 39*(5), 764–787. doi: 10.1177/0011000010385849

Solomon, D. H., & Samp, J. A. (1998). Power and problem appraisal: Perceptual foundations of the chilling effect in dating relationships. *Journal of Social and Personal Relationships, 15*(2), 191–209. doi: 10.1177/0265407598152004

Sprecher, S. (2001). Equity and social exchange in dating couples: Associations with satisfaction, commitment, and stability. *Journal of Marriage and the Family, 63*, 599–613. doi: 10.1111/j.1741-3737.2001.00599.x

Wagner, W., Kirchler, E., Clack, F., Tekarslan, E., & Verma, J. (1990). Male dominance, role segregation, and spouses' interdependence in conflict: A cross-cultural study. *Journal of Cross–Cultural Psychology, 21*(1), 48–70. doi: 10.1177/0022022190211002

Walster, E., & Walster, G. W. (1975). Equity and social justice. *Journal of Social Issues, 31*(3), 21–43.

Willemyns, M., Gallois, C., & Callan, V. J. (2003). Trust me, I'm your boss: Trust and power in supervisor–supervisee communication. *The International Journal of Human Resource Management, 14*(1), 117–127. doi: 10.1080/09585190210158547

Worley, T. R., & Samp, J. A. (2016). Complaint avoidance and complaint-related appraisals in close relationships: A Dyadic Power Theory perspective. *Communication Research, 43*, 391–413. doi:10.1177/0093650214538447

6

COMPLAINT EXPRESSION IN CLOSE RELATIONSHIPS

A Dependence Power Perspective

Timothy R. Worley

Power has been identified as one of the defining features of human relationships (Russell, 1938; Kelley & Thibaut, 1978). While power permeates all interpersonal encounters to a greater or lesser degree (Burgoon & Hale, 1984; Dillard et al, 1996), the experience of conflict brings power to the forefront as a factor shaping communicators' decisions to communicate – *or not* – about problematic issues. The *chilling effect* (Roloff & Cloven, 1990) refers to the way in which a partner's relational power may encourage individuals to avoid communication about sensitive relational topics, such as complaints about a partner's behavior. When a partner is particularly powerful, individuals may fear that expressing complaints to that partner may lead to negative consequences such as physical or verbal punishment (Cloven & Roloff, 1993).

While power may be defined by a partner's ability to mete out punishment (Cloven & Roloff, 1993), power in intimate relationships may also take more subtle forms. To cast the issue in the form of a popular idiom, relational power consists in both "sticks" (punitive behaviors) and "carrots" (providing a partner with access to valued resources). The potential for coercive behavior gives rise to *punitive power*, while the ability to withhold valued resources gives rise to *dependence power* (Lawler & Bacharach, 1987). This chapter considers dependence power arising from relational dependence – that is, partners' dependence on one another for such resources as affection, belonging, sex, finances, and social opportunities that are available only through continued association with that partner.

Explicating Dependence Power

The principle of *dependence power* states that the more dependent one is on a partner for valued resources, the more power that partner accrues (Emerson, 1962; Kelley & Thibaut, 1978). Dependence power is rooted in a partner's commitment to the association, and one's own alternatives to the relationship. Individuals who are relatively uncommitted, have good alternatives to their current romantic relationship, and have partners who are highly committed, gain relational power over their more dependent partners (Cloven & Roloff, 1993). For powerful partners, dependence power grants them implicit control of the relationship; they are relatively free to act without concern that their behavior will impact their likelihood of receiving continued relational rewards (Roloff & Cloven, 1990). To the extent that one's partner is highly committed, one can likely count on receiving continued benefits from that association. Should the partner decide to leave the relationship, one has ample alternatives to satisfy one's relational needs.

Conversely, the more dependent an individual is on his or her romantic partner for access to valued resources, the more that individual stands to lose if the partner withdraws these resources or terminates the relationship (Roloff & Cloven, 1990). Thus, individuals who are highly committed and/or perceive that they have poor alternatives for finding these resources in another relationship (whether due to a dearth of attractive others or to their own perceived undesirability) may be more likely to endure a partner's costly relational behavior if the costs incurred to receive these resources are perceived to be lower than the cost of seeking such resources in another relationship, or going without an equivalent relationship (Roloff & Cloven, 1990; Rusbult & Martz, 1995). Researchers have noted a variety of ways in which dependence power influences cognitions, behaviors, and communication in the context of problematic behavior in close relationships. The following section reviews this literature, with an eye toward the role of dependence power in shaping interpersonal conflict.

Dependence and Relational Cognition

Cognition has been recognized as a central factor mediating the links between relational events and communicative responses to those events (e.g., Solomon & Theiss, 2007). One factor which may influence individuals' relational cognitions is their dependence power. Many individuals report withholding complaints about a partner's behavior because they do not consider the behavior serious enough to warrant confrontation (Cloven & Roloff, 1993; Roloff & Solomon, 2002). That said, research suggests that appraisals of problem severity are influenced by dependence-related factors. For instance, Roloff and Solomon (2002) observed that commitment was positively associated with withholding complaints because a problem was deemed minor. While it is undoubtedly the case that many problems in committed relationships *are* minor, the fact that commitment was associated with increased likelihood of avoiding *because* a problem was considered minor suggests that highly dependent individuals may subjectively bias their own appraisals of problem severity.

In line with this view, other research provides direct evidence of the cognitive biases associated with dependence power. Solomon and Samp (1998) observed that a partner's dependence power was associated with perceiving that partner's problematic behavior as less severe. Regarding individuals' *own* problematic relational behaviors, Samp and Solomon (2001) found that the quality of a partner's alternatives was positively associated with appraisals of the severity of one's transgressions. In a follow-up study comparing offenders' and observers' (i.e., romantic partners') appraisals of problematic events, Samp (2001) observed that offenders' perception of partners' commitment was negatively associated with perceived event severity, while their perception of partners' alternatives was positively associated with severity appraisals. Conversely, observers' perception of partner commitment was positively associated with their perception of event severity, while observers' perception of partners' alternatives was negatively associated with severity appraisals. This study provided a robust comparison of the ways in which dependence power may influence cognitions for both offenders and observers of negative relational behaviors. In sum, it appears that possessing dependence power attenuates the perceived seriousness of one's own negative behaviors, while heightening the perceived seriousness of a partners' transgressions. Conversely, less powerful individuals may exaggerate the severity of their own misdeeds while downplaying the seriousness of a partner's harmful behaviors.

Additionally, Knobloch and Solomon (2002) argued that dependence power may also influence cognitive processes involved in the management of relational uncertainty. They posited that powerless individuals may fear that they will not be able to cope with sensitive relational information, and may therefore be less likely to seek information directly. Conversely, powerful partners should be more immune to the effects of discovering troubling information, and thus less averse to seeking relational information directly when uncertain. Although no published work has examined these propositions, partial support is provided in unpublished data collected by the current author (Worley & Samp, 2011). In this data, 163 individuals reflected on a time when they were uncertain whether a romantic partner had engaged in a problematic behavior. In this context, individuals' commitment was positively associated with the belief that seeking information about the behavior would yield positive outcomes. At the same time, quality of partners' alternatives was associated with *desiring greater uncertainty* about the partner's behavior. Finally, a partner's perceived commitment was negatively associated with anxiety felt due to uncertainty about the partner's behavior. While the authors did not observe interactions between individuals' commitment, partners' commitment, and partners' alternatives (as in Solomon & Samp, 1998), the pattern of results is consistent with Knobloch and Solomon's contention that dependence power may influence cognitive processes involved in uncertainty management.

Dependence and Behavioral Accommodation

Dependence has also been linked to individuals' willingness to accommodate a partner's problematic relational behavior. For instance, commitment, investment size, relational satisfaction, and poor alternatives have been observed to be positively associated with accommodative responses to partners' destructive behavior (Rusbult et al., 1991) as well as with greater willingness to sacrifice one's own interests in favor of a partner's (Van Lange et al, 1997). While accommodation and sacrifice may certainly play a role in promoting relational well-being (Rusbult et al, 1994), in the context of conflict these responses may also perpetuate a dependent partner's powerlessness by preempting attempts to change the relationship for the better (Cloven & Roloff, 1993).

One area in which accommodation has been particularly linked to dependence power concerns the experience of physical violence. Although violence is often implicitly associated with punitive forms of power (e.g., Cloven & Roloff, 1993; Stets & Pirog-Good, 1987), dependence power has also been linked to the experience of intimate violence. Research indicates that, in particular, women often remain in violent relationships because they are committed to a partner and/or lack adequate alternatives to the relationship (Follingstad et al, 1988; Rusbult & Martz, 1995). The link between dependence and remaining in abusive relationships is not limited to heterosexual associations, but has also been documented among gay men (Cruz, 2003). Samp and Abbott (2011) recently documented among a community sample of at-risk mothers that dependence on a child's father was positively associated with tolerating physical and psychological violence from the father. Further, while many explorations of dependence and violence have focused on women's tolerance of male violence, Samp and Abbott also observed that a mother's dependence power was positively associated with *her own* use of violent child discipline tactics. In essence, the more powerful the mother was (as defined by her relationship to her child's father), the more likely she was to engage in physically violent discipline toward her child. Together, these results illustrate that dependence power may embolden individuals to engage in violent behavior toward romantic partners and others, while powerlessness is associated with tolerating violence.

Dependence and the Chilling Effect

At least in the United States, romantic relationships are often understood through an "ideology of intimacy," according to which total openness is perceived as the paradigm for communication between intimate partners (Parks, 1982). While conflict has the potential for fostering greater openness and honesty (Siegert & Stamp, 1994), ample evidence attests that withdrawal (Gottman, 1994) and avoidance (Afifi, 2009) are frequent experiences in conflict. Avoiding communication about important relational issues is generally associated with decreased relational satisfaction and emotional closeness (Caughlin & Golish, 2002; Dailey & Palomares, 2004).

Why are individuals often reluctant to speak their minds during conflict? A variety of factors have been associated with communicative avoidance during conflict, including family communication orientations (Koerner & Fitzpatrick,

1997), relational schemata (Solomon et al, 2004), perceiving a problem as unimportant (Roloff & Solomon, 2002), and the desire to protect a partner (Afifi et al, 2005). However, one of the most documented reasons for withholding complaints during conflict is the perception of a partner's power. A number of studies within the chilling effect tradition have indicated that a partner's dependence power is positively associated with withholding complaints about the partner's behavior (Cloven & Roloff, 1993; Roloff & Cloven, 1990; Solomon & Samp, 1998). Similarly, Samp and Solomon (2001) observed that when individuals were highly committed but perceived their partners as uncommitted, they were less likely to communicate with partners about their *own* problematic behaviors. These results point to the way in which dependence power may influence the degree to which individuals discuss problematic relational issues with intimate partners.

A Spotlight Examination of Dependence Power

Past research on the chilling effect has largely been conducted using data from only one member of a dyad. A series of studies by Afifi and colleagues (Afifi & Afifi, 2009; Afifi et al, 2009; Afifi & Olsen, 2005) has examined communicative avoidance in romantic or family dyads; however, these studies have focused on factors other than dependence power. Similarly, Samp (2001) conducted a dyadic study investigating the influence of dependence power on offenders' and observers' appraisals of problematic relational events. While this study did assess dependence power in a dyadic sample, it did not directly investigate the chilling effect (i.e., communicative avoidance). There is currently a lacuna in the literature on dependence and the chilling effect due to the dearth of dyadic analyses to date. As power is an inherently relational phenomenon (Thibaut & Kelley, 1978), a full assessment of the chilling effect must involve consideration of *both* partners' power and communicative decisions.

Research indicates that individuals' own and partners' power may have unique contributions to relational phenomena. Some conceptualizations view relational power as a zero-sum entity, such that one's power is the inverse of a partner's power (Dunbar, 2004). However, Bacharach and Lawler (1981) demonstrated that self and partner dependence are both conceptually and empirically distinct, such that one's own power is not simply the inverse of a partner's. They observed that in bargaining contexts, individuals' own dependence power, but *not* a partner's dependence power, served as the primary criterion by which individuals formed predictions about a partner's likely conflict tactics. Similarly, self and partner power have been observed to predict different types of emotion during dyadic interaction (Langner & Keltner, 2008). The ability to observe such dynamics is obscured when power is conceived in a zero-sum manner or when conclusions are based on reports of only one dyad member.

Accordingly, the current study sought to understand the relative contributions of individuals' own and a partners' power to verbal avoidance about relational complaints. The analytic approach is rooted in the Actor-Partner Interdependence Model (APIM) (Kenny et al, 2006), which accounts for interdependence between dyadic partners' characteristics and outcomes. According to the APIM, relational phenomena may be categorized as *actor effects* or *partner effects*. Actor effects refer to the influence of an individual's characteristics on his or her own outcomes. Partner effects refer to the influence of a partner's characteristics on an individuals' outcomes. Utilizing this framework, I hypothesized that individuals' own dependence power would be negatively associated with complaint withholding (*actor effect*: H1), while a partner's power would be positively associated with complaint withholding (*partner effect*: H2).

A second impetus for the current study concerns the operationalization of dependence power. Prior research has largely observed dependence power as a three-way interaction between individuals' commitment, perceived partner commitment, and perceived partner alternatives (Cloven & Roloff, 1993; Samp & Solomon, 2001; Solomon & Samp, 1998). While this approach captures the substantive dynamic of dependence power, both the computation and interpretation of the 3-way interaction become prohibitively complex within the context of a dyadic framework. A promising alternative to the 3-way interaction approach has been developed by Samp and Abbott (2011). Samp and Abbott operationalized dependence power as a formative index[1] composed of individuals' commitment, perceived partner commitment, and perceived partner alternatives. Using this index, they observed theoretically anticipated associations of mothers' dependence power with tolerance for violence from a partner. No previous studies have assessed the utility of a dependence power index for studying the chilling effect. As such, this study utilized a formative index to quantify each partner's dependence power and its associations with complaint avoidance.

Method

Participants

The sample consisted of 182 heterosexual couples (364 total participants), all of whom defined themselves as currently involved in a romantic relationship with one another, as they defined "romantic." Participants were recruited from the undergraduate research pool in the communication department at a large southeastern U.S. university. Eligible participants received credit toward a research requirement for communication courses (other research and non-research options were also available to fulfill this course component).

Procedures

Partners were distributed surveys, which they completed separately. As a prompt to stimulate reflection on their responses to relational complaints, participants were first instructed to create a list of up to five complaints they currently had about their partners' behavior, or had had at some time in the past. Participants were instructed that these could be issues that both partners were aware of, or issues that only one partner was aware of. If participants were unable to think of five issues, they were instructed to list as many as they could think of. Following this task, participants completed a survey designed to assess perceptions of communicative avoidance and relational characteristics.

Measures

Complaint avoidance. Complaint avoidance was assessed using a four-item measure, adapted from Solomon and Samp (1998). Participants responded to the following prompt, "In my relationship with my romantic partner," using a seven-point Likert-type scale (1 = *strongly disagree*; 7 = *strongly agree*). Participants reported on the following statements: (a) I voice my opinion to my partner about problematic issues (reverse scored); (b) I express my feelings to my partner about problematic issues (reverse scored); (c) I avoid talking to my partner about problematic issues; and (d) I "hold my tongue" rather than telling my partner what I really think about problematic issues. This scale had high reliability ($M = 2.79$, $SD = 1.27$, $\alpha = .87$).

Dependence power. Consistent with the conceptualization of dependence power as a multidimensional construct composed of individuals' commitment, partners' commitment, and partners' alternatives (Cloven & Roloff, 1993), dependence power was operationalized via a formative index developed by Samp and Abbott (2011). The index was based upon Likert-type measures of commitment and relational alternative reported by Solomon and Samp (1998) (1 = *strongly disagree*; 6 = *strongly agree*). Individuals' commitment was measured using three items (e.g., "I am very committed to my partner"; $M = 5.23$, $SD = 1.05$, $\alpha = .89$). Three items assessed perceived partner commitment (e.g., "My partner is very committed to me"; $M = 5.22$, $SD = .95$, $\alpha = .86$). Perceived partner alternatives was measured via three items (e.g., "My partner's alternatives to our relationship are quite appealing"; $M = 2.23$, $SD = 1.07$, $\alpha = .75$). To compute the index, the measures for partner commitment and partner alternatives were first reverse-scored. The three dependence-related measures were then summed to derive individuals' dependence power scores, with higher scores indicating greater dependence power ($M = -2.22$, $SD = 1.45$).

Results

Preliminary analyses examined whether males and females differed in dependence power and complaint avoidance. A paired-samples t-test indicated no differences between males ($M = -2.27$, $SD = 1.47$) and females ($M = -2.21$, $SD = 1.44$) on dependence power, $t(148) = 0.36$, $p = .72$. However, males ($M = 2.93$, $SD = 1.27$) reported significantly higher levels of complaint avoidance than did females ($M = 2.64$, $SD = 1.26$), $t(179) = 2.42$, $p = .01$.

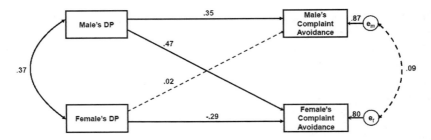

FIGURE 6.1 Actor-partner interdependence model for dependence power and complaint avoidance

Note: The parameters above are standardized estimates. Bold lines represent significant paths, and dotted lines represent non-significant paths. All significant parameters are significant at the $p < .001$ level.

Hypotheses were tested via an APIM path model using structural equation modeling (SEM) in LISREL 9.1. SEM is the preferred method for dyadic analyses when members are distinguishable by sex (i.e., heterosexual) (Kenny et al, 2006). Accordingly, actor and partner effects for males and females within each couple were examined. Results are summarized in Figure 6.1.[2]

Results indicated two significant actor effects and one significant partner effect. As predicted (H1), females' dependence power was negatively associated with their own complaint avoidance (actor effect). In line with H2, males' dependence power was positively associated with females' complaint avoidance (partner effect). In contrast to initial predictions (H1), males' dependence power was *positively* associated with their own complaint avoidance (actor effect); the more powerful males perceived themselves to be, the *less* they voiced complaints to their partners. Contrary to H2, females' dependence power was not associated with males' complaint avoidance.

Discussion

This study provided an initial exploration of dependence power and complaint avoidance within a dyadic framework. An APIM analysis illuminated the unique insights that a dyadic perspective offers into the dependence-based processes underlying the chilling effect. The study also provides further evidence of the utility of formative measures of dependence power (see Samp & Abbott, 2011) for examining dependence power within complex models.

Theoretical Implications

The current results highlight that both actor and partner dependence power may influence individuals' complaint expression. However, the associations between dependence and the chilling effect differed somewhat for males and females.

Females' dependence power appeared to have an "enabling effect" on their own willingness to voice complaints (see Samp, 2001). Conversely, males' dependence power was associated with *greater* complaint avoidance. This pattern for males may reflect the view that powerful individuals see less need to attempt to change a partner's behavior, because their power grants them implicit control of the relationship (Dunbar, 2004; Roloff & Cloven, 1990). Yet it is intriguing that while there were no sex differences in overall levels of dependence power, males' and females' power had opposite effects on their own communication. If the positive association between males' dependence power and complaint avoidance were simply due to implicit control rendering influence attempts unnecessary (Dunbar, 2004; Roloff & Cloven, 1990), this pattern should have emerged for females as well. That it did not suggests that perhaps the *subjective implications* of similar *objective levels* of dependence power may differ for men and women.

Post hoc analyses of additional data provided by the participants appear to support this explanation. Within the data set reported here, females ($M = 5.75$, $SD = 1.22$) rated their complaints as more important than did males ($M = 5.12$, $SD = 1.73$), $t(316) = 3.72$, $p < .001$. At the same time, females ($M = .97$, $SD = 1.53$) were also more optimistic about the potential for favorable outcomes of complaint expression than were men ($M = .28$, $SD = 1.64$). Research on demand-withdraw patterns in conflict suggests that women frequently demand in an effort to change relational dynamics, while men frequently withdraw from conflict in order to maintain the relational status quo (Christensen & Heavey, 1990; Klinetob & Smith, 1996). To the extent that the relational status quo tends to favor men in heterosexual associations (Peplau & Gordon, 1985), women will have more to gain from influence attempts (e.g., complaining), and men will be motivated to preserve their power by avoiding discussion of relational problems. As females in this sample considered their complaints relatively more important than did males, they may have been more motivated to *use* their power to address problematic issues, particularly given their greater optimism about the outcomes of complaint expression.

Additional support for this interpretation comes from research on power and verbal aggression. Sagrestano et al (1999) conducted an interactive study involving conflict discussions between marital partners. They observed that wives' power was positively associated with both wives, and husbands' verbal aggression, while husbands' power had non-significant negative associations with husbands, and wives' verbal aggression. The authors interpreted these patterns as indicating that male verbal aggression (of which complaining may be considered a form) is driven more by males' *desire* for power, rather than their *actual* power. If this perspective is correct, it may help to explain the differing effects of dependence power on men's and women's complaint expression in the current study. The positive association between men's dependence power and complaint avoidance may be interpreted in terms of its inverse: *men's powerlessness was associated with greater complaint expression*. This is congruent with the view that males who lack relational power utilize verbal aggression in an attempt to acquire it. Conversely, females appear to avoid verbally aggressive influence attempts unless they perceive themselves as possessing sufficient power to "get away with it."

Methodological Challenges and Opportunities for Future Research

Dependence is Resource-Specific

Dependence, in its classical formulation (e.g., Emerson, 1962), is dependence on a partner *for desired resources*. This conceptualization implies that individuals in intimate relationships may be dependent on one another for a variety of relationally-linked outcomes. To date, communication research on dependence and conflict has tended to highlight almost exclusively dependence as continued romantic attachment in the face of potential relational alternatives (either one's own alternatives or a partner's). While romantic attachment (e.g., having someone to date) represents one potential relationally linked resource, a host of other resources may serve as bases of dependence in intimate relationships (Safilios-Rothschild, 1976). For instance, individuals may depend on partners for financial support (Rusbult & Martz, 1995), childrearing assistance (Samp & Abbott, 2011), sexual satisfaction (Baumeister & Vohs, 2004), social activities and prestige (Rusbult, 1983), and even a sense of existential identity (Simon & Oakes, 2006). Although research employing global measures of dependence (i.e., global commitment and alternatives) has revealed important associations between these constructs and communication in conflict, it is possible that such a global view may obscure differences in communicative decisions based on the specific types of resources for which individuals depend on a partner. In the future, researchers are encouraged to consider a broader range of dependence bases in their research.

Dependence is Relationship-Specific

Further, the nature of dependence and its influence on communicative decisions may differ across relationship types (Solomon et al, 2004). For instance, the greater structural commitment often implied in marriage may render *affective* dependence less salient for married individuals than for dating individuals (Solomon et al, 2004), while rendering economic dependence more central (Rusbult & Martz, 1995). Additionally, as relationships vary in the degree to which partners value interdependence versus autonomy (Fitzpatrick, 1988), the influence of dependence power on communication may vary depending on communicators' relational schemata. Although Solomon et al (2004) did not observe that married individuals' relational schemata moderated the influence of dependence power on the chilling effect, it is possible that within the more precarious context of dating relationships (Knobloch & Solomon, 2004), relational schemata may moderate the extent to which dependence impacts individuals' communicative decisions.

Dependence Power as Both Cause and Effect of Communication

A further area ripe for theoretical and methodological advancement concerns the potential for a bidirectional relationship of dependence power and communication. Within communication scholarship (and, indeed, the social sciences as a whole; Simon & Oakes, 2006), power is generally treated as an antecedent condition that *explains* communicative action, rather than as something to be *explained by* communicative action. While some scholars in the rhetorical tradition have explored the potential for communication to contribute to power (e.g., McKerrow, 1989; Phillips, 2006), this emphasis has been relatively lacking among scholars of interpersonal communication and conflict. Certainly, power does contribute to communicative decisions in close relationships. However, it is almost certainly the case that communicative acts, particularly when carried out over time in close relationships, have implications for subsequent perceptions of power (including dependence power). For instance, how might discussions of relational commitment influence partners' appraisals of one another's dependence power? How might observing a partner's communication with an attractive rival shift one's perceptions of that partner's alternatives? These acts represent merely a slice of the various communicative phenomena that may serve to shape relational power dynamics.

Taking a bidirectional view of power and communication necessitates methodological advancements over current practices in the literature. At the very least, examining a bidirectional model with cross-sectional data could be carried out using non-recursive SEM modeling (Bollen, 1989), which involves reciprocal feedback loops in which two variables serve simultaneously as cause and effect of one another. Using this approach, researchers could model dependence power and communication variables (e.g., verbal aggression, nonverbal dominance, etc.) as simultaneously influencing and being influenced by one another. However, non-recursive models require stringent data assumptions that cannot generally be tested within cross-sectional data (Kline, 2010). Further, model identification can be challenging for non-recursive models, and even properly identified models frequently encounter empirical problems such as non-convergence and inadmissible solutions (Kline, 2010). At a more basic level, cross-sectional data limit the ability to forward causal claims, making them less than ideal for testing ostensibly *causal* bidirectional relations between communication and power.

A more robust analysis of bidirectional relations between power and communication would require collecting data at multiple time points. Using longitudinal data, researchers could examine causal links between power and communication using methods such as cross-lagged panel modeling (Finkel, 1995) or growth curve modeling (Curran et al, 2010). Additionally, longitudinal data would allow for robust mediation analyses (e.g., Hayes, 2013) to determine whether communication processes mediate over-time changes in dependence power (and vice versa). Further, video-assisted recall techniques (Keck & Samp, 2007;

Waldron, 1997) would enable researchers to track the ways in which observed communication behaviors and subjective power appraisals covary over time within discrete interactions (Bakeman & Quera, 2011). Using such methods, communication scholars would be equipped to explore the extent to which communication both *reflects* and *constructs* power relations within dyadic relationships.

Notes

1. A formative approach to measurement differs from the reflective approach traditionally associated with scale development (see Bollen & Lennox, 1991). Within a reflective framework, indicators (e.g., measurement items or lower-level factors) are presumed to *flow from* an underlying latent construct (Nunnally, 1978). In contrast, within a formative framework indicators are presumed to causally influence a latent construct (Diamontopoulos & Winklhofer, 2001). For instance, socioeconomic status is generally assumed to be *caused by* (rather than *to cause*) its components of education, income, and occupational prestige (Hauser & Goldberger, 1971). Analogously, while it makes little sense to say that an underlying dependence power construct causally influences individuals' commitment, partners' commitment and partners' alternatives, it does seem to be the case that commitment and alternatives causally influence individuals' dependence power. As such, parallelism and internal consistency are not required for formative measures, although conceptual validity of the measurement approach is necessary (Bollen & Lennox, 1991).
2. Cases with missing data ($n = 32$) were handled using full information maximum likelihood (FIML) estimation (Enders & Bandalos, 2001). Because the APIM is a saturated model, it is just-identified and therefore has only one unique solution. A just-identified model has trivially perfect fit; therefore, information about model fit (e.g., RMSEA, CFI, etc.) is uninformative for the standard APIM, and is not reported (Kenny, 2012). Instead, model evaluation is based on the magnitude and significance of the path estimates.

References

Afifi, W. A., & Afifi, T. D. (2009). Avoidance among adolescents in conversations about their parents' relationship: Applying the Theory of Motivated Information Management. *Journal of Social and Personal Relationships*, 26(4), 488–511. doi: 10.1177/0265407509350869

Afifi, T. D., & Olson, L. (2005). The chilling effect in families and the pressure to conceal secrets. *Communication Monographs*, 72(2), 192–216. doi: 10.1080/03637750500111906

Afifi, T. D., Olson, L. N., & Armstrong, C. (2005). The chilling effect and family secrets: Examining the role of self protection, other protection, and communication efficacy. *Human Communication Research*, 31(4), 564–598. doi: 10.1093/hcr/31.4.564

Afifi, T. D., McManus, T., Steuber, K., & Coho, A. (2009). Verbal avoidance and dissatisfaction in intimate conflict situations. *Human Communication Research*, 35, 357–383. doi: 10.1111/j.1468-2958.2009.01355.x

Bacharach, S. B., & Lawler, E. J. (1981). Power and tactics in bargaining. *Industrial and Labor Relations Review*, 34(2), 219–233. doi: 10.2307/2522537

Bakeman, R., & Quera, V. (2011). *Sequential analysis and observational methods for the behavioral sciences*. New York: Cambridge University Press.

Baumeister, R. F., & Vohs, K. D. (2004). Sexual economics: Sex as female resource for social exchange in heterosexual interactions. *Personality and Social Psychology Review, 8,* 339–363. doi: 10.1207/s15327957pspr0804_2

Bollen, K. A. (1989). *Structural equations with latent variables.* New York: Wiley and Sons.

Bollen, K. A., & Lennox, R. M. (1991). Conventional wisdom on measurement: A structural equation perspective. *Psychological Bulletin, 110*(2), 305–314. doi: 10.1037/0033-2909.110.2.305

Burgoon, J. K., & Hale, J. L. (1984). The fundamental topoi of relational communication. *Communication Monographs, 51,* 193–214. doi: 10.1080/03637758409390195

Caughlin, J. P., & Golish, T. D. (2002). An analysis of the association between topic avoidance and dissatisfaction: Comparing perceptual and interpersonal explanations. *Communication Monographs, 69*(4), 275–295. doi: 10.1080/03637750216546

Christensen, A., & Heavey, C. L. (1990). Gender and social structure in the demand/withdraw pattern of marital conflict. *Journal of Personality and Social Psychology, 59,* 73–81. doi: 10.1037//0022-3514.59.1.73

Cloven, D. H., & Roloff, M. E. (1993). The chilling effect of aggressive potential on the expression of complaints in intimate relationships. *Communication Monographs, 60,* 199–219. doi: 10.1080/03637759309376309

Cruz, M. (2003). "Why doesn't he just leave?" Gay male domestic violence and the reasons victims stay. *Journal of Men's Studies, 11*(3), 309–323. doi: 10.3149/jms.1103.309

Curran, P. J., Obeidat, K., & Losardo, D. (2010). Twelve frequently asked questions about growth curve modeling. *Journal of Cognition and Development, 11*(2), 121–136. doi: 10.1080/15248371003699969

Dailey, R. M., & Palomares, N. A. (2004). Strategic topic avoidance: An investigation of topic avoidance frequency, strategies used, and relational correlates. *Communication Monographs, 71*(4), 471–496. doi: 10.1080/0363452042000307443

Diamontopoulos, A., & Winklhofer, H. M. (2001). Index construction with formative indicators: An alternative to scale construction. *Journal of Marketing Research, 38*(2), 269–277. doi: 10.1509/jmkr.38.2.269.18845

Dillard, J. P., Solomon, D. H., & Samp, J. A. (1996). Framing social reality: The relevance of relational judgments. *Communication Research, 23,* 703–723. doi: 10.1177/009365096023006004

Dunbar, N. E. (2004). Dyadic Power Theory: Constructing a communication-based theory of relational power. *Journal of Family Communication, 4,* 235–248. doi: 10.4135/9781412959384

Emerson, R. M. (1962). Power-dependence relations. *American Sociological Review, 27*(1), 31–41. doi: 10.2307/2089716

Enders, C. K., & Bandalos, D. L. (2001). The relative performance of full information maximum likelihood estimation for missing data in structural equation models. *Structural Equation Modeling, 8*(3), 430–457. doi: 10.1207/s15328007sem0803_5

Finkel, S. (1995). *Causal analysis with panel data.* London: Sage.

Fitzpatrick, M. A. (1988). *Between husbands and wives: Communication in marriage.* Newbury Park, CA: Sage.

Follingstad, D. R., Rutledge, L. L., Polek, D. S., & McNeill-Hawkins, K. (1988). Factors associated with patterns of dating violence toward college women. *Journal of Family Violence, 3*(3), 169–182. doi: 10.1007/bf00988973

Gottman, J. M. (1994). *What predicts divorce? The relationship between marital processes and marital outcomes.* Hillsdale, NJ: Lawrence Erlbaum.

Hauser, R. M., & Goldberger, A. S. (1971). The treatment of unobserved variables in path analysis. *Sociological Methodology*, *3*, 81–117. doi: 10.2307/270819

Hayes, A. F. (2013). *Introduction to mediation, moderation, and conditional process analysis: A regression-based approach*. New York: Guilford.

Keck, K. L., & Samp, J. A. (2007). The dynamic nature of goals and message production as revealed in a sequential analysis of conflict interaction. *Human Communication Research*, *33*, 27–47. doi: 10.1111/j.1468-2958.2007.00287.x

Kelley, H. H., & Thibaut, J. W. (1978). *Interpersonal relations: A theory of interdependence*. New York: Wiley.

Kenny, D. A. (2012, April 30). Dyadic data analysis: Chapter 7 elaborations. Retrieved from http://davidakenny.net/kkc/c7/c7.htm

Kenny, D. A., Kashy, D. A., & Cook, W. L. (2006). *Dyadic data analysis*. New York: Guilford Press.

Kline, R. B. (2010). Reverse arrow dynamics: Feedback loops and formative measurement. In G. R. Hancock & R. O. Mueller (Eds.), *Structural equation modeling: A second course* (2nd ed.) (pp39–77). Charlotte, NC: Information Age Publishing.

Klinetob, N. A., & Smith, D. A. (1996). Demand-withdraw communication in marital interaction: Tests of interspousal contingency and gender role hypotheses. *Journal of Marriage and the Family*, *58*, 945–957. doi: 10.2307/353982

Knobloch, L. K., & Solomon, D. H. (2002). Information-seeking beyond initial interaction: Negotiating relational uncertainty within close relationships. *Human Communication Research*, *28*(2), 243–257. doi: 10.1093/hcr/28.2.243

Koerner, A. F., & Fitzpatrick, M. A. (1997). Family type and conflict: The impact of conversation orientation and conformity orientation on conflict in the family. *Communication Studies*, *48*, 59–78. doi: 10.1080/10510979709368491

Langner, C. A., & Keltner, D. (2008). Social power and emotional experience: Actor and partner effects within dyadic interactions. *Journal of Experimental Social Psychology*, *44*(3), 848–856. doi: 10.1016/j.jesp.2007.08.002

Lawler, E. J., & Bacharach, S. B. (1987). Comparison of dependence and punitive forms of power. *Social Forces*, *66*(2), 446–462. doi: 10.2307/2578749

McKerrow, R. E. (1989). Critical rhetoric: Theory and praxis. *Communication Monographs*, *56*, 98. doi: 10.1080/03637758909390253

Nunnally, J. C. (1978). *Psychometric theory* (2nd ed.). New York: McGraw-Hill.

Parks, M. R. (1982). Ideology in interpersonal communication: Off the couch and into the world. In M. Burgoon (Ed.), *Communication Yearbook 6* (pp79–107). Beverly Hills, CA: Sage.

Peplau, L. A., & Gordon, S. L. (1985). Women and men in love: Gender differences in close heterosexual relationships. In V. E. O'Leary, R. K. Unger, & B. S. Wallston (Eds.), *Women, gender and social psychology* (pp257–291). Hillsdale, NJ: Lawrence Erlbaum.

Phillips, K. R. (2006). Rhetorical maneuvers: Subjectivity, power and resistance. *Philosophy and Rhetoric*, *39*(4), 310–332. doi: 10.1353/par.2007.0005

Roloff, M. E., & Cloven, D. H. (1990). The chilling effect in interpersonal relationships: The reluctance to speak one's mind. In D. D. Cahn (Ed.), *Intimates in conflict: A communication perspective* (pp49–76). Hillsdale, NJ: Erlbaum.

Roloff, M. E., & Solomon, D. H. (2002). Conditions under which relational commitment leads to expressing or withholding relational complaints. *International Journal of Conflict Management*, *13*(3), 276–391. doi: 10.1108/eb022877

Rusbult, C. E. (1983). A longitudinal test of the investment model: The development (and deterioration) of satisfaction and commitment in heterosexual involvements. *Journal of Personality and Social Psychology, 45,* 101–117. doi: 10.1037/0021-9010.68.3.429

Rusbult, C. E., & Martz, J. M. (1995). Remaining in an abusive relationship: An investment model analysis of nonvoluntary commitment. *Personality and Social Psychology Bulletin, 21,* 558–571. doi: 10.1177/0146167295216002

Rusbult, C. E., Verette, J., Whitney, G. A., Slovik, L. F., & Lipkus, I. (1991). Accommodation processes in close relationships: Theory and preliminary empirical evidence. *Journal of Personality and Social Psychology, 60,* 53–78. doi: 10.1037//0022-3514.60.1.53

Rusbult, C. E., Drigotas, S. M., & Verette, J. (1994). The investment model: An interdependence analysis of commitment processes and relationship maintenance phenomena. In D. Canary & L. Stafford (Eds.), *Communication and relational maintenance* (pp115–139). New York: Academic Press.

Russell, B. (1938). *Power: A new social analysis.* New York: Norton.

Safilios-Rothschild, C. (1976). A macro-and micro-examination of family power and love: An exchange model. *Journal of Marriage and the Family, 37,* 355–362. doi: 10.2307/350394

Sagrestano, L. M., Heavey, C. L., & Christensen, A. (1999). Perceived power and physical violence in marital conflict. *Journal of Social Issues, 55(1),* 65–79. doi: 10.1111/0022–4537.00105

Samp, J. A. (2001). Dependence power, severity appraisals, and communicative decisions about problematic behaviors in dating relationships. *Communication Studies, 52(1),* 17–36. doi: 10.1080/10510970109388538

Samp, J. A., & Abbott, L. (2011). An examination of dependence power, father involvement, and judgments about violence in an at-risk community sample of mothers. *Journal of Interpersonal Violence, 26(18),* 3682–3698. doi: 10.1177/0886260511403746

Samp, J. A., & Solomon, D. H. (2001). Coping with problematic events in dating relationships: The influence of dependence power on severity appraisals and decisions to communicate. *Western Journal of Communication, 65(2),* 138–160. doi: 10.1080/10570310109374697

Siegert, J. R., & Stamp, G. H. (1994). "Our first big fight" as a milestone in the development of close relationships. *Communication Monographs, 61,* 345–360. doi: 10.1080/03637759409376342

Simon, B., & Oakes, P. (2006). Beyond dependence: An identity approach to social power and domination. *Human Relations, 59,* 105–139. doi: 10.1177/0018726706062760

Solomon, D. H., & Samp, J. A. (1998). Power and problem appraisal: Perceptual foundations of the chilling effect in dating relationships. *Journal of Social and Personal Relationships, 15,* 191–209. doi: 10.1177/0265407598152004

Solomon, D. H., & Theiss, J. A. (2007). Cognitive foundations of communication in close relationships. In D. R. Roskos-Ewoldson, & J. L. Monahan (Eds.), *Communication and social cognition: Theories and methods* (pp117–140). Mahwah, NJ: Erlbaum.

Solomon, D. H., Knobloch, L. K., & Fitzpatrick, M. A. (2004). Relational power, marital schema, and decisions to withhold complaints: An investigation of the chilling effect on confrontation in marriage. *Communication Studies, 55(1),* 146–167. doi: 10.1080/10510970409388610

Stets, J. E., & Pirog-Good, M. A. (1987). Violence in dating relationships. *Social Psychology Quarterly, 50(3),* 237–246. doi: 10.2307/2786824

Van Lange, P. A. M., Rusbult, C. E., Drigotas, S. M., Arriaga, X. B., Witcher, B. S., & Cox, C. L. (1997). Willingness to sacrifice in close relationships. *Journal of Personality and Social Psychology, 72,* 1373–1395. doi: 10.1037/0022-3514.72.6.1373

Waldron, V. R. (1997). Toward a theory of interactive conversational planning. In J. O. Greene (Ed.), *Message production: Advances in communication theory* (pp195–220). Mahwah, NJ: Lawrence Erlbaum Associates.

Worley, T. R., & Samp, J. A. (2011). *Study of dependence power and information management.* Unpublished raw data.

SECTION 3
Conflict as an Ongoing Process

7

SERIAL ARGUMENTS IN INTERPERSONAL RELATIONSHIPS

Relational Dynamics and Interdependence

Amy Janan Johnson and Ioana A. Cionea

Trapp and Hoff (1985)'s initial findings, that people often referred to ongoing arguments when asked to describe one such exchange, paved the way for an exciting line of research into what they called *serial arguments*. These arguments are ongoing discussions of the same issue with the same person that attempt to resolve some perceived incompatibility between the two parties involved (Trapp & Hoff, 1985).

Research on serial arguments has grown exponentially in the past decade, moving beyond Trapp and Hoff's (1985) initial model. Our goal in this chapter is to provide a summary of the main lines of research focused on relational dynamics that have spun from Trapp and Hoff's initial model in order to facilitate an understanding of the current state of research in this area.

We then explore a new avenue for explaining the underlying processes that characterize serial arguments: focusing more specifically on the interdependence (Hocker & Wilmot, 1978) between arguers. We present an analysis of serial arguments in close relationships in which we focus on the role arguers have in the argumentative episode in order to illustrate the idea of interdependence. Finally, we present several methodological and theoretical implications regarding serial arguments research and the potential directions for future research in this area.

A Summary of Serial Argument Research Focused on Relational Dynamics

Trapp and Hoff (1985) proposed a descriptive model of the process involved in serial arguments that focused on antecedent and consequent conditions of arguing as well as the primary and secondary processes involved in arguing. In short, according to Trapp and Hoff, arguing arises because people believe some incompatibility exists between them (an antecedent to arguing) and one party decides to confront the other party about it (primary process involved in arguing). If the incompatibility between the two parties cannot be resolved via argumentation, arguers need to weigh yet another matter: "Is the issue and/or the relationship important enough to try again to resolve the incompatibility?" (secondary process involved in arguing; Trapp & Hoff, 1985, p. 4). If no, avoidance occurs. If yes, as Trapp and Hoff explained, arguments "simmer down" and parties try to resolve the issue via reason-giving again. This loop, caused by the inability to move towards resolution in the first place and the decision to try again at a later time, is essential for serial arguments. It captures the cyclical nature of such arguments, continuously revolving around the incompatibility that cannot be resolved. If, at any point, the parties are able to resolve their incompatibility through argumentation (either because they have reached a consensus, a compromise, or because one party conceded), resolution occurs (a consequence condition; Trapp & Hoff, 1985).

This initial model of serial arguments highlights several key features that have been explored in more detail in later research. One line of research, which we focus on in this review, examines the effects of such repetitive arguments on relationships.

Initial Investigations: Outcomes of Serial Arguments

The initial research following Trapp and Hoff's (1985) model emphasized outcomes of serial arguing. Of particular interest was the perceived resolvability of a serial argument and its connections to relational satisfaction. In addition, consequences for the health of the arguers and the health of the relationship were studied (e.g., Johnson & Roloff, 1998; Johnson et al, 2011).

Perceived Resolvability and Relational Satisfaction

Johnson and Roloff (1998) utilized Trapp and Hoff's (1985) model distinctions (antecedent conditions, primary processes, secondary processes, and consequence conditions) to predict perceived resolvability of a serial argument. They found that resolvability was positively associated with relational satisfaction, whether a relationship was currently intact, negatively associated with the antecedent condition of argument issue (whether the argument was about violated expectations), and not associated with the argument's frequency. In a subsequent study, Johnson and Roloff (2000a) found that perceived resolvability was related positively to the use of confirming behaviors. Later on, Malis and Roloff (2006a) found that perceived resolvability of the argument was negatively associated with the demand/withdraw pattern, regardless of who demanded and who withdrew from the argument. Malis and Roloff (2006b) found that resolvability of a perceived stressor related positively to such coping strategies as optimistic comparisons, and negatively with resignation, perceived stress from the serial argument, and hyperarousal.

In terms of secondary processes involving how arguments heat up or simmer down, Johnson and Roloff (1998) found that people's belief that they could predict the occurrence of a serial argument episode and what would be said during the argument related negatively to resolvability. Mulling between episodes and the number and frequency of additional episodes were also negatively related to resolvability. The authors also found that resolvability was negatively related to avoiding a relational partner after a serial argument episode (consequent condition).

So, initially, this line of research correlated resolvability with other variables of interest. In research conducted more recently, the interest has shifted towards predicting resolvability based on the processes involved in arguing. For example, Bevan et al (2008) found that both integrative and distributive tactics led to higher resolvability. Other studies have found that resolvability of the serial argument decreased with the use of distributive tactics (Hample & Allen, 2012; Hample et al, 2012; Hample & Richards, 2015) but increased with the use of integrative tactics (Hample & Allen, 2012; Hample et al, 2012; Hample & Richards, 2015). Thus, the general findings regarding perceived resolvability suggest that constructive, positive behaviors tend to increase the perception of resolvability of a serial argument.

Relational Harm, Personal Harm, and Coping Strategies

Closely related to the idea of perceived resolvability was the idea of analyzing the harm that serial arguments can inflict on the arguers' relationship. Johnson and Roloff (2000a) found that hostility was positively associated with relational harm and that confirming behaviors were negatively related to such harm.

Johnson et al (2011) examined several other variables related to relational harm, including type of argument (Johnson, 2002), argument function (Johnson, 2009), and argumentativeness (Infante & Rancer, 1982). Personal-issue arguments (those involving issues internal to the arguing dyad) with low levels of perceived resolvability had higher levels of relational harm than personal-issue arguments with high levels of perceived resolvability or public-issue arguments (those involving issues external to the arguing dyad) at all levels of resolvability. In addition, reporting that the argument fulfilled the function of solving behavioral incompatibilities was positively related to relational harm, while reporting that the argument fulfilled the function of gaining or giving knowledge was negatively related to relational harm.

Besides relational harm, personal harm caused by serial arguments has also been examined extensively. Malis and Roloff (2006a) started this line of research that examined how serial arguments are related to a "person's psychological and physical well-being" (p. 198). They analyzed stress and stress-related symptoms experienced after a serial argument episode, including hyperarousal, avoidance of thoughts about the serial argument, intrusion of thoughts about the serial argument on one's consciousness, and disruptions to everyday activities caused by serial argument stress. Thought avoidance, intrusive thoughts, hyperarousal, and "limitation on activities" (p. 211) were positively related to the pattern of self-demand/partner withdrawal, and stress related positively to partner-demand/self-withdrawal. The authors concluded that perceived resolvability of a serial argument and the role that one plays in the serial argument can predict relational outcomes and personal outcomes (stress and stress-related symptoms) of a serial argument.

In another study, Malis and Roloff (2006b) examined one's coping mechanisms, stress, and stress-related symptoms resulting from serial arguments. Overall, resigned stance positively predicted stress and stress-related symptoms, whereas selective ignoring negatively predicted these symptoms. This latter negative relationship was unexpected. The authors suggested that this coping strategy may be effective in helping individuals "distract themselves from their stress-related problems" (p. 59). The research on coping thus shows that resigned stance is negatively related to both relational harm (Johnson & Roloff, 2000a) and personal harm (Malis & Roloff, 2006b). Optimistic comparisons, though, predict relational harm (Johnson & Roloff, 2000a) and perceived resolvability (Johnson & Roloff, 2000a; Malis & Roloff, 2006b) but are not associated to most stress-related symptoms (Malis & Roloff, 2006b).

To explore further the relationship between serial arguments and mental and physical health, Roloff and Reznik (2008) and Reznik et al (2010) examined destructive and constructive conflict strategies. Roloff and Reznik found that frequency of arguing was related to hostility, constructive communication was negatively related to hyperarousal and thought avoidance, and hostility was positively associated to a host of stress-related problems. The authors also found an interaction between constructive communication and hostility on hyperarousal and intrusion. Constructive communication was negatively related to these variables at low levels of hostility but positively related to them at high levels of hostility. Roloff and Reznik (2008) concluded that the "benefits of constructive communication largely disappear with increasing levels of mutual hostility" (p112). Reznik et al (2010) found that distributive and avoidance conflict tactics were positively associated with stress-related symptoms, and that hyperarousal mediated the relationship between conflict tactics and reported health problems related to a serial argument. However, they unexpectedly found that integrative conflict tactics were also positively associated with stress-related problems, supporting the belief that constructive tactics can be stressful sometimes.

To explore this unexpected connection in more detail, Reznik, Roloff, and Miller (2010, 2012) explored when constructive communication may be stressful to enact. They proposed, based on cognitive depletion theory, that people's attempts at self-regulation can cause stress, especially when people try to deviate from their usual behaviors. In a serial argument, one may be stressed if having to respond positively when one's usual responses would have been negative (Reznik et al, 2012). The results confirmed that integrative conflict tactics were associated with post-episodic stress and health problems, such as hyperarousal and intrusive thoughts. Reznik et al (2012) expanded on this research by determining whether certain integrative tactics are more stressful to use than others. They found that problem-solving was positively related to stress and stress-related problems, whereas active listening had a negative relationship (contrary to their expectations). Reznik et al concluded that seeking to solve a serial argument may lead to stress, and that individuals may need to accept that actively listening to one another's viewpoint may be the best solution.

Other factors that have been found to influence the perceived levels of stress and stress-related problems resulting from a serial argument include type of argument, argument function, and argumentativeness (Johnson et al, 2011). Similar to their findings for relational harm, Johnson et al found that type of argument and perceived resolvability interacted to predict what they termed *personal harm*, an aggregate variable composed of stress, thought intrusion, thought avoidance, and hyperarousal. Whether the argument was perceived to function to resolve behavioral incompatibility, or to portray oneself in a positive light, were each positively related to personal harm.

Thus, the research into relational or personal harm and coping strategies suggests that serial arguments can cause harmful consequences depending on the strategies used in the argument (and, contrary to expectations, it is not only distributive tactics that increase stress), and depending on how resolvable an argument is perceived to be. Serial arguments are, overall, related to a series of stressful outcomes. So, why do individuals continue to engage in such exchanges? The next section will develop the idea that interdependence between arguers is an important variable to consider when examining why serial arguments occur. One aspect of prior research that focuses on such interdependence is the role one takes in a serial argument and how this role relates to perceptions of resolvability, harm, and relational satisfaction. First, the pertinent literature on serial arguments and role is reviewed. Second, the argument concerning interdependence is detailed and hypotheses are presented.

Summary of Findings Regarding Role in Serial Arguments

There are only a few studies that have analyzed the connections between role and serial argument behaviors. In terms of secondary processes involving how arguments heat up or simmer down, Johnson and Roloff (1998) found that resolvability was negatively related to avoiding a relational partner after a serial argument episode (consequent condition). These initial results paved the way for subsequent research in which more attention was paid to whether such perceptions differ depending on the role partners have in the serial argument.

Johnson and Roloff (2000b) focused specifically on the effects that the role one took in the first episode of a serial argument (resistor or initiator) had on serial argument behaviors. Role affected approaches to the argumentative episode. Initiators reported bringing up the issue of the serial argument because they were "becoming more upset about the problem" and "couldn't keep quiet any longer" (Johnson & Roloff, 2000b, p8). Initiators also reported planning the interaction in advance. Compared to resistors, initiators demanded more, whereas resistors withdrew more. Finally, resistors perceived arguments to be less resolvable as the frequency of the episodes increased. Role was only determined in this study by the stance (initiator or resistor) one took in the initial episode of the serial argument.

Closely related to the idea of perceived resolvability was the idea of analyzing the harm that serial arguments can inflict on the arguers' relationship. Johnson and Roloff (2000b) also found that one's role in the argument affected perceived relational harm. Resistors only (not initiators) reported that higher argument frequency was associated with greater relational harm. The authors concluded that resistors appear to have more negative views of serial arguments than initiators, which translates into greater perceived harm that may lead them to end the relationship. This action may surprise initiators who do not believe the argument is as serious. Once again, role results in different perceptions of the consequences serial arguments have on the relationship.

Regarding personal harm caused by serial arguments, Malis and Roloff (2006a) found that perceived resolvability of the argument was negatively associated with the demand/withdraw pattern, regardless of who demanded and who withdrew from the argument. They also found that initiators of the serial argument reported using more demanding strategies while their partners withdrew, whereas resistors in the serial argument reported using more withdrawal strategies while their partners demanded that they change. This latter pattern, withdrawing while the other person demands, the authors found, was strongly correlated with stress.

In their subsequent study, Malis and Roloff (2006b) examined several strategies that predicted stress. Although not directly focusing on role, the study is still important because it highlights several possible explanations for differences in health and well-being between initiators and resistors. If role were taken into account, it could be the case that, for example, initiators may be able to reduce the stress of ruminating over a troublesome behavior by selective ignoring. Resistors, who have been the targets of the same demanding behavior over and over again, may adopt the strategy of resigned stance, which, according to this study, leads to stress.

Another study, Reznik et al's (2012) exploration of situations in which constructive communication may be stressful to enact, concluded, as previously mentioned, that seeking to solve a serial argument may lead to stress. This finding is relevant to the role that one takes in the argument. For example, initiators who may believe that bringing up the serial argument can solve the problem may actually be experiencing more stress as they try to self-regulate or plan how to bring up the issue. It may be the case that they need a different strategy.

Overall, serial arguments are related to a series of stressful outcomes for both initiators and resistors. Although initiators may have more optimistic views about the effects of serial arguments on their relationship, they, nevertheless, are victims of increased levels of stress associated with hyperarousal and intrusive thoughts related to the bothersome behavior. Resistors have more negative views in respect to the harm such arguments inflict on their relationships or the resolvability of such issues, and they also engage in more withdrawal following demanding from their initiating partners. Are there any circumstances of serial arguments in which these negative effects may be reduced? Are there any relational features that may help ameliorate the multitude of negative consequences serial arguments appear to have on relationships? In what follows, we propose that alternating roles, or bringing up the issue of the serial argument relatively evenly between the two partners, may be a constructive alternative due to the underlying assumption of mutual management of problematic issues in a relationship: interdependence between partners.

Interdependence in Serial Arguments

When considering *why* individuals engage in serial arguments, a key element to consider is the interdependence between the two partners. Interdependence is a necessary condition for conflict between individuals to occur (Hocker & Wilmot, 1978). The question arises, how does one person's motivation to argue interact with his or her partner's motivation to engender the repetitive pattern of a serial argument?

A limited amount of research in serial arguments has examined how arguments tend to heat up and simmer down (Trapp & Hoff, 1985). For example, Carr et al (2012) examined two factors believed to predict a continued cycle of serial argumentation: motivation to continue the argument and likelihood of continuing the argument. In addition, Miller and Roloff (2006) proposed that intractable conflicts often involved "issues interactants perceive as central" (p. 295). Thus, one's own beliefs about the serial argument topic can contribute to whether a serial argument continues. This is similar to suppositions by Johnson et al (2014) who discuss how interpersonal arguments differ in the degree of *involvement* that individuals feel in respect to certain argument topics.

In addition to considering an individual's perspective about the serial argument, Carr et al (2012) claimed that individuals also considered their partner's views. Prior research related to interdependence theory (Kelley & Thibaut, 1978) may help us to understand this process. When one is interdependent with someone, the rewards and costs associated with the relationship are dependent on the other's actions (Kelley & Thibaut, 1978). Rusbult et al (1982) explained that factors related to the interdependence between individuals influence how people seek to deal with relational dissatisfaction: whether they *exit* the relationship, *voice* their concerns, stay *loyal* in hopes that circumstances will improve, or *neglect* the relationship and let it disintegrate. In this model, *voice* seems particularly relevant to serial arguments, and two factors were found to relate to the tendency to voice concerns: how satisfied individuals were with the relationship before they began experiencing problems, and how much one had invested in the relationship up to the current point. As some topics of serial arguments may be associated with areas of greater interdependence with one's partner than others, such considerations should affect the occurrence and recurrence of serial arguments, how serial arguments heat up or simmer down over time. Hence, to understand why serial arguments reoccur over time, one must consider one's own feelings and beliefs about the issue, in addition to one's degree of dependence with his or her partner concerning the desired outcomes related to the argument's topic. When an issue is very involving and it pertains to an area of great overlap between the two partners (their interdependence is high in regards to the issue), the likelihood of a serial argument developing and continuing should be high. The amount of interdependence between the individuals should predict how the argument develops and the outcomes associated with the serial argument, both for the relationship and the individuals' personal health.

In addition to these more general claims, this chapter presents data that examine interdependence between the arguing parties as manifested in the roles that individuals take during serial argument episodes. Prior research has examined whether individuals are the initiator or resistor during an initial serial argument episode (Johnson & Roloff, 2000b; Reznik & Roloff, 2008). However, previous research has not acknowledged the possibility that these roles may change over time. We believe this possibility to be particularly important because it highlights the interdependence of the two individuals involved in a serial argument. We gave participants the option to indicate whether they brought up the issue, whether the other person brought up the issue, or whether who brought up the issue was pretty even between partners. If both individuals are motivated to initiate a topic, then this case may be a particular instance where positive outcomes of the serial argument, such as movement toward resolution and lack of relational harm, may be more likely to occur.

Whether the issue is perceived as resolvable should be positively influenced by the commitment of both partners to work towards that resolution. The argument may transform from a perceived unilateral push (by initiators onto resistors) into a mutual effort. Instead of a "me versus you" mentality, partners who bring up the issues that bother them evenly may be working with a "we" mentality that actually has a positive effect on resolvability but also on their satisfaction. Bringing up issues that are known to affect their relationship may be interpreted as commitment and willingness to work through problems. Arguing, in this case, may have positive qualities, such as providing a means to address on-going issues. To analyze these possibilities, we posit that perceived resolvability (H1) and relational satisfaction (H2) will be higher when both partners bring up the serial argument issue equally as compared to when only one of the partners tends to bring it up, whereas relational harm (H3) will be lower when both partners bring up the serial argument issue equally as compared to when only one of the partners tends to bring it up.

Finally, we also propose that the stress (H4) arguers experience will be reduced if an issue is brought up by both partners as opposed to just one of them. We test here Malis and Roloff's (2006) conclusion that role predicts the personal harm inflicted by a serial argument. A unilateral repetition of the argument can create stress, regardless of the role. Therefore, we propose that perceived stress will be lower when both partners bring up the serial argument issue equally as compared to when only one of the partners tends to bring it up.

A Spotlight Examination of Interdependence in Serial Arguments

In what follows we present data from two studies on serial arguments in interpersonal relationships (i.e., romantic relationships, friendships, and family relationships). Previously reported analyses involving these two data sets can be found in Johnson et al (2010; 2011; 2014) but the current analysis is the first time that any analyses have been completed on the data sets together. The same procedures and measures were used in each of the data collections, except that the second data collection only involved serial arguments that occurred in families (see Johnson et al, 2014).

Participants

In the combined data set used for this study, 345 undergraduates from the research participation pool at a midsized southwestern university were asked to recall a serial argument that occurred with an interpersonal partner. Forty-eight percent recalled a serial argument with a friend, 32 percent with a family member, 15 percent with a romantic partner, and 5 percent did not specify their argumentation partner. Fifty-eight percent of the participants were women, whereas the remaining 42 percent were male. Seventy-five percent were Caucasian, 7 percent were African American, 5 percent were Hispanic, 4 percent were Asian American, 4 percent were Native American/Pacific Islander, 4 percent indicated another ethnicity, and 1 percent did not answer the question. The average age of the sample was 20.40 ($SD = 2.66$).

Procedures and Measures

The questionnaire asked participants to recall a serial argument they had experienced recently with a friend, romantic partner, or family member. Serial arguments were defined for participants as follows: "A serial argument exists when individuals argue or engage in conflict about the same topic over time, during which they participate in several (at least two) arguments about the topic" (Johnson & Roloff, 1998, p. 333). Participants were randomly assigned to recall a serial argument about either a public-issue or personal-issue topic. If participants reported not having a serial argument about any of the topics listed on their assigned questionnaire (public- or personal-issue argument topics), they were given the other questionnaire. Participants briefly described the argument and reported with whom they argued. Then, they answered questions regarding their serial argument. Likert-type scales were used for all measures, unless otherwise specified, ranging from 1 = strongly disagree to 7 = strongly agree. Means, standard deviations, Cronbach's alpha scores, as well as confirmatory factor analyses (CFA) results for all scales are reported in Table 7.1. All reliabilities were acceptable.

Role in the argument was measured by asking individuals when they argued about the issue, who tended to bring the issue up, themselves ($n = 84$), their partner ($n = 107$), or both ($n = 154$). *Perceived resolvability* was measured with two items taken from Johnson and Roloff (1998) and four items taken from Johnson et al (2011). *Relational harm* was measured with items from Johnson and Roloff (2000a). Respondents indicated on a seven-point scale if the relationship became close/more distant, stronger/weaker, and sadder/happier. *Relational satisfaction* was measured in two ways: as an overall variable with scales used in previous research [four items from Johnson's (2001) scale] and a specific variable that measured the immediate effect of the serial argument on the argument dyad. The first author created a scale with three items (e.g., "This argument will change the satisfaction level that we have") for this purpose. *Stress* was measured with 14 items from Cohen et al's (1983) global stress measure. CFA results indicated several problems with this scale. First, items four, eight, and twelve loaded poorly in the analyses and were dropped from further analyses. Second, a one-factor model was not supported by the data. We therefore employed a two-factor structure, *perceived stress* and *coping with stress*, in our subsequent analyses.

Results

Analyses of variance were conducted to test H1 through H4. H1 posited that perceived resolvability would be higher when both individuals bring up the serial argument as compared to only initiators or only resistors. This prediction was not supported, though, as results indicated no significant difference between the three roles, $F(2, 340) = 2.36$, $p = .10$. The mean resolvability score was actually lowest when both partners brought up the issue.

H2 posited that relational satisfaction would be higher when both partners bring up the issue instead of only one of them. This hypothesis was tested in two ways, depending on which measure of satisfaction was analyzed. Overall satisfaction was affected by one's role, $F(2, 272) = 7.27$, $p = .001$, and, indeed, higher

TABLE 7.1 Means, Standard Deviations, Reliabilities, and CFA Results for Dependent Variables

	N	No. items	M	SD	α	df	χ^2	p	CFI	RMSEA	SRMR
Resolvability[a]	344	6	4.10	1.66	.93	7	28.90	.00	.99	.09	.02
Overall satisfaction[b]	276	4	5.34	1.44	.87	1	0.70	.40	1.00	.00	.01
Post-argument satisfaction[c]	276	3	3.35	1.77	.87		Just-identified model, no fit indices available
Relational harm	342	3	3.99	1.14	.86		Just-identified model, no fit indices available
Perceived stress[d]	345	4	2.64	0.83	.75	1	1.12	.29	1.00	.02	.01
Coping stress[e]	345	7	2.56	0.84	.90	13	29.23	.01	.99	.05	.02

Notes: CFA $N = 345$.
[a] Reported CFA results are for the revised model in which covariances were permitted between the errors of the first and third, and fifth and sixth indicators.
[b] Reported CFA results are for the revised model in which a covariance was permitted between the errors of the first fourth indicators.
[c] Lower numbers indicate more satisfaction.
[d] Reported CFA results are for the revised model in which a covariance was permitted between the errors of the first and third indicators.
[e] Lower numbers indicate less coping. Reported CFA results are for the revised model in which a covariance was permitted between the errors of the fifth and sixth indicators.

when both partners brought up the serial argument ($p < .01$) as compared to when a participant brought up the issue or when the partner brought up the issue. Thus, H2 was supported. Whether individuals reported that the argument was likely to affect the satisfaction level of the dyad (second satisfaction measure) was also related to one's role, $F(2, 272) = 11.82$, $p = .00$. The mean score was significantly lower ($p < .001$) when both partners brought up the issue as compared to when a participant or the partner brought up the issue. This result actually supported H2, because individuals were least likely to indicate that the argument would affect their satisfaction when both individuals brought up the argument topic equally.

H3 proposed that relational harm would be lower when both partners bring up the issue as opposed to only one of them bringing it up. The hypothesis was supported. There was a difference in harm based on one's role, $F(2, 338) = 8.93$, $p = .00$, and the mean score for relational harm was significantly lower for both partners bringing the topic up ($p < .01$) than the mean for initiators or the mean for resistors.

H4 proposed that perceived stress would be lower when both partners bring up the issue as opposed to only one of them. The omnibus F-test was significant, indicating a difference in perceived stress depending on role, $F(2, 342) = 4.56$, $p = .01$. The hypothesis was supported, given that the mean score for stress when both partners brought up the issue was significantly lower ($p < .05$) than when either of the partners mainly brought up the issue.

Finally, we examined whether the second factor of the stress measure (coping with stress) would be lower when both partners bring up the issue as compared to only one of the partners. Results indicated a significant difference existed in coping based on role, $F(2, 342) = 3.83$, $p = .02$. Post-hoc comparisons, however, indicated that the mean coping score was significantly higher (meaning that coping was poorer, $p < .05$) when the partner brought the issue up as compared to initiators or to both partners bringing the issue up (who did not significantly differ from each other).

Discussion

Our goal in this chapter was to highlight the importance of acknowledging that during the course of a serial argument partners may change roles: sometimes one person brings up the issue, other times the other person does. We have argued that this possibility is a fundamental characteristic of the interdependence that characterizes relationships and serial arguments and helps us understand the processes by which serial arguments heat up and simmer down over time.

Our results suggest positive effects occur when both partners initiate episodes of a serial argument. Relational satisfaction levels are higher, and individuals are less likely to say that the serial argument has affected their satisfaction levels (presumably negatively, as measured with our specific satisfaction items). The negative effects of serial arguments (relational harm and stress) are reduced, which is extremely important given that prior research (Johnson & Roloff, 2000b) has indicated a discrepancy in these variables existed between the perceptions of initiators and resistors.

The lack of significance in respect to resolvability is a surprising result. It is possible that, when both partners bring up a serial argument, the perception of resolvability decreases because both partners believe the issue is something that must be addressed. In other words, the similar thinking that a particular topic is a recurring issue actually works against partners' perception that they can settle the matter in the future.

Finally, our findings in respect to stress also indicate the importance of analyzing effects of serial arguments based on interdependence. When both partners bring up the issue, stress is significantly reduced, and coping with stress increases for resistors. The shared role seems to reduce negative feelings, nervousness, and anger. In the long-run, being mutually involved in a serial argument may be less detrimental to the arguers' mental well-being.

Methodological areas and challenges of examining interdependence in serial arguments in the future

Our review of the serial arguments literature and our analysis of role's effects for relational outcomes suggest important methodological implications for research on serial arguments. A first implication concerns how role in serial arguments is measured. It is important to move beyond the dichotomous conceptualization of role as fixed and unilateral. Although participants in a serial argument may be initiators during the first episode or at a later time when researchers ask them to report their role, it is possible, given the ongoing nature of such arguments, that participants change roles. This possibility is not accounted for right now in research on serial arguments and future research should incorporate a measurement of alternating roles in serial argument studies. Our study indicates outcomes differ (and several of them improve) if partners alternate roles, and the results give us optimistic hopes in respect to ameliorating the negative effects that serial arguments can have on relationships.

A second methodological implication that follows from the idea that partners alternate roles throughout serial arguments is that longitudinal studies ought to offer better information about the dynamics of such role shifts and the connections with heating up and simmering down processes than cross-sectional studies. Alternating roles implies that an individual's goals within a serial argument may also change. For example, some goals may be important when one is the initiators, such as changing the target or determining if one wants to remain in a relationship, whereas other goals may be important when one is the resistor, such as expressing positive or negative feelings. This suggests cross-sectional studies on goals are able to catch only a momentary glimpse of participants' serial argument behaviors, whereas longitudinal studies would be able to explicate how goals are formed, evolve, and are met (or not). Such longitudinal studies would also help researchers explain what heats up or simmers down a serial argument; in other words, what behaviors determine arguers to bring up the issue again as opposed to letting it go, and how does this dynamic compare when partners alternate roles as opposed to holding unilateral roles in the argument.

A third methodological implication that derives from our study concerns the idea of interdependence. We did not measure interdependence directly in our study but rather used alternating roles as a proxy to indicate interdependence. A direct test of the effects of interdependence is needed, though. Researchers ought to test how various forms of interdependence, such as relational interdependence (i.e., the degree to which one conceptualizes one's self by the relationships with close others; Cross et al, 1999) or outcome interdependence (i.e., the degree to which outcomes depend on other people's behavior, not just an individual's behavior; Wageman, 1995) affect serial argument processes and outcomes. Based on our results, we would expect more interdependence to have more positive outcomes given that the two partners need each other or depend on each other for solving the issue.

Conclusion

In this chapter, we have reviewed the main lines of research related to relational dynamics that have developed following Trapp and Hoff's (1985) initial investigation into serial arguments. We also developed an idea that we believe is capable of uncovering essential features of the serial argument process: focusing more on the degree of interdependence between partners regarding the argument issue, as illustrated in this study by alternating roles in a serial argument. We propose that interdependence is closely connected with the functioning of a relationship. Unlike arguments with strangers or even colleagues in the workplace, friendships, romantic relationships, and families have an inherently interdependent assumption that accompanies them. People in such relationships have ongoing contact and share certain activities, goals, and emotional bonds. Thus, serial arguments are likely influenced by these innate characteristics of these interpersonal relationships.

In addition to the methodological issues highlighted above, our review and analysis also suggests several theoretical implications regarding serial argument research. An immediate observation is that, despite increasing research on the topic, the theoretical underpinning of the research is not yet strongly developed. Trapp and Hoff's (1985) model utilized a cost-benefit framework of analysis. Other studies (Bevan and colleagues, Hample and colleagues) included connections to the goals-plans-action model (Dillard, 2004). Roloff and colleagues have referenced cognitive depletion theory and Gottman's (1994) cascade model of relational dissolution. Overall, though, the larger question of *why* serial arguments continue to occur needs to be explored further. The research has accumulated to a point where scholars need to start articulating theories specific to the serial argument phenomenon. In other words, what can we theorize about the reasons, the processes, and the outcomes of serial arguments in interpersonal relationships?

One of the theoretical concepts that may explain processes associated with serial arguments is Singer's (1974) notion of involvement. Singer proposed that people become invested in an exchange, and this involvement can explain several outcomes or characteristics of their behavior. It would be interesting to analyze serial argument behaviors in terms of involvement. Are initiators more invested in a serial argument than resistors? Mutual investment also connects to our proposed framework of interdependence and the possibility of both partners bringing up the argument. Both theoretical ideas would help detail the primary and secondary processes that underlie serial arguments, as proposed by Trapp and Hoff's (1985) model.

The serial argument literature is a young, incipient area of research. Significant contributions have been made by scholars thus far in explaining the phenomenon and exciting new avenues of research are still ahead. We have suggested several main directions for future research, both methodological and theoretical. Researchers should start analyzing serial arguments brought up by both partners throughout their repetitions, examine interdependence between partners, and engage in longitudinal research on this topic. Issues of interdependence and involvement are promising for explaining the processes at work during serial arguments. Most important, however, is that we need to begin articulating a theory of serial arguments in interpersonal research.

References

Berger, C. R. (1997). *Planning strategic interaction: Attaining goals through communicative action.* Mahwah, NJ: Erlbaum.

Bevan, J. L., Hale, J. L., & Williams, S. L. (2004). Identifying and characterizing goals of dating partners engaging in serial argumentation. *Argumentation and Advocacy, 41*(1), 28–40.

Bevan, J. L., Tidgewell, K. D., Bagley, K. C., Cusanelli, L., Hartstern, M., Holbeck, D., & Hale, J. L. (2007). Serial argumentation goals and their relationships to perceived resolvability and choice of conflict tactics. *Communication Quarterly, 55*, 61–71. doi: 10.1080/0146337 0600998640

Bevan, J. L., Finan, A., & Kaminsky, A. (2008). Modeling serial arguments in close relationships: The serial argument process model. *Human Communication Research, 34*, 600–624. doi: 10.1111/j.1468-2958.2008.00334.x

Carr, K., Schrodt, P., & Ledbetter, A. M. (2012). Rumination, conflict intensity, and perceived resolvability as predictors of motivation and likelihood of continuing serial arguments. *Western Journal of Communication, 76*, 480–502. doi: 10.1080/10570314.2012.689086

Cohen, S., Kamarck, T., & Marmelstein, R. (1983). A global measure of perceived stress. *Journal of Health and Social Behavior, 24*, 385–396. doi: http://dx.doi.org/10.2307/2136404

Cross, S. E., Bacon, P. L., Morris, M. L. (1999). The relational-interdependent self-construal and relationships. *Journal of Personality and Social Psychology, 78*, 791–808. doi: 10.1037/0022-3514.78.4.791

Dillard, J. P. (2004). The goals-plans-action model of interpersonal influence. In J. S. Seiter & R. H. Gass (Eds.), Perspectives on persuasion, social influence, and compliance gaining (pp185–206). Boston, MA: Allyn & Bacon.

Gottman, J. M. (1994). *What predicts divorce? The relationship between marital processes and marital outcomes.* Hillsdale, NJ: Erlbaum.

Hample, D., & Allen, S. (2012). Serial arguments in organizations. *Journal of Argumentation in Context, 1,* 312–330. doi: 10.1075/jaic.1.3.03ham

Hample, D., & Cionea, I. A. (2012). Serial arguments in inter-ethnic relationships. *International Journal of Intercultural Relations, 36,* 430–445. doi: 10.1016/j.ijintrel.2011.12.006

Hample, D., & Krueger, B. (2011). Serial arguments in classrooms. *Communication Studies, 62,* 597–617. doi: 10.1080/10510974.2011.576746

Hample, D., & Richards, A. S. (2015). Attachment style, serial argument, and taking conflict ersonally. *Journal of Argumentation in Context, 4,* 63–86. doi: 10.1075/jaic.4.1.04ham

Hample, D., Richards, A. S., & Na, L. (2012). A test of the conflict linkage model in the context of serial arguments. *Western Journal of Communication, 76,* 459–479. doi: 10.1080/10570314.2012.703361

Hocker, J. L., & Wilmot, W. W. (1978). *Interpersonal conflict.* New York, NY: McGraw-Hill.

Infante, D. A., & Rancer, A. S. (1982). A conceptualization and measure of argumentativeness. *Journal of Personality Assessment, 46,* 72–80. doi: 10.1207/s15327752jpa4601_13

Johnson, A. J. (2001). Examining the maintenance of friendships: Are there differences between geographically close and long-distance friends? *Communication Quarterly, 49,* 424–435. doi: 10.1080/01463370109385639

Johnson, A. J. (2002). Beliefs about arguing: A comparison of public-issue and personal-issue arguments. *Communication Reports, 15,* 99–112. doi: 10.1080/08934210209367757

Johnson, A. J. (2009). A functional approach to interpersonal argument: Differences between public- and personal-issue arguments. *Communication Reports, 22,* 13–28. doi: 10.1080/08934210902798528

Johnson, K. L., & Roloff, M. E. (1998). Serial arguing and relational quality: Determinants and consequences of perceived resolvability. *Communication Research, 25,* 327–343. doi: 10.1177/009365098025003004

Johnson, K. L., & Roloff, M. E. (2000a). Correlates of the perceived resolvability and relational consequences of serial arguing in dating relationships: Argumentative features and the use of coping strategies. *Journal of Social and Personal Relationships, 17,* 676–686. doi: 10.1177/0265407500174011

Johnson, K. L., & Roloff, M. E. (2000b). The influence of argumentative role (initiator vs. resistor) on perceptions of serial argument resolvability and relational harm. *Argumentation, 14,* 1–15. doi: 10.1023/A:1007837310258

Johnson, A. J., Averbeck, J. M., Kelley, K. M., & Liu, S. (2010). Serial arguments and argument type: Comparing serial arguments about public and personal issue argument topics. In D. S. Gouran (Ed.), The functions of argument and social context: Selected papers from the 16th biennial conference on argumentation (pp211–218). Washington, DC: National Communication Association.

Johnson, A. J., Averbeck, J. M., Kelley, K. M., & Liu, S. (2011). When serial arguments predict harm: Examining the influences of argument function, perceived resolvability, and argumentativeness. *Argumentation and Advocacy, 47(4),* 214–217.

Johnson, A. J., Hample, D., & Cionea, I. A. (2014). Understanding argumentation in interpersonal communication: The implications of distinguishing between public and personal topics. *Communication yearbook, 38,* 144–173.

Johnson, A. J., Kelley, K., Liu, S., Averbeck, J., King, S., & Bostwick, E. N. (2014). Family serial arguments: Beliefs about the argument and perceived stress from the argument. *Communication Reports, 27*, 116–128. doi: 10.1080/08934215.2014.927517

Kelley, H. H., & Thibaut, J. W. (1978). *Interpersonal relations: A theory of interdependence.* New York, NY: Wiley.

Malis, R. S., & Roloff, M. E. (2006a). Demand/withdraw patterns in serial arguments: Implications for well-being. *Human Communication Research, 32*, 198–216. doi: 10.1111/j.1468-2958.2006.00009.x

Malis, R. S., & Roloff, M. E. (2006b). Features of serial arguing and coping strategies: Links with stress and well-being. In B. A. LePoire & R. M. Dailey (Eds.), *Applied interpersonal communication matters: Family, health, and community relations* (pp39–66). New York, NY: Peter Lang.

Miller, C. W., & Roloff, M. E. (2006). The perceived characteristics of irresolvable, resolvable, and resolved intimate conflicts: Is there evidence of intractability? *International Journal of Conflict Management, 17*, 291–315. doi: 10.1108/10444060610749464

Reznik, R. M., Roloff, M. E., & Miller, C. W. (2010). Communication during interpersonal arguing: Implications for stress symptoms. *Argumentation and Advocacy, 46(4)*, 193–213.

Reznik, R. M., Roloff, M. E., & Miller, C. W. (2012). Components of integrative communication during arguing: Implications for stress symptoms. *Argumentation and Advocacy, 48(3)*, 142–158.

Roloff, M. E., & Reznik, R. M. (2008). Communication during serial arguments: Connections with individuals' mental and physical well-being. In M. T. Motley (Ed.), *Studies in applied interpersonal communication* (pp97–119). Thousand Oaks, CA: Sage. doi: http://dx.doi.org/10.4135/9781412990301

Rusbult, C. E., Zembrodt, I. M., & Gunn, L. K. (1982). Exit, voice, loyalty, and neglect: Responses to dissatisfaction in romantic involvements. *Journal of Personality and Social Psychology, 43*, 1230–1242. doi: 0022-3514/82/4306-1230

Singer, M. T. (1974). Presidential address – Engagement-involvement: A central phenomenon in psychophysiological research. *Psychosomatic Medicine, 36*, 1–17.

Trapp, R., & Hoff, N. (1985). A model of serial argument in interpersonal relationships. *Journal of the American Forensic Association, 22(1)*, 1–11.

Wageman, R. (1995). Interdependence and group effectiveness. *Administrative Science Quarterly, 40*, 145–180. doi: 10.2307/2393703

8

ROMANTIC SERIAL ARGUMENT PERCEIVED RESOLVABILITY, GOALS, RUMINATION, AND CONFLICT STRATEGY USAGE

A Preliminary Longitudinal Study

Jennifer L. Bevan, Megan B. Cummings, Makenna L. Engert, and Lisa Sparks

In 1985, Trapp and Hoff (1985) embarked on a study that explored argumentation in relationships. Their interviews with 12 relational pairs, including family members, friends, and romantic partners, revealed an unexpected pattern: many reported that their arguments consisted of serial episodes that reoccurred on a regular basis throughout the course of their relationships, which Trapp and Hoff labeled as serial arguments. These serial arguments, inherently defined by their ongoing nature, did not reflect the dominant view at that time of interpersonal conflict occurring in only a single, autonomous episode.

Until Johnson and Roloff (1998) took up the scholarly cause, little research attention was paid to serial arguments. They formally defined serial arguments as a set of argument episodes about the same topic that occur over time and without resolution. Now, serial argumentation is an active, diverse research area that has exponentially grown and significantly contributed to our understanding of the cognitions, behaviors, and individual and relational correlates and outcomes of engaging in ongoing conflict. For example, serial arguments occur in romantic (Bevan et al, 2007; Johnson & Roloff, 2000a), family (Bevan, 2010; Gaze et al, 2015), and intercultural (Hample & Cionea, 2012) relationships, in organizational (Hample & Allen, 2013) and educational (Hample & Krueger, 2011) settings, and about a variety of topics (Bevan et al, 2014b; Janan Johnson et al, 2011). In this chapter, we overview this body of research by focusing on the two most commonly studied serial argument variables – perceived resolvability and communication behaviors – and also present original longitudinal data that explores how serial argument thoughts and behaviors are linked over time.

Explicating Serial Arguments: A Focus on Communication Patterns

Serial arguing is fundamentally an act of communication, and research attention has accordingly focused primarily on how individuals communicate during serial argument episodes. The messages that have been the predominant focus in serial argument research are logically drawn from the interpersonal conflict literature, specifically Sillars's (1980) avoidance-distributive-integrative conflict strategy typology, and the demand/withdraw communication pattern (Christensen & Heavey, 1993). We thus explore each type of message in the context of serial arguments below.

Conflict Strategies

Sillars's (1980) typology contains three conflict strategies that have been frequently adapted to how individuals communicate during serial arguments:

1. integrative, or positive, direct messages;
2. distributive, or direct, destructive messages; and
3. avoidant, or indirect, primarily negative messages.

Across studies, integrative communication is the most commonly reported strategy used by individuals in their serial argument episodes (e.g., Bevan, 2014; Bevan et al, 2007; Hample & Allen, 2012), regardless of relationship type (Bevan, 2010), and is also more likely to be used in serial than in non-serial arguments (Bevan et al, 2014b).

Integrative communication involves aspects of disclosures, discussions, and prosocial messages. It makes sense, then, that using this conflict strategy in serial arguments is positively associated with pursuing positive goals such as a mutual understanding/resolution (Bevan et al, 2008), higher relational satisfaction (Hample & Cionea, 2012), greater civility (i.e., being well-mannered), more positive educational (Hample & Krueger, 2011) and organizational (Hample & Allen, 2012) climates, and with possessing a horizontal collectivist cultural orientation (Radanielina-Hita, 2010). Integrative communication was also more likely in serial arguments about personal topics compared with workplace or public issue arguments (Cionea & Hample, 2013). In contrast, the integrative conflict strategy is less likely to be employed in a serial argument episode when the individual seeks to accomplish negative goals, such as hurting the partner or gaining control (Bevan et al, 2007), and is negatively associated with having an individualistic cultural orientation (Radanielina-Hita, 2010).

However, this pattern is not the whole story about integrative communication. For example, integrative strategy usage has been linked with increased serial argument-related stress and physical health issues in one study (Reznik et al,

2010), negatively associated in other research (Reznik et al, 2012), and unrelated in yet another study (Bevan & Sparks, 2014). Integrative communication also positively predicts rumination about the serial argument (Bevan et al, 2008). The overall negative nature of serial arguments overriding usage of specific positive argument messages may help to explain these findings.

Distributive conflict strategies can include elements of threats, hostility, and antisocial messages. Use of this conflict strategy in serial arguments is positively related to the importance of negative serial argument goals such as expressiveness negative or changing the partner (Bevan et al, 2007), greater rumination (Bevan et al, 2008), and the experience of serial argument-related stress and self-reported health issues (Reznik et al, 2010). On the other hand, using distributive communication in a serial argument is inversely related to constructive coping strategies (Johnson & Roloff, 2000a), pursuing positive serial argument goals such as positive relational expression (Bevan et al, 2007), greater civility, more positive organizational (Hample & Allen, 2012) and classroom (Hample & Krueger, 2011) climates, and constructive argument outcomes such as reconciliation (Reznik & Roloff, 2011). Findings do, however, conflict for distributive communication and relationship satisfaction: studies have observed positive (Hample & Cionea, 2012), negative (Johnson & Roloff, 2000a), and no (Bevan et al, 2014a) association.

Further, the less individuals used distributive communication, the more likely their serial arguments were to have been resolved (Bevan et al, 2008) and the less likely their relationships had ended (Reznik et al, 2010). Distributive communication was more likely in workplace serial arguments and about public issues than about personal issues (Cionea & Hample, 2013). However, the distributive strategy was less likely to be used in serial arguments, compared to non-serial arguments (Bevan et al, 2014b).

These two direct conflict strategies are also the central components of Bevan et al's (2008) serial argument process model, which depicts a specific serial argument episode in either a family or romantic relationship. One's pursuit of one or more serial argument goals sets the process into motion. These goals then predict conflict strategy usage, with positive goals predicting integrative communication, and negative goals predicting distributive communication. Next, integrative communication usage leads to increased perceived resolvability, and both integrative and distributive communication positively predict rumination about the serial argument. This rumination, then, increases the likelihood that individuals will be motivated to pursue their serial argument goals. The paths set forth by the serial argument process model have been supported in dyadic (Bevan, 2014), educational (Hample & Krueger, 2011), organizational (Hample & Allen, 2012), and intercultural (Hample & Cionea, 2012) studies, demonstrating the model's scope and utility.

As opposed to the integrative and distributive strategy findings, avoidance's role in serial arguments is much murkier. For example, being avoidant during a serial argument is positively related to the importance of both positive and negative goals (Bevan et al, 2007) and greater thought avoidance and hyperarousal (Reznik et al, 2010). Former relationship partners also used avoidance in their serial arguments more than current relational partners (Reznik et al, 2010), and avoidance was a more common strategy in non-serial, rather than serial, arguments (Bevan et al, 2014b). However, avoidance's nonsignificant links with rumination and the other two conflict strategies prevented its inclusion in the serial argument process model (Bevan et al, 2008). What contributes to serial argument avoidance may be clarified by the recent finding that romantic relationship satisfaction was a strong, negative predictor of avoidance usage, leading Bevan et al (2014a) to suggest that serial argument avoidance may be better understood via relationship, rather than individual, characteristics.

The Demand/Withdraw Pattern

Another commonly-studied communicative facet of serial arguments is the enactment of the demand/withdraw pattern, where the demander is the instigator who criticizes and condemns the withdrawer, who tries to avoid and circumvent the conflict (e.g., Caughlin, 2002). In addition, Johnson and Roloff (2000b) studied what they coined the "initiator" and "resistor" roles in serial arguments. The initiator is more likely to demand, in that the initiator makes complaints that spark an argument episode (Johnson & Roloff, 2000b). On the other hand, the resistor is more likely to withdraw because the resistor is being confronted and is fighting the change demanded by the initiator (Johnson & Roloff, 2000b). In other words, the person who adopts the initiator role is a change agent, whereas the person who chooses to respond by not complying or via withdrawal is the resistor.

Enacting the demand/withdraw pattern in a serial argument has been found to be negatively associated with relational satisfaction (e.g., Malis & Roloff, 2006a), perceived resolvability (e.g., Johnson & Roloff, 1998), and civility (e.g., Hample & Allen, 2012). Using the demand/withdraw pattern, in contrast, is positively related to experiencing stress about the serial argument (Malis & Roloff, 2006a), being preoccupied with relationships (DiDomencio & Roloff, 2011), the pursuit of negative serial argument goals (e.g., Hample et al, 2012), the cultural orientation of vertical individualism (Radanielina-Hita, 2010), and the number of serial argument episodes (e.g., Reznik & Roloff, 2011). Demanding individuals are also more likely to argue about topics related to the workplace and about personal topics (Cionea & Hample, 2013).

However, there is a counterintuitive pattern, where the other demand/self withdraw pattern was associated with increased relationship satisfaction and the pursuit of the positive relational expression goal (Hample et al, 2012). Self-demand and other demand behaviors are also positively related to the importance of multiple positive serial argument goals (Hample & Allen, 2012). The specific other demand/self withdraw pattern can also be beneficial when an individual is attempting to end a destructive argument episode, and ultimately a negative attack cycle between the partners (Reznik & Roloff, 2011). These findings indicate that, though general demand/withdraw is accompanied by a number of negative implications, it is not an entirely destructive pattern, particularly when an individual is in the withdrawal position.

Perceived Resolvability

To date, research on serial arguments has also consistently emphasized the significance of perceived resolvability (PR), defined as "the degree to which individuals believe they are making progress toward resolving their disagreement" (Johnson & Roloff, 1998, p. 329). As a serial argument-specific concept, PR is a better predictor of relational quality than serial argument frequency (Johnson & Roloff, 1998). Subsequent research has found that PR is also positively related to constructive communication (e.g., Bevan et al, 2008), higher relationship quality, the use of positive coping strategies (e.g., Johnson & Roloff, 2000a), the pursuit of positive goals such as mutual understanding/resolution (e.g., Bevan et al, 2007), and increased civility and positive climate (e.g., Hample & Krueger, 2011).

Conversely, PR is negatively associated with negative coping strategies, greater experience of stress and hyperarousal (e.g., Malis & Roloff, 2006b), pursuing negative goals such as dominance and hurting the partner, engaging in conflict avoidance (e.g., Bevan et al, 2007), destructive communication (Johnson & Roloff, 1998), and demand patterns (e.g., Hample ·& Allen, 2012), argument frequency (Johnson & Roloff, 1998), and the likelihood of argument continuation (Carr et al, 2012). Further, PR is central to personal topic arguments, and to topics that are relevant to one's values (e.g., Janan Johnson et al, 2011).

Those who view their conflicts as irresolvable also feel more hopeless and are more resistant to resolution than those involved in arguments they believe are resolvable (Miller & Roloff, 2006). Recent research has additionally observed dyadic PR effects: the more that Partner A perceives that Partner B uses integrative conflict strategies, and does not use distributive strategies, in a serial argument, the higher Partner B's PR (Bevan, 2014). Together, these findings suggest that perceiving that one's serial argument cannot be resolved is related to a series of destructive goals, communication strategies and patterns, and relationship and argument features. Further, research (e.g., Bevan et al, 2008) suggests that perceived resolvability is a motivating force that impels partners to reach a mutual understanding. Based on these studies, Roloff (2009) prescribed perceived resolvability as the single most important buffer against the relationship damage that can be caused by a serial argument.

Longitudinal Research

The ongoing, unresolved nature of serial arguments means it is an ideal context to examine using longitudinal research methods. However, only one study has thus far tracked serial arguments over time. Namely, Hample et al (2012) found that having imagined interactions about a serial argument was related to serial argument goal importance one month later, providing initial evidence that an individual thinks about a serial argument between argument episodes and these thoughts then contribute to the goals pursued in a future episode.

A Spotlight Study on Serial Arguments and Rumination Over Time

To continue understanding what occurs between serial argument episodes and why episodes continue to arise, we offer two research questions that will be tested using longitudinal data. First, following the relationships specified by Bevan et al's (2008) serial argument process model, RQ1 asks: Is t_1 conflict strategy usage and rumination related to t_2 perceived resolvability? Second, we are interested in which serial argument components may contribute to whether individuals engage in a serial argument episode. Such information is important to untangle, because cognitive or behavioral "triggers" in one episode may make a subsequent episode more or less likely. Thus, RQ2 asks: Is perceived resolvability, serial argument goal importance, conflict strategy usage, and rumination about a serial argument episode at t_1 related to whether a serial argument episode has occurred between t_1 and t_2?

Method

Participants and Procedures

Adult participants currently in romantic relationships were invited to complete two surveys by students in a Chapman University undergraduate communication research capstone class led by the first author. Those who provided their email addresses to these students, or who responded to social networking posts about the study, were directed to the t_1 survey on the online platform SurveyMonkey.com. Participants provided consent and confirmed that they qualified, answered a series of items about an ongoing conflict in their romantic relationships, and provided their email address to receive the link to the second survey.

In accordance with Konstan et al (2005), t_1 responses were manually validated by the first author.[1] After validation ($N = 287$), most t_1 participants were female ($n = 188$, male $n = 70$), heterosexual ($n = 238$, homosexual $n = 8$, bisexual $n = 9$), white/Caucasian ($n = 201$, Hispanic/Latino/a $n = 21$, Asian $n = 18$, Bi/multiracial $n = 13$, other $n = 2$, Black/African American $n = 1$), and were university students ($n = 179$, not students $n = 79$). Participants averaged 25.54 years of age (range $= 18$-65, $SD = 9.87$) and were involved in a variety of romantic relationships (casual dating $n = 6$, serious or exclusive dating $n = 149$, living together but not engaged or married $n = 40$, engaged $n = 10$, married $n = 47$, other $n = 6$)

that were of varying lengths (less than 6 months $n = 27$, 6 months to 1 year $n = 40$, between: 1 to 2 years $n = 42$, 2 to 4 years $n = 71$, 4 to 6 years $n = 28$, 6 to 10 years $n = 14$, 10 to 15 years $n = 13$, 15 to 20 years $n = 6$, over 20 years $n = 12$).[1] Ten participants who reported that their serial arguments had occurred once were removed (2 to 5 times $n = 109$, 6 to 10 times $n = 77$, 11 to 20 times $n = 51$, 21 to 30 times $n = 13$, over 30 times $n = 27$), leaving a final t_1 sample of 277.[2]

Individuals who provided validated t_1 survey responses were sent an email with a link to the second survey approximately eight to ten weeks after the first data collection. Confidential participation at t_1 and t_2 was voluntary and each survey took 15 to 20 minutes to complete. A total of 147 validated participants completed both surveys (female $n = 113$, male $n = 34$, age $M = 26.89$, $SD = 11.30$, range = 18-65), and received a $10 Amazon.com gift card via email.

Measures

Perceived Resolvability

Johnson and Roloff's (1998) four-item Likert-type scale assessed perceived resolvability at t_1 and t_2 (e.g., I believe that the argument will be resolved in the future). Higher values indicate greater perceived resolvability (1 = strongly disagree, 7 = strongly agree; t_1 $M = 4.23$, $SD = 1.68$, $\alpha = .87$; t_2 $M = 4.34$, $SD = 1.69$, $\alpha = .91$).

Goal Importance

T_1 serial argument goal importance was measured via Bevan et al's (2008) revised Likert-type (1 = strongly disagree, 7 = strongly agree) scale. Three items each measured expressiveness negative (e.g., to express frustration; $M = 4.16$, $SD = 1.58$, $\alpha = .75$), change target (e.g., to change my partner's habits; $M = 4.22$, $SD = 1.67$, $\alpha = .74$), dominance/control (e.g., to not lose the serial argument; $M = 2.88$, $SD = 1.34$, $\alpha = .58$), and mutual understanding/resolution (e.g., to negotiate with my partner; $M = 4.98$, $SD = 1.51$, $\alpha = .79$). Positive relational expression (e.g., to let my partner know that I care about him or her; $M = 5.11$, $SD = 1.67$, $\alpha = .86$) and relationship termination (e.g., to terminate our relationship; $M = 1.48$, $SD = 1.03$, $\alpha = .83$) were each assessed via four items. The hurt partner/benefit self scale includes seven items (e.g., to put my partner down; $M = 1.36$, $SD = .86$, $\alpha = .93$).

Conflict Strategies

The integrative, distributive, and avoidance conflict strategies were measured at t_1 with Likert-type items (1 = strongly disagree, 7 = strongly agree) from Bevan and Sparks (2014). Avoidance was measured via seven items (e.g., I made excuses; M

= 2.16, SD = 1.11, α = .85). Twelve items comprised the integrative conflict strategy scale (e.g., I listened to my partner's point of view; M = 4.78, SD = 1.11, α = .90) and 13 items assessed the distributive conflict strategy (e.g., I insulted my partner; M = 2.68, SD = 1.06, α = .88).

Rumination

Cloven and Roloff's (1991) five-item semantic differential mulling scale assessed rumination at t_1 (e.g., 1 = Never thought about this argument, 7 = thought about this argument all the time; M = 4.42, SD = 1.44, α = .90).

Argument Occurrence between T_1 and T_2

T_2 Ps were asked if they could recall a time when they argued with their romantic partner about the topic since they completed the first survey. Those who responded yes (n = 103, no n = 44) were classified as having engaged in a serial argument episode between t_1 and t_2.

Results

Analysis Plan

A series of two-tailed, bivariate correlations tested the individual relationships investigated in both research questions. For RQ1, the t_1 usage of the three conflict strategies and rumination about the serial argument were each examined in relation to t_2 perceived resolvability. For RQ2, t_1 goal importance, conflict strategy usage, and rumination were examined in relation to whether or not a participant had been in a serial argument episode between t_1 and t_2 (1 = no, 2 = yes). See Table 8.1 for the correlation matrix.

Research Question 1

Usage of the t^1 integrative conflict strategy was positively related (r = .29, p < .001) to t^2 perceived resolvability, which was negatively related to distributive conflict strategy usage (r = -.19, p < .05). T^1 avoidance (r = -.15, p = .08) and rumination (r = -.15, p = .08) were unrelated to t^2 perceived resolvability.

Research Question 2

Three t^1 goals — mutual understanding/resolution (r = .17, p < .05), expressiveness negative (r = .19, p < .05), and change target (r = .19, p < .05) — and rumination (r = .17, p < .05) were significantly, positively related to whether an argument episode had occurred between t^1 and t^2. The remaining goals (positive

TABLE 8.1 Correlations between study variables

	_1_	_2_	_3_	_4_	_5_	_6_	_7_	_8_	_9_	_10_	_11_	_12_	_13_	_14_
1. T_1 Perceived Resolvability	1	.33***	.16*	-.17**	-.20**	-.15*	-.08	-.14*	.37***	-.11	-.23***	-.26***	.56***	-.16
2. T_1 Positive Relational Expression Goal		1	.59***	.06	.08	.11	-.07	-.08	.59***	-.03	-.04	.18**	.19*	.16
3. T_1 Mutuality Goal				.11	.09	.07	-.14*	-.10	.49***	-.04	.01	.20**	.04	.17*
4. T_1 Expressiveness Negative Goal					.48***	.35***	.20**	.15*	-.03	.08	.45***	.15*	-.19*	.19*
5. T_1 Change Target Goal						.27***	.11	.09	-.05	-.11	.45***	.13*	-.19*	.19*
6. T_1 Dominance/Control Goal							.39***	.28***	-.02	.31***	.43***	.12	-.27**	.12
7. T_1 Hurt Partner Goal								.82***	-.10	.45***	.44***	.05	-.08	.07
8. T_1 Relationship Termination Goal									-.09	.44***	.33***	.08	-.13	.10
9. T_1 Integrative Conflict Strategy										-.14*	-.22***	.02	.29***	.03
10. T_1 Avoidance Conflict Strategy											.32***	.14*	-.15	.09
11. T_1 Distributive Conflict Strategy												.29***	-.19*	.15
12. T_1 Rumination													-.15	.17*
13. T_2 Perceived Resolvability														-.32***
14. Argument Occurred between T_1 and T_2														1

Note. * $p < .05$, ** $p < .01$, *** $p < .001$

relationship expression $r = .15$, $p = .05$, dominance/control $r = .12$, $p = .16$, hurt partner/benefit self $r = .07$, $p = .42$, and relationship termination ($r = .10$, $p = .23$) and all three of the conflict strategies (integrative $r = .03$, $p = .69$, distributive $r = .15$, $p = .07$, avoidance $r = .09$, $p = .28$) at t^1 were unrelated to whether an argument episode had occurred between t^1 and t^2.

Discussion

In this chapter, we have reviewed the growing body of scholarship on the process and enactment of serial arguments in interpersonal relationships. We also explored a number of longitudinal associations between the cognitions and behaviors that occurred during a romantic serial argument episode and perceived resolvability eight to ten weeks later, as well as in relation to whether a subsequent episode had occurred in that same time period. Here, we will discuss our longitudinal findings in light of previous serial argument research, consider how serial argument scholarship can expand methodologically, and offer suggestions for future research.

Findings for RQ1, the logic of which was guided by the relationships predicted by Bevan et al's (2008) serial argument process model, revealed that the more romantic partners used integrative communication, and the less they used distributive communication, during the t^1 serial argument episode, the greater their perceived resolvability at t^2. Avoidance usage and rumination about the serial argument at t^1 were unrelated to t^2 perceived resolvability. These findings indicate that the positive relationship from integrative communication to perceived resolvability as specified in Bevan et al's (2008) serial argument process model also endures over time. As PR is an integral buffer to the potential destructive effects of serial arguments (Roloff, 2009), integrative communication can be a useful tool for sustaining increased PR levels for romantic partners between serial argument episodes. The previously-observed negative link between PR and distributive communication (e.g., Bevan et al, 2007) also spans time, further emphasizing the potential destructive nature of these hostile messages in serial arguments.

The relationships between avoidance (e.g., Bevan et al, 2007) and PR have been inconsistent (e.g., Bevan et al, 2007; Hample & Krueger, 2011), and PR is unrelated to rumination (Bevan et al, 2008; Carr et al, 2012) in cross-sectional studies. Thus, it is not surprising that these associations also did not emerge in our longitudinal data. Our findings, though preliminary, suggest that though avoidance and rumination are typically negative aspects of serial arguments, they have little impact on how resolvable the argument is perceived to be.

Although we know that serial arguments recur multiple times about a particular topic, we do not know which specific serial argument thoughts and behaviors that occur during one serial argument episode will increase the likelihood that the argument will continue. As such, RQ2 found that cognitions in the form of three t^1 episode goals and rumination increased the likelihood that an argument had taken place by t^2. Specifically, when an individual indicated that mutual understanding/resolution, expressing negative feelings, and changing the partner were important serial argument goals, another argument episode by t^2 was more likely. Interestingly, no t^1 communication behaviors predicted the occurrence of a future serial argument episode. Rather, our findings tentatively suggest that cognitions may be more central than communication to understanding if and why our participants engage in multiple argument episodes over time.

One explanation for this finding may be that the individual felt that his or her goal of resolution was unfulfilled during the t^1 argument episode, and this goal frustration then increased the importance of the two negative goals during and after the episode. The expressiveness negative and change target goals are typically carried out in ways that are destructive to the argument (e.g., Bevan et al, 2007, 2008; Hample & Allen, 2012) because individuals focus their efforts on communicating negative emotions and altering their partners' behavior. As such, achieving these goals may not be possible in one argument episode, which can arouse rumination for one or both partners, thereby leaving the issue unsettled and likely to occur again. Of course, these longitudinal relationships are preliminary and should be examined in future research.

Methodological Considerations

Our review of serial argument research has identified a number of sets of research findings that have considerably increased scholarly understanding of how we communicate during serial arguments, how our thoughts and motivations are related to serial argument messages, and the individual and relationship implications of engaging in serial arguments in a variety of contexts. However, this review has also revealed that serial argument scholars are not utilizing diverse research methods. Indeed, every known serial argument study has relied in some way upon the self-report survey methodology, and only a handful of these have done so longitudinally (Hample et al, 2012), dyadically (e.g., Bevan, 2014), or by using randomly assigned, manipulated conditions (e.g., Bevan, 2010; Miller & Roloff, 2006).

Findings from longitudinal data, such as the results we report in this chapter, are beginning to emerge, however, and are vital to the continued growth of serial argument research. Quite simply, how can we confidently draw empirical conclusions about serial arguments – which by their very nature span multiple time periods and can last for years – until we are consistently conducting research that follows these arguments as they emerge and change over time? Employing longitudinal research methods is thus vital and should be the primary methodological priority as the study of serial arguments moves forward.

Further, no known research has examined serial arguments using content analysis, in-depth interviews, laboratory observation, or experimental techniques. Delving into greater detail about how partners actually interact during a serial argument episode is thus another crucial methodological area that needs expansion. In particular, observing and coding relational partners' serial argument sequential messages as they unfold would provide valuable information. Though it involves more time and resources than survey research, employing this method is certainly viable, as other observational laboratory conflict studies ask couples to discuss a conflict that has occurred more than once (e.g., Keck & Samp, 2007); in other words, ones that are serial in nature. Information derived from these methods would advance the study of serial arguments considerably.

Suggestions for Future Research

In addition to methodological considerations, we offer a number of future serial argument research suggestions. First, the roles that each partner occupies in an argument are important to understand because they influence each person's experiences and communication in an argument episode. Though a great deal of research has been conducted on the enactment of the demand/withdraw pattern and the initiator/demand roles in serial arguments, many questions remain unanswered. Namely, we do not know whether these roles are reoccurring throughout varying serial argument topics and between argument episodes. For example, does the same relational partner, regardless of the topic, consistently occupy either the initiator/resistor role? On the same note, do the demanding and withdrawing individuals enact this pattern regardless of argument episode or topic? Greater understanding of how these argument roles and topics interact is important, as the specific topic of a serial argument has the potential to dramatically influence the communication during the argument and the possibility of resolution.

The manner in which these roles are enacted, and how they are projected onto the other partner, can also have significant implications regarding the argument's longevity, perceived resolvability, important goals, relationship quality, and stress and well-being of the participants. For example, although withdrawers remove themselves from a serial argument, they could still ruminate about argument episodes, and this could increase individual stress and relationship strain. These patterns also need to be examined in relation to goal importance, as well as how they shape and alter communication throughout the life of the serial argument.

Second, as with most interpersonal communication research, serial argument researchers have thus far focused exclusively on heterosexual relationships. This, of course, excludes the substantial number of same-sex romantic relationships that exist today. Gay marriage is now legal in the United States and in many other countries. In addition, most modern societies are generally more accepting of same-sex relationships than in the past. Therefore, it is essential for serial argument research to include this increasingly prominent population in order to understand the similarities and differences in serial arguing between individuals of different sexual orientations. Relatedly, how serial arguments would uniquely unfold between friends and adult children and their aging parents are also topics that deserve future research attention.

In conclusion, we know a considerable amount about the process of ongoing, unresolved conflict in a variety of relationships and contexts. These serial arguments can have significant relationship and individual implications, particularly when destructive messages are used and perceived resolvability is low. However, there is still more to learn about serial arguments, and these questions should be investigated using a greater variety of research methods. Additional concepts found to be relevant in interpersonal conflict, and that can certainly also inform our understanding of serial arguments, include competence (e.g., Canary et al, 2001), emotion (e.g., Hample et al, 2005), and forgiveness (e.g., Kelley & Waldron, 2005). Overall, though the state of serial argument research is currently sound, there remain many interesting avenues for continued growth and understanding of this dynamic area of interpersonal conflict scholarship.

Acknowledgment

The study upon which this chapter is based was funded by a 2012–2013 Chapman University Faculty Scholarly/Creative Activity Grant that was awarded to the fourth author. The authors thank Cassandra Basile, Danica Beener, Monika Bik, Cristina Chan, Alexandra Chrystal, Kristen Furr, Matthew Gibeson, Brogyn Gage, Whitney Hubbell, Erin Jenkins, Kaz Koltai, Cynthia Lesher, Alexandra Murrel, Jennifer Nadler, Kaitlin Olson, Daniel Pokorski, Hilary Smith, Sabrina Stanley-Katz, Malia Tanaka, Alison Teague, Racquel Thompson, Hannah Torrance, Sabrina Walker, Carlee Wallace, Nicole Weiss, Natalie Wentworth, Alexandria Wood, and Emily Zelden for their assistance in data collection.

Notes

1 For full details about the survey validation process, please contact the first author.
2 Totals do not add up to the sample size because some participants did not complete the demographic items, which were at the end of the online survey.

References

Bevan, J. L. (2010). Serial argument goals and conflict strategies: A comparison between romantic partners and family members. *Communication Reports, 23*, 52–64. doi: 10.1080/08934211003598734

Bevan, J. L. (2014). Dyadic perceptions of goals, conflict strategies, and perceived resolvability in serial arguments. *Journal of Social and Personal Relationships, 31*, 773–795. doi:10.1177/0265407513504653

Bevan, J. L., Della Ripa, A., Boulger, A., Tuazon, A., Simmons, C., & Levine, D. (2014a). An exploration of the extent to which serial argument thoughts and behaviors are relationally disturbing. In C. Palczewski (Ed.), *Disturbing argument: Selected papers from the*

2013 *meeting of the NCA/AFA summer conference on argumentation.* Washington, DC: National Communication Association.

Bevan, J. L., Finan, A., & Kaminsky, A. (2008). Modeling serial arguments in close relationships: The serial argument process model. *Human Communication Research, 34,* 600–624. doi: 10.1111/j.1468-2958.2008.00334.x

Bevan, J. L., Hale, J. L., & Williams, S. L. (2004). Identifying and characterizing goals of dating partners engaged in serial argumentation. *Argumentation and Advocacy, 41,* 28–40. Retrieved from http://www.americanforensics.org/AA/aa_info.html

Bevan, J. L., Hefner, V., & Love, A. (2014). An exploration of topics, conflict styles, and rumination in romantic non-serial versus serial arguments. *Southern Communication Journal, 79,* 347–360. doi:10.1080/1041794X.2014.918645

Bevan, J. L., & Sparks, L. (2014). The relationship between accurate and benevolently biased serial argument perceptions and individual negative health perceptions. *Communication Research, 41,* 257–281. doi: 10.1177/0093650212438391

Bevan, J. L., Tidgewell, K. D., Bardull, K. C., Cusanelli, L., Hartsern, M., Holbeck, D., & Hale, J. L. (2007). Serial argumentation goals and their relationships with perceived resolvability and choice of conflict tactics. *Communication Quarterly, 55,* 61–77. doi: 10.1080/01463370600998640

Canary, D. J., Cupach, W. R., Serpe, R. T. (2001). A competence-based approach to examining interpersonal conflict. *Communication Research, 28,* 79–104. doi: 10.1177/009365001028001003

Carr, K., Schrodt, P., & Ledbetter, A. M. (2012). Rumination, conflict intensity, and perceived resolvability as predictors of motivation and likelihood of continuing serial arguments. *Western Journal of Communication, 76,* 480–502. doi: 10.1080/10570314.2012.689086

Caughlin, J. P. (2002). The demand/withdraw pattern of communication as a predictor of marital satisfaction over time: Unresolved issues and future directions. *Human Communication Research, 28,* 49–85. doi: 10.1111/j.1468-2958.2002.tb00798.x

Christensen, A., & Heavey, C. L. (1993). Gender differences in martial conflict: The demand/withdraw interaction pattern. In S. Oskamp & M. Costanzo (Eds.), *Gender issues in contemporary society* (pp113–141). Newbury Park, CA: Sage.

Cionea, I., & Hample, D. (2013, August). Serial argument topics. Paper presented at the biennial meeting of the NCA/AFA Conference on Argumentation, Alta, UT.

Cloven, D. H., & Roloff, M. E. (1991). Sense-making activities and interpersonal conflict: Communicative cures for the mulling blues. *Western Journal of Speech Communication, 55,* 134–158. doi: 10.1080/10570319109374376

DiDomencio, S., & Roloff, M. E. (2011, May). Preoccupation with relationships and serial arguing: Implications for post-episodic stress and pursuer/distancer and demand/withdraw patterns. Paper presented at the annual meeting of the International Communication Association, Boston, MA.

Gaze, C. M., Reznik, R. M., Miller, C. W., & Roloff, M. E. (2015). The role of communication and coping in emerging adults' serial arguments with parents. *Journal of Argumentation in Context, 4,* 21–41. doi:10.1075/jaic.4.1.02gaz.

Gold, D. B., & Wegner, D. M. (1995). Origins of ruminative thought: Trauma, incompleteness, nondisclosure, and suppression. *Journal of Applied Social Psychology, 25,* 1245–1261. doi: 10.1111/j.1559-1816.1995.tb02617.x

Hample, D., & Allen, S. (2013). Serial arguments in organizations. *Journal of Argumentation in Context, 1,* 312–330. doi: 10.1075/jaic.1.3.03ham

Hample, D., & Cionea, I. A. (2012). Serial arguments in inter-ethnic relationships. *International Journal of Intercultural Relations*, 36, 430–445. doi: 10.1016/j.ijintrel.2011.12.006

Hample, D., & Krueger, B. (2011). Serial arguments in classrooms. *Communication Studies*, 62, 597–617. doi: 10.1080/10510974.2011.576746

Hample, D., Thompson-Hayes, M., Wallenfelsz, K., Wallenfelsz, P., & Knapp, C. (2005). Face-to-face arguing is an emotional experience: Triangulating methodologies and early findings. *Argumentation and Advocacy*, 42, 74–93. Retrieved from http://www.americanforensics.org/AA/aa_info.html

Hample, D., Richards, A. S., & Na, L. (2012). A test of the conflict linkage model in the context of serial arguments. *Western Journal of Communication*, 76, 459–479. doi: 10.1080/10570314.2012.703361

Janan Johnson, A., Averbeck, J. M., Kelley, K. M., & Liu, S. (2011). When serial arguments predict harm: Examining the influences of argument function, topic of the argument, perceived resolvability, and argumentativeness. *Argumentation and Advocacy*, 47, 214–227. Retrieved from http://www.americanforensics.org/AA/aa_info.html

Johnson, K. L., & Roloff, M. E. (1998). Serial arguing and relational quality: Determinants and consequences of perceived resolvability. *Communication Research*, 25, 327–343. doi: 10.1177/009365098025003004

Johnson, K. L., & Roloff, M. E. (2000a). Correlates of the perceived resolvability and relational consequences of serial arguing in dating relationships. *Journal of Social and Personal Relationships*, 17, 676–686. doi: 10.1177/0265407500174011

Johnson, K. L., & Roloff, M. E. (2000b). The influence of argumentative role (initiator vs. resistor) on perceptions of serial argument resolvability and relational harm. *Argumentation*, 14, 1–15. doi: 10.1023/A:1007837310258

Keck, K. L., & Samp, J. A. (2007). The dynamic nature of goals and message production as revealed in a sequential analysis of conflict interactions. *Human Communication Research*, 33, 27–47. doi: 10.1111/j.1468-2958.2007.00287.x

Kelley, D. L., & Waldron, V. R. (2005). An investigation of forgiveness-seeking communication and relational outcomes. *Communication Quarterly*, 53, 339–358. doi: 10.1080/01463370500101097

Konstan, J. A., Rosser, B. R. S., Ross, M. W., Stanton, J., & Edwards, W. M. (2005). The story of subject naught: A cautionary but optimistic tale of internet survey research. *Journal of Computer-Mediated Communication*, 10, article 9. doi: 10.1111/j.10836101.2005.tb00248.x

Malis, R. S., & Roloff, M. E. (2006a). Demand/withdraw patterns in serial arguments: Implications for well-being. *Human Communication Research*, 32, 198–216. doi: 10.1111/j.1468-2958.2006.00009.x

Malis, R. S., & Roloff, M. E. (2006b). Features of serial arguing and coping strategies: Links with stress and well-being. In B. A. LePoire & R. M. Dailey (Eds.), *Applied interpersonal communication matters: Family, health, and community relations* (pp39–66). New York: Peter Lang.

Miller, C. W., & Roloff, M. E. (2006). The perceived characteristics of irresolvable, resolvable, and resolved intimate conflicts: Is there evidence of intractability? *International Journal of Conflict Management*, 17, 291–315. doi: 10.1108/10444060610749464

Radanielina-Hita, M. L. (2010). Let's make peace! A cross-cultural analysis of the effects of serial arguing behaviors in romantic relationships: The case of Malagasy romantic partners. *Journal of Intercultural Communication Research*, 39, 81–103. doi: 10.1080/17475759.2010.526314

Reznik, R. M., & Roloff, M. E. (2011). Getting off to a bad start: The relationship between communication during an initial episode of a serial argument and argument frequency. *Communication Studies*, 62, 291–306. doi: 10.1080/10510974.2011.555491

Reznik, R. M., Roloff, M. E., & Miller, C. W. (2010). Communication during interpersonal arguing: Implications for stress symptoms. *Argumentation and Advocacy, 46,* 193–213. Retrieved from http://www.americanforensics.org/AA/aa_info.html

Reznik, R. M., Roloff, M. E., & Miller, C. W. (2012). Components of integrative communication during arguing: Implications for stress symptoms. *Argumentation and Advocacy, 48,* 142–158. Retrieved from http://www.americanforensics.org/AA/aa_info.html

Roloff, M. E. (2009). Links between conflict management research and practice. *Journal of Applied Communication Research, 37,* 339–348. doi: 10.1080/00909880903233200

Sillars, A. L. (1980). Attributions and communication in roommate conflicts. *Communication Monographs, 47,* 180–200. doi: 10.1080/03637758009376031

Trapp, R., & Hoff, N. (1985). A model of serial argument in interpersonal relationships. *Journal of the American Forensic Association, 22,* 1–11. Retrieved from http://www.americanforensics.org/AA/aa_info.html

9

WORTH FIGHTING FOR

The Correlates, Context, and Consequences of Avoiding Versus Enacting Domestic Labor Conflict

Kendra Knight and Jess K. Alberts

Domestic labor conflict arises when parties have incompatible goals or interests with regard to the achievement of household and care-related tasks. This can include household "chores," such as cooking and laundry, as well as care for children and other dependents. Common sources of domestic labor conflict include dissatisfaction with the cleanliness of the home, perceived unfairness in household labor performance, desire for one or more parties to increase their performance and responsibility for domestic tasks, and complaints and disputes about standards for the performance of domestic tasks and care work.

Domestic labor conflict has been most often studied among heterosexual cohabiting and married couples, and to a lesser extent among homosexual couples, roommates, and siblings. Although the study of domestic labor conflict has primarily concerned conflict over the tasks contained within one household or within a family's shared space, domestic labor conflict also arises between parties who do not share living space, such as between individuals who co-parent one or more children but live in separate residences, or adult siblings providing care for aging family members.

Research on domestic labor conflict has a decades-long history and is multidisciplinary, with contributions from scholars in the fields of sociology, economics, family studies, gender studies, psychology and communication. Domestic labor conflict research often focuses on the relationship of conflict behavior to relational outcomes (e.g., satisfaction), personal health outcomes (e.g., stress, immune function), and the ability to affect change in labor allocation. Given the importance of domestic labor to family functioning, and considering that domestic labor conflicts interpenetrate issues of relational power and identity, family/household decision-making, and material resources and rewards (e.g., personal comfort, leisure time), the study of domestic labor conflict has the potential to greatly improve interpersonal relating among spouses and family members. In this chapter, we focus on domestic labor conflict that is enacted among heterosexual cohabiting and married couples.

Domestic Labor Conflict in Heterosexual Couples

Women and men's roles in society have changed considerably over the past three decades. Despite the important changes that have occurred in political, employment and domestic spheres, women still experience inequities in each. For many women, however, perceived inequities in the domestic realm are the most problematic, because not only must these inequities be confronted daily, they also occur in a space where one is most likely to expect fairness and equitable treatment. Women are likely to feel this way because, as most researchers report, women in cohabiting heterosexual relationships on average perform two-thirds of household labor and childcare (Alberts et al, 2011; Parker & Wang, 2013). In addition, an assumption exists and some research suggests that women perform the lion's share of emotional labor and take primary responsibility for planning and scheduling family tasks and events (Wiesmann et al, 2008). As a result, women often experience role overload due to their contributions to domestic labor and concomitantly report increased feelings of stress and burnout and higher rates of depression as well as physical and mental health problems (Glass & Fujimoto, 1994).

When women perceive inequity in spousal performances of household labor, they experience emotional distress and anger as well as increased marital dissatisfaction and thoughts of divorce (Frisco & Williams, 2003; Mirowsky & Ross, 1995). Nonetheless, dissatisfaction with a partner's household task performance in and of itself need not lead to such negative outcomes or cause serious damage to one's relationship. For example, Folger et al (1979) found support for a *voice effect* among couples who experienced inequities in household task performance. That is, independent of actual differences in spouses' performance of household labor, wives' satisfaction in their marriages and their perception of fairness were related to whether the couple engaged in constructive discussions of the problem.

Thus, *how* couples managed their conflict over household labor seemed to have more impact on their relationships than did the presence of inequities. This finding is consistent with Gottman's (1979) claim that how couples manage conflict is one of the most important determinants of relationship quality.

More specifically, researchers have found that, as with other conflict topics, mutually integrative communication behaviors enacted during division of domestic labor conflict associate directly with productive outcomes, such as increased understanding and perceptions of compromise (Kluwer et al, 1997), and the development of a clear-cut plan that leads to more equal sharing (Wiesmann et al, 2008). Also, mutually integrative behaviors are inversely associated with negative outcomes related to division of domestic labor conflict, such as relationship disruption (Kluwer et al, 1997). These findings suggest that mutually integrative communication during housework conflicts could stave off some of the adverse consequences of dissatisfaction with housework allocation.

A couple's ability to talk productively about division of labor conflict has other important ramifications as well. For example, healthy immune function is associated with how couples communicate, independent of their marital quality. That is, even among highly satisfied couples, negative or hostile behavior is significantly related to physiological changes such as depressed immune functions and increased blood pressure, and these changes persist for up to 24 hours after a 30-minute conversation (Kiecolt-Glaser et al, 1996).

Finally, the ability to communicate about the division of domestic labor is important because it provides a significant way for women to break through traditional gender roles that can interfere with their personal and marital happiness as well as their professional success (Alberts et al., 2011; Kluwer et al, 1996). Wiesmann et al (2008) found that the most egalitarian couples engaged in explicit discussions about domestic labor and that they made specific plans as to how housework would be carried out. Deutsch's (1999) study of dual-earning parents found that truly equal sharing of family work was enabled through early and frequent discussions of expectations, as well as course-correcting discussions when one partner began to dominate or take too much responsibility for childcare or domestic work.

An Unspoken "Agreement"

Despite the advantages of constructive, explicit discussion of household labor conflict, couples typically do not engage in explicit negotiations regarding the allocation of household labor prior to or at the onset of cohabitation. Rather, for most couples, early decisions regarding the allocation of domestic tasks occur implicitly and indirectly (Alberts et al, 2011). Implicit decision-making among couples often entails "silent agreement," or a consensus reached without verbal agreement (Scanzoni & Szinovacz, 1980; Sillars & Kalbfleisch, 1989). Silent agreement frequently occurs as a result of an evolved precedent. A particular course of action, uncontested, over time develops into an unarticulated relationship rule. This precedent can become so engrained that later diversion from it will elicit the same reaction as if an explicitly established rule had been violated (Sillars & Kalbfleisch, 1989).

Adherence to precedent appears to be an important predictor of domestic labor performance. Alberts et al (2011) theorize that to the extent that an individual completes a household task repeatedly, the task comes to be defined as "belonging" to him/her, which in turn deters other members of the household from performing the same behavior, in a self-organizing process referred to as a negative feedback loop (Fewell, 2003). Interviews with couples in a Dutch study provide support for the role of precedent in allocating domestic labor. Participants in the study commented on a process by which one member of the couple took on a task initially, and then both members of couple understood it to be his/her responsibility, in a self-perpetuating cycle (Wiesmann et al, 2008). The couples reported that divisions of labor in their households occurred "naturally," "without thinking", and in a "taken-for-granted" fashion. Although they had general expectations regarding the allocation of domestic labor prior to moving in together, no clear rules or divisions were discussed, and couples lacked general awareness of the need to discuss domestic labor arrangements (Wiesmann et al, 2008). Similarly, Becker and Moen (1999) found that among dual-earner couples, implicit agreement was the prevailing strategy for making decisions regarding the management of paid and unpaid work. The researchers found that couples engaged in a general strategy of "scaling back" (e.g., one partner works reduced hours, or one partner works a "job" rather than a "career") in order to meet the demands of paid work and domestic labor. Becker and Moen pointed out that although the decision to scale back was enacted consciously and deliberately in response to perceived need, the question of who would do the scaling back – which disproportionately fell to women – was often "pragmatic and unremarked," (p383).

In some cases, implicit agreement reflects true agreement. A fortunate few couples find that household labor "sorts itself out" in a manner that is acceptable and equitable to all parties. Unfortunately, research suggests that it is also possible that implicit agreement represents a surface-level agreement, under which disagreement and unexpressed conflict reside (Devault, 1990; Kluwer et al, 1997; Wiesmann et al, 2008). For example, Benin and Agostinelli (1988) found that wives' dissatisfaction with division of labor did not associate with husbands' perceived frequency of open conflict, indicating that a lack of expressed conflict does not necessarily reflect true agreement between spouses about labor allocation. In the study conducted by Wiesmann et al (2008), participants initially reported a natural and seamless allocation of labor. However, when participants continued to discuss their division of labor, they revealed that there actually were discrepancies and disagreements under the surface of the relationship, which were managed via conflict avoidance.

Avoiding Overt Domestic Labor Conflict

Conflict avoidance has been represented in previous literature in two basic forms. First, avoidance occurs when a topic is brought up for discussion, or arises in conversation, and one or both partners evade partial or full discussion of it. This type of avoidance can take several behavioral forms, including subtleties such as changing the topic or deflecting with humor, or more explicit evasions such as challenging the eligibility of a topic for discussion, declaring a topic taboo or "off-limits", or physically withdrawing from the interaction (Afifi et al, 2008; Baxter & Wilmot, 1985; Christensen, 1987; Sullaway & Christensen, 1983; Wile, 1981).

Second, avoidance occurs in the form of withheld or suppressed complaints, as when a topic is never brought to the table at all. If a conversation topic becomes salient to one individual, but he/she refrains from raising the issue, the issue is confined to the mind of one party and thus discussion is preempted. In the context of household labor conflict, avoidance can take either form. Avoidance through evasion occurs when one partner complains about household labor allocation, standards, or performance, and the other's communication tactics (e.g., through a humorous or abbreviated response) shut down or dilute the force of the complaint or discussion (Eldridge & Christensen, 2002). Avoidance through suppression occurs when, despite perceived differences in labor performance expectations and reality, the topic is not raised at all (also referred to as stoicism; Komter, 1989; Wiesmann et al, 2008).

Conflict avoidance leads to a number of negative outcomes, including relationship dissatisfaction, decreased cohesion (Bodenmann et al, 1998), and relational distress (Crohan, 1992). In the realm of household labor, avoidance has been associated with destructive outcomes such as unresolved conflict, resentment, and lack of change (Kluwer et al, 1997; Wiesmann et al, 2008). Although conflict avoidance negatively affects both men and women, women are more negatively affected. Specifically, women are more dissatisfied by their own and their partner's avoidance, especially in response to a conflict that is important to them (Afifi, et al, 2008). Moreover, when domestic labor is avoided, women are more likely than men to make concessions in paid work to accommodate domestic labor inequities at home (Becker & Moen, 1999; Stone, 2007; Wiesmann et al, 2008). Given that women's marital satisfaction is central to both partner's satisfaction and women are more likely to seek divorce (Afifi et al, 2012), it is important to understand why couples choose to avoid conflict on such an important issue.

Reasons for Avoiding Domestic Labor Conflict

Research has tended to focus on different causes of household labor conflict avoidance for men and women. Research examining why men chose to avoid discussions of household labor suggests that men avoid doing so because it is to their advantage. That is, since men usually perform less household labor, conflict discussions on the topic may lead to a demand for or an actual increase in their contributions, which is characterized as a negative outcome; thus, men are better off if they avoid addressing the topic at all (Eldridge & Christensen, 2002). Research on demand-withdraw in domestic labor conflict, for example, has shown that men are more likely to withdraw because they benefit from a less-than-equal share of household labor (Christensen & Heavey, 1990; Eldridge & Christensen, 2002; Eldridge et al, 2007; Heavey et al, 1993; Walczynski, 1997).

Fewer studies have examined why women might avoid a conflict that possesses the potential to provide favorable outcomes for them. Those that have suggest that women perform cognitive work in response to domestic labor inequities that permit or encourage them to avoid domestic labor conflict (Johnson & Huston, 1998; Komter, 1989; Wiesmann et al, 2008). For example, Komter (1989) argued that wives cultivate fairness out of inequity by cultivating a preference to do household work themselves, claiming greater enjoyment of the work or their greater skill. Wiesmann's et al (2008) study argued that women avoid conflict and accept an inequitable share of household burdens because they perceive that the cost of engaging in conflict with their partners outweighs any benefits they might achieve.

Housework-Conflict-Related Cognitions and Conflict Avoidance.

The objective of the present study is to extend research on the role of conflict-related cognitions in determining household labor conflict avoidance. Individuals' cognitions about the world influence their expectations about and responses to events they encounter. Similarly, through their lived experiences and their interactions with one another, couples develop relatively fixed sets of cognitions about marital roles and relationships generally and about the nature of their relationship specifically (Baucom et al, 1989). Based on these templates, couples develop expectations regarding how relational partners are supposed to act as well as how they should relate to one another. These cognitions act as templates couples use to solve problems and make decisions within their marriages. Therefore, to understand why couples make the choices they do, one must understand their underlying belief structures.

Based on extant literature, we identified three housework conflict-related cognitions that we expected would influence an individual's tendency to avoid overt conflict over household labor. The three cognitions we investigate converge on the question of whether or not conflict over household labor seems to be "worth" engaging in (Wiesmann et al, 2008). Other research on topic avoidance has focused on reasons specific to those topic domains. Afifi and et al (2008), for example, examined anxiety and desire for self-protection as reasons motivating adolescents' avoidance of their divorced parents' relationship. Our focus on beliefs about the "worthwhile" nature of domestic labor conflict derives from the fact that at its heart, domestic labor conflict is often about two underlying interests: the material resources one has to devote to performing household labor, and the implications of one's labor load for one's feelings about the relationship (Alberts et al, 2011). Therefore, we suspect that relevant cognitions in household labor conflict are those that help an individual decide whether he/she will accrue a gain in material resources (e.g., time gained because one's spouse takes over a larger share of the work) or emotional resources (e.g., an increased sense that one is appreciated), not the costs associated with engaging in conflict.

The first cognition we expected to be relevant relates to whether or not an individual believes that the conflict will lead to positive change. An individual's assumptions about whether marital conflict, generally, or a conflict over a specific topic is resolvable influences their willingness to confront their partners (Crohan, 1992; Fincham et al, 1990). In the realm of household labor, it is likely that previous experiences with division of labor conflict, and/or how fixed existing patterns appear to be, influence the degree of "hope" that a partner possesses for improvements over the status quo resulting from overt conflict. We expect that individuals will avoid to the extent that they believe that expressed conflict won't lead to improvements in the division of domestic labor.

Second, we expect that individuals weigh the emotional costs of engaging in conflict with the material costs of completing housework oneself. One of the sentiments expressed by Wiesmann and colleagues' (2008) participants, and implied in other research (van Doorne-Huiskes, 1992), is that engaging in conflict is *more work* than performing domestic labor tasks. Individuals may believe that the benefits gained in "help" with housework are not worth risking the state of marital harmony by open argument.

Finally, we expect that avoidance will be a preferred strategy to the extent that individuals perceive that explicit negotiation of household labor is inappropriate or incompatible with a highly functioning and loving marital relationship. It has been argued, for example, that explicit decision-making is a first sign of disorganization in the family system (Reiss, 1981; Watzlawick et al, 1967). Additionally, both legal jurisprudence and norms of domesticity depict the family home and the marital relationship as a "last holdout" from the harsh negotiations of the public sphere, rendering explicit exchange and negotiation processes incompatible with the "haven" that home life ought to represent (Drago, 2007; Williams, 2000). Recent research demonstrates that such perceptions do exist in contemporary households. For instance, Wiesmann et al (2008) suggested that their respondents believe that housework is an expression of love, and "rational bargaining about who spends how much time on which task is incompatible with a romantic relationship" (p358).

A Spotlight Study On Domestic Labor Conflict

Each of the cognitions we have identified has been examined or implied in previous research. However, these belief structures have been limited to explaining *women's* decision to avoid domestic labor conflict, and primarily through suppression or stoicism. In other words, research has found preliminary evidence that cognitions play a role in women's decisions to withhold complaints and refrain from initiating household labor conflict, but have not examined the role of cognitions in evasion behaviors or the role of husbands' beliefs on their use of avoidance. Thus, in this chapter, we examine the effect of housework conflict-related cognitions on both husbands' and wives' avoidance of domestic labor conflict. Specifically, we predicted that individuals' reports of avoidant behaviors during division of labor conflict would associate positively with their own endorsement of the following household labor conflict (HLC) beliefs:

1. engaging in household labor conflict will not lead to positive change;
2. it is easier to perform household labor than to engage in conflict about it; and
3. household labor is not a worthy conflict topic.

Additionally, because conflict is a dyadic interchange, we believe that the decision for any one partner to avoid is likely a function of her or his own as well as his/her partner's conflict-related cognitions. Our cognitions not only affect our own behavior but also affect our partner through our behavior and through the relationship climate (Baucom et al, 1989), therefore we believe it is important to examine how husbands' and wives' avoidance behavior is affected by *each other*'s housework-conflict-related cognitions. Thus, we predicted that individuals' reports of avoidant behaviors during division of labor conflict would associate positively with *their partners*' endorsement of the following household labor conflict (HLC) beliefs:

1. engaging in household labor conflict will not lead to positive change;
2. it is easier to perform household labor than to engage in conflict about it; and
3. household labor is not a worthy conflict topic.

Finally, in order to investigate whether housework-related cognitions (their own or their partner's) affect husbands' and wives' conflict avoidance differently, we posed two research questions:

1. Do the effects of actors' HLC beliefs on conflict avoidance differ by role (husbands versus wives)?
2. Do the effects of partners' HLC beliefs on conflict avoidance differ by role (husbands versus wives)?

Method

Participants

Data were collected using a social networking sample. Undergraduate students in a communication department at a large university in the southwestern United States were asked to recruit one heterosexual married couple to complete a web survey. Students were offered extra credit in a communication course in exchange for recruiting a couple to the study. Participants were 155 heterosexual married couples. Dyads had been married an average of 19.98 years (SD = 9.99), and the vast majority of dyads (n = 116) were reporting on their first marriage. Male participants' age ranged from 22 to 77 years, with a mean age of 49.69 years (SD = 9.73). Female participants' age ranged from 20 to 69 years, with a mean age of 46.92 years (SD = 8.84). Collectively, 3.3 percent of this sample identified as Asian, 3.9 percent as Black or African American, 2.6 percent as Latino or

Hispanic, 85.6 percent as White or European American, 4.6 percent as other or more than one category. Among males, 83.9 percent were employed full time and 3.9 percent were employed part time. Among females, 49.0 percent were employed full time and 20.6 percent were employed part time.

Measures

Housework conflict-related cognitions were measured using an eight-item scale developed from extant literature. As this scale had not been used previously, the items were subjected to an exploratory factor analysis (EFA) using maximum likelihood estimation and oblique (oblimin) rotation. Criteria for determining factors were:

1. Kaiser's criterion of an eigenvalue of 1 or greater;
2. at least two items per component;
3. primarily loadings of .60 or greater and secondary loadings less than .40; and
4. conceptual coherence among items forming each component.

One of nine initial items that did not meet these criteria was dropped from the analysis, which was then rerun. The final three-component solution accounted for 67.28 percent of the variance. The first component (variance = 25.62 percent, loadings = .68 to .84) contained three items reflecting a perception that it is easier to simply do the work than ask for help (i.e., *easier to do it myself*). The second component (variance = 21.64 percent, loadings = .83) contained two items reflecting a perception that engaging in conflict won't improve the situation (i.e., *not going to improve*). Finally, the third component (variance = 20.01 percent, loadings = .66 to .81) contained three items reflecting a perception that it is not appropriate to engage in conflict over household labor (i.e., *not worth fighting about*).

Conflict behavior was measured using an adapted version of the Communication Patterns Questionnaire-Short Form (CPQ-SF; Christensen & Heavey, 1990; Heavey et al., 1993). The CPQ-SF was revised to include six items that measure individual avoidance behaviors (e.g., "When issues or problems arise related to housework or household chores, how likely is it that... *You don't initiate a discussion about the problem?*") Answer choices formed a Likert scale (1= *very unlikely*; 7 = *very likely*; Cronbach's alpha = .79).

Results

The influence of housework conflict-related cognitions on conflict avoidance was measured via a series of actor-partner-interdependence models using multilevel modeling (MLM). The APIM allows for the simultaneous estimation of actor, partner, and role (e.g., husband vs. wife) effects, as well as actor-partner and actor-partner-role interactions. MLM allows for the estimation of these effects while controlling for non-independence in dyad members' scores. Following Kenny et al's (2006) recommendation, predictor variables were centered at the grand mean prior to conducting analyses.

"Won't Lead To Positive Change."

Hypotheses 1a and 2a predicted that actors' and partners' belief that household labor conflict does not lead to positive change would associate positively with avoidance of domestic labor conflict. Our results supported these hypotheses: actors' reported conflict avoidance associated positively with their *own* perception that conflict doesn't improve the situation, $F(1,299.55) = 13.06$, $\beta = .12$, $p < .001$, $\eta^2 = .04$ as well as their partners' belief of the same $F(1,286.35) = 4.57$, $\beta = .07$, $p = .033$, $\eta^2 = .02$. Thus, hypotheses 1a and 2a are supported. No significant actor- or partner-by-role effects were obtained.

"It Is Easier To Do It Myself."

Hypotheses 1b and 2b predicted that actors' endorsement of the belief that performing housework is less costly than engaging in conflict would associate positively with actors' reported avoidance of domestic labor conflict. Again, the APIM obtained significant actor and partner effects such that actors' reported conflict avoidance positively associated with their *own* perception that performing labor is less costly than engaging in conflict, $F(1,300.20) = 55.50$, $\beta = .22$, $p < .001$, $\eta^2 = .16$, as well as their partners' belief of the same $F(1,278.13) = 4.90$, $\beta = .07$, $p = .028$, $\eta^2 = .02$. No significant actor- or partner-by-role effects were obtained.

"Not Worth Arguing About."

Finally, hypotheses 1c and 2c predicted that dyad members' endorsement of the belief that division of labor conflict is not an appropriate or worthwhile conflict topic would associate positively with their reported conflict avoidance. The APIM produced a significant actor effect: actors' reported conflict avoidance associates positively with their own endorsement of this belief, $F(1,289.75) = 16.45$, $\beta = .13$, $p < .001$, $\eta^2 = .06$. No significant partner effect was obtained, but the APIM obtained a significant interaction effect for actor-role-by-partner-belief, $F(1,288.51) = 7.10$, $\beta = -.17$, $p = .008$, $\eta^2 = .02$. That is, a significant interaction effect indicated that the influence of partner's belief on actor avoidance differed for husbands and wives. The significant interaction was interpreted by plotting simple slopes using an Excel program developed by Dawson (2012; 2013) in accordance with methods suggested by Aiken and West (1991) and Dawson and Richter (2006; see Figure 9.1). Examination of the simple slopes revealed that wives' use of avoidance positively associates with their husbands'

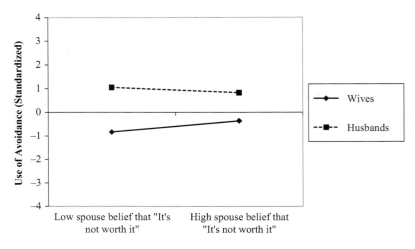

FIGURE 9.1 Actor Role by Partner "Not Worth It" Belief on Use of Avoidance

belief that division of labor is not a worthwhile or appropriate conflict topic. By contrast, husbands' use of avoidance is relatively unaffected by this belief among wives.

Discussion

Previous literature has suggested that the beliefs individuals hold about household labor conflict affect their propensity to avoid it, even when facing inequity and dissatisfaction. Based on this research, three housework conflict-related cognitions were assessed and tested in our study. Support was found for all three – the perception that household labor conflict will not lead to positive change, the perception that it is easier to perform household labor oneself than to engage in conflict about it, and the perception that household labor is not a worthy or appropriate topic for conflict. Moreover, it was found that not only do individuals' own beliefs associate with their tendency to avoid domestic labor conflict, individuals' *partners'* endorsement of housework conflict-related beliefs are also related to use of avoidance. Taken together, these findings expand our understanding of the dynamics of domestic labor conflict. Although there are demonstrated negative outcomes for avoiding domestic labor conflict, our results suggest that dyads may engage in relatively rational assessments of the costs and benefits of engaging in overt domestic labor conflict. One interpretation of our results is that marital dyads appear to be weighing the physical labor of performing common household tasks against the emotional labor (Erickson, 2005; Hochschild, 1983) associated with explicit negotiations about housework. In the remainder of the chapter, we discuss three broader issues connected to the study of household labor conflict avoidance in marriage: using dyads as the unit of analysis, the problem of studying avoidance, and the importance of research that connects "private" conflict interactions to the broader social contexts in which couples lead their lives.

Methodological Challenges and Studying Conflict in the Future

Studying Conflict Dyadically

A unique challenge of studying interpersonal conflict is the dyadic nature of interaction. In conflict, as with other arenas of relational life, the "roles that individuals construct and enact are most strongly influenced by the relationship partner" (Golden, 2001, p251). When attempting to observe and depict the nature of interpersonal conflict, employing dyads as the unit of analysis provides a considerable advantage. In the present study, a dyadic focus permits us to examine the mutual impact of individuals' own cognitions, and their spouses' cognitions, on an individual's elected conflict behaviors. This is but one of the functions of dyadic analyses. Other functions include:

1. Comparing dyad members. Dyadic methods are useful for comparing dyad members on conflict-relevant behaviors and cognitions (e.g., comparing women and men on frequency of housework-related complaints).
2. Comparing types of dyads. Dyadic research also allows for researchers to assess the differences between types of intact dyads. To continue the example from above, say a researcher also wished to investigate whether frequency of housework-related complaints differs between dyads in which both partners work full time and those in which one partner works part time.
3. Examining the impact of continuous between-dyads variables. If instead of, or in addition to, assessing the differences between dyads based on whether both partners work full time (as described above), a researcher wanted to assess the impact of duration of relationship on the frequency of housework-related complaints. Dyadic analyses enable a researcher to examine the effects on the dependent variable of some interval- or ratio-level between-dyads variable (e.g., length of relationship, annual household income, number of children in the home).

Difficulty in "Capturing" Avoidance

A central methodological problem for researchers who study conflict avoidance is how to measure what is not said. In some cases, avoidance can be detected by focusing on evasion strategies employed to forestall a discussion topic raised by an interlocutor. Afifi et al (2008) identified five such avoidance tactics: changing the topic ("S/he gave responses that were not related to the other person's questions"), brevity or evasiveness ("S/he gave very short responses to the other person's questions"), humor ("S/he used humor in a way that distracted the other person from the issue"), challenging the validity of the topic ("S/he questioned why they should be discussing the issue"), and hostility ("S/he made the other person feel uncomfortable talking about the issue"). These strategies may be relatively easy for survey respondents to recall about their partners if they are primed as well as for researchers to observe in laboratory studies. However, more subtle avoidance behaviors, such as silence or leaving the room, may not be attended to by participants or performed in laboratory settings (Eldridge & Christensen, 2002).

The problem of "capturing" avoidance is particularly pronounced in instances in which the would-be initiator suppresses a complaint to or query of his/her partner. For example, in the second author's study of everyday interaction among married couples, audio-recordings revealed instances of withdrawal during conflict, but they not could not capture occasions when a partner wanted to initiate a discussion or conflict but chose not to do so. This inability to observe avoidance in the form of suppression can be especially problematic for scholars who examine conflict over household labor, because research suggests that in large part the allocation of domestic tasks takes place absent explicit discussion.

For these reasons, surveying participant's perceptions of conflict avoidance over domestic labor is preferable over laboratory or observational studies. It allows participants to reflect on their behavior to identify times when disagreements arose but they chose to evade overt conflict or refrain from initiating a discussion. Even in this case, however, participants may not remember every instance (or perhaps any instance) where they avoided conflict by suppressing their feelings and desire for discussion. Therefore, it would be maximally effective to study conflict avoidance by either conducting a diary study or adding it to survey studies of conflict behavior. Like survey methods, diary methods enable the measurement of avoidance behaviors that are not directly or readily observable, and also attenuate the recall concerns present when simply asking participants to reflect on previous interactions.

Studying Micro-Interaction within Socio-Cultural Contexts

Finally, when investigating conflict in applied contexts, it is important to recognize that the motivations for avoiding or engaging in conflict are rooted in larger social practices and beliefs that are rarely acknowledged consciously. For instance, both men and women frequently subscribe to the belief that performing household labor is a personal choice. Coontz (2005) suggests that men often make sense of inequitable labor allocation by arguing "it [an undone household task] doesn't bother me, so I shouldn't have to do it." This comment reflects a common sense notion of how the world works – "if it bothers you, you should fix it" (Alberts et al, 2011, 32). Although this kind of belief glosses over the importance and necessity of most domestic work, it structures thinking such that for many people, asking a partner to participate more actively in household labor feels inappropriate.

The "worth" of engaging in overt conflict over household labor should also be considered in its historical context. The perception that household labor is not a worthy or appropriate source or topic of conflict is at least partly a remnant of thinking about the private sphere that emerged in the United States as a result of the industrial revolution (Williams, 2000). Prior to the Industrial Revolution, there was no division of public and private spheres of work, as families in agrarian economies worked as a unit to feed, clothe, and provide shelter for members. Whatever could not be produced by the family unit could be traded or bartered for with other families in the community. With the advent of industrialization, however, the shift to mass production divided family members into those who worked in public production for pay, and those who worked in familial production for the upkeep of the household (Folbre, 1991). As sociologists and historians have pointed out (Siegel, 1994; Williams, 2000), the cultural legacy of this logistical change was that the private sphere came to be understood as a place of refuge or respite from the harried life of the public sphere. As Siegel explains, in the post-industrial private sphere, a husband found he could:

> [Seek] refuge from the vexations and embarrassments of business, an enchanting repose from exertion, a relaxation from care by the interchange of affection: where some of his finest sympathies, tastes, and moral and religious feelings are formed and nourished, – where is the treasury of pure disinterested love, such as is seldom found in the busy walks of a selfish and calculating world (p1196).

As such, the private sphere was transformed from a place in which business transactions were a regular part of everyday life, to a place not to be sullied by rational bargaining. The result of this ideology has been observed throughout American political culture, not least in American family law, where attempts to collect entitlements for domestic work – say, in the case of a failed marriage – have been labeled "cold" or "calculated" (Williams, 2000).

We argue that traces of this ideology also permeate interpersonal interactions surrounding household labor, and such is the reason that we see participants avoiding division of labor conflict because it they believe it is not "appropriate." Individuals' reticence to engage in overt negotiations of "who will do what" reflects an ideology that in so doing, the concept of marriage or romance is somehow corrupted or demeaned. The material consequence of such a belief, of course, is that couples are more likely to rely on implicit arrangements that tend to perpetuate inequality.

We believe that there is a tremendous benefit to be gained by conducting applied conflict research that fully considers the socio-contextual factors that impact conflict behavior. To date, most of the research on domestic labor conflict that does examine societal level factors focuses on demographic characteristics such as trends in women's employment. However, communication scholars are uniquely poised to examine the interrelationships among seemingly "private" interaction and choices within marriages and broader systems of meaning.

Conclusion

Sheer lack of time and resources entails that dyads cannot raise every decision to the level of explicit discussion (Sillars & Kalbfliesch, 1989). Domestic labor, despite its importance to marital functioning, is one of the topics relegated to implicit agreement for all but the most conscientious couples. Research over the past two-and-a-half decades has given form to the factors that lead couples to avoid division of labor conflict. The present study contributes to that research, providing empirical evidence of the influence of both dyad members' perceptions of the costliness, appropriateness, and effectiveness of household labor conflict on avoidant behavior. Our hope is that this work, in addition to expanding understanding of the dynamics of domestic labor conflict, underscores the benefits and challenges of studying what is "not said" in domestic labor conflict, using dyads as the unit of analysis, and considering how the socio-cultural meanings imbued in particular topics affect our ability to communicate about them.

References

Afifi, T. D., Afifi, W. A., Morse, C., & Hamrick, K. (2008). Adolescents' avoidance tendencies and physiological reactions to discussions about their parents' relationship: Implications for post-divorce and non-divorced families. *Communication Monographs*, 75, 290–317. doi: 10.1080/03637750802342308.

Afifi, T. D., Joseph, A., & Aldeis, D. (2012). The "standards for openness hypothesis": Why women find (conflict) avoidance more dissatisfying than men. *Journal of Social and Personal Relationships*, 29, 102–127. doi: 10.1177/0265407511420193.

Aiken, L. S., & West, S. G. (1991). *Mutiple regression: Testing and interpreting interactions.* Newbury Park, London: Sage.

Alberts, J. K., Tracy, S. J., & Trethewey, A. (2011). An integrative theory of the division of household labor: Threshold level, social organizing, and sensemaking. *Journal of Family Communication*, 11, 21–38. doi: 10.1080/15267431.2011.534334.

Baucom, D. H., Epstein, N., Sayers, S. L., & Sher, T. G. (1989). The role of cognitions in marital relationships: Definitional, methodological and conceptual issues. *Journal of Consulting and Clinical Psychology*, 57, 31–38. doi: 10.1111/j.1752-0606.2005.tb01539.x.

Baxter, L., & Wilmot, W. (1985). Taboo topics in close relationships. *Journal of Social and Personal Relationships*, 2, 253–269. doi: 10.1177/0265407585023002.

Becker, P. E., & Moen, P. (1999). Scaling back: Dual-earner couples' work-family strategies. *Journal of Marriage and Family*, 61, 995–1007. doi: 10.2307/354019.

Benin, M. H., & Agostinelli, J. (1988). Husbands' and wives' satisfaction with the division of labor. *Journal of Marriage and the Family*, 50, 349–361. doi: 10.2307/352002.

Bodenmann, G., Kaiser, A., Hahlweg, K., & Fehm-Wolfsdorf, G. (1998). Communication patterns during marital conflict: A cross-cultural replication. *Personal Relationships*, *5*, 343–356. doi: 10.1111/j.1475–6811.1998.tb00176.x.

Christensen, A. (1987). Detection of conflict patterns in couples. In K. Hahlweg & M. J. Goldstein (Eds.), *Understanding major mental disorder: The contribution of family interaction research* (pp250–265). New York: Family Process Press.

Christensen, A., & Heavey, C. L. (1990). Gender and social structure in the demand/withdraw pattern of marital conflict. *Journal of Personality and Social Psychology*, *59*, 73–81. doi: 10.1037/0022–3514.59.1.73.

Coontz, S. (2005) *Marriage, A History: From Obedience to Intimacy, or How Love Conquered Marriage*. New York: Viking.

Crohan, S. E. (1992). Conflict: A longitudinal investigation. *Journal of Social and Personal Relationships*, *9*, 9–102. doi: 10.1177/0265407592091005.

Dawson, J. F. (2012). Interpreting interaction effects, http://www.jeremydawson.co.uk/slopes.htm

Dawson, J. F. (2013). Moderation in management research: What, why, when and how. *Journal of Business and Psychology*, *29*, 1–19. doi: 0.1007/s10869-10013-9308-9307.

Dawson, J. F., & Richter, A. W. (2006). Probing three-way interactions in moderated multiple regression: Development and application of a slope difference test. *Journal of Applied Psychology*, *91*, 917–926. doi: 10.1037/0021–9010.91.4.917.

Deutsch, F. M. (1999). *Halving it all: How equally shared parenting works*. Cambridge, MA: Harvard University Press.

Devault, M. L. (1990). Conflict over housework: The problem that still has no name. In L. Kriesberg (Ed.), *Research in social movements, conflict and change* (pp182–202). Greenwood, CT: JAI.

Drago, R. W. (2007). *Striking a balance: Work, family, life*. Boston, MA: Dollars & Sense.

Eldridge, K. A., & Christensen, A. (2002). Demand-withdraw communication during couple conflict: A review and analysis. In P. Noller & J. A. Feeney (Eds.), *Understanding marriage: Developments in the study of couple interaction* (pp289–322). Cambridge: Cambridge University Press.

Eldridge, K. A., Sevier, M., Jones, J., Atkins, D. C., & Christensen, A. (2007). Demand-withdraw communication in severely distressed, moderately distressed, and nondistressed couples: Rigidity and polarity during relationship and personal problem discussions. *Journal of Family Psychology*, *21*, 218–226. doi: 10.1037/0893–3200.21.2.218.

Erickson, R. J. (2005). Why emotion work matters: sex, gender, and the division of household labor. *Journal of Marriage and Family*, *67*(2), 337–351. doi: 10.1111/j.0022–2445.2005.00120.x.

Fewell, J. H. (2003). Social insect networks. *Science*, *301*, 1867–1870. doi: 10.1126/science.1088945.

Fincham, F. D., Bradbury, T. N., & Scott, C. K. (1990). Cognition in marriage: Retrospect and prospect. In F. D. Fincham & T. N. Bradbury (Eds.), *The psychology of marriage*. New York, NY: Guilford Publications.

Folbre, N. (1991). The unproductive housewife: Her evolution in nineteenth-century economic thought. *Signs: Journal of Women in Culture and Society*, *16*, 463–484. doi: 10.1086/494679.

Folger, R., Rosenfield, D., Grove, J., & Corkran, L. (1979). Effects of "voice" and peer opinions on responses to inequity. *Journal of Personality and Social Psychology*, *37*, 2243–2261. doi: 10.1037/0022–3514.37.12.2253.

Frisco, M. L., & Williams, K. (2003). Perceived housework equity, marital happiness, and divorce in dual-earner households. *Journal of Family Issues*, *24*, 51–73. doi: 10.1177/0192513X02238520.

Glass, J., & Fujimoto, T. (1994). Housework, paid work, and depression among husbands and wives. *Journal of Health and Social Behavior*, *35*, 179–191. doi: 10.2307/2137364.

Golden, A. G. (2001). Modernity and the communicative management of multiple roles: The case of the worker-parent. *Journal of Family Communication*, *1*, 233–264. doi: 10.1207/S15327698JFC0104_02.

Gottman, J. M. (1979). *Marital interaction: Experimental investigations*. San Diego, CA: Academic Press.

Heavey, C. L., Layne, C., & Christensen, A. (1993). Gender and conflict structure in marital interaction: A replication and extension. *Journal of Consulting and Clinical Psychology*, *61*, 16–27. doi: 10.1037/0022–006X.61.1.16.

Hochschild, A. R. (1983). *The managed heart*. Berkeley, CA: University of California Press.

Johnson, E. M., & Huston, T. L. (1998). The perils of love, or why wives adapt to husbands during the transition to parenthood. *Journal of Marriage and Family*, *60*, 195–204. doi: 10.2307/353451.

Kenny, D. A., Kashy, D. A., & Cook, W. L. (2006). *Dyadic data analysis*. New York: Guilford Press.

Kiecolt-Glaser, J. K., Newton, T., Cacioppo, J. T., MacCallum, R. C., Glaser, R., & Malarkey, W. B. (1996). Marital conflict and endocrine function: Are men really more physiologically affected than women? *Journal of Consulting and Clinical Psychology*, *64*, 324–332. doi: 10.1037//0022–0006x.64.2.324.

Kluwer, E. S., Heesink, J. A. M., & Van de Vliert, E. (1996). Marital conflict about the division of household labor and paid work. *Journal of Marriage and Family*, *58*, 958–969. doi: 10.2307/353983.

Kluwer, E. S., Heesink, J. A. M., & Van de Vliert, E. (1997). The marital dynamics of conflict over the division of labor. *Journal of Marriage and Family*, *59*, 635–653. doi: 10.2307/353951.

Komter, A. (1989). Hidden power in marriage. *Gender & Society*, *3*, 187–216. doi: 10.1177/089124389003002003.

Mirowsky, J., & Ross, C. E. (1995). Sex differences in distress: Real or artifact? *American Sociological Review*, *60*, 449–468. doi: 10.2307/2096424.

Parker, K., & Wang, W. (2013). *Modern parenthood: Roles of moms and dads as they balance work and family*. Pew Research Retrieved from http://www.pewsocialtrends.org/2013/03/14/modern-parenthood-roles-of-moms-and-dads-converge-as-they-balance-work-and-family/2/

Reiss, D. (1981). *The family's construction of reality*. Cambridge, MA: Harvard University Press.

Scanzoni, J., & Szinovacz, M. (1980). *Family decision-making: A developmental sex role model*. Beverly Hills, CA: Sage.

Sillars, A. L., & Kalbfleisch, P. J. (1989). Implicit and explicit decision-making styles in couples. In D. Brinberg & J. Jaccard (Eds.), *Dyadic decision making* (pp179–215). New York: Springer-Verlag.

Siegel, R. B. (1994) "The rule of love": Wife beating as prerogative and privacy. *The Yale Law Journal*, *105*, 2115–2227.

Stone, P. (2007). *Opting Out? Why women really quit careers and head home*. Berkeley, CA: University of California Press.

Sullaway, M., & Christensen, A. (1983). Assessment of dysfunctional interaction patterns in couples. *Journal of Marriage and Family*, *38*, 15–28. doi: 10.2307/351670.

van Doorne-Huiskes, A. (1992). *Betaalde en onbetaalde arbeid: Over oude spanningen en niuewe uitdagingen*. Rotterdam, Netherlands: Erasmus Universiteit.

Walczynski, P. T. (1997). *Power, personality, and conflictual interaction: An exploration of demand/withdraw interaction in same-sex and cross-sex couples*. PhD thesis, University of California, Los Angeles, CA.

Watzlawick, P., Beavin Bavelas, J., & Jackson, D. D. (1967). *Pragmatics of Human Communication*. New York, NY: W. W. Norton & Company.

Wiesmann, S., Boeije, H., van Doorne-Huiskes, A., & den Dulk, L. (2008). "Not worth mentioning": The implicit and explicit nature of decision-making about the division of paid and domestic work. *Community, Work & Family*, *11*, 341–363. doi: 10.1080/13668800802361781.

Wile, D. B. (1981). *Couples therapy: A non-traditional approach*. New York: Wiley.

Williams, J. (2000). *Unbending gender: Why family and work conflict and what to do about it*. New York, NY: Oxford University Press.

SECTION 4
Conflict in Families

10

DEMAND AND WITHDRAW BEHAVIOR AND EMOTION IN MOTHER–ADOLESCENT CONFLICT

Christin E. Huggins, Melissa Sturge-Apple, and Patrick T. Davies

Adolescence is a point of transition for families that can create turbulence in the parent-child relationship as both parties work to successfully navigate changing relational dynamics (Branje, 2008; Branje et al, 2013; Knobloch & Solomon, 2004). Conflict is characteristic of this developmental stage due to the high levels of interdependence and emotional involvement between parents and adolescent children (Braiker & Kelly, 1979; Laursen & Collins, 2004; Sillars et al, 2004). Indeed, adolescents report experiencing interpersonal conflict most often with mothers, followed by fathers and close friends (Laursen & Collins, 1994). Parent–child conflicts can increase in both frequency and intensity during early adolescence with the topics of conflict often centering on mundane issues such as cleanliness, chores, and curfews (Adams & Laursen, 2001). The conflictual discussions between parents and adolescents are of substantial import to adolescent development as children seek to obtain autonomy from parents through these interactions (Branje, 2008). Efforts to gain autonomy must be strategically managed to preserve the parent-adolescent relationship and the individuals' well-being. However, parent–child conflict interactions are often resolved through the use of negative communication behaviors including power displays and withdrawal (Adams & Laursen, 2001). As such these conflict interactions are punctuated by the use of *demand* and *withdraw* behaviors (Caughlin & Malis, 2004a; 2004b; Caughlin & Ramey, 2005).

Prior efforts by Caughlin and colleagues have established the presence of these communicative behaviors in the parent-adolescent relationship (Caughlin & Ramey, 2005) as well as the association of the dyadic pattern of demand-withdraw with adjustment and relational outcomes (Caughlin & Malis, 2004a; 2004b). Despite the established presence of the maladaptive conflict behaviors of demand and withdraw within these relationships, scarce research has continued to examine these behaviors within parent–adolescent conflict interactions. The aim of the current chapter is to provide a focused review of demand and withdraw behavior within the context of parent–adolescent relationships and address a limitation of previous research by examining the connection between these behaviors and emotion experience during conflict. The chapter is divided into three segments. In the first portion, we review the current state of research specific to demanding and withdrawing during conflict between parents and their adolescent children. The second section presents a study of the association between the use of demands and withdrawal in mother–adolescent conflict with the experience of negative emotion and perceptions of conflict resolution. The concluding remarks place the results of the current study within the larger context of parent–adolescent conflict and provide future directions for the study of demand and withdraw behaviors in this context.

Explicating Demand and Withdraw Behavior in Parent–Adolescent Conflict

The behaviors of demand and withdraw, though often enacted within close relationships (Caughlin, 2002), are maladaptive approaches to conflict engagement. Demand behavior includes complaining, nagging, or commanding of another, while withdraw behavior is manifest through disengaging or avoiding an issue under discussion (Caughlin, 2002; Christensen, 1988; Malis & Roloff, 2006; Vogel & Karney, 2002). Though conflict during adolescence may not be particularly severe (Caughlin & Ramey, 2005), conflict is characteristic of family relationships and for adolescents occurs more often within the parent–child relationship than in other close relations (Branje et al, 2013). When conflicts are managed through the employment of demands and withdrawal, the individuals within the relationship and the relationship overall may be adversely affected.

Initial efforts by Caughlin and Ramey (2005) to explore demand and withdraw behavior within parent-adolescent relationships demonstrate that both parties engage in these behaviors during conflict. Specifically, adolescents were more likely to withdraw from conflict than were parents, while parents engaged in demanding more so than did adolescents. The authors also examined differences in employment of these behaviors according to topic ownership. Parents were more likely to engage in demanding behavior when discussing a topic in which they were seeking a change from their child. In turn, adolescents demanded more and withdrew less when engaged in discussion of an issue in which they desired a change in their parent. Together, the results of Caughlin and Ramey's (2005) analysis indicate the conditions under which parents and adolescent children enact demand and withdrawal communication behaviors.

The work of Caughlin and Malis (2004a; 2004b) furthered understanding of demanding and withdrawing within parent-adolescent relationships by illustrating the detrimental outcomes associated with the enactment of these behaviors during conflict. When examining audio recordings of conflicts between a parent and a child 13 to 16 years of age, the authors identified parents' and adolescents' retrospective self-reports of the dyadic pattern of demand-withdraw along with adolescents' post-conversation reports of the pattern to be negatively associated with parents' perceived relational satisfaction. Additionally with regard to adolescents' satisfaction, retrospective and post-conversation self-reports of the demand-withdraw pattern were negatively associated with adolescents' relational satisfaction (Caughlin & Malis, 2004a). Not only may engagement in the dyadic pattern of demand-withdraw be detrimental to perceptions of the parent–child relationship, but also may have negative implications for the individual's adjustment. Caughlin and Malis (2004b) noted frequent implementation of the dyadic pattern of demand-withdraw in the parent-adolescent relationship was associated with low self-esteem and high substance use (i.e., alcohol and drugs) for both parents and adolescents.

Global examinations of conflictual interactions between parents and early adolescents are consistent with the work of Caughlin and colleagues as well. For instance, Branje (2008) conducted a study of conflict discussions of 30 dyads consisting of a mother and her 12-year-old daughter. Branje (2008) noted that when mothers and daughters perceived their relationship to be characterized by open communication, daughters were more actively engaged in conflict interactions whereas mothers were more passive. Additionally, high levels of variability in the dyadic interaction were associated with mothers and daughters perceiving one another as dominant in the relationship. Branje's (2008) results, though not specific to the behaviors of demand and withdraw, suggest a pattern similar to that identified in earlier work of communication behavior during parent-adolescent conflict.

Though previous efforts provide insight into the use of demands and withdrawal within parent-adolescent conflict, evidence is limited regarding associations to episodic conflict outcomes. Considering, conflict is an emotional experience for individuals and that the enactment of conflict behaviors is often tied to one's experience of various emotions (Jones, 2001); it is of interest to delineate the connection between demand and withdraw behaviors and subjective emotion experience within the context of parent-adolescent conflict.

A Spotlight Study of Demand and Withdraw Behavior with Episodic Conflict Outcomes

As demand and withdraw behaviors are primarily studied within the marital and romantic relationship contexts (e.g., Caughlin & Huston, 2002; Heavey et al, 1995; Vogel & Karney, 2002), a limited number of studies have linked romantic partners' use of these behaviors to emotion experience (Huggins & Samp, 2014; Tashiro & Frazier, 2007; Verhofstadt et al, 2005). For example, Verhofstadt and colleagues (2005) analyzed marital partners' discussions of a problem in their relationship with partners' subsequent experience of negative affect. Wives' use of demand behavior influenced self-reported experience of negative affect, while withdraw behavior was not a significant predictor. Additionally, Tashiro and Frazier

(2007) experimentally manipulated romantic dating partners' emotion experience prior to discussions of problematic areas in the couples' relationship. The emotion condition was found to be a significant predictor of one's use of both demand and withdraw behavior, such that those in the negative emotion condition exhibited more demanding and withdrawing than did those in the positive emotion condition. Finally, exploring romantic partners' discrete emotion experience during conflict, Huggins and Samp (2014) identified the experience of both anger and sadness as positively associated with demanding; however, the experience of these emotions was not significantly associated with withdrawal.

Despite prior evidence for the association of demand and withdraw behaviors to emotion experience, the reviewed studies are specific to romantic attachments and do not speak to the potential relationship among these variables in the mother–adolescent conflict context. Work in the field of family psychology provides indirect evidence for the potential association between a parent's demands and withdrawal to influence child emotional response during conflict. For example, interparental conflict behaviors such as hostility and withdrawal have been positively associated with child emotional reactions, child distress symptoms, and negative adolescent outcomes (Cummings et al, 2008; Davies et al, 2006; Miga et al, 2012). Nevertheless, scarce research explores the reciprocal nature of the mother-adolescent relationship with regard to emotion experience during conflict. Examination of this reciprocal relationship has the potential to shed light on how emotions may be linked to functional and dysfunctional conflict behaviors and episodic conflict outcomes (Emery, 2014). Therefore, we consider both mothers' and adolescents' use of demands and withdrawal in relation to subjective emotion experience for a more comprehensive assessment of conflict dynamics.

Our focus on mothers as the parent of interest stems from the understanding that both sons and daughters experience more conflict and are more openly expressive with their mothers than with their fathers during adolescence (Branje, 2008; Caughlin & Ramey, 2005; Collins & Laursen, 2004; Noller & Callan, 1988). Following the assumption from family systems theory that understanding of perceptions and actions of individuals within a family should account for the mutual influence of family members (Emery, 2014; Minuchin, 1985), we examine how the reciprocal parent–adolescent relationship may be associated with functional and dysfunctional conflict behaviors and outcomes. Specifically, we seek to elucidate the relationship of mothers' and adolescents' use of demanding and withdrawing behavior to their subjective experience of negative emotion and perceptions of conflict resolution.

Negative Emotion Experience

Much relationship research explores the association between the utilization of destructive approaches to conflict and negative emotion as conflict is considered to be challenging process for relationships that is tied to emotion experience. Negative emotion, specifically, has been linked to damaging outcomes to close relationships (Martini & Busseri, 2012); yet, this association has not been demonstrated in the context of interest: mother-adolescent conflict. Included in negative emotion is the experience of anger and sadness, two fundamental negative emotions (Ortony & Turner, 1990) that may be detrimental to both general relationship functioning and the specific process of conflict in close relationships (Mikulincer & Shaver, 2005). Negative emotion, which also involves feeling frustrated or upset, may be positively associated with the use of destructive communication behaviors such as demands and withdrawal considering negative emotion may be externally conveyed via dominance (Gottman, 1994) and blaming one's partner (Sanford, 2007; Smith & Lazarus, 1990). For example, Creasey and Hesson-McInnis (2001) studied romantic partners' retrospective accounts of conflict, finding participants' self-reports of trying to dominate one's partner were positively correlated with self-reported experience of anger. The characterization of demand behavior as blaming, criticizing, and pressuring a partner to change aligns with the dominant and destructive behaviors associated with anger experience in past close relationship conflict research (Heavey et al, 1993). Thus, we propose:

H1a: A mother's use of demand behavior will be positively associated with her own experience of negative emotion.
H1b: An adolescent's use of demand behavior will be positively associated with his/her own experience of negative emotion.

Though demand behavior has been associated with negative emotion experience in prior examinations of close relationship conflict, the evidence for the relationship between withdrawal and the experience of negative emotion is less clear. For example, studies of romantic relationship partners have outlined a significant positive association between demanding behavior and negative emotion experience, while also reporting the association to be non-significant for withdrawal (Huggins & Samp, 2014; Verhofstadt et al., 2005). The absence of significant relationships between withdraw behavior and negative emotion experience in previous investigations may be due in part to the nature of withdrawal as a signifier of apathy and indifference (Gottman, 1993). According to this characterization, enactment of withdrawal would not be significantly associated with emotion response and instead would imply a lack of emotional involvement in the conflict and perhaps the relationship as a whole. Yet, an association between withdrawing and negative emotion experience has been established in prior research (Tashiro & Frazier, 2007). Considering the inconsistent findings in previous studies between the use of withdrawing and negative emotion experience, we question:

RQ1a: What is the association (if any) between a mother's use of withdraw behavior and her negative emotion experience?
RQ1b: What is the association (if any) between an adolescent's use of withdraw behavior and his/her negative emotion experience?

We also seek to understand how the enactment of destructive conflict behaviors by one's family member may influence one's self-reported experience of negative emotion. According to family systems theory, understanding of individuals within the family must account for the interdependence and mutual influence of family members (Emery, 2014; Minuchin, 1985); therefore, we seek to determine how a mother's demand and withdraw behavior may influence an adolescent's negative emotion experience (and vice versa). Yet, prior research tends to focus exclusively on the influence of parental behavior on child outcomes. For example, Davies and colleagues (2006) identified interparental hostility, as defined by the use of demands and disengagement (i.e. withdrawal), as predicting child emotional reactivity both concurrently and prospectively. Additional studies indicate the influence of interparental conflict on child and adolescent adjustment including negative emotional reactivity (Goeke-Morey et al, 2013; Miga et al, 2012). Together, these results point to the potential for a mother's demand and withdraw behavior to be positively associated with her adolescent child's experience of negative emotion. Though not explicitly examined in earlier studies, the assumptions of family systems theory would lead us to believe that this relationship may also be observed from adolescent child to parent, such that an adolescent's use of demanding and withdrawing should be positively associated with a mother's negative emotion experience. We put forth the following predictions:

H2: Mother (a) demand and (b) withdraw behavior will be positively associated with adolescent negative emotion experience.

H3: Adolescent (a) demand and (b) withdraw behavior will be positively associated with mother negative emotion experience.

Perceived Conflict Resolution

As both demand and withdraw behaviors are considered to be detrimental approaches to conflict as well as destructive to relationship functioning (Eldridge et al, 2007; Heavey et al, 1995), it is of interest to examine the association of these behaviors to one's own and one's family member's evaluations of the conversation. Prior research has explored perceived conflict resolvability (i.e., one's beliefs about potential resolution of the issue in the future) in connection with communication behavior but only through retrospective reports of serial arguments (e.g., Bevan et al, 2008; Hample et al, 2012; Malis & Roloff, 2006). Therefore, previous investigations of perceived resolvability have not identified the degree to which a singular conflict discussion leads to resolution of a problematic relational issue. Here, we assess both mother and adolescent perceptions of the extent to which discussion of a conflictual topic lead to issue resolution immediately after interaction.

Prior research of the relationship between demand behavior and perceptions of conflict resolution has elicited varied results. For example, scholars specifically examining self-reported use of the dyadic pattern of demand-withdraw found the association with perceived resolvability to be non-significant (Hample et al, 2012; McGinn et al, 2009). Additionally, when explicitly studying demand behavior in romantic relationship conflict, a significant association did not emerge between demanding and either self or partner perceptions of resolution (Huggins & Samp, 2013). Conversely, Heavey and colleagues (1993) observed demand behavior decreased perceptions of progress toward issue resolution. The limited support for the influence of demand behavior on perceptions of conflict resolution coupled with the examination of these behaviors in an understudied context of mother-adolescent conflict, we query:

RQ2: What is the association between mother demand behavior and (a) her own and (b) her adolescent child's perceptions of conflict resolution?
RQ3: What is the association between adolescent demand behavior and (a) his/her own and (b) his/her mother's perceptions of conflict resolution?

The evidence connecting withdrawal to perceptions of conflict resolution is more consistent than that for demand behavior. Research points to the negative association between self-reported avoidance and perceived resolvability of serial arguments (Bevan et al, 2007; Malis & Roloff, 2006), demonstrating the potential for withdrawal during a mother-adolescent conflict to be negatively related to self-reported perceptions of conflict resolution. Additionally, one's own withdrawal may lead to negative responses by a partner (Overall et al, 2010), suggesting withdrawal may also be negatively correlated with partner perceptions of resolution. Indeed, Huggins and Samp (2014) uncovered romantic partners' enactment of withdrawal to be negatively associated with both self and partner perceptions of conflict resolution. Thus, we assert:

H5: Mother withdraw behavior will be negatively associated with (a) her own and (b) her adolescent child's perceptions of conflict resolution.
H6: An adolescent's withdraw behavior will be negatively associated with (a) his/her own and (b) his/her mother's perceptions of conflict resolution.

Method

Participants

The community-based sample included 65 mother–adolescent dyads (33 mother–daughter dyads, 32 mother–son dyads) drawn from a larger data collection project. Families were recruited through community flyers and local school districts in a moderate-sized metropolitan area in the northeast. Families who demonstrated interest were included if they met the following criteria:

1. the adolescent and parents had lived together for the past three or more years;
2. one parent was the biological or adoptive parent of the adolescent;

3. the adolescent was between the ages of 12 and 15; and
4. all participants were fluent in English.

Efforts were made to obtain a sample of families representative of the county where data was collected. Mothers identified as White (83 percent), Black (11 percent), Asian (2 percent), American Indian or Alaska Native (2 percent), and more than one race (3 percent). The majority of mothers reported being the birth parent of the child (92 percent) with the remainder identifying as a step-parent (3 percent) or grandparent (5 percent). Median family income was in the range of $55,000 to $74,999 with 14 percent of the sample reporting a household income below $23,000.

Procedures

Families arrived at a laboratory space of a local community center to complete all tasks and measures for the larger data collection project. Upon arrival, families were provided with a tour of the facility and an overview of the visit. Mothers completed an informed consent process and provided permission for the adolescent to participate. After providing consent, mothers completed a survey of demographic information and measures for another study.

Conflict Interaction

Participants completed a 7-minute triadic, family conflict interaction task, where they were instructed to discuss a problematic issue specific to their relationship as parents and child. They were provided with a list of common issues parents and children may disagree about in the event that they had difficulty generating a topic for discussion. Participants were also instructed on the importance of every person "getting their point across." Common discussion topics included but were not limited to: school, chores/responsibilities, and siblings. Interactions were video and audio recorded for 7 minutes regardless of whether the discussion was completed by the end of the time period. At the conclusion of discussion, participants were separated to complete measures of subjective emotion experience and perceived resolvability of the conflict along with measures for another study. Based on a preliminary examination of the data and the understanding that adolescent children are more openly expressive with their mothers than with their fathers (Collins & Laursen, 2004; Noller & Callan, 1988), we elected to focus specifically on the exchange between the mother and adolescent child.

Independent Variables

Demand and Withdraw Behaviors

Two independent coders assessed mother and adolescent demand and withdraw behavior using a cultural informants approach, whereby coders were provided with minimal training (Caughlin, 2002; Christensen & Heavey, 1990). Coders were instructed to assess the degree to which an individual displayed the behavior at 1-minute intervals using a five-point, Likert-type scale (0 = did not display this behavior at all; 4 = intensely expressed). Interrater reliability was assessed using intra-class correlations. For each dimension, ratings were summed across all time points of assessment to create a total score for each dimension. Demand behavior was assessed based on two dimensions: *blame* (r_k = .86, M = 2.96, SD = 3.14) (i.e., blaming, accusing, criticizing a partner) and *pressure for change* (r_k = .75, M = 3.86, SD = 3.83) (i.e., hostile communication through demanding, nagging, pressuring for a change). Withdraw behavior was rated according to the dimensions of *avoidance* (r_k = .84, M = 5.38, SD = 5.03) (i.e., hesitating, changing topics, delaying discussion) and *withdrawal* (r_k = .88, M = 6.17, SD = 5.38) (i.e., disengaging, becoming silent, refusing to discuss the topic). Ratings for each dimension of the behavior were summed (range 0–37) to create a total score for demand (M = 6.79, SD = 5.91) and withdraw behavior (M = 11.55, SD = 8.26). A one-way ANOVA indicated that for adolescents, demand and withdraw behavior did not significantly differ according to gender (demand: $F(1, 59)$ = 3.51, p = .07, *ns*; withdraw: $F(1, 59)$ = 3.32, p = .07, *ns*).

Dependent Variables

Negative Emotion Experience

After completion of the conflict interaction, participants reported the extent to which they experienced negative emotion during the interaction. Participants were instructed: "How much did you feel each emotion during the discussion with your child (parent)?" Emotion experience was rated on a six-point, Likert-type scale (0 = not at all, 5 = a whole lot). Responses for each item (i.e., angry, sad, upset) were summed to create an overall score for negative emotion experience (α = .80, M = 3.12, SD = 3.22, range 0–14).

Perceived Conflict Resolution

Perceived conflict resolution was assessed using a single item stating, "How much did the discussion of the topic help you resolve this issue?" Perceived conflict resolution was rated on a six-point, Likert-type scale (0 = not at all, 5 = a whole lot). An independent one-sample *t*-test comparing resolution scores to the scale midpoint (= 3) indicated that on average (M = 1.35, SD = 1.30) participants did not view the conflict as resolved ($t(129)$ = −14.46, p < .001).

Results

To account for interdependence of reports from family members, multi-level modeling (MLM) analyses treated individual participants as nested within family.

Analyses were conducted specific to the behavior of interest (i.e., demand or withdraw) with the individual total score for the behavior entered as the dependent variable and the score for negative emotion experience or perceived resolvability entered as a fixed factor. For all hypotheses and research questions, two analyses were conducted: one for mothers and one for adolescents.

Demand and Withdraw Behavior, Negative Emotion Experience

Self-Behavior

H1 asserted (a) mother and (b) adolescent demand behavior would be positively associated with one's own experience of negative emotion. For *mothers*, the association between demand behavior and one's experience of negative emotion was non-significant ($\beta = .13$, $t(60) = 1.78$, $p = .08$, ns). However for *adolescents*, one's own demand behavior was positively associated with one's experience of negative emotion ($\beta = .29$, $t(61) = 3.96$, $p < .001$). *H1b* is supported.

RQ1 sought to understand the potential association between (a) mothers' and (b) adolescents' use of withdrawal and their own negative emotion experience. For both mothers and adolescents, withdraw behavior was not significantly correlated with one's experience of negative emotion (mothers: $\beta = .05$, $t(60) = .70$, $p = .48$, ns; adolescents: $\beta = -.01$, $t(61) = -.14$, $p = .92$, ns).

Partner Behavior

H2 proposed that both mother (a) demand and (b) withdraw behavior would be positively associated with adolescent self-reported negative emotion experience. Mother demand was not significantly associated with adolescent's reports of negative emotion experience ($\beta = .30$, $t(60) = .58$, $p = .56$, ns). Thus, *H2a* was not supported. However, consistent with predictions, mother withdrawal was positively associated with adolescent's experience of negative emotion ($\beta = 1.20$, $t(60) = 2.38$, $p = .02$). *H2b* was supported.

H3 put forth that adolescent (a) demand and (b) withdraw behavior would be positively associated with mother self-reported negative emotion experience. In alignment with *H3*, adolescent demand behavior was positively associated with mother's negative emotion experience ($\beta = 1.23$, $t(61) = 2.30$, $p = .025$). However, adolescent withdraw behavior was not significantly associated with mother experience of negative emotion ($\beta = -.03$, $t(61) = -.08$, $p = .94$, ns). As such, *H3a* was supported.

Demand and Withdraw Behavior, Perceived Conflict Resolution

Demand

RQ2 questioned the possible association between mother demand behavior and (a) her own and (b) her adolescent child's perceptions of conflict resolution.

Mother demand behavior was not a significant predictor of one's own ($\beta = -.01$, $t(60) = -.44$, $p = .66$, ns) or one's adolescent child's perceptions of resolution ($\beta = -.0001$, $t(60) = -.04$, $p = .97$, ns).

RQ3 sought to determine the potential association between adolescent demand behavior and (a) his/her own and (b) his/her mother's perceptions of conflict resolution. A significant association did not emerge between adolescent enactment of demand behavior and one's own perception of resolvability ($\beta = -.01$, $t(61) = -.55$, $p = .59$, ns). Yet, adolescent use of demand behavior was negatively associated with mother's perceptions of resolution ($\beta = -.07$, $t(61) = -3.07$, $p = .003$).

Withdrawal

H5 hypothesized that a mother's withdrawal would be negatively associated with (a) her own and (b) her adolescent child's perceptions of conflict resolution. Consistent with predictions, mothers' use of withdrawal was negatively associated with one's own perceptions of conflict resolution ($\beta = -.06$, $t(60) = -2.47$, $p = .02$). However, this association was non-significant for adolescent's perception of resolution ($\beta = .004$, $t(60) = .22$, $p = .83$, ns). H5a was supported.

H6 proposed that an adolescent's withdrawal would be negatively associated with (a) his/her own and (b) his/her mother's perceptions of conflict resolution. Adolescent withdrawal behavior was not a significant predictor of one's own or one's mother's perceptions of resolution (self: $\beta = .001$, $t(61) = .43$, $p = .67$, ns; mother: $\beta = .01$, $t(61) = .62$, $p = .54$, ns).

Discussion of Implications for Parent–Adolescent Conflict

After a review of prior work outlining the use of demand and withdraw behavior within the parent-adolescent relationship, we presented a study of the association of demand and withdraw behaviors of a mother and her adolescent child with their self-reported negative emotion experience and perceptions of conflict resolution in an effort to better understand conflict dynamics within this relational context. One's enactment of demand behavior was positively associated with negative emotion experience for adolescents, while one's family member's use of destructive conflict behavior was associated with one's own experience of negative emotion. More specifically, mother withdraw behavior was positively associated with adolescent negative emotion experience, while adolescent demand behavior was positively associated with mother negative emotion experience. Concerning perceptions of resolution, the interdependence of mother and adolescent behavior emerged such that enactment of adolescent demand and mother withdraw behavior were negatively correlated with mother's perceptions of conflict resolution. We now present the implications of these results for a more nuanced understanding of the dynamics of mother-adolescent conflict.

Self-Demand and Withdraw Behavior, Negative Emotion Experience

Demand

Adolescents' use of demand behavior during conflict was positively associated with self-reported experience of negative emotion; however, the association between demand behavior and emotion experience was non-significant for mothers. Our findings point to the potential for power in the relationship to differentiate the association between demand behavior and one's negative emotion experience. For instance, prior research of parent–adolescent conflict indicates the dyadic pattern of parent-demand/adolescent-withdraw occurs more frequently than adolescent-demand/parent-withdraw (Caughlin & Ramey, 2005). The prevalence of parent-demand behavior suggests demanding during conflict may be more normative for mothers than for adolescents. Thus, mothers' demanding behavior may not be significantly associated with their experience of negative emotion, which is often elicited by disruption of both one's goals (Guerrero & LaValley, 2006; Lazarus, 1991) and one's expected patterns of behavior (Fehr & Harasymchuk, 2005). Conversely, for adolescents, engaging in demand behavior may be non-normative and reflect a disturbance in typical patterns of behavior which may be concurrently associated with negative emotion experience. A goals-based approach to demand and withdraw behavior could also serve as an explanation for this pattern of results, such that mothers' and adolescents' motivations for engaging in demand behavior may elicit different emotional responses (Caughlin & Scott, 2010). For example, in romantic relationship conflict, the goals to dominate/control the conversation and to express frustration were both positively associated with demand behavior (Huggins & Samp, 2013). If applied to mother–adolescent conflict, these goals may elucidate the differential relationship between self-demand behavior and experience of negative emotion for mothers and adolescents.

Withdrawal

Consistent with the non-significant association demonstrated in some prior investigations of romantic relationship conflict (Huggins & Samp, 2014; Verhofstadt et al., 2005), a significant correlation between withdrawal and negative emotion experience did not emerge. These results are reflective of the characterization of withdrawal as indicative of indifference and apathy toward the conflict situation (Gottman, 1993). Rather than being associated with the experience of negative emotion, withdrawal may instead point to an absence of emotion experience and indifference toward one's partner and the relationship (Davies et al, 2006; Gottman, 1993). Additionally, when enacted by mothers, withdrawal may reflect a level of ease or comfort in allowing the adolescent child to assert autonomy in the relationship and a more smooth transition toward a horizontal mother–child relationship (Branje, 2008).

Partner Demand and Withdraw Behavior, Negative Emotion Experience

Demand

We explored the reciprocal relationship between the behaviors of mothers and adolescents during conflict to elucidate how emotions may be linked to dysfunctional conflict dynamics. Although mother demand behavior was predicted to be positively associated with adolescent negative emotion experience, this relationship was non-significant in the current study. Although speculative, in the context of parent–adolescent conflict, adolescent children may be "immune" to mother's demand behavior as mothers' pressuring for change and blaming a child may be consistent with adolescents' expectations for parental behavior. Indeed, Noller and Callan (1988) state that adolescents tend to overestimate negativity in the parent–child relationship. Hence, being presented with a mother's overtly negative, demanding behavior may not elicit negative emotion from adolescents because this behavior by mothers is expected.

On the other hand, adolescent demand behavior may come as a surprise to mothers who may be expecting to control the conversation. For example, though adolescence is socially accepted as a time period of establishing autonomy from one's parents, mothers and adolescents may differ in their perceptions of when and how autonomy is established (Van Doorn et al, 2011). If this is the case, an adolescent's demanding of his/her mother as a means of asserting autonomy during conflict may be distressing to the mother. Sillars et al (2010) also point to parents' feelings of responsibility for adolescent adjustment. Though speculative, displays of directly hostile behavior by an adolescent child may lead to a mother's negative emotion experience as a reaction to feeling responsible for the adolescent's use of destructive behavior. In all, our results are consistent with the assumption of family systems theory of the interdependence of individual members within a family unit.

Withdrawal

The reciprocal relationship between mothers and adolescents was also supported by the findings concerning the influence of family member withdrawal on one's negative emotion experience. Mother withdraw behavior was positively associated with adolescent experience of negative emotion. Considering mother demand was not significantly associated with adolescent negative emotion experience, our results suggest a mother's withdrawal from a conflict may be more detrimental to an adolescent child's functioning than overtly hostile demand behavior. In support of this assertion, Fehr and Harasymchuk (2005) note that when an individual expresses dissatisfaction, a neglect response from a romantic relationship partner elicits strong negative emotion when compared to a neglect response from a friend. Davies and colleagues (2006) also state a positive association between parental disengagement and child emotional reactivity. Accordingly, withdrawal by one's mother during a conflict interaction may be particularly distressing to an adolescent child. Together our results point to the mutual influence of mother and adolescent behavior on negative emotion experience during conflict interactions.

Demand and Withdraw Behavior, Perceived Conflict Resolution

Demand

Corresponding to prior research (Huggins & Samp, 2014), one's demand behavior was not significantly associated with one's own perception of conflict resolution. These results suggest that although individuals may employ demand behavior during conflict, they still may not believe this behavior to be an effective form of conflict management. However, the use of demand behavior by one's family member may be detrimental to one's perceptions of the conflict as progressing toward resolution. Here, adolescent demand behavior was negatively associated with a mother's perception of resolution. Our results for adolescent demand behavior add nuance to the understanding of the mutual influence of mother and adolescent behavior by indicating the potential for adolescents to shape mothers' cognition in response to conflict. Adolescent influence on mothers may be indicative of the increased engagement with mothers during this period of transition and may also reflect that as children mature, approaches to conflict shift from vertical to horizontal (Van Doorn et al., 2011).

Withdrawal

One's enactment of withdrawal was predicted to be negatively correlated with one's own and one's family member's perceptions of resolution. For mothers, withdrawal was negatively associated with one's perceptions of conflict resolution, consistent with the findings of prior research linking self-reported avoidance to perceptions of serial argument resolution (Bevan et al, 2007; Malis & Roloff, 2006). For adolescents, the non-significant relationship between withdrawal and perceptions of resolution may result from withdraw behavior being viewed as a normative response to parent–child conflict, which would be consistent with research stating withdrawal from one's parents increases during adolescence (Caughlin & Malis, 2004b; Van Doorn et al, 2011). Additionally, the results concerning the influence of one's withdraw behavior on one's family member's perception of resolution were non-significant, counter to both our prediction and prior research of romantic relationship conflict. Though speculative, significant results may not have emerged due to distinctions between romantic and parent–child attachments. For instance, romantic relationships may require higher levels of engagement from a communicative partner than may be expected in mother–adolescent interactions which, in turn, may lead to more detrimental outcomes being associated with withdraw behavior in romantic relationships.

Limitations

The current study examining a community sample of mother–adolescent child dyads contributes to understanding of parent-adolescent conflict by highlighting the influence of demands and withdrawal on negative emotion experience and perceptions of conflict resolution. Still, limitations of our investigation should be noted. First, our sample focused on the mother-adolescent dyad specifically, limiting generalizability to overall parent–child conflict. Therefore, the current findings should be applied with caution to communicative interactions between fathers and adolescent children. Second, the use of a single-item to assess perceptions of conflict resolution should be altered in the future for a more comprehensive measure of perceived resolvability of the conflict topic. Third, it would be beneficial to evaluate mothers' and adolescents' post-conversation reports of the use of demands and withdrawal as a counterpoint to the observer judgments of the behaviors, as individuals within the dyad are able to frame interaction-specific behavior within the context of overarching relationship dynamics (Caughlin & Ramey, 2005; Sillars et al, 2004).

Next Steps in the Analysis of Parent–Adolescent Conflict

Our study refines understanding of conflict dynamics in the mother-adolescent child relationship and expands understanding of the influence of demand and withdraw behavior to negative emotion experience, which is underexplored in prior research. Consistent with the understanding that parent behavior shapes child outcomes, mother withdrawal was positively associated with adolescent negative emotion experience. In addition, our results contribute to the understanding that children also exert an influence on their parents. The effect of adolescent behavior on parent outcomes is demonstrated in the current study by the significant positive association of adolescent demand behavior with both one's own and one's mother's negative emotion experience, along with the significant negative relationship between adolescent demand and mother perceptions of conflict resolution. The findings of our investigation shed new light on the ability of adolescents to shape mothers' emotional experience and cognitions in response to parent-adolescent conflict. Additionally, the significant positive association between mother withdraw behavior and adolescent negative emotion experience suggests a mother's withdrawal from a conflict interaction may be more detrimental to adolescent functioning than overtly aggressive conflict behavior. Even still, much remains to be uncovered concerning conflict in the close relationship context of parent-adolescent relationships.

For example, as the current study examined families with early adolescent children, these results do not speak to the changing nature of parent-child conflict which may include alterations in the use of demand and withdraw behaviors and the association to episodic outcomes over time. Understanding of the changes in parent-child relational dynamics as children mature from early adolescence to young adulthood is an important avenue for future study as prior research indicates conflict frequency and intensity levels off as children mature (Branje et al, 2013). However, longitudinal research can be challenging for scholars to conduct due to time and financial restraints for obtaining parent-adolescent dyads to complete laboratory-based interaction studies. These difficulties may explain, in part, the limited amount of communication-specific research of parent-adolescent conflict.

Though examination of changing dynamics of parent-adolescent conflict as children mature presents a challenge to communication scholars, cross-sectional interaction research presents the opportunity to elucidate the variability of conflict behaviors and emotional responses across a single-interaction. Future efforts should include sequential analysis of conflict behaviors to more closely outline how parents' and adolescents' strategic management of problem discussions influences one another's emotion experience and perceptions of conflict resolution as an interaction progresses (e.g., Branje, 2008). As conflict is often the result of perceived incompatibility of goals between interactants (Canary, 2003; Dillard et al, 1989; Samp, 2009), next steps should explore how parents' and adolescents' goals for the interaction may vary across the conflict and, in turn, may influence changes in behaviors enacted and emotions expressed.

Finally, the results of our study point to the potential of and continued need for investigation of father–adolescent dyads and exploration of the more complex dynamics of parents-adolescent triads which could provide additional depth of understanding regarding conflict between parents and children. Family systems theory suggests individual family members are interdependent such that the behaviors of a single person must be placed in the context of overarching family dynamics (Emery, 2014; Minuchin, 1985). Analyzing the interplay among all individuals in the triad would therefore provide a fuller picture of the parent–adolescent relationship, particularly given the evidence that dynamics within the marital relationship may be consequential to child adjustment outcomes (Cummings et al, 2008; Davies et al, 2006; Goeke-Morey et al, 2013). Overall, the results of this chapter demonstrate the reciprocal nature of the mother–adolescent relationship with regard to conflict behavior, negative emotion experience, and perceptions of conflict resolution, while highlighting the potential for future exploration of conflict within the close relationships between parents and adolescent children.

References

Adams, R. & Laursen, B. (2001). The organization and dynamics of adolescent conflict with parents and friends. *Journal of Marriage and Family, 63*, 97–110.

Bevan, J. L., Finan, A., & Kaminsky, A. (2008). Modeling serial arguments in close relationships: The serial argument process model. *Human Communication Research, 34,* 600–624. doi: 10.1111/j.1468-2958.2008.00334.x

Bevan, J. L., Tidgewell, K. D., Bagley, K. C., Cusanelli, L., Hartstern, M., Holbeck, D., & Hale, J. L. (2007). Serial argumentation goals and their relationships to perceived resolvability and choice of conflict tactics. *Communication Quarterly, 55,* 61–77. doi: 10.1080/01463370600998640

Braiker, H. B., & Kelley, H. H. (1979). Conflict in the development of close relationships. In R. L. Burgess & T. L. Huston (Eds.), *Social exchange in developing relationships* (pp135–168). New York: Academic Press.

Branje, S. J. T. (2008). Conflict management in mother-daughter interactions in early adolescence. *Behaviour, 145,* 1627–1651.

Branje, S., Laursen, B., & Collins, W. A. (2013). Parent–child communication during adolescence. In A. L. Vangelisti (Ed.), *The Routledge handbook of family communication,* (pp271–286). New York: Routledge.

Canary, D. J. (2003). Managing interpersonal conflict: A model of events related to strategic choices. In J. O. Greene & B. R. Burleson (Eds.), *Handbook of communication and social interaction skills* (pp515–550). Mahwah, NJ: Lawrence Erlbaum.

Caughlin, J. P. (2002). The demand/withdraw pattern of communication as a predictor of marital satisfaction over time: Unresolved issues and future directions. *Human Communication Research, 28(1),* 49–85. doi: 10.1111/j.1468-2958.2002.tb00798.x

Caughlin, J. P., & Huston, T. L. (2002). A contextual analysis of the association between demand/withdraw and marital satisfaction. *Personal Relationships, 9,* 95–119. doi: 10.1111/1475-6811.00007

Caughlin, J. P., & Malis, R. S. (2004a). Demand/withdraw communication between parents and adolescents as a correlate of relational satisfaction. *Communication Reports, 17,* 59–71. doi: 10.1080/08934210409389376

Caughlin, J. P., & Malis, R. S. (2004b). Demand/withdraw communication between parents and adolescents: Connections with self-esteem and substance use. *Journal of Social and Personal Relationships, 21(1),* 125–148. doi: 10.1177/0265407504039843

Caughlin, J. P., & Ramey, M. E. (2005). The demand/withdraw pattern of communication in parent-adolescent dyads. *Personal Relationships, 12,* 337–355.

Caughlin, J. P., & Scott, A. M. (2010). Toward a communication theory of the demand/withdraw pattern of interaction in interpersonal relationships. In S. W. Smith & S. R. Wilson (Eds.), *New directions in interpersonal communication research* (pp180–200). Thousand Oaks, CA: Sage.

Christensen, A. (1988). Dysfunctional interaction patterns in couples. In P. Noller & M. A. Fitzpatrick (Eds.), *Perspectives on marital interaction* (pp31–52). Philadelphia: Multilingual Matters.

Christensen, A., & Heavey, C. L. (1990). Gender and social structure in the demand/withdraw pattern of marital conflict. *Journal of Personality and Social Psychology, 59,* 73–81. doi: 10.1037/0022-3514.59.1.73

Collins, W. A., & Laursen, B. (2004). Parent–adolescent relationships and influences. In R. M. Lerner & L. Steinberg (Eds.), *Handbook of adolescent psychology* (2nd ed., pp331–361). Hoboken, NJ: Wiley.

Creasey, G., & Hesson-McInnis, M. (2001). Affective responses, cognitive appraisals, and conflict tactics in late adolescent romantic relationships: Associations with attachment orientations. *Journal of Counseling Psychology, 48,* 85–96. doi: 10.1037//0022- O167.48.1.85

Cummings, E. M., Goeke-Morey, M. C., & Papp, L. M. (2008). A family-wide model for the role of emotion in family functioning. *Marriage and Family Review, 34*(1/2), 13–34. doi: 10.1300/J002v34n01_02

Davies, P. T., Sturge-Apple, M. L., Winter, M. A., Cummings, E. M., & Farrell, D. (2006). Child adaptational development in contexts of interparental conflict over time. *Child Development, 77,* 218–233. doi: 009–3920/2006/7701–0015

Dillard, J. P., Segrin, C., & Harden, J. M. (1989). Primary and secondary goals in the production of interpersonal influence messages. *Communication Monographs, 56,* 19–38.

Eldridge, K. A., Sevier, M., Jones, J., Atkins, D. C., & Christensen, A. (2007). Demand-withdraw communication in severely distressed, moderately distressed, and nondistressed couples: Rigidity and polarity during relationship and personal problem discussions. *Journal of Family Psychology, 21,* 218–226. doi: 10.1037/0893–3200.21.2.218

Emery, R. E. (2014). Families as systems: Some thoughts on methods and theory. In S. M. McHale, P. Amato, & A. Booth (Eds.), *National symposium on family issues: Vol. 4. Emerging methods in family research* (pp109–124). doi: 10.1007/978-3-319-01562-0_7

Fehr, B., & Harasymchuk, C. (2005). The experience of emotion in close relationships: Toward an integration of the emotion-in-relationships and interpersonal script models. *Personal Relationships, 12,* 181–196. doi: 10.1111/j.1350–4126.2005.00110.x

Goeke-Morey, M. C., Papp, L. M., & Cummings, E. M. (2013). Changes in marital conflict and youth's responses across childhood and adolescence: A test of sensitization. *Development and Psychopathology, 25,* 241–251. doi: 10.1017/S0954579412000995

Gottman, J. M. (1993). The roles of conflict engagement, escalation, and avoidance in marital interaction: A longitudinal view of five types of couples. *Journal of Consulting and Clinical Psychology, 61,* 6–15.

Gottman, J. M. (1994). *What predicts divorce? The relationship between marital processes and marital outcomes.* Hillsdale, NJ: Lawrence Erlbaum.

Guerrero, L. K., & La Valley, A. G. (2006). Conflict, emotion, and communication. In J. G. Oetzel & S. Ting-Toomey (Eds.). *The SAGE handbook of conflict communication: Integrating theory, research, and practice* (pp69–96). Thousand Oaks, CA: SAGE.

Hample, D., Richards, A. S., & Na, L. (2012). A test of the conflict linkage model in the context of serial arguments. *Western Journal of Communication, 76*(5), 459–479. doi: 10.1080/10570314.2012.703361

Heavey, C. L., Christensen, A., & Malamuth, N. M. (1995). The longitudinal impact of demand and withdrawal during marital conflict. *Journal of Consulting and Clinical Psychology, 63,* 797–801. doi: 10.1037//0022–0006X.63.5.797

Heavey, C. L., Layne, C., & Christensen, A. (1993). Gender and conflict structure in marital interaction: A replication and extension. *Journal of Consulting and Clinical Psychology, 61,* 16–27. doi: 10.1037/0022-3514.59.1.73

Huggins, C. E., & Samp, J. A. (2013, November). A multiple goals approach to demand-withdraw within close relationship conflict. Paper to be presented to the Interpersonal Communication Division of the National Communication Association, Washington, DC.

Huggins, C. E. & Samp, J. A. (2014, April). Emotion experience as a predictor of demand and withdraw behavior within conflict. Paper presented to the Interpersonal Communication Division of the Southern States Communication Association, New Orleans, LA.

Jones, T. S. (2001). Emotional communication in conflict: Essence and impact. In W. F. Eadie & P. E. Nelson (Eds.), *The Language of Conflict and Resolution* (pp81–104). Thousand Oaks, CA: Sage Publications.

Knobloch, L. K., & Solomon, D. H. (2004). Interference and facilitation from partners in the development of interdependence within romantic relationships. *Personal Relationships, 11*, 115–130.

Laursen, B., & Collins, W. A. (1994). Interpersonal conflict during adolescence. *Psychological Bulletin, 115*, 197–209.

Laursen, B., & Collins, W. A. (2004). Parent–child communication during adolescence. In A. L. Vangelisti (Ed.), *Handbook of family communication* (pp333–348). Mahwah, NJ: Erlbaum.

Lazarus, R. S. (1991). Progress on a cognitive-motivational-relational theory of emotion. *American Psychologist, 46*, 819–834. doi: 10.1037/0003-066X.46.8.819

Malis, R. S., & Roloff, M. E. (2006). Demand/withdraw patterns in serial arguments: Implications for well-being. *Human Communication Research, 32*, 198–216. doi: 10.1111/j.1468-2958.2006.00009.x

Martini, T. S., & Busseri, M. A. (2012). Emotion regulation and relationship quality in mother-young adult child dyads. *Journal of Social and Personal Relationships, 29*(2), 185–205. doi: 10.1177/0265407511431056

McGinn, M. M., McFarland, P. T., & Christensen, A. (2009). Antecedents and consequences of demand/withdraw. *Journal of Family Psychology, 23*(5), 749–757. doi: 10.1037/a0016185

Miga, E. M., Gdula, J. A., & Allen, J. P. (2012). Fighting fair: Adaptive marital conflict strategies as predictors of future adolescent peer and romantic relationship quality. *Social Development, 21*(3), 443–460. doi: 10.1111/j.1467-9507.2011.00636.x

Mikulincer, M., & Shaver, P. R. (2005). Attachment theory and emotions in close relationships: Exploring the attachment-related dynamics of emotional reactions to relational events. *Personal Relationships, 12*, 149–168. doi: 10.1111/j.1350-4126.2005.00108.x

Minuchin, P. (1985). Families and individual development: Provocations from the field of family therapy. *Child Development, 56*, 289–302.

Noller, P., & Callan, V. J. (1988). Understanding parent-adolescent interactions: Perceptions of family members and outsiders. *Developmental Psychology, 24*, 707–714.

Ortony, A., & Turner, T. J. (1990). What's basic about basic emotions? *Psychological Review, 97*, 315–331. doi: 10.1037/0033-295X.97.3.315

Overall, N. C., Sibley, C. G., & Travaglia, L. K. (2010). Loyal but ignored: The benefits and costs of constructive communication behavior. *Personal Relationships, 17*, 127–148. doi: 10.1111/j.1475-6811.2010.01257.x

Samp, J. A. (2009). Communication goal theories. In S. Littlejohn & K. Foss (Eds.), *The encyclopedia of communication theory* (Vol. 1, pp129–132). Thousand Oaks, CA: Sage.

Sanford, K. (2007). Hard and soft emotion during conflict: Investigating married couples and other relationships, *Personal Relationships, 14*, 65–90. doi: 10.1111/j.1475-6811.2006.00142.x

Sillars, A. L., Canary, D. J., & Tafoya, M. (2004). Communication, conflict, and the quality of family relationships. In A. L. Vangelisti (Ed.), *Handbook of Family Communication* (pp413–446). Mahwah, NJ: Lawrence Erlbaum.

Sillars, A., Smith, T., & Koerner, A. (2010). Misattributions contributing to empathic (in)accuracy during parent-adolescent conflict discussions. *Journal of Social and Personal Relationships, 27*, 727–747. doi: 10.1177/0265407510373261

Smith, C. A., & Lazarus, R. S. (1990). Emotion and adaptation. In L. A. Pervin (Ed.), *Handbook of personality: Theory and research* (pp609–637). New York: Guilford.

Tashiro, T., & Frazier, P. (2007). The causal effects of emotion on couples' cognition and behavior. *Journal of Counseling Psychology, 54*, 409–422. doi: 10.1037/0022-0167.54.4.409

Van Doorn, M. D., Branje, S. J. T., & Meeus, W. H. J. (2011). Developmental changes in conflict resolution styles in parent-adolescent relationships: A four-wave longitudinal study. *Journal of Youth and Adolescence*, *40*, 97–107. doi: 10.1007/s10964–10010–9516–9517

Verhofstadt, L. L., Buysse, A., de Clercq, A., & Goodwin, R. (2005). Emotional arousal and negative affect in marital conflict: The influence of gender, conflict structure, and demand-withdrawal. *European Journal of Social Psychology*, *35*, 449–467. doi: 10.1002/ejsp.262

Vogel, D. L., & Karney, B. R. (2002). Demands and withdrawal in newlyweds: Elaborating on the social structural hypothesis. *Journal of Social and Personal Relationships*, *19*, 685–701. doi: 10.1177/0265407502195008

11

THE ROLE OF PERCEPTION IN INTERPARENTAL CONFLICT

Tamara D. Afifi, Shardé Davis, Anne F. Merrill, and Samantha Coveleski

An incredible amount of research has examined the impact of divorce and parents' conflict on children. While conflict is a natural and often productive part of families, negative forms of interparental conflict adversely affects children's relational and mental health (Fabricius & Luecken, 2007). Unfortunately, parents are often unaware of how they communicate during conflict and the effect it has on their children, particularly if their children become enmeshed in it. Children who feel caught between their parents' conflict tend to avoid talking about their feelings in an effort to minimize the conflict. Partially due to this avoidance, parents continue to communicate in ways that place their children in the middle of their disputes (see Afifi, 2003).

But what if parents and adolescents were asked to have a conversation about the parents' conflict and then reflect on how they communicated together about it? What would the adolescents think about their parents' communication? What would the parents think of their adolescents' communication? The goal of the current chapter is to shed light on these questions by examining the role of parents' and adolescents' perceptions via video recall procedures during such a discussion task. Researchers commonly use video recall procedures with conflict and have shown that people are not very good at deciphering what the other person is thinking during a conflict. This research also shows that people tend to make attributional errors about the other person's conflict behaviors and thoughts. Much of the video recall research has been conducted with couples or with parents and adolescents and shows that romantic partners often tend to blame their partner for negative conflict patterns, particularly when the couple is dissatisfied or in a turbulent relationship (e.g., Sillars et al, 2000). The research with parents and adolescents demonstrates, among other findings, that parents do not readily understand what their adolescents are thinking about their family conflict patterns (e.g., Sillars et al, 2005). But, no research, to our knowledge, has used video recall with parents and adolescents who are asked to reflect on parents' conflict. Introducing the adolescents' perspective could provide another important perspective on the parents' conflict that could be informative for parents and children alike. Before addressing the role of perception in interparental conflict, however, the research on parents' conflict in divorced and non-divorced families is discussed briefly.

Explicating Interparental Conflict in Divorced and Non-Divorced Families

Much of the research that has examined interparental conflict involves divorce. Even though divorce is important and it can have a direct impact on children (see Amato, 2000), interparental conflict is often more important than family structure in determining children's adaptation. Nevertheless, there are some noteworthy differences between divorced and non-divorced families that shape the nature of the conflict and how it affects children. Overall, children of divorce tend to report greater avoidance, feelings of being caught, and greater parental demand–withdraw patterns than children from first marriage families (Afifi & Schrodt, 2003). For instance, the top topics that children of divorce report avoiding with their parents are talking about money (e.g., child support payments) and the parents' relationship in an effort to prevent conflict between the parents and maintain the status quo of the family (Golish & Caughlin, 2002). These topics are often not the ones most commonly avoided in first marriage families. When examining topic avoidance across families more broadly, topics like sex, failure events, and activities with friends often surface (Guerrero & Afifi, 1995).

Conflict may also be more prevalent and problematic in divorced families compared to non-divorced families because of the focus of the parents' conflict. Specifically, conflict over co-parenting between spouses may be more common in divorced families than in non-divorced families. Conflict about co-parenting is a particularly important issue for families because conflict over child rearing has been found to be a stronger predictor of children's adjustment than either global levels of marital distress or conflicts in areas other than child rearing (Jouriles et al, 1991). In addition, parents' conflicts that involve their children elicit greater shame, self-blame, feelings of being caught, and symptoms of depressive and anxiety disorders in children than conflict that does not involve the children (Buchanan et al, 1991). In divorced families, research has consistently found that parents who cooperatively co-parent enhance children's well-being (Adamsons & Pasley, 2006). However, effective co-parenting can be difficult for some divorced parents, with approximately one third of them reporting highly antagonistic and unsupportive co-parenting (Maccoby & Mnookin, 1992). Antagonistic, unsupportive co-parenting relationships are not only harmful for children's adjustment, but for parents' post-divorce adjustment as well (Adamsons & Pasley, 2006; Amato, 2000).

Divorce also involves topics, behaviors, and other situational variables that shape conflict in ways that are different than in non-divorced families. Children and parents face numerous unique stressors that can create conflict (see Amato, 2000). Children after a divorce often engage in conflict with their siblings and parents because they have to learn how to live in two different households. They might also be experiencing loneliness and upheaval due to not being able to see both parents every day like they used to before the divorce. This stress can reveal itself in conflict with parents and siblings. They probably are also feeling financial restraints because their standard of living has changed. Children also tend to be very uncertain about the future of their family and their relationships, which can create stress and conflict within and between households. These are just a few examples of the unique stressors children of divorce face. These stressors change and often become magnified if the parents remarry. Children, for example, are often on a different "time clock" of divorce compared to their parents. Parents might be ready to remarry quicker than the children anticipate because the parents have been grieving the loss of their prior relationship much longer. Divorced parents often have additional stressors compared to parents who are still married. Following a divorce, parents' psychological, emotional, and financial resources may be drained (Barber & Demo, 2006), resulting in more stress, conflict and difficulties parenting. All of these stressors can be managed so that conflict is manageable, but their very nature makes conflict somewhat unique in divorced families.

In addition, while children from divorced and non-divorced families can both feel caught between their parents (Afifi & Schrodt, 2003), this issue tends to be more prominent in divorced families. Children feel caught, torn, or put in the middle of their parents when they experience divided loyalties to both parents (Buchanan et al, 1991). Children tend to feel caught between their parents when their parents request information about the other parent, disclose negative things about the other parent, ask the child to choose loyalties, and/or ask children to carry messages to the other parent (Buchanan et al, 1991). When children feel caught, it can negatively affect children's physical and mental health and weaken the parent-child relationship (Amato & Afifi, 2006). Research shows, however, that children's feelings of being caught dissipate approximately ten years after a divorce (Amato & Afifi, 2006). To the contrary, some children whose parents have a highly turbulent relationship and who remain married may never be able to escape their parents' conflict.

How do children tend to respond when they feel caught? Children often avoid talking about one parent in front of the other or engage in escape behaviors and activities to minimize conflict and maintain family harmony (Afifi, 2003; Afifi & Schrodt, 2003). Unfortunately, because children avoid talking about how uncomfortable they feel with their parents' conflict, parents are unaware of how damaging it is to their children and continue to disclose negative information about the other parent in front of the children. Feeling caught creates cognitive dissonance for children. One way to settle the dissonance is to side with one parent over the other (Kalmijn, 2013). Children often disengage from one parent and interact more with the other parent to restore a sense of balance – within themselves and their family as a whole (Kalmijn, 2013). In addition to avoidance, children sometimes respond to their parents' conflict with their own aggression. Children may socially model their parents' conflict when they do not even realize they are doing it. A final response to feeling caught is children directly confronting their parents and telling them to leave them out of their disputes. This typically happens as children get older and generate more communication competence to talk to their parents in this manner.

Theoretical Frameworks

Several theoretical frameworks can be used to help understand why children react to their parents' conflict the way they do. One such framework is Grych and Fincham's (1990) cognitive-contextual framework. This framework maintains that children's appraisals of marital conflict mediate the association between the state of the marriage and child well-being and adjustment. That is, as children try to make sense of their parents' conflict, they often blame themselves for the conflict and feel threatened by the conflict. A similar theoretical framework is Davies and Cumming's (1994) emotional security hypothesis. The emotional security hypothesis suggests that children's emotional security is threatened by parents' conflict. When parents' fight in an unhealthy manner, it makes children question their parents' marriage, their family life, and their attachments with their parents. Children, in turn, tend to respond physically, emotionally, and physiologically with extreme reactions. According to Schrodt and Afifi (2007), offspring of divorced families are more likely than those from intact families to report higher levels of marital conflict, lower levels of family satisfaction and higher levels of feeling caught. Because feeling caught occurs to the degree that children *perceive* themselves to be in the middle of marital conflict, it may explain why some, but not all, marital conflict directly affects children's relational and mental health (Schrodt & Afifi, 2007).

Similarities in Conflict Patterns between Children of Divorced and Non-Divorced Families

While there are differences in conflict between divorced and non-divorced families, research has revealed important similarities in conflict patterns between divorced and non-divorced families. Margolin et al (2001) found that for both divorced and married spouses, contentious conflict about issues such as finances can negatively spill over into how they interact about co-parenting. Most research shows that interparental conflict is a more important predictor of children's adjustment than divorce *per se* (Amato, 2000; Booth & Amato, 2001; Jekielek, 1998). In fact, children who tend to fare the worst are those whose parents have a highly conflicted marriage who never divorce (Amato & Afifi, 2006). Research continues to be necessary that examines the potential differences (as well as similarities) between divorced and non-divorced families' experiences of conflict.

The degree to which parents are able to communicate effectively with their children predicts children's well-being and social skills. Problematic parenting techniques (e.g., permissive or authoritarian parenting) have been linked to children's poor social skills (Davies & Cummings, 1994). Furthermore, parents' lack of communication skills, such as aggressiveness, abuse, negativity, criticism, demand-withdraw patterns, and lack of impulse control, can make the marital conflict environment even more harmful for children (Afifi & Hamrick, 2006). More effective conflict skills, however, such as taking the perspective of the other person, problem solving, collaboration, and emotion regulation, can help families function more effectively (Afifi & Hamrick, 2006). Therefore, the way in which parents approach conflict can either buffer or exasperate the impact of marital conflict on children.

Parents who are warm and confirming with their children can bolster overall family satisfaction and help children cope in stressful situations like divorce (Afifi & Hamrick, 2006; Schrodt & Ledbetter, 2012). Schrodt and Ledbetter (2012) examined parental confirmation (e.g., validation and respect) as a buffer against the harm that feeling caught has on children's family satisfaction. They found that family satisfaction was lowest when children who felt caught had disconfirming parents. Similar to parental disconfirmation, parental rejection is problematic for children, particularly if rejection is repetitive and long term, because it threatens children's emotional security (Davies & Cummings 1994). Parental rejection tends to be associated with internalizing and externalizing problems in children (Davies & Cummings, 1994).

The quality of parents' conflict resolution is also extremely important for how children perceive the conflict. Exposure to successful interparental conflict resolution can help children learn how to cope more effectively with conflict and teach them skills for how to manage it when it emerges in their own relationships (Kitzmann & Cohen, 2003). Therefore, both quality conflict resolution and parental confirmation are important factors that can help children feel more emotionally secure and satisfied in their families, even in presence of conflict or stress.

Certainly, then, the degree to which parents are skilled communicators, whether in divorced or non-divorced families, should shape the experience of interparental conflict in the family system. However, the level of parents' awareness or understanding of the effects of their conflict on others – particularly as it reflects on their own communication skills – is likely another vital factor in predicting the harmful effects of interparental conflict on the family.

A Spotlight Study of Parents' and Children's Perceptions of Interparental Conflict

There is a growing amount of research on children's feelings and perceptions about interparental conflict, but there is far less information on parents' perceptions of their conflict and its effects on their children. As a result, it is important for researchers to explore not only how children perceive interparental conflict, but also how the parents themselves think about the way they communicate in order to identify areas of parent–child misperception and the potential for increasing parents' awareness of the effects of their communication patterns on their children.

Children's perceptions and understanding of conflict are critical for understanding its impact upon children (Cummings et al, 1994; Grych et al, 1992). In fact, research has found that children's appraisals of marital conflict are often more accurate predictors of their adjustment than parents' reports of the same conflict. Cummings et al (1994) found that boys' appraisals of conflict were better predictors of their adjustment than their mothers' reports of the same conflict. In addition, compared to parents' perceptions, children's perceptions of interparental conflict were more strongly related to the relational quality of their friendships (Kitzmann & Cohen, 2003). Furthermore, while research has shown that family members tend to have congruency in their ratings of overt dimensions of family conflict, such as frequency and intensity (Grych et al, 1992), parents' and adolescents' ratings of children's subjective distress in response to the conflict are more incongruent (Kitzmann & Cohen, 2003). These findings highlight that children and parents may perceive interparental conflict in meaningfully different ways.

These differences between parents' and children's perceptions of interparental conflict beg the question as to whether many parents are fully aware of the effects of their conflict on their children. For example, research has found that parents are unaware of the appropriateness of their disclosures to their children (Sandler et al, 1985), the child's awareness of the conflict (Grych et al, 1992), and the child's discomfort with such interactions (Golish, 2003). However, there is some evidence that children's and mothers' perceptions of interparental conflict may be more similar than children's and fathers' perceptions given mothers' different roles in parenting and greater emotional connection with their children (Kitzmann & Cohen, 2003).

Furthermore, parents' lack of "awareness" of the effects of their conflict on their children may be more or less intentional. According to the DDM (Afifi et al, 2009), the motivations behind parents' decisions to expose their children to negative disclosures about the other parent/the divorce range from intentional and strategic to mindless. For example, some parents may simply have a lack of impulse control and unwittingly disclose too much or inappropriate information to their children (Afifi et al, 2009). From a fever model perspective, parents may engage in inappropriate disclosures to their children as a way to disclose the stress and emotions they have been harboring in an effort to feel better (i.e., catharsis). Finally, parents may also strategically and intentionally disclose negative information about the other parent to their child as a way to take control over their relational identities (e.g., strengthen the bond with their child, damage the identity of the other parent).

Interestingly, there may be important distinctions between parents who talk negatively about the other parent intentionally compared to those who accidently disclosed negative information. Afifi et al (2007) found that when former spouses who had a healthy or less strained relationship with each other appeared to be distressed by their inappropriate disclosures about the other parent to their children. Alternately, former spouses who had a strained relationship were not personally affected by their inappropriate disclosures. Former spouses who have a strained relationship may be less mindful of, or may be become habituated to, their inappropriate disclosures over time compared to former spouses who have a better relationship. These findings underscore the importance of understanding more about parents' perceptions and awareness of their own conflict communication patterns, given their strong impact on the children's and the entire family's well-being. Given that children's most frequent response to feeling caught between their parents' conflict is to avoid talking about it (Afifi, 2003), it is equally important to unearth what children are thinking when they are talking with their parent about the parents' relationship and how it is aligned or misaligned with their parent. Consequently, this chapter addresses the following research questions: What do parents and adolescent think about the parents' conflict and the way they talk about it with each other? How are these perceptions similar and different over the course of the conversation?

Method

Participants

The participants included 118 parents and one of their adolescent children (ages 15–22; M age = 16.5). Only one of the parents per family participated in the study with his/her child. Approximately half of the parents were married (n = 57) and half were divorced (n = 61). The divorced families experienced physical separation an average of 3.3 years prior. The majority of the parents (n = 30 or 49 percent) had primary physical custody of the children who were still residing in their house. Only 15 percent of the divorced parents were remarried. The sample consisted of a comparable amount of female (n = 64, 55 percent) and male (n = 53, 45 percent) adolescents, but most of the parents were mothers (n = 91 or 71 percent; fathers = 27 or 23 percent). The majority of the adolescents (n = 73; 62 percent) and parents (n = 82 or 70 percent) were Caucasian or Latino (adolescents = 27 or 23 percent; parents = 24 or 20 percent). The parents were also quite educated, with most of them having some college or an Associate's degree (n = 42 or 36 percent) or a Bachelor's degree (n = 36 or 31 percent). The median household income was $65,000.

Procedures

The families resided in southern California and were recruited through newspaper advertisements, social media, announcements at the local university, and flyers placed in local non-profit organizations and businesses. The study was advertised as a study on parent-child relationships. The parent and adolescents came to the university laboratory for a one-time visit lasting approximately 3 hours. After completing their consent form and an initial pre-interaction survey, the parents and adolescents sat together on a couch and engaged in small talk for seven minutes. They were then asked to talk with each other about something that was stressful and conflict inducing related to the parents' relationship for as long as they liked, up to 20 minutes (M length of interaction = 16 minutes). The parents and adolescents discussed this topic in private, but were informed that their discussion was being videotaped. The parents and adolescents then completed a post-interaction survey about the conversation. After completing the post-interaction survey, the parents and adolescents were separated into private rooms for the video recall portion of the study. A research assistant played back the video of their interaction, stopping it every minute. In addition to completing some Likert-type items (not reported here), the parents and adolescents were each asked to write down in an open-ended fashion what they were thinking during that minute of the conversation. The adolescents were also asked to think specifically about what the parent was disclosing in that moment and how they felt about it. The parents were asked to think about what they were disclosing and how they felt about it. All of the families were debriefed thoroughly before they left the laboratory.

Data Analysis

For this chapter, we used an interpretive method to examine the open-ended comments in the video recall. Open-ended coding and the constant comparative method (Glaser, 1992) were used to generate themes. Two of the authors read through the data independently of each other, reading the child and parent's responses minute after minute, with the parents' responses next to the child's responses. The researchers wrote down rough notes about key insights as they emerged within each dyad and across the transcripts. The researchers then came together and discussed their thoughts, slowly grouping their insights into broader concepts or themes, while continually comparing and contrasting the themes and accounting for discrepant cases (Strauss & Corbin, 1990; Glaser, 1978; Glaser & Strauss, 1967). The researchers then read through the data a second time, refining the themes that surfaced in the data. Some of the themes were combined and the themes were further developed into properties and sub-properties (Strauss & Corbin, 1990). Efforts were made to account for divergent cases and to best represent the data in its entirety. The themes were further developed by inserting quotes into each theme to demonstrate its properties. Special attention was also given to axial coding as much as possible by examining the larger theoretical connections across the themes and situating them within the context in which they occurred (Glaser, 1978; Strauss & Corbin, 1990).

Results

The parents' and adolescents' video recalls revealed a host of reactions about the way they communicated with each other during the interaction and the nature of the parents' conflict. Many of the reports conveyed parents' lack of understanding of children's stress during the parents' conflict and their awareness of the issues involved in the conflict, individual complicity in the disintegration of the conversation about the conflict, reflection on the quality of the parent–adolescent relationship, and contemplation about the effectiveness of the communication practices. A number of themes were identified from the video recall and are discussed below.

Varying Perceptions of the Conversation

Escalating Spiral of Negativity

Perceptions of the conversation assumed many forms for parents and adolescents during the video recall session. Some parents were reminded that their family endured a difficult time (e.g., divorce) in their lives. As parents became more aware, a high proportion of their thoughts during the video recall were negatively valenced and became progressively worse minute after minute. In this group, parents attended to a few negative aspects of the conversation and fixated on those aspects throughout the video recall. For this particular group of parents, the video recall exacerbated the parent's feeling of inadequacy about his/her communication patterns and the child's reaction to them. As one parent wrote, "Didn't really know [my] daughter felt THIS much pain" (Mother 58, minute 5).

Another significant contributor to the steady decline in parents' negative feelings about the conversation was the parents' lack of ability to effectively discuss (or communication efficacy) a stressful topic with their child. They knew that the topic needed to be discussed but did not know what to say or how to maneuver the awkward overtone permeating the conversation. The lack of communication efficacy was amplified by the child's disengagement. Many parents did not recognize their child's withdrawal from the conversation until they watched the video; they felt overwhelmed by the glaring reality that their desire to facilitate a fruitful discussion was trumped by their family situation and the fact that their child was not engaged in the conversation. Being asked to talk about something conflict inducing and stressful in the parents' relationship, matched with simultaneous disengagement by the child, negatively affected the parents' ability to effectively introduce and maintain a conversation with their child.

Consistently Positive and Uplifting

Not all conversations were cast in a negative light; there were a host of parents and adolescents who engaged in uplifting and hopeful discussions, with messages that progressed positively or remained consistently positive over time. Families with difficult family situations often started the conversation negatively, but became increasingly hopeful that their family would endure. As one mother mentioned, "I felt comfortable talking with him [son] ... I felt more confident in his values and how they have changed and I felt hopeful" (Mother 21, minute 17). Parents' hopefulness resulted from a realization that they employed good parenting practices and shared a strong emotional bond with their child. As this same parent indicated, "It seems we have a good relationship. [My son] always makes me laugh. He's a good kid" (Mother 21, minute 12). The conflict in their family reminded parents of their family's resiliency and family members' abundant love for one another. It also shed light on personality characteristics their child developed unbeknownst to the parent: "[My daughter] is such a young bright ... woman" (Mother 1, minute 12). Even though most families did not reach a positive conclusion until the end of the conversation, there were a handful of parents and children that expressed these sentiments throughout the video recall.

Children Caught in the Middle

The recall session not only increased awareness of the conflict situation and the parent's relationship with the child, it also helped parents to identify their child's position in the middle of the conflict, especially for divorced parents. For example, many divorced parents were saddened by their child's involuntary participation in the emotionally taxing process of divorce. Parents' feelings of guilt and shame surfaced in their video recalls as the parents began to align their child's despondency during the discussion to their marital discord, episodic verbal arguments, and derogation of the other parent. Children also expressed feeling caught in the middle of a family situation that did not directly concern them. Consider the following excerpt from a daughter responding to a discussion about divorce with her mother.

Adolescent thinks (family 118):

> [minute 3] I can't give advice about what my parents should do. I'm so tired of being so involved in the divorce.
> [minute 4] I feel we should not have to talk about what is happening with the divorce/court so often.
> [minute 5] It looks like I am bored because I don't want to be [giving] advice.
> [minute 6] All the details of the figures and the medical insurance shouldn't be my worries.
> [minute 7] My parent was expressing feelings [of] anxiety and stress. I have enough personal worries [without] trying to absorb hers.
> [minute 8] I am not equipped to be a therapist.
> [minute 9] I gave advice again, what if I need advice ... Would I have to give it to myself?

[minute 13] It's ok when we aren't talking about the divorce, but I shouldn't have to be the happy/funny one always.

The video recall brought out the child's feelings of being put in the middle. These were feelings that were never expressed during the interaction, but were cognitions that could only be gathered by specifically asking the child to reflect back on what he/she was thinking during the interaction. A number of parents were upset for putting the child and the child's siblings in this precarious position, but hopeful that their family could collectively manage the situation.

Parents and Adolescents' Shock by Poor Communication Practices

Regardless of the positive or negative reaction to the videotaped conversation, both parents and adolescents confessed employment of poor communication strategies. One of the most common reactions from parents was their tendency to talk more than the child. Parents often dominated the conversation by:

1. expressing their emotional reactions to the conflict;
2. describing the conflict in more detail with the hopes of bringing clarity to the situation;
3. justifying inappropriate or hurtful behaviors before, during, or after the conflict; and
4. talking to fill the silence.

A few parents weighed the cost of talking excessively with the benefit of experiencing immediate relief from "telling their side of the story". Most parents, however, were frustrated and saddened by the degree to which they spoke more and listened less with their child, sometimes referring to themselves as "bad parents" and confessing that they need professional help. Consider the following excerpt from a mother–daughter interaction.

Mother thinks (family 77):

> [minute 6] It's like I'm trying to be a "psychologist" (and doing it poorly!) when I asked those questions. Perhaps I should have kept quiet.
> [minute 7] Not focusing on my daughter's feelings. Yapping about what she already knows.
> [minute 8] Not getting at the real issue.
> [minute 9] She knows what these problems are; I'm not addressing *her* issues.
> [minute 10] I took some of the heat, but again not addressing *her* needs.
> [minute 11] I need to *shut up*. Not hearing her at all. This is dismal.
> [minute 12] All about *me, me, me*. She is sitting there being talked at; *pitiful*.
> [minute 13] Am I insane? *All about me.*

[minute 14] No help for the ones who need it – *my daughter*. She looked disturbed by my rantings.

[minute 15] Finally focusing on her.

[minute 16] The silence works until blabbermouth starts up again.

[minute 17] Make this woman shut up.

[minute 18] I am leading up to something but not fully disclosing yet. But what about my daughter's feelings? No room to get in the [conversation].

[minute 19] Oh poor *me*. It's all about me. I'm drawing out her feelings but ranting about my own. This is every depressing.

[minute 20] She knows all this x 15 years. No way for her to enter the conversation.

Many parents realized that their child was disengaged during the conversation, but after watching the videotaped conversation, they recognized that their child's behavior was a reaction to their poor communication practices.

The adolescents' self-reports revealed a congruent sentiment. Many children admitted during the video recall that their disengagement, sheer boredom, avoidance, and anger about the conversation were often because their parents were exhibiting poor listening skills and dominating the discussion. Consequentially, children maintained the same negative reaction from the beginning to the end of the conversation. This was particularly evident during the following minute-by-minute response from a mother–son interaction. The mother was incredibly emotional about her poor listening skills and excessive talking during the conversation as she watched herself, and feared that her ineffective communication would have an adverse impact on her son's well-being. Conversely, the son did not react to his behaviors or his communication practices, but continued to mention, after each minute passed, his sincere desire to leave. Not simply to end the conversation, but to leave the premises and go home. While separately reviewing the videotaped interaction, they each reported the following, simultaneous thoughts.

Adolescent thinks (family 6) …..	Mother thinks ….
	[minute 1] Hurt, angry at his spouse. Embarrassed about our situation.
	[minute 2] Worried about my son. Sad for him and his dad. Worried about his sadness and ability to (cope).
	[minute 3] Confused. Torn. Unsure. Bad parent (me).
	[minute 4] I hate myself right now! Confused. Confused. Confused. Defensive. People have no clue. I feel misunderstood, no one understands.

[minute 5] Every second I want to leave

[minute 6] I want to leave

[minute 9] I want to leave.

[minute 11] I want to leave, thank you.

[minute 12] I want to leave, that is all I can think.

[minute 13] I want to leave, this is hard on my head.

[minute 14] I can't stand it anymore.

[minute 15] I don't have a ride to Elwood.

[minute 16] I need a ride to Elwood.

[minute 17] I can't walk to Elwood, too far.

[minute 5] Wanting to talk. Old news. No one wants to leave; hear about it, move on. Get over it.

[minute 6] I don't know. Wanting some solutions. Don't know what to do about it.

[minute 7] Worried for [my son]. This is hard.

[minute 8] Trying to enlighten him, break through, figure him out too. I feel like a bad parent. To talk about this all the time. I bring it up probably every day.

[minute 9] Old news. Repeating myself. Wanting [my son] to change. Wanting to manipulate his feelings. Make him ok.

[minute 10] Really sad and confused feelings right now. Poor [son] he shouldn't have to hear this stuff. I'm bludgeoning him to death. I need help.

[minute 11] Now: I really need some professional help. My kids shouldn't have to hear it.

[minute 12] I'm so sad; self-obsessed somehow ... Sad for (my son) and my other son.

[minute 13] I'm not really listening to him. Terrible. He didn't do anything wrong. Casualty of war.

[minute 14] Confused, overwhelmed. Now I see what I am doing. It's wrong. I'm really not listening to him at all. I feel awful!

[minute 15] Ashamed of myself. Worried about him. Sad for him. Confused.

[minute 16] Most enlightening of the whole conversation.

[minute 17] Worried for him. Worried I made him think and feel this way.

[minute 18] New feelings. Different idea, thought. First time (my son) told me that I shouldn't have divorced his dad.

[minute 19] I feel like everything I'm saying and doing is wrong while I watch this. At the time I was trying to get insight into him but I'm not a very good listener.

[minute 20] Thank you.

[minute 20] Wish I made different choices wish I had thought about the (kids') future and relationship with (their father). Realized now that I need to get help, professionally. Not putting my kids through this stuff.

Some adolescents expressed the same avoidance and consistent negative emotions during the video recall as they did during the conversation. But other adolescents were surprised by their avoidance, admitting their obliviousness to their disengaged demeanor during the interaction. Some children also mentioned that they did not know how to talk about the topic, prompting them to disengage from the conversation. This shows that parents not only lacked communication efficacy, but the children did as well. A few adolescents even expressed remorse for their actions. As one adolescent reflected, "I'm mean to my mom. I don't like talking to my mom in that way" (Daughter 3, minute 1). Whether it was prompted by oblivion or poor communication practices, children were very avoidant during the conversation, and this behavior set the "tone" of the conversation. During the video recall adolescents, as well as parents, were able to recognize their involvement in a difficult and sometimes awkward conversation.

Parent Underestimating Child's Knowledge of Conflict

The conflicts that were introduced in the study often revolved around difficult and sensitive family issues concerning the parents, such as financial difficulties, tumultuous family relationships, and divorce. The seriousness of the topic sometimes meant that children did not have direct verbal communication about the issue with their parents at home and thus were not privy to all the information surrounding the topic. As parents discussed these topics with their children during the lab discussion task, many parents assumed the child did not understand the situation in its entirety and misjudged the knowledge the child acquired over the years. The parents often belabored points about the conflict during the conversation, relayed information that was common knowledge by the time of the discussion, and treated their child like an uninformed bystander. The children expressed irritation with the parent's misjudgment. A few even exhibited their knowledge of the situation in the video recall by articulating the ideas that the parents were trying to convey during the conversation. The adolescents felt comfortable expressing these feelings in written form, but only a few verbally communicated these feelings to their parents. The following mother–son excerpt illustrates these points.

Adolescent thinks (family 6)	Mother thinks ....
[minute 1] Overwhelming agreement over divorce.	[minute 1] He looked amused, like "Here we go over divorce go again."
[minute 2] Money is too much responsibility.	[minute 2] I was redundant. He was politely responsibly bored.
[minute 3] A lot of financial management is needed.	[minute 3] I should be less animated. Less repetitive. He heard it all before. The processing of accessing money doesn't matter to him.
[minute 4] Sister is pulled apart daily [and the] fights are tense.	[minute 4] He's very bored. Solution [is] being worked out.
[minute 5] One parent talking down another parent, inappropriate.	[minute 5] Very, very bored and disinterested in hearing another word.
[minute 6] Blame other parent, uncomfortable/uninterested.	
[minute 7] Finances are difficult to talk about.	[minute 7] I wonder what he is thinking. I should have noticed him looking down, not at me and I should have stopped talking. He know it all it is hopeless, so I should shut up.
[minute 8] It's a hard transition.	[minute 8] He is disinterested. I have lost him. His shoes are more interesting than me. He'll make a typical husband. Listening, smiling. Stays in his own world.
[minute 10] She lashes out and blames the other parent; much disagreement.	[minute 10] Bored, he failed to participate.

The son in this excerpt has similar responses to other self-reports from adolescents, such that he willingly shared perceptions of the conflict in written form but appeared bored and apathetic during the conversation itself. The mothers' response in the excerpt illustrates the stark contrast between the parent's estimation of the child's knowledge versus the children's actual knowledge. It also demonstrates the misinterpretation of the child's behavior – the parent thought the child was bored and the topic did not matter to him. The child was thinking about the parents' finances and family members' conflict during the conversation, but he did not convey these feelings verbally or non-verbally during the conversation. What is also particularly interesting throughout the themes is that children may be avoiding for different reasons. Some children appear to avoid because they are sad or anxious, others are angry at the parent, and still others are truly bored or preoccupied with something else.

Stable versus Erratic Emotional Reactions

Perceptions of the 20-minute interaction sparked oppositional emotional responses from the parents and adolescents. Parents tended to report a wide array of emotions, whereas the children's emotional expressions were stable and consistent. Many children maintained the same, often negative, sentiment from the beginning to the end of the conversation. Their minute-by-minute responses to the discussion were often static and unwavering, despite the dynamic emotions of their parent and the tangential turns of the conversational. In the excerpt below, the son reiterates the same four emotions as each minute passed.

Adolescent thinks (family 55)	Mother thinks .....
[minute 1] Confused and nervous didn't know where to start.	[minute 1] Had so much to think about.
[minute 2] Didn't know what to say.	[minute 2] My mind went back to five years ago to remember what happened.
[minute 3] Confused.	[minute 3] Putting things in order of how it happened.
[minute 4] Sad, confused.	[minute 4] That it happened five years ago.
[minute 5] Confused.	[minute 5] Was feeling upset because I remember that day.
[minute 6] Confused.	[minute 6] I was clueless of the date my ex met his new partner.
[minute 7] Nervous, upset.	[minute 7] Felt weird remembering this thing.
[minute 8] Mad and confused.	[minute 8] Felt very anxious.
[minute 9] Mad and confused.	[minute 9] I was thinking of my step-kids.
[minute 10] Curious mad.	[minute 10] I was just (thinking) of that day.
[minute 11] Mad, curious.	[minute 11] Feeling upset at what happened to them.
[minute 12] Mad and confused.	[minute 12] I felt upset by the way things had to be.
[minute 13] Mad and confused.	[minute 13] I was feeling upset when thinking what happened to my step-kids.
[minute 14] Very upset and confused.	[minute 14] Full disappointment of things occurred.

[minute 15] Mad and pissed off.

[minute 16] Upset and confused.

[minute 15] How people make the wrong choices in life

[minute 16] I felt upset just to think about my ex.

Conversely, parents often relayed a 20-minute emotional rollercoaster taking them up through moments of happiness and relaxation to downturns of despondency and grief. Parents felt anxious about their child's avoidant behavior during the interaction and they were worried about the impact of the conflict upon their child's well-being. Parents were also saddened that their child was caught in the middle of a difficult family issue. For example, many parents from divorced families wrote that they were upset for casting their former spouse in a negative light in front of the child. The video recall allowed parents to witness how their communication behaviors during the conversation affected the child's reaction to the conversation and the entire conflict situation. Many parents confessed that reliving the conversation was difficult, but a few admitted that watching the conversation was "painful but necessary." The excerpts below demonstrate emotional reactions from two different mothers that not only changed every minute, but were also quite mixed within each minute.

Parent thinks (family 57):

[minute 1] Self concerned, optimistic.
[minute 2] Nervous, happy, sad, hopeful, silly, happy.
[minute 3] Optimistic, happy, proud, concerned, sad, good feeling, optimistic.
[minute 4] Happy, sad, hopeful.
[minute 5] Sad.

Parent thinks (family 59):

[minute 6] Happy, good, concerned, sad, sad, sad, very sad, I feel like crying.
[minute 7] Concerned, sad, sad, sad, very sad, very sad, very sad.
[minute 8] Happy, concerned, happy, happy, happy, happy.
[minute 9] Happy, happy, happy, tense, stress, happy, loving.
[minute 10] Happy, happy, happy.
[minute 11] Happy.

The video recall aroused strong emotional responses from parents and children alike, however the type and range of emotions differentiated parents from children.

Methodological Challenges and Future Directions for Examining Children and Parents' Perceptions of Interparental Conflict

Researchers have long emphasized the important role of perception in conflict. Most of this research focuses on misperceptions within marital couples, dating couples, or parent–adolescent dyads (e.g., Sillars et al, 2000; Sillars et al, 2005). But what if there is a third party (i.e., child) who is witness to the conflict that is occurring between two other people? Even though the conflict being emphasized is between two parents, the child plays a crucial role in the family system and the parent(s) may have a different perception about the conflict than the child because of the different roles the parents and child assume in the family.

The findings presented here confirm the research on feeling caught (Afifi, 2003; Afifi et al, 2006) that has found that parents are often unaware that their children feel caught. Children want their parent to stop putting them in the middle of their disputes, but often do not have the communication efficacy to do so. They also think that if they talk about their feelings of being caught, it will escalate the conflict. As a result, they avoid talking about their feelings. Children's avoidance was also evident in the video recall here. The children themselves, however, were not even fully aware of their avoidance until they watched the video. The parents also realized for the first time by watching the video recall that their children felt uncomfortable with the way their parent was communicating.

The video recall procedure is a valuable method of collecting data on conflict. Part of the difficulty with researching conflict is determining what people are thinking when they are in a conflict. Typically, researchers do not have access to this information in the moment. The video recall method, however, allows for retrospective data that is very close to the time of the conflict that allows for observation and reflection of one's self and others. This method often examines differences in perception between participants (typically quantitatively) and how this is associated with personal and relational health. These perceptions are often compared minute by minute and then an overall difference score is created. A less common, but equally important, way of examining the perceptions might be to gauge how the perceptions change or remain consistent over the course of the conversation. Even though we cannot show that the video recall changed participants' perceptions (without any quantitative changes in perception and lack a control group), the qualitative results suggested important changes in perspectives within and between the parents and children.

In the current study, parents experienced multiple, often conflicting, emotions that changed frequently over time. Adolescents, on the other hand, were very stable in their emotions across the video recall. An interesting avenue of future research would be to investigate why parents' emotions were so erratic and why adolescents' emotions were so stable. One possible explanation is that parents' identity is being threatened because they are the topic of the conversation. Indeed, the stimulus of asking the parent and child to talk about something stressful and conflict inducing in the parents' relationship could make parents sensitive to the way they are communicating. Parents also want to believe they are good parents and the very nature of the topic could threaten their schemata for parenting. The parents may have been happy in certain moments because they found pieces of the conversation affirming and were sad and angry in other parts because the information was identity threatening. The discussion task could have also been potentially identity threatening for the child for different reasons. The task could have been identity threatening for the adolescents because it introduced a previously avoided topic.

Parents and adolescents alike were often surprised at the way they communicated and wished they had communicated differently by the end of the video. But, their reactions to the videos were different across the families. Some parents and adolescents were extremely positive and hopeful from the beginning of the conversation to the end while other parents and adolescents eventually reached that point. The other group of parents and adolescents felt worse after watching their videotapes. An important question that remains is why some families were more positive than others. Part of the reason could be that there was less conflict in the families that were more positive and hopeful. Many of the families in this positive group were ones where the parents were still married. However, there were also divorced families in this group who realized how resilient they were in the face of divorce and how much they grew from the process. It is important to figure out why some parents are able to communicate in ways that promote resilience despite difficult circumstances while other parents communicate in ways that place their children at risk.

Finally, children are extremely perceptive and can typically detect nonverbally when their parents are fighting. Parents often felt as if they hid their conflict from their children and that their children did not fully understand the issue as a result. However, the adolescents and young adults in this sample were very aware of the source of their parents' conflict. Interestingly, they avoided bringing up the fact that they knew the information in the conversations, but instead wrote it down in the video recall. This finding illustrates the importance of potentially using the video recall method as a stimulus for conversations between parents and adolescents and for clinicians to figure out what a child really thinks about his/her parents' communication.

The Video Recall Method as an Intervention

While video recall procedures are sometimes used in clinical work for behavioral modification and this work is mentioned in research and shown to the lay public (e.g., John Gottman's work), these procedures could be used as interventions in research. The video recall method could help parents be more mindful of their communicative tendencies – both good and bad. In many instances, as our results demonstrate, parents became increasingly aware that their communication needed to improve by the end of the video. Researchers tend to focus on adults and their awareness of their behaviors. However, the adolescents also became aware of the fact that they were despondent or avoidant, often felt bad for their parent that they were communicating that way, and recognized that they needed to alter their communication to more effectively respond to their parents' requests for information. Many of the families in this sample did not have very intense levels of conflict. The findings would probably be even more pronounced in samples where there was more intense and chronic conflict. The video recall procedure could be used for families who have significant levels of conflict as a way to help family members recognize and change maladaptive conflict tendencies. The procedure could enhance family members' awareness of their conflict patterns and, in turn, increase their efficacy to change them, as long as researchers then provide them with information on how to change them. An interesting future study would be to determine if the video recall procedure alone is enough to change people's conflict tendencies. The video recall procedure might help families, but providing educational sessions after the video recall would provide additional information and encouragement that could make the behavior changes more long-lasting.

As the results from the current analysis also suggest, however, one cannot assume that the video recall procedure will make people feel good about their communication. While the video recall procedure may help families become more aware of their communication, it may make them feel bad about it in so doing. As some parents in the sample became increasingly aware of their communicative tendencies as they watched the videos, they simultaneously became angry at themselves, sad, and embarrassed by their behavior. These negative feelings were exacerbated as they watched their child's reactions to the conversation. As the parents watched the video, they became increasingly aware of their child's avoidance and their own communicative tendencies, which intensified their negative emotions. Consequently, there are ethical implications with this procedure that need to be taken into account. The video recall method alone as an intervention may help some family members' communication but hurt others, unless there is training afterward that gives them efficacy and hope.

References

Adamsons, K., & Pasley, K. (2006). Coparenting following divorce and relationships dissolution. In M. A. Fine, & J. H. Harvey (Eds.) *Handbook of divorce and relationship dissolution* (pp241–262). Mawah, NJ: Lawrence Erlbaum Associates, Inc.

Afifi, T. D. (2003). "Feeling caught" in stepfamilies: Managing boundary turbulence through appropriate communication privacy rules. *Journal of Social and Personal Relationships*, 20, 729–755. doi: 10.1177/0265407503206002

Afifi, T. D. & Hamrick, K. (2006). Communication processes that promote risk and resiliency in postdivorce families. In M. A. Fine, & J. H. Harvey (Eds.) *Handbook of divorce and relationship dissolution* (pp435–456). Mawah, NJ: Lawrence Erlbaum Associates, Inc.

Afifi, T. D., & Schrodt, P. (2003). "Feeling caught" as a mediator of adolescents' and young adults' avoidance and satisfaction with their parents in divorced and non-divorced households. *Communication Monographs*, 70, 142–173. doi: 10.1080/0363775032000133791

Afifi, T. D., Hutchinson, S., & Krouse, S. (2006). Toward a theoretical model of communal coping in postdivorce families and other naturally occurring groups. *Communication Theory*, 16(3), 378–409. doi.org/10.1080/10502550902970496

Afifi, T. D., McManus, T., Hutchinson, S., & Baker, B. (2007). Inappropriate parental divorce disclosures, the factors that prompt them, and their impact on parents' and adolescents' well-being. *Communication Monographs*, 74, 78–102. doi: 10.1080/03637750701196870

Afifi, T. D., Schrodt, P., & McManus, T. (2009). The divorce disclosure model (DDM): Why parents disclose negative information about the divorce to their children and its effects. In T. D. Afifi & W. A. Afifi (Eds.), *Uncertainty, Information Management, and Disclosure Decisions* (pp403–425). New York, NY: Routledge.

Amato, P. R. (2000). The consequences of divorce for adults and children. *Journal of Marriage and the Family*, 62, 1269–1287. doi: 10.1111/j.1741-3737.2000.01269.x

Amato, P. R., & Afifi, T. D. (2006). Feeling caught between parents: Adult children's relations with parents and subjective well-being. *Journal of Marriage and Family*, 68, 222–235. doi: 10.1111/j.1741-3737.2006.00243.x

Barber, B. L., & Demo, D. H. (2006). The kids are alright (at least, most of them): Links between divorce and dissolution and child well-being. In M. A. Fine, & J. H. Harvey (Eds.) *Handbook of divorce and relationship dissolution* (pp289–312). Mawah, NJ: Lawrence Erlbaum Associates, Inc.

Booth, A., & Amato, P. R. (2001). Parental predivorce relations and offspring postdivorce well-being. *Journal of Marriage and the Family*, 63, 197–212. http://dx.doi.org/10.1111/j.1741-3737.2001.00197.x

Buchanan, C. M., Maccoby, E. E., & Dornbusch, S. M. (1991). Caught between parents: Adolescents' experience in divorced homes. *Child Development*, 62, 1008–1029. doi: 10.2307/1131149

Cummings, E. M., Davies, P. T., & Simpson, K. S. (1994). Marital conflict, gender, and children's appraisals and coping efficacy as mediators of child adjustment. *Journal of Family Psychology*, 8, 141–149. doi: 10.1037//0893-083200.8.2.141

Davies, P. T., & Cummings, E. M. (1994). Marital conflict and child adjustment: An emotional security hypothesis. *Psychological Bulletin*, 116, 387–411. doi: 10.1037/0033-2909.116.3.387

Fabricius, W. V., & Luecken, L. J. (2007). Postdivorce living arrangements, parent conflict, and long-term physical health correlates for children of divorce. *Journal of family psychology*, 21(2), 195. doi.org/10.1037/0893-3200.21.2.195

Golish, T. D. (2003). Stepfamily communication strengths: Understanding the ties that bind. *Human Communication Research*, 29, 41–80. http://dx.doi.org/10.1093/hcr/29.1.41

Golish, T. D., & Caughlin, J. (2002). "I'd rather not talk about it": Adolescents' and young adults' use of topic avoidance in stepfamilies. *Journal of Applied Communication Research*, 30, 78–106. http://dx.doi.org/10.1080/00909880216574

Glaser, B. G. (1978). *Theoretical sensitivity*. Mill Valley, CA: Sociology Press.

Glaser, B. G. (1992). *Basics of grounded theory analysis*. Mill Valley, CA: Sociology Press.

Glaser, B. G. & Strauss, A. (1964). Awareness contexts and social interaction. *American Sociological Association*, 29, 669–679.

Glaser, B. G. & Strauss, A. (1967). *The discovery of grounded theory: Strategies for qualitative research*. Chicago, IL: Aldine.

Grych, J. H., & Fincham, F. D. (1990). Marital conflict and children's adjustment: A cognitive-contextual framework. *Psychological Bulletin*, 108, 267–290. doi: 10.1037/0033-2909.108.2.267

Grych, J. H., Seid, M., & Fincham, F. D. (1992). Assessing marital conflict from the child's perspective: The Children's Perception of Interpersonal Conflict Scale. *Child Development*, 63, 558–572. http://dx.doi.org/10.1111/j.1467-8624.1992.tb01646.x

Guerrero, L. K., & Afifi, W. A. (1995). What parents don't know: Topic avoidance in parent–child relationships. In T. Socha & G. Stamp (Eds.), *Parents, children, and communication: Frontiers of theory and research* (pp219–247). Mahwah, NJ: Lawrence Erlbaum Associates.

Kalmijn, M. (1999). Father involvement in childrearing and the perceived stability of marriage. *Journal of Marriage and the Family, 5*, 409–421. doi.org/10.2307/353758

Kerig, P. K. (1996). Assessing the links between interparental conflict and child adjustment: The conflicts and problem-solving scales. *Journal of Family Psychology, 10*, 454–473. doi: 10.1037//0893-083200.10.4.454

Kitzmann, K. M., & Cohen, R. (2003). Parents' versus children's perceptions of interparental conflict as predictors of children's friendship quality. *Journal of Social and Personal Relationships, 20*, 689–700. doi: 10.1177/02654075030205007

Jekielek, S. (1998). Parental conflict, marital disruption and children's emotional well-being. *Social Forces, 76*, 905–936. doi: 10.2307/3005698

Maccoby, E. E., & Mnookin, R. H. (1992). *Dividing the child: Social and legal dilemmas of custody*. Cambridge, MA: Harvard University Press.

Margolin, G., Gordis, E. B., & John, R. S. (2001). Coparenting: A link between marital conflict and parenting in two-parent families. *Journal of Family Psychology, 15*, 3–21. doi: 10.1037//0893-083200.15.1.3

Sandier, I., Wolchik, S., & Braver, S. (1985). Social support and children of divorce. In I. Sarason & B. Sarason (Eds.), *Social support: Theory, research, and applications* (pp371–389). Boston, MA: Martinus Nijhoff Publishers.

Schrodt, P., & Afifi, T. D. (2007). Communication processes that predict young adults' feelings of being caught and their associations with mental health and family satisfaction. *Communication Monographs, 74*, 200–228. doi: 10.1080/03637750701390085

Schrodt, P., & Ledbetter, A. M. (2007). Communication processes that mediate family communication patterns and mental well-being: A mean and covariance structures analysis of young adults from divorced and non-divorced families. *Human Communication Research, 33*, 330–356. doi: 10.1111/j.1468-2958.2007.00302.x

Schrodt, P., & Ledbetter, A. M. (2012). Parental confirmation as a mitigator of feeling caught and family satisfaction. *Personal Relationships, 19*, 146–161. doi: 10.1111/j.1475-6811.2010.01345.x

Sillars, A., Roberts, L. J., Leonard, K. E., & Dun, T. (2000). Cognition during marital conflict: The relationship of thought and talk. *Journal of Social and Personal Relationships, 17*, 479–502.

Sillars, A., Koerner, A., & Fitzpatrick, M. A. (2005). Communication and understanding in parent-adolescent relationships. *Human Communication Research, 31*, 102–128.

Strauss, A., & Corbin, J. (1990). *Basics of qualitative research: Techniques and procedures for developing grounded theory*. Newbury Park, CA: Sage.

12

FAMILY CONFLICT IS DETRIMENTAL TO PHYSICAL AND MENTAL HEALTH

Chris Segrin and Jeanne Flora

Improving people's physical and mental health is a major public health concern. Most people who are concerned about their physical health are likely to think of commonly touted messages about a balanced diet, regular exercise, or adequate sleep rather than the quality of their close personal relationships. When it comes to mental health, social stigma, denial, or the painful distress of actually experiencing a mental health problem may keep people from seeking treatment or considering the possibility that troubled family or romantic interactions may trigger, aggravate, or prolong the problem.

This chapter is devoted to exploring the ways in which physical and mental health are intertwined with conflicted family interactions. In many cases, scholars have been able to show that it is not simply conflict per se that is damaging to physical and mental health, but rather certain forms of conflict. Specifying these destructive forms and describing how they are tied to health problems helps elevate the study of conflict to a public health issue. In the past 20 years scientists have made astonishing discoveries of possible pathophysiological mechanisms linking marital and family conflict with poor physical health outcomes. The first half of this chapter describes these links in both adults and children. The second half of the chapter attempts to promote greater understanding and appreciation for the constellation of mental health problems that accompany certain destructive forms of family conflict.

Explicating Conflict in the Developmental Course of Family Members' Physical Health

Family conflict, when dealt with poorly, threatens the physical health of adults and children, often in ways that people do not foresee. Physical health can be measured in a variety of ways, meaning that some physical health outcomes are more obvious than others. Robles, Slatcher, Trombello, and McGinn (2013) describe how physical health can be operationalized by making important distinctions between clinical endpoints, surrogate endpoints, and biological mediators. Clinical endpoints are typically objective and observable measures of functioning, such as a hospitalization, heart attack, or mortality, though they may also include self-rated changes in quality of life. Surrogate endpoints are objective biological processes such as blood pressure or cholesterol levels that, if measured to be at unsafe levels, can predict clinical endpoints. Finally, biological mediators involve physiological responses, such as increased stress hormones or compromised immune functioning, affected by acute stressors such as a conflict interaction. As Robles et al explain, biological mediators may not necessarily lead to clinical endpoints, but over time the load or stress put on the body by such events could play a role in compromised health. In the sections that follow, we explore the pathways, some physiological and others behavioral, by which toxic conflict can compromise physical health. We also show that the consequences of destructive conflict on physical health can be far reaching. As evidence, we close the first half of the chapter by presenting findings from a study conducted out of our lab that indicates a family system-wide effect of conflict on physical health.

Marital Conflict and Adult Physical Health

People in low-quality marriages tend to have more physical health problems than people in high-quality marriages. Although the link between marital quality and physical health is complex and bidirectional, conflict patterns have been targeted as one key to understanding how marital quality and physical health are related. Besides the fact that low-quality marriages are typically characterized by self-reports of low satisfaction and negative attitudes about the partner/relationship, the conflict interactions in such marriages are marked by hostility, criticism, and rapid escalation of negativity (Robles et al, 2013). This stands in contrast to high-quality marriages that tend to be defined by positive sentiment, high satisfaction, as well as conflict interactions that are characterized by support, affection, and regulation of negative emotion. Destructive marital conflict patterns appear to compromise spouses' physical health by way of major pathophysiological mechanisms that include endocrine, immune, and cardiovascular functioning (Robles & Kiecolt-Glaser, 2003; Robles et al, 2013). Further, significant impairments in any one of these mechanisms is sufficient to cause morbidity or even mortality in the case of extreme disruption.

Neuroendocrine Functioning

The endocrine system involves glands that secrete hormones in the bloodstream, often at the signaling of the nervous system. Couples who enact more hostile, negative, and controlling behaviors during problem-solving discussions experience increased secretion of stress hormones (Malarkey et al, 1994). In one premier study, Kiecolt-Glaser et al (2003) followed 90 couples over the course of their first ten years of marriage and studied how their stress hormone levels in their first year of marriage predicted later marital outcomes. Compared to intact couples, couples who divorced over the course of the 10-year study had 34 percent higher epinephrine levels during a conflict discussion in their first year of marriage. Their stress hormones were also significantly higher throughout the day and at night in their first year of marriage. Kiecolt-Glaser et al (2003, p187) concluded that "stress hormones may function as a kind of bellwether in early marriage". In other words, heightened stress hormones may foreshadow negative relationship changes that spouses themselves do not even foresee. Next, these researchers looked closer at the couples in the study who were still married ten years later. They compared those who were married but in distressed marriages versus those who were in non-distressed marriages. Among women whose marriages were distressed, ACTH (adrenocorticotropic hormone) levels during the conflict discussion in the first year were twice as high as those whose marriages were not troubled ten years later. The couples who were still married, but distressed ten years later, indeed displayed higher rates of negative behaviors when observed interacting in the conflict discussion during their first year of marriage.

Incidentally, young or newlywed couples are not the only ones who experience increased stress hormones during negative conflict interactions. Heffner et al (2006) examined the cortisol levels of older couples (mean age: 66.75 years) and found that wives who perceived high levels of the wife demand-husband withdrawal conflict pattern also experienced elevated cortisol responses. Heffner et al's concern is that persistently high cortisol responses can compromise immune functioning, slow wound healing, and provoke a variety of other health concerns, some of which are already age-related.

Immune Functioning

As suggested in the previous section, many of the neuroendocrine responses to hostile interpersonal conflict are thought to promote compromised responses to infection and injury (Kiecolt-Glaser et al, 1993). Neuroendocrine responses can prompt inflammation, one part of immune functioning. Acute, short-term inflammation is what helps the body respond to infection and injury, but elevated inflammation over prolonged periods of time taxes the body and creates risks for a variety of health problems. Chronic inflammation can also literally impair the healing process (Kiecolt-Glaser et al, 2010). To demonstrate this, Graham et al (2009) and Gouin et al (2010) brought married couples to a hospital lab for 24-hour visits during which they inflicted blister wounds on their arms. Shortly thereafter the couples had a discussion about an area of conflict in their relationship. Most participants in these studies evidenced increased levels of pro-inflammatory cytokines, as would be expected for people undergoing stressful procedures. However, the level of these cytokines was higher among those who engaged in hostile behavior during the conflict interaction and lower among those who used a lot of words suggestive of cognitive processing (e.g., "because," "think," "ought") during the conflict (Graham et al, 2009). The retarded wound-healing associated with the stress of marital conflict can be thought of as an expression of endocrine disruptions associated with hostility and conflict in marriage. The Graham et al study further revealed that extensive cognitive processing during conflict and minimization of hostility can literally have anti-inflammatory effects on the body. Hostile marital conflict has been linked with declines in fitness of the immune system over the ensuing 24 hours, as indicated by natural killer cell lysis and high antibody titers to latent Epstein-Barr virus (Keicolt-Glaser et al, 2003). Such findings, coupled with those on degraded wound healing, provide compelling examples of how hostile marital conflicts can generate susceptibility to, and impaired recovery from, illnesses.

Cardiovascular Functioning

In addition to increased circulation of stress hormones and compromised immune functioning, couples that enact more hostile, negative, and controlling behaviors during problem solving discussions also have higher increases in blood pressure and their blood pressure remains elevated for a longer time after the interaction (Brown & Smith, 1992). The heightened blood pressure is a reaction to the stress induced by negative affect. Heightened blood pressure and heart rates are particular risk factors in the course of hypertension and cardiovascular disease. Whisman et al (2010) studied 671 married couples where both spouses were between 52 and 79 years of age. They looked for markers of metabolic syndrome: central obesity, high blood pressure, elevated triglycerides and glucose in the blood, and decreased HDL (or "good") cholesterol in the blood. This constellation of symptoms is a potent risk factor for heart disease, diabetes, and stroke. As part of their research, spouses were asked questions about the quality of their marriage. These questions were often indicators of disagreement or conflicts (e.g., "How much does your spouse really understand the way you feel about things?" and "How much does your spouse criticize you?"). Women, but not men, who reported higher scores in response to these questions were more prone to having metabolic syndrome than those women who reported higher quality, less conflicted marriages. Both perceptions of marital hostility and actual interactions that involve marital disagreements can impact cardiovascular health. For example, Smith et al (2009) examined the cardiovascular reactivity (e.g., heart rate, blood pressure) of middle-aged and older couples after an interaction that involved discussing a current, ongoing area of disagreement. After the disagreement discussions, both men and women experienced greater cardiovascular reactivity, as compared to measures taken after a collaborative discussion.

Mortality

There is no health outcome variable more consequential than mortality. Aside from those who die from injuries due to accidents or violence, mortality for most people follows some form of compromised health. In general, marriage reduces mortality risk. Findings from the National Longitudinal Mortality Study reveal that the relative risk of mortality for unmarried versus married people 45–64 years of age is 1.24–1.39 (Johnson et al, 2000). However, people in marriages with a high level of conflict do not enjoy this survival effect, and conflict-laden marriages might actually generate an increased risk of mortality. These mortality risks are most evident in people who otherwise have a chronic health condition. For example, women with end stage renal disease who reported low levels of marital conflict survived significantly longer than a comparable group of women who experienced high levels of marital conflict (Kimmel et al, 2000). Among patients with congestive heart failure, marital quality is negatively related to 4-year mortality (Coyne et al, 2001).

It is not just the mere presence of marital conflict that is associated with mortality, but also how conflicts are handled. Middle-aged women who report that they usually self-silence and keep things to themselves during marital conflict are four times more likely to die over the ensuing ten years than women who openly express themselves during conflicts (Eaker et al, 2007). What is particularly noteworthy about this finding is the fact that these women actually did not all have chronic health conditions and the effect of self-silencing on mortality held after controlling for age, systolic blood pressure, body mass index, cigarette smoking, diabetes, and cholesterol level. In a closely related study, participants were asked "Imagine that you were doing something outside and your husband/wife yelled in anger or blew up at you for something that wasn't your fault, how would you feel?" (Harburg et al, 2008). People in marriages where both spouses were suppressors – that is, they keep their anger inside, had a rate of all-cause mortality almost five times higher than those where one or both spouses were expressive of their anger. These findings show that the ill effects of conflict cannot be avoided by simply keeping issues bottled up. In the long run, that approach to marital conflict poses a serious mortality risk.

Family Conflict and Poor Child Health Outcomes

Family conflict, especially when it is severe, is detrimental to children's health. The upcoming section highlights research that shows how family conflict and children's physiological functioning are related. We also explore the fascinating idea that family conflict can damage children's health by first compromising parenting behaviors, which then affect child health. Finally, we consider the way a family's communication climate is related to the health of multiple members of the family system, parents and children alike.

Children's Physiology

Exposure to family conflict upsets children's normal physiology, just as it does with married couples. Family conflict is positively associated with children's physical symptoms such as headaches and stomach aches (Mechanic & Hansell, 1989). In Mechanic and Hansell's investigation, the children of divorced parents rated family conflict as significantly more unpleasant than their parents' actual divorce. In fact, the adolescents from high conflict intact families had more physical ailments than those from low conflict-divorced families. In a unique experimental study, children were exposed to angry or friendly interactions between two adult research assistants who, unbeknownst to the children, were just role-playing these emotional reactions (El-Sheikh et al, 1989). Children in the angry interaction condition showed more behavioral signs of distress and had higher blood pressure than those who were exposed to the friendly exchange. In a related investigation, boys who came from families that were low in supportiveness and positive involvement with the child showed more anger and hostility, and had greater cardiovascular arousal in response to simple laboratory stressors such as an isometric handgrip exercise or counting backwards by sevens (Woodall & Matthews, 1989).

Family conflict has far reaching effects on children's health. Lundberg (1993) analyzed longitudinal data on family living conditions and health for over 4,000 people in Sweden. He examined the effect of economic hardship, growing up in a large family (e.g., four or more siblings), parental divorce, and family conflict. Of these four stressful family processes, family conflict had the most powerful effect on subsequent physical illnesses. Children who grew up in a family marked by high levels of conflict were in a worse state of health 13 years later. Miller and Chen (2010) asked 15- to 19-year-olds about their exposure to family hostility and conflict as young children, as indicated by questions such as "How often did a parent or other adult in the household swear at you, insult you, put you down, or act in a way that made you feel threatened?" and "How often would you say that a parent or other adult in the household behaved violently toward a family member or visitor in your home?" Being reared in such an environment as a child was associated with a dysregulation of stress hormones in response to psychological stresses as a late adolescent. In particular, late adolescents' immune cells exhibited increasing resistance to anti-inflammatory signals from cortisol. Over the long haul, this dysregulation could make people vulnerable to later life chronic diseases.

The increased sympathetic arousal evidenced by children exposed to unsupportive and conflicted family interactions is functional in the short run for activating resources to deal with the stressor. The problem, however, is when this heightened responsiveness of the nervous system becomes permanently altered. This is a process known as allostasis or allostatic load, and family scientists believe that chronic exposure to stressful family environments is responsible for increased allostatic load in children, making them vulnerable to subsequent health problems. The wearing down of the nervous system associated with allostasis is exceptionally taxing on children's physiology and this can culminate in illness through compromised immune response or dysfunction in the same physiological systems that are affected by the sympathetic arousal (e.g., heart, gastro-intestinal system, etc.).

Compromised Parenting.

In addition to chronic physiological arousal and sensitivity to stress, another attractive hypothesis linking family conflict to poor child health is behavioral in nature. It has been suggested that marital conflict and disruption compromise parenting practices. As they deal with their own marital problems, parents may become less available and responsive and more angry, depressed, or and irritable. This, in turn, may lead to offspring deficits in affective, behavioral, and cognitive domains (Troxel & Matthews, 2004). These deficits can increase risk of poor health by corrupting young people's health behaviors as well as their aforementioned physiological stress responses. The idea is that with less parental monitoring and supervision, children may be more prone to engage in behaviors that would risk their physical health (e.g., more injuries, risky substance use or sexual behavior). Children may turn to health-compromising behaviors as a way of self-medicating or coping with parental conflict. There is also the chance that children will relate in their own peer relationships using some of the same aggressive or physically damaging conflict behaviors exposed to them by their parents. This behavioral hypothesis is useful in that it specifies consequences of family conflict (i.e., compromised parenting practices) that have potentially detrimental developmental effects. Naturally, this also specifies a point of entrance for family interventions that could be developed for at-risk youth and their families.

A Spotlight Study on the Family System-Wide Effects of Conflict

Previously unpublished findings from a study conducted at our lab indicate what may be a family system-wide effect of conflict on health. As our findings suggest, the physical health of the family as a whole may be linked to a family's conflict climate. Participants were 169 young adults (mean age 21) and 148 parents (mean age 52) who were participating in a larger study on loneliness and health in families (Segrin et al, 2012). Young adults completed a measure of their satisfaction with the family's communication that included three items specific to conflict: "our family's ability to resolve conflict," "the way problems are discussed," and "the fairness of criticism in our family." Young adults and their parents also completed a symptom-based measure of health (e.g., upset stomach, headache) and a health related quality of life measure (e.g., "My health is excellent").

Further details on these measures can be found in Segrin et al (2012). To parsimoniously test the association between family conflict and health we created a family conflict latent variable, indicated by each of the three conflict items, and a health latent variable, indicated by the symptom-based and health quality of life measures. The association between these two latent variables was tested in structural equation modeling. The proposed model fit the sample data well, $\chi^2 = 4.73$, $df = 4$, $p = .31$, $\chi^2/df = 1.18$, CFI = .99, RMSEA = .03, and revealed a significant association between young adults' satisfaction with their family's conflict handling and their own reports of health, $\beta = .41$, $p < .01$. Next we tested a comparable model, but this time with parents' health. Once again the proposed model provided an excellent fit to the sample data, $\chi^2 = 3.07$, $df = 4$, $p = .55$, $\chi^2/df = 0.77$, CFI = 1.00, RMSEA = .01, revealing a significant association between young adults' satisfaction with their family's conflict handling and their parents' health, $\beta = .25$, $p < .01$. What is striking about this second association is that young adults' perceptions of the family's conflict handling reveal information about not just their own health but also the health of their parents.

Family Conflict in the Developmental Course of Family Members' Mental Health

Just as there is a clear connection between the experience of family conflict and the physical health of family members, there is perhaps an equally clear connection between family conflict and the mental health of family members. Simply put, family conflict can be detrimental to the psychological well-being of both child and adult family members. The noxious effects of family conflict on the mental health of children were demonstrated in a recent longitudinal study that followed over 3,000 people from birth through age 21 (Hayatbakhsh et al, 2013). Children reared in a family marked by a high level of disagreement and discord, or whose parents divorced (a plausible proxy for exposure to marital conflict), evidenced elevated symptoms of a broad range of psychopathologies. Indicators of such mental health problems were apparent in measures of depression, anxiety, aggression, delinquency, internalizing, and externalizing (Hayatbakhsh et al, 2013). The sensitization hypothesis indicates that exposure to hostile conflict between parents increases children's negative emotionality, threat, self-blame, and skepticism about the possibility of conflict resolution (e.g., Goeke-Morey et al, 2013). These psychological responses may play an etiologic role in subsequent mental health problems, especially if parental conflict persists and intensifies. Even in adults, chronic entanglement in conflict has significant implications for the experience of mental health and psychopathology (Fincham, 2003).

In this section we examine specific family conflict forms and processes including expressed emotion, conflict stabilization, exaggeration of aggression, and exposure to interparental and/or family conflict during early developmental stages. The findings associated with all of these phenomena converge to indicate that family conflict is a powerful concomitant and, in some cases, risk factor to psychopathology in family members.

Expressed Emotion

A family dynamic that psychologists refer to as expressed emotion and its counterpart in verbal behavior, negative affective style, has been implicated in a number of mental health problems experienced by the offspring reared in such families. Expressed emotion (EE) is an attitude of hostility, criticism, and over-involvement expressed by a family member (usually a parent) about another family member (usually a child), and is commonly operationalized through interviews with the parent (Hooley, 2007). Critical comments about the child (e.g., "She never listens when you tell her what to do") and expression of disliking of the child (e.g., "He's so irresponsible – it's just obnoxious") are characteristic of high EE families. Affective style (AS) is the family interaction counterpart of expressed emotion. Negative AS is evident in family members' negative verbal behaviors (e.g., personal criticism, guilt induction, and intrusiveness), and lack of positive verbal behaviors (e.g., support) during family conflicts (Doane et al, 1981).

Research on family AS has identified verbal "intrusiveness" from a parent as part of a constellation of behaviors that can predict both the onset and course of schizophrenia in offspring (Doane et al, 1981). In its most pernicious form intrusiveness has a harsh and critical component (e.g., "You enjoy being mean to others."). This type of mindreading behavior, when coupled with attributions of negative intent and motivation, is destructive to the psychological well-being of children in the family. For those with predispositions toward schizophrenia, this behavior may precipitate onset and relapse. There is often a vicious cycle of negative AS and psychiatric symptoms whereby the symptoms of the child prompt negative comments during family conflicts and negative comments during family conflicts also promote the expression of psychiatric symptoms (Cook et al, 1991; Woo et al, 2004).

The criticism and hostility that is part and parcel of high family EE has been implicated in a surprising range of child mental health problems that include schizophrenia, depression, anxiety disorders, eating disorders, substance use disorders, and personality disorders (Hooley, 2007). For example, a review of 25 studies on family EE indicated a 50 percent relapse rate, over a period of 9 to 12 months, among schizophrenia patients discharged to a high EE family, but only 21 percent among those with low EE relatives (Bebbington & Kuipers, 1994).

Some of the same corrosive elements of family expressed emotion evidenced in families of people with schizophrenia can be found in families of young people with eating disorders. For example, the criticism component of expressed emotion is often evident in family conflicts that include offspring with an eating disorder. Mothers' openly critical comments during a family interaction assessment were a better predictor of patients' healthy or disordered eating than a variety of other predictors such as body weight prior to onset of the disorder, duration of illness, body mass index, and age at onset (van Furth et al, 1996). Family expressed emotion may be problematic in part because it is associated with high levels of conflict and poorer levels of organization in families of people with eating disorders (Hedlund et al, 2003). In particular, the criticism element of expressed emotion appears to run rampant in families of young people with eating disorders.

Research shows that family expressed emotion contributes to disordered attitudes toward food and eating through diminished social competence and increased psychological distress (Arroyo & Segrin, 2013). That is, young adult women who came from families with high levels of EE, as rated by both the women themselves and one of their siblings, reported lower social competence, that in turn predicted greater psychological distress (depression, loneliness, low self-esteem), and ultimately, disordered eating attitudes and behaviors (e.g., excessive dieting, food preoccupation). Thus, family EE may be caustic to the development of social competence, generating a risk for psychological distress and perhaps disordered eating as a response to this distress. In the Arroyo and Segrin investigation, expressed emotion, but not a generic measure of family conflict (e.g., "We fight a lot in our family," "Family members often try to one-up or outdo each other") predicted diminished social competence and disordered eating attitudes. So, there is something unique about expressed emotion in particular, in contrast to family conflict in general, that generates a risk for eating disorders.

Family-expressed emotion and negative affective style represent a stressor that can interact with various genetic, temperamental, etc. predispositions to enhance the likelihood of a child experiencing a significant mental health problem. The criticism, hostility, and intrusiveness inherent in this type of communication are harmful to the developing psyche of a young family member, which is sometimes ultimately expressed in significant social and psychological problems.

Conflict Stabilization and Exacerbation of Aggression Associated with Alcoholism

Alcoholism and family conflict often go hand in hand, but not always in the most obvious ways. For instance, early research revealed that the interactions of alcoholics and their family members were more patterned, organized, and predictable while the alcoholic member was intoxicated (Steinglass, 1981; Steinglass & Robertson, 1983). So in some cases, at least, alcoholism may bring a degree of stability and predictability to certain families. However, the cost associated with this stabilizing function appears to be paid in disagreements, negativity, and aggression. Alcoholics and their spouses will often disagree about family matters, including their own relationship. In one investigation alcoholics described themselves as more loving, affectionate, and understanding than non-alcoholics did (Neeliyara et al, 1989). However, their spouses sharply disagreed with the alcoholics' self-perceptions, perceiving them as less loving and more aggressive. In the areas of affective involvement (e.g., "we are too self-centered") and behavior control (e.g., "anything goes in our family") alcoholics and their spouses showed very low agreement (McKay et al, 1993). These differing perceptions hold considerable potential to produce marital conflicts and distress.

It is unfortunately the case that alcoholism is often accompanied by physical and verbal aggressiveness in husbands and negatively toned marital interactions (Murphy & O'Farrell, 1997). When discussing a marital problem, couples with an aggressive and alcoholic husband showed a higher rate of negative communication behaviors (e.g., blaming, criticizing, put downs) and more negative reciprocity in their communication compared to couples with a non-aggressive alcoholic husband. There is also a positive association between frequency of male alcoholics' drinking and their own and their wives' verbal aggressiveness (O'Farrell et al, 2000).

Negativity in marital interaction also seems to be prevalent when the wife is alcoholic. In a rare comparison of female and male alcoholics, couples with a female alcoholic were found to be more negative in their conversations than those with a male alcoholic or no alcoholic, so long as they were not drinking (Haber & Jacob, 1997). When they drank, differences from male-alcoholic couples disappeared. For concordant couples (both husband and wife alcoholic), negativity in communication behaviors escalated when they were allowed to drink. A related study showed greater negativity during a 10-minute conflict resolution discussion among maritally distressed couples in which the wife was alcoholic, compared to non-distressed, nonalcoholic couples (Kelly et al, 2002). Among these distressed couples with a female alcoholic, the men had high rates of negative encoding behaviors (e.g., criticize, offer negative solution), but not negative decoding behaviors (e.g., disagree, justify, withdraw). In contrast, their alcoholic wives had high rates of negative decoding behaviors but not encoding behaviors.

Family of Origin Conflict and Mood Disorders

When children grow up in family environments that are strained by high levels of conflict they are at risk for mood disorders both during childhood, as well as later adulthood. Mood disorders are emotional problems such as depression, anxiety, and loneliness. High levels of family conflict appear to compromise the supportive social architecture that allows children to grow into adolescents and young adults with healthy emotional development.

Interparental conflict is positively associated with adolescents' depression, both concurrently and prospectively (Sheeber et al, 1997), and this effect may be explainable by parental rejection that is concomitant to interparental conflict (Shelton & Harold, 2008). In other words, adolescents who are exposed to high levels of interparental conflict also perceive higher levels of rejection (e.g., "Almost always complains about what I do"), and this in turn promotes symptoms of depression and anxiety in adolescents. Another factor that has been implicated in the association between family conflict and depression in offspring is disrupted attachment. In a sample of African-American adolescent females, Constantine (2006) found that family conflict was associated with weaker attachment between child and parent, and this weak attachment in turn predicted greater depression in adolescents. Constantine observed that Black adolescent females have frequent, but not very intense conflict with their parents over issues such as completing household chores. However, when these conflicts reach high levels, they become injurious to girls' emotional well-being. It is interesting to note that parental attachment has also been implicated in the association between family conflict and emotional problems in young adults (Feeney, 2006). However, in Feeney's investigation with Australian young adults, parents' insecure attachment was associated with greater conflict that was in turn associated with their young adult children's higher loneliness.

Conflict in the family of origin has been implicated in problems with loneliness and social anxiety experienced by late adolescents and young adults (Johnson et al, 2001). In a unique investigation of Asian immigrant families, parent-child conflict about acculturation (e.g., "Your parents want you to sacrifice your personal interests for the sake of the family, but you feel this is unfair") was concurrently associated with Asian-American adolescents' depression and loneliness, and predictive of subsequent anxiety over the following three years. Poor communication skills may at least partially explain the family conflict-child emotional distress association. In young adults, higher levels of family conflict, as reported by father-mother-adult child triads, were predictive of lower social skills in adult children that in turn were associated with higher levels of loneliness in those adult children (Burke, Woszidlo, & Segrin, 2012).

Family Conflict as a Disrupter of the Developing Personality

A personality disorder is an enduring and stable pattern of behavior and cognition that deviates from normative standards and expectations in one's culture (American Psychiatric Association, 2013). This pattern of behavior and experience is inflexible, pervasive, has its onset during adolescence or early adulthood, and leads to tangible distress and impairment. The *Diagnostic and Statistical Manual of Mental Disorders* (DSM-5; American Psychiatric Association, 2013) recognizes ten distinct personality disorders. Family conflict has been found to be predictive of dependent, narcissistic, and antisocial personality disorder, but never more so than with borderline personality disorder (BPD). The principal features of this personality disorder include instability of interpersonal relationships, affect, and self-image. People with BPD exhibit intense and variable mood, generally aberrant and aloof behavior, excessive daydreaming, a dissociated self-image, frantic efforts to avoid abandonment, impulsivity, feelings of emptiness, and problems with anger control. It could almost go without saying, given this constellation of symptoms, that people with BPD frequently experience turbulent interpersonal relationships.

Symptoms of BPD are positively associated with social conflict and feelings of loneliness (Johnson et al, 2000). Interpersonal conflict is also a common theme in retrospective descriptions of family of origin relationships provided by people with BPD (Gunderson & Lyoo, 1997). For example, people with this diagnosis report that their mothers were autonomous and hostile toward them (Benjamin & Wonderlich, 1994). A similar theme is evident in findings of Stern et al (1997) whose borderline personality disorder patients described their fathers and mothers as attacking and rejecting. Incidentally, these same patients also indicated that they too were attacking and rejecting toward their parents. This illustrates how the antecedents to the conflictual adult personal relationship may have their origins in early family of origin relationships.

One problem that has plagued researchers interested in family of origin conflict and offspring BPD is the tendency for people with BPD to retrospectively describe their family of origin relationships with a bias toward chaos and conflict. A study recently conducted in England addressed this matter by following 6000 expecting mothers though the first 11 years of their child's life, assessing family adversity, family conflict, and ultimately, symptoms of BPD in the children when they reached age 11 (Winsper et al, 2012). Children exposed to high levels of family of origin conflict were at elevated risk for exhibiting symptoms of BPD at age 11, even after controlling for child IQ and a number of other sociodemographic factors. Because the initial wave of assessment in this investigation was conducted during pregnancy, before the child was even born, the reverse causality argument can be effectively discarded.

Winsper et al (2012) argued that family environments marked by conflict, anger, and hostility, especially when directed at the child, will disrupt the normal emotional and cognitive development of that child. They suggest that alternations occur in the development of internal schemata of behavior and relationships, exacerbation of stress responses, and interactions with genes that may generate certain temperaments that can all compromise emotional and cognitive regulation. It is this cognitive and emotional dysregulation that lies at the core of virtually all personality disorders. Findings for the Winsper et al investigation are particularly noteworthy for they clearly implicate a family communication variable in the etiology of borderline personality disorder.

Methodological Challenges and Areas for Examining Conflict and Health in the Future

As researchers continue to investigate the pathogenic role of family conflict in various health problems, it will be important to be mindful of several methodological issues. The first, and perhaps most fundamental of these issues, is the assessment of conflict itself. There will always be inherent tradeoffs between laboratory-based observations and self-reports. Observations of family conflict use "thin slices" of family behavior to predict health problems. Observational methods are particularly powerful for assessing how family members actually behave, rather than how they say that they behave. Unfortunately, observational assessments are often made in unnatural laboratory settings, and even when they occur in more realistic settings, or even family homes, they still provide only a narrow field of vision on the family's conflict patterns. In contrast, self-reports of family conflict have the benefit of providing information on more general and recurring patterns of family interaction. Unfortunately, these come with price tags of their own, most notably perceptual and social desirability biases. Any useful line of inquiry into family conflict and health will need to generate evidence from multiple methodological perspectives that counter the weaknesses of any particular method.

A second issue concerns data that are appropriate for making causal inferences. Research on family conflict and health is dominated by investigations with cross-sectional designs. Studies that have used longitudinal designs, many of which are reviewed in this chapter, provide extremely useful information for understanding the causal ordering of conflict and health problems. This is an especially consequential issue in the domain of mental health problems where it is entirely reasonable to expect that the problem itself could become a source of conflict.

Finally, the assessment of health and well-being is something of a new frontier in the study of family conflict and health. Researchers are currently using physiological indicators of health that would have been hard to even imagine 25 years ago. As new methods are developed and simplified for assessing neuroendocrine, cardiovascular, and immunological fitness, it will obviously be useful for researchers interested in family conflict and health to adopt and test these methods in this context.

Conclusion

It is safe to say that family conflict, especially when hostile and severe, is detrimental to the physical and mental health of both adults and children. As demonstrated in the first half of this chapter, marital quality in general functions to minimize rates of health problems, whereas being in a strained and conflict-laden marriage is a risk factor for physical health problems, often by means of compromising endocrine, immune, and cardiovascular functioning. The negative physical reactions to marital conflict may show up even before spouses are willing to acknowledge that their marriage is distressed. Conflict compromises children's physiological functioning in much the same way as adults. Over time, the body is worn down from the stress of marital and family conflict. In the case of both children and adults, this stress can exacerbate the course of existing physical problems or in some extreme cases lead to the development of physical health problems. Perhaps less obvious are the ideas that marital conflict damages children's health by way of compromising parenting behavior or that family conflict can have system-wide effects.

The latter half of this chapter describes how ongoing engagement in toxic family conflict is damaging to mental health. The parallels between family conflict and physical versus mental health likely come as no surprise to those who understand that the mind-body distinction is a false dichotomy. The criticism, hostility, and intrusiveness characteristic of expressed emotion injure the psyche of children and generate health risks that have both mental and physical consequences, for example, in the form of eating disorders. The tendency for conflict stabilization or exaggeration of aggression in families with an alcoholic member is not only a mental health concern, but can also lead to physical health consequences in the case of physical violence. In addition, conflict in the family of origin is implicated in the development of other personality and mood disorders. The pathways between conflict, physical health, and mental health can be complicated, unforeseen, and far-reaching, making the study of these connections a serious concern for public health.

References

American Psychiatric Association. (2013). *Diagnostic and statistical manual of mental disorders* (5th ed.). Washington, DC: Author.

Arroyo, A., & Segrin, C. (2013). Family interactions and disordered eating attitudes: The mediating roles of social competence and psychological distress. *Communication Monographs, 80*, 399–424. doi: 10.1080/03637751.2013.828158

Bebbington, P., & Kuipers, L. (1994). The predictive utility of expressed emotion in schizophrenia: An aggregate analysis. *Psychological Medicine, 24*, 707–718. doi: 10.1017/S0033291700027860

Benjamin, L. S., & Wonderlich, S. A. (1994). Social perceptions and borderline personality disorder: The relation to mood disorders. *Journal of Abnormal Psychology, 103*, 610–624. doi: 10.1037//0021–843x.103.4.610

Brown, P. C., & Smith, T. W. (1992). Social influence, marriage, and the heart: Cardiovascular consequences of interpersonal control in husbands and wives. *Health Psychology, 11*, 88–96. doi: 10.1037//0278–6133.11.2.88

Burke, T. J., Woszidlo, A., & Segrin, C. (2012). Social skills, family conflict, and loneliness in families. *Communication Reports, 25*, 75–87. doi 10.1080/08934215.2012.719461

Constantine, M. G. (2006). Perceived family conflict, parental attachment, and depression in African American female adolescents. *Cultural Diversity and Ethnic Minority Psychology, 12*, 697–709. doi: 10.1037/1099–9809.12.4.697

Cook, W. L., Kenny, D. A., & Goldstein, M. J. (1991). Parental affective style risk and the family system: A social relations model analysis. *Journal of Abnormal Psychology, 100*, 492–501. doi: 10.1037/0021–843x.100.4.492

Coyne J. C., Rohrbaugh, M. J., Shoham, V., Sonnega, J. S., Nicklas, J. M., & Cranford, J. A. (2001). Prognostic importance of marital quality for survival of congestive heart failure. *American Journal of Cardiology, 88*, 526–529. doi: 10.1016/s0002–9149(01)01731–01733

Doane, J. A., West, K. L., Goldstein, M. J., Rodnick, E. H., & Jones, J. E. (1981). Parental communication deviance and affective style: Predictors of subsequent schizophrenia spectrum disorders. *Archives of General Psychiatry, 38*, 679–685. doi: 10.1037/0021–843X.92.4.399

Eaker, E. D., Sullivan, L. M., Kelly-Hayes, M., D'Agostino, R. B., & Benjamin, E. J. (2007). Marital status, marital strain, and risk of coronary heart disease or total mortality: The Framingham offspring study. *Psychosomatic Medicine, 69*, 509–513. doi: 10.1097/psy.0b013e3180f62357

El-Sheikh, M., Cummings, E. M., & Goetsch, V. L. (1989). Coping with adults' angry behavior: Behavioral, physiological, and verbal responses in preschoolers. *Developmental Psychology, 25*, 490–498. doi: 10.1037//0012-1649.25.4.490

Feeney, J. A. (2006). Parental attachment and conflict behavior: Implications for offspring's attachment, loneliness, and relationship satisfaction. *Personal Relationships, 13*, 19–36. doi: 10.1111/j.1475-6811.2006.00102.x

Fincham, F. D. (2003). Marital conflict: Correlates, structure, and context. *Current Directions in Psychological Science, 12*, 23–27. doi: 10.1111/1467-8721.01215

Finger, B., Kachadourian, L. K., Molnar, D. S., Eiden, R. D., Edwards, E. P., & Leonard, K. E. (2010). Alcoholism, associated risk factors, and harsh parenting among fathers: Examining the role of marital aggression. *Addictive Behaviors, 35*, 541–548. doi: 10.1016/j.addbeh.2009.12.029a

Gavazzi, S. M., McKenry, P. C., Jacobson, J. A., Julian, T. W., & Lohman, B. (2000). Modeling the effects of expressed emotional, psychiatric symptomology, and marital quality levels on male and female verbal aggression. *Journal of Marriage and the Family, 62*, 669–682. doi: 10.1111/j.1741-3737.2000.00669.x

Goeke-Morey, M. C., Papp, L. M., & Cummings, E. M. (2013). Changes in marital conflict and youths' responses across childhood and adolescence: A test of sensitization. *Developmental Psychopathology, 25*, 241–251. doi: 10.1017/s0954579412000995

Gouin, J. P., Carter, C. S., Pournajafi-Nazarloo, H., Glaser, R., Malarkey, W. B., Loving, T. J., Stowell, J., & Kiecolt-Glaser, J. K. (2010). Marital behavior, oxytocin, vasopressin, and wound healing. *Psychoneuroendocrinology, 35*, 1082–1090. doi: 10.1016/j.psyneuen.2010.01.009

Graham, J. E., Glaser, R., Loving, T. J., Malarkey, W. B., Stowell, J. R., & Kiecolt-Glaser, J. K. (2009). Cognitive word use during marital conflict and increases in proinflammatory cytokines. *Health Psychology, 28*, 621–630. doi: 10.1037/a0015208

Gunderson, J. G., & Lyoo, K. (1997). Family problems and relationships for adults with borderline personality disorder. *Harvard Review of Psychiatry, 4*, 272–278. doi: 10.3109/10673229709030553

Haber, J. R., & Jacob, T. (1997). Marital interactions of male versus female alcoholics. *Family Process, 36*, 385–402. doi: 10.1111/j.1545-5300.1997.00385.x

Harburg, E., Kaciroti, N., Gleiberman, L., Julius, M., & Schork, M. A. (2008). Marital pair anger-coping types may act as an entity to affect mortality: Preliminary findings from a prospective study (Tecumseh, Michigan, 1971–1988). *Journal of Family Communication, 8*, 44–61. doi: 10.1080/15267430701779485

Hayatbakhsh, R., Clavarino, A. M., Williams, G. M., Bor, W., O'Callaghan, M. J., & Najman, J. M. (2013). Family structure, marital discord and offspring's psychopathology in early adulthood: a prospective study. *European Child and Adolescent Psychiatry, 22*, 693-700. doi: 10.1007/s00787-00013-0464-0

Hedlund, S., Fichter, M. M., Quadflieg, N., & Brandl, C. (2003). Expressed emotion, family environment, and parental bonding in bulimia nervosa: A 6-year investigation. *Eating and Weight Disorders, 8*, 26–35. doi: 10.1007/bf03324986

Heffner, K. L., Loving, T. J., Kiecolt-Glaser, J. K., Himawan, L. K., Glaser, R., & Malarkey, W. B. (2006). Older spouses' cortisol responses to marital conflict: Associations with demand-withdrawal communication patterns. *Journal of Behavioral Medicine, 29*, 317–325. doi: 10.1007/s10865-10006-9058-9053

Hooley, J. M. (2007). Expressed emotion and relapse of psychopathology. *Annual Review of Clinical Psychology, 3*, 329–352. doi: 10.1146/annurev.clinpsy.2.022305.095236

Johnson, H. D., LaVoie, J. C., & Mahoney, M. (2001). Interparental conflict and family cohesion: Predictors of loneliness, social anxiety, and social avoidance in late adolescence. *Journal of Adolescent Research, 16*, 304–318. doi: 10.1177/0743558401163004

Johnson, N. J., Backlund, E., Sorlie, P. D., & Loveless, C. A. (2000). Marital status and mortality: The National Longitudinal Mortality Study. *Annals of Epidemiology, 10*, 224–238. doi: 10.1016/s1047-2797(99)00052-00056

Kelly, A. B., Halford, W. K., & Young, R. M. (2002). Couple communication and female problem drinking: A behavioral observation study. *Psychology of Addictive Behaviors, 16*, 269–271. doi: 10.1037/0893-164x.16.3.269

Kiecolt-Glaser, J., Malarkey, W. B., Chee, M. A., Newton, T., Cacioppo, J. T., Mao, H. Y., Glaser, R. (1993). Negative behavior during marital conflict is associated with immunological down-regulation. *Psychosomatic Medicine, 55*, 395–409. doi: 10.1097/00006842-1993090 000-00001

Kiecolt-Glaser, J. K., Bane, C., Glaser, R., & Malarkey, W. B. (2003). Love, marriage, and divorce: Newlyweds' stress hormones foreshadow relationship changes. *Journal of Consulting and Clinical Psychology, 71*, 176–188. doi: 10.1037//0022-006x.71.1.176

Kiecolt-Glaser, J. K., Gouin, J. P., & Hantsoo, L. (2010). Close relationships, inflammation, and health. *Neuroscience and Biobehavioral Reviews, 35*, 33–38. doi: 10.1016/j.neubiorev.2009.09.003

Kimmel, P. L., Peterson, R. A., Weihs, K. L., Shidler, N., Simmens, S. J., Alleyne, S., Cruz, I., Yanovshl, J. A, Veis, J. H, Phillips, R. M. (2000). Marital conflict, gender and survival in urban hemodialysis patients. *Journal of the American Society of Nephrology, 11*, 1518–1525.

Lundberg, O. (1993). The impact of childhood living conditions on illness and mortality in adulthood. *Social Science Medicine, 8*, 1047–1052. doi: 10.1016/0277-9536(93)90122-k

Malarkey, W. B., Kiecolt-Glaser, J. K., Pearl, D., & Glaser, R. (1994). Hostile behavior during marital conflict alters pituitary and adrenal hormones. *Psychosomatic Medicine, 56*, 41–51. doi: 10.1097/00006842-199401000-00006

McKay, J. R., Maisto, S. A., Beattie, M. C., Longabaugh, R., & Noel, N. E. (1993). Differences between alcoholics and spouses in their perceptions of family functioning. *Journal of Substance Abuse Treatment, 10*, 17–21. doi: 10.1016/0740-5472(93)90094-i

Mechanic, D., & Hansell, S. (1989). Divorce, family conflict, and adolescents' well-being. *Journal of Health and Social Behavior, 30*, 105–116. doi: 10.2307/2136913

Miller, G. E., & Chen, E. (2010). Harsh family climate in early life presages the emergence of a proinflammatory phenotype in adolescence. *Psychological Science, 21*, 848–856. doi: 10.1177/0956797610370161

Murphy, C. M., & O'Farrell, T. J. (1997). Couple communication patterns of maritally aggressive and nonaggressive male alcoholics. *Journal of Studies on Alcohol, 58*, 83–90.

Neeliyara, T., Nagalakshmi, S. V., & Ray, R. (1989). Interpersonal relationships in alcohol dependent individuals. *Journal of Personality and Clinical Studies, 5*, 199–202.

O'Ferrell, T. J., Murphy, C. M., Neavins, T. M., & Van Hutton, V. (2000). Verbal aggression among male alcoholic patients and their wives in the year before and two years after alcoholism treatment. *Journal of Family Violence, 15*, 295–310.

Robles, T. F., & Kiecolt-Glaser, J. K. (2003). The physiology of marriage: Pathways to health. *Physiology and Behavior, 79*, 409–416. doi: 10.1016/S0031-9384(03)00160-00164

Robles, T. F., Slatcher, R. B., Trombello, J. M., & McGinn, M. M. (2013). Marital quality and health: A meta-analytic review. *Psychological Bulletin*. Advance online publication. doi: 10.1037/a0031859

Segrin, C., Burke, T. J., & Dunivan, M. (2012). Loneliness and poor health within families. *Journal of Social and Personal Relationships, 29*, 597–611. doi: 10.1177/0265407512443434

Sheeber, L., Hops, H., Alpert, A., Davis, B., & Andrews, J. (1997). Family support and conflict: Prospective relations to adolescent depression. *Journal of Abnormal Child Psychology, 25*, 333–344. doi: 10.1023a:1025768504415

Shelton, K. H., & Harold, G. T. (2008). Interparental conflict, negative parenting, and children's adjustment: Bridging links between parents' depression and children's psychological distress. *Journal of Family Psychology, 22*, 712–724. doi: 10.1037/a0013515

Smith, T. W., Uchino, B. N., Berg, C. A., Florsheim, P., Pearce, G., Hawkins, M., Henry, N. J. M., Beveridge, R. M., Skinner, M. A., Ko, K. J., & Olsen-Cerny, C. (2009). Conflict and collaboration in middle-aged and older couples: II. Cardiovascular reactivity during marital interaction. *Psychology and Aging, 24*, 274–286. doi: 10.1037/a0016067

South, S. C., Turkheimer, E., & Oltmanns, T. F. (2008). Personality disorder symptoms and marital functioning. *Journal of Consulting and Clinical Psychology, 76*, 769–780. doi: 10.1037/a0013346

Steinglass, P. (1981). The impact of alcoholism on the family. *Journal of Studies on Alcohol, 42*, 288–303. doi: 10.1001/archpsyc.1980.01780300090011

Steinglass, P., & Robertson, A. (1983). The alcoholic family. In B. Kissin & H. Begleiter (Eds.), *The biology of alcoholism: Vol. 6. The pathogenesis of alcoholism: Psychosocial factors* (pp243–307). New York: Plenum Press. doi: 10.1007/978-1-4684-4274-8_7

Stern, M. I., Herron, W. G., Primavera, L. H., & Kakuma, T. (1997). Interpersonal perceptions of depressed and borderline inpatients. *Journal of Clinical Psychology, 53*, 41–49. doi: 10.1002/(sici)1097-4679(199701)53:aid-jclp6>3.3.co;2-t

Troxel, W. M., & Matthews, K. A. (2004). What are the costs of marital conflict and dissolution to children's physical health? *Clinical Child and Family Psychology Review, 7*, 29–57. doi: 10.1023/b:ccfp.0000020191.73542.b0

van Furth, E. F., van Strien, D. C., Martina, L. M. L., van Son, M. J. M., Hendrickx, J. J. P., & van Engeland, H. (1996). Expressed emotion and the prediction of outcome in adolescent eating disorders. *International Journal of Eating Disorders, 20*, 19–31. doi: 10.1002/(sici)1098-1108x(199607)20:1<19:aid-eat3>3.3.co;2-r

Whisman, M. A., Uebelacker, L. A., & Settles, T. D. (2010). Marital distress and the metabolic syndrome: Linking social functioning with physical health. *Journal of Family Psychology, 24*, 367–370. doi: 10.1037/a0019547

Winsper, C., Zanarini, M., & Wolke, D. (2012). Prospective study of family adversity and maladaptive parenting in childhood and borderline personality disorder symptoms in a non-clinical population at 11 years. *Psychological Medicine, 42*, 2405–2420. doi: 10.1017/s0033291712000542

Woo, S. M., Goldstein, M. J., & Neuchterlein, K. H. (2004). Relatives' affective style and the expression of subclinical psychopathology in patients with schizophrenia. *Family Process, 43*, 233–247. doi: 10.1111/j.1545-5300.2004.04302008.x

Woodall, K. L., & Matthews, K. A. (1989). Familial environment associated with type A behaviors and psychophysiological responses to stress in children. *Health Psychology, 8*, 403–426. doi: 10.1037//0278-6133.8.4.403

Wickrama, K. A. S., Lorenz, F. O., Conger, R. D., & Elder, G. H. (1997). Marital quality and physical illness: a latent growth curve analysis. *Journal of Marriage and the Family, 59*, 143–155. doi: 10.2307/353668

SECTION 5
Forgiveness as Part of Interpersonal Conflict

13

FORGIVENESS FOLLOWING CONFLICT
What It Is, Why It Happens, and How It's Done

Andy J. Merolla

Depending upon one's perspective, forgiveness is many things: something we request, desire, need, discuss, reflect upon, question, reject, fear, or celebrate. Forgiveness involves deliberation as well as automaticity, introspection as well as communication, biology as well as culture. It waxes and wanes over time, is sensitive to personality differences, contextualized by religious doctrines, and deeply personal. And while often considered divine, it also appears remarkably commonplace (McCullough, 2008).

Explicating Forgiveness Following Interpersonal Conflict

Scholars suggest that when we are working with complex concepts, such as conflict and forgiveness, we can learn much by simply listening to people's stories (Cloke & Goldsmith, 2000). Stories of forgiveness reveal the ways that people work through hurt to strengthen their relationships. Consider the story of Samuel Taylor and his mother Connie Casey. The two of them struggled greatly with Connie's rejection of Samuel's homosexuality, as well as Connie's sending of Samuel to conversion therapy. Years later, Samuel and Connie recounted their long road from fear and pain to forgiveness and gratitude on the oral history program, *StoryCorps* (Belcher, 2013).

"I don't think I've ever told you," said Samuel, "that, I completely, and 100 percent, forgive you. It's part of what we had to go through to get to where we are today. And for that, I'm not only forgiving, I'm grateful."

"If this were to be the last five minutes of conversation that I ever got to have with you," replied Connie, "and I think you already know these things, but it doesn't hurt to say it again, I'm so sorry, and I could not be more proud of the human being that you are. You're just an amazing, awesome human being."

Samuel and Connie's story demonstrates how forgiveness is critical to relationship repair. By listening to their story, we hear how Connie and Samuel reimagined their relationship's past, present, and future, and renegotiated their value systems to transcend their discord (Waldron & Kelley, 2008). The story also touches upon several of the topics discussed in this chapter, including cognition, emotion, temporality, meaning, and communication.

Borrowing the approach of Worthington (2005), this chapter begins by answering a series of questions of interest to anyone writing about or researching interpersonal forgiveness from a social scientific perspective. This chapter then examines the utility of examining communicative aspects of the forgiveness process. In addition to reviewing existing communication perspectives, such as Waldron and Kelley's (2008) Negotiated Morality Theory, I describe forgiveness as a meaning-making process – rooted in everyday talk – that is critical to people's unique understandings of themselves, their partners, and their relationships (Duck, 1994).

Critical Questions in the Study of Interpersonal Forgiveness

What is Forgiveness?

Despite frequent mentions in the literature that there is little agreement about what forgiveness entails, Worthington et al (2007) suggested that by the mid-2000s, there was, in fact, consensus amongst many scholars. Scholars agreed that forgiveness is different than such actions as excusing, condoning, or ignoring an offense. Many also agreed that interpersonal forgiveness involves a victim's emotional and motivational transformations following the experience of hurt caused by an offender. As McCullough et al (2003) put it, "nearly every theorist appears to concur that when people forgive, their responses (i.e., thoughts, feelings, behavioral inclinations, or actual behaviors) toward a transgressor become more positive and/or less negative" (p540).

Forgiveness, then, involves the reduction of negative motivations and emotions, as well as the enhancement of positive emotions. Additionally, individuals may feel an increased desire to reconcile with their offender. This last point speaks to many scholars' assertion that forgiveness and reconciliation are distinct concepts (Enright & Fitzgibbons, 2000). From a therapeutic perspective, it makes sense to clearly distinguish forgiveness and reconciliation. In some situations, reconciliation would indeed be harmful and put victims at risk of re-traumatization. Reconciliation, moreover, is not always possible (e.g., forgiving the dead; Enright & Fitzgibbons, 2000).

But many writers suggest that in people's day-to-day experiences with conflict in personal relationships, forgiveness and reconciliation are highly intertwined (Holmgren, 2012; Hook et al, 2012). McCullough (2008), for instance, noted that reconciliation "seems to be the point of forgiveness" and that "the main adaptive function of forgiveness seems to be helping individuals preserve their valuable relationships" (p116). Gerlach et al (2012) noted that forgiveness in close relationships "cannot easily be thought of without the restoration of warm-hearted feelings or one's desire to be close to the person again" (p379). Prototype studies also suggest that many people view reconciliation as a central feature of forgiveness (e.g., Friesen & Fletcher, 2007). Hook et al (2012) showed that some people have an inherently "interpersonal conceptualization of forgiveness" – they view forgiveness as necessarily involving the reestablishment of interaction between offenders and victims. Individuals from collectivistic cultures seem especially likely to have an interpersonal conceptualization of forgiveness (Hook et al, 2009).

Amongst the many definitions of forgiveness that exist, I find Fehr et al's (2010) to be particularly enlightening, comprehensive, and inclusive, as it takes into account emotion, motivation, and interaction between victims and offenders:

> Victims who forgive their offenders become motivated to act prosocially toward them by reconciling their differences, cooperating on interdependent tasks, and admonishing ill will. Victims who fail to forgive their offenders conversely become motivated to act antisocially by avoiding them or even taking revenge.
>
> *(p896)*

How Common Is Forgiveness?

Logically, it would seem that the frequency of forgiveness in close relationships is correlated with the frequency of partners' conflict and hurtful actions. Some studies suggest that partners average only about one or two conflict episodes per month, while other studies suggest conflict is much more frequent (e.g., several conflicts per week; see Caughlin & Vangelisti, 2006). Related research on hurtful events indicates that partners typically experience about two hurtful episodes per month (Feeney & Hill, 2006). Based on this work, we might assume people typically experience forgiveness no more than a few times per month in their close relationships.

But this logic might underestimate the frequency of forgiveness because it assumes that forgiveness is only germane to clearly-identifiable and memorable hurtful events and conflicts. What if it is the case that forgiveness often occurs beyond consciousness and careful deliberation, perhaps even on a daily basis? McCullough (2008) asserts just that, arguing forgiveness is far more common that most of us realize. "Everyday acts of forgiveness are so commonplace", he argued, "that we scarcely take notice" (p14). Preliminary research appears to corroborate McCullough's position, demonstrating that forgiveness can occur automatically in the context of close relationships (Karremans & Aarts, 2007).

When considering how common forgiveness is, it is important to keep in mind that not all offenses are created equal. As a result, forgiveness takes different forms in response to different types of events. Scobie and Scobie (1998) provided a useful distinction between four levels of transgressions: *apology automatic, apology dependent, forgiveness level 1,* and *forgiveness level 2.* Apology automatic and apology dependent offenses are considered minor, and lead to short-term psychological pain. Forgiveness level 1 offenses are considered relational in nature, and cause moderate pain because the offender inflicted intentional harm. Forgiveness level 2 offenses are of the highest severity and considered traumatic. The major difference between forgiveness levels 1 and 2 is that level 2 offenses require a long-term healing process (irrespective of factors such as offender remorse and apology). Thus, we might experience forgiveness much more frequently (and remember it less vividly) in the context of apology automatic and apology dependent transgressions compared to forgiveness levels 1 and 2 transgressions.

Is Forgiveness Always Positive and Appropriate?

The benefits of forgiveness are widely recognized. It has been suggested that forgiveness can benefit people physically, mentally, relationally, and spiritually (Worthington, 2005). Particularly intriguing is research suggesting forgiveness supports a range of positive health outcomes, ranging from improved cardiovascular health (Lawler et al, 2003) to lower inclination toward substance abuse (Lin et al, 2004). Summarizing this burgeoning area of research, Worthington et al (2007) said, "Forgiveness may serve as an antidote to the health-eroding processes of stress, hostility, and rumination, and as an agonist for the health-promoting processes of positive other-oriented emotion" (p296).

Yet, just because forgiveness appears be correlated to positive health outcomes, does not mean that it is inherently positive or appropriate across social situations. Philosophers debate, for instance, virtue, utilitarian, and retributivist perspectives on forgiveness. At the heart of the debate is the extent to which forgiveness and resentment can be viewed as positive, functional, and necessary (Haber, 1991; Holmgren, 2012; Murphy, 2005). One prominent voice in this debate is that of Margaret Holmgren (2012) whose virtuist stance advocates that "unconditional genuine forgiveness is always appropriate and desirable from a moral point of view" (p10). Holmgren cautions, though, that true forgiveness can only be experienced after victims work through a series of steps, including the consideration of whether or not punishment of the offender is needed. "A victims' forgiveness," said Holmgren, "is genuine only if she regards herself with sufficient self-respect, and if she does not condone the wrong, engage in self-deception, or evade any of the issues she needs to address" (p63).

Holmgren's (2012) work is fascinating in the way it carefully explores the nature of forgiveness and resentment. Other writers, working from various disciplinary perspectives, have also provocatively called for a re-examination of our taken-for-granted assumptions about forgiveness (as well as its counterpart, revenge). Adopting an evolutionary perspective, McCullough (2008) argues that we too often conceptualize forgiveness as righteous and divine, and revenge as depraved and diseased. McCullough suggests that both forgiveness and revenge are functional and serve important purposes that can lead to positive or negative outcomes for individuals and groups. McCullough et al (2013) put it this way: "revenge and forgiveness result from psychological adaptions that became species-typical because of their ancestral efficacy in solving recurrent social problems that humans encountered during evolution (Williams, 1966)" (p2). Revenge, in other words, is a normal impulse when someone wrongs us, and is functional insofar as it wards off repeat offenses. Revenge, of course, also has its costs, such that it can promote "counter-revenge" or cause the dissolution of valuable relationships. McCullough et al. (2013) argue that to operate successfully in the social world, people calculate the costs and benefits of revenge; when the costs are too high, forgiveness emerges as a functional alternative.

McCullough and colleagues are not alone in their value-neutral stance on forgiveness. Research by James McNulty and his colleagues (2008, 2010a; Luchies et al, 2010) suggests that under certain circumstances forgiveness can reduce relationship quality and undermine self-esteem. In one of the initial tests of this hypothesis, McNulty (2008) conducted a study of 72 newlywed couples who completed an initial survey and laboratory visit, as well as mail-in questionnaires every six months. Results showed that whereas forgiveness was significantly correlated with positive outcomes cross-sectionally, more complex results emerged in longitudinal analyses. An interaction effect showed that forgiveness benefited relationships characterized by infrequent negative partner behavior, but detracted from relationships in which negative partner behavior was common.

McNulty (2010a) followed up this work with a seven-day diary study. He hypothesized that partners will act more negatively on days after they have been forgiven (relative to days after which they have not been forgiven). Based on his analysis, McNulty reported that "spouses were more than six times more likely to report that their partners had engaged in a negative behavior on days after they had forgiven those partners" (p789). Luchies et al (2010) also examined the potentially negative effects of forgiveness. Their study included four experimental and longitudinal analyses as well as a meta-analysis across three of the four studies. The authors found evidence for a "bolstering effect", as well as a "doormat effect". The bolstering effect suggests forgiveness enhances victims' self-respect when their offenders show sufficient remorse. The doormat effect suggests forgiveness detracts from victims' self-respect when offenders make weak amends. McNulty (2010b) speculated that partners that have high levels of conflict in their relationship might actually experience better outcomes from less rather than more forgiveness.

Why Do People Forgive?

There is a rather large body of research linking forgiveness (both state and trait) to a host of antecedent variables. McCullough et al (1998) offered a useful four-category system to capture the range of forgiveness antecedents. The four categories – in order of least to most proximal to people's forgiveness decision making – are *personality*, *relational*, *offense-related*, and *social-cognitive*. Personality variables include the Big Five factors, religiosity, and dispositional empathy. Relational variables include closeness, commitment, and social embeddedness. Offense-related variables include offense severity and offender apology. Finally, social-cognitive variables include empathy, blame attributions, and rumination. In lieu of an exhaustive review of this research, I summarize the results of two recent meta-analyses by Fehr et al (2010) and Riek and Mania (2011).

Riek and Mania (2011) used McCullough et al's (1998) four-category framework to guide their meta-analysis of the antecedents and consequences of forgiveness. Their analysis was based on 103 articles (158 total samples). Their findings demonstrated that variables in the four categories consistently predicted state and trait forgiveness. Overall, state empathy was the strongest predictor of forgiveness ($r = .50$). This finding fits with McCullough et al's (1998) assertion that empathy is the "governor of forgiving" (p1588). Other good predictors at the social-cognitive level were attribution ($r = .37$) and anger ($r = -.37$). Among the personality variables, agreeableness ($r = -.37$) was the best predictor of forgiveness. At the relationship level, commitment – the only variable examined in that category – was associated with forgiveness at $r = .34$. Consistent with much research, apology, an offense-level variable, was also moderately correlated with forgiveness ($r = .33$).

Fehr et al's (2010) meta-analysis analyzed results from 175 studies to cast light on the "situational and dispositional correlates" of forgiveness. Fehr et al. utilized a framework that was slightly different from McCullough et al's (1998) four-category system. Fehr et al proposed three overarching categories of antecedents: *cognition* (i.e., "What happened?"), *affect* (i.e., "How do I feel?"), and *constraints* (i.e., "What if I do not forgive?"). Then, as opposed to conceptualizing personality as a fourth distinct category, Fehr et al. embedded it within the three categories, such that they assessed state and trait variables at the cognitive, affective, and constraint levels. Consistent with Riek and Mania (2011), state empathy was the strongest correlate with forgiveness ($r = .53$). Consistent, too, were Fehr et al.'s findings that attribution (i.e., intent, $r = -.50$), anger ($r = -.45$), and apology ($r = .40$) were amongst the strongest correlates of forgiveness. In general, situational (i.e., more proximal) variables were better predictors of forgiveness than were dispositional variables.

Before concluding this section, it is essential to consider time. If time, as the saying goes, "heals all wounds", does it also promote forgiveness? Although some research suggests that people become more forgiving over time, Fehr et al's (2010) meta-analysis indicated that time is not significantly related to forgiveness. The reason time is not consistently related to forgiveness in research could be due to the way in which time has been measured. McCullough et al (2003) showed that to effectively test the effects of time on forgiveness, three specific estimates are needed. First, researchers must assess *forbearance*, which is individuals' initial emotional response to an offense. Next, researchers must assess *trend forgiveness*, which is individuals' degree of change over time from their baseline forbearance. Finally, *temporary forgiveness* must be measured, which captures individuals' upward or downward fluctuations in forgiveness based on an expected trend. In other words, temporary forgiveness estimates the extent to which individuals have days when their retaliatory or unforgiving motivations spike. Based on McCullough et al's (2003) research using these three estimates, it appears many people's road to forgiveness is a winding one.

What is the Role of Culture in Forgiveness?

Most cross-cultural research on forgiveness explores the role of individualistic versus collectivist ideals (Merolla et al, 2013). As noted by Sandage and Williamson (2005), cultural individualism and collectivism are essential factors in the function and performance of forgiveness. The researchers suggested that in individualistic cultures, the central driver of forgiveness is the restoration of personal well-being. But in collectivistic cultures, forgiveness is primarily motivated by social well-being. "The collectivistic goal of forgiveness," said Sandage and Williamson, "will prioritize restoring social harmony and well-being above personal benefits" (p45). Further, they said that whereas individualists tend to perceive forgiveness and reconciliation as distinct, collectivists tend to perceive them as largely indistinguishable.

Hook et al (2009) forwarded a theoretical model of collectivistic forgiveness. Hook et al's goal was help counseling psychologists better understand the varying orientations that might exist toward forgiveness around the world. Consistent with Sandage and Williamson (2005), Hook and colleagues defined collectivistic forgiveness as motivated by social harmony, relationship repair, and in-group relationship concerns. Consistent with this theorizing, recent research demonstrates that social harmony is indeed a more robust predictor of forgiveness decisions in collectivistic than individualistic cultures (Karremans et al, 2011; cf. Merolla et al, 2013). It should also be noted that researchers have also done interesting cross-cultural research on forgiveness and dispositional variables (e.g., Paz et al, 2008). Nevertheless, there is much work left to be done on the role of culture in the forgiveness process.

The Communication of Forgiveness

Researchers in the field of communication typically assume that communication is not merely a one-way process that expresses thoughts conjured in the mind. Communication also creates, enables, and constrains reality. Acknowledging this perspective, there are at least three general ways to conceptualize and study forgiveness communication. First, forgiveness is self-presentational, comprised of identifiable and meaningful speech acts (Haber, 1991). Second, forgiveness emerges in partners' relational negotiation process (Waldron & Kelley, 2008).

Third, forgiveness is socially constructed and given meaning over time through talk (Duck, 1994). The remainder of this chapter describes each of these approaches to forgiveness, followed by a discussion of theoretical and methodological challenges and opportunities for researchers of forgiveness communication.

The Communicative Performance of Forgiveness

In addition to experiencing forgiveness, people can also perform it verbally and nonverbally (Scobie & Scobie, 1998; Waldron & Kelley, 2005). Although the performance of forgiveness might align with one's actual feelings, people can also engage in verbal and nonverbal behaviors reflective of forgiveness when they do not, in fact, feel it (Merolla, 2014). It is important, then, to differentiate the intra- and interpersonal experiences of forgiveness.

Forgiveness as a Speech Act

When examining the expressive elements of forgiveness, it is helpful to first turn to the work of Haber (1991). Haber, a philosopher, began examining communication aspects of forgiveness as a way to define forgiveness as something more than just a motivational or emotional construct. He set out to "examine what it is one does when one performs the linguistic act of expressing forgiveness" (p29). Drawing on speech act theory (Austin, 1962), Haber suggested that forgiveness can be analyzed as a performative utterance. The "I forgive you" phrase, Haber argued, is the prototypical way a victim communicates his or her forgiveness to an offender. And the very utterance of this phrase carries with it a certain set of assumptions that, if met, suggest one's forgiveness is genuine.

Of course, uttering "I forgive you" does not *necessarily* mean one's forgiveness is genuine, just as one can say "I love you" and not actually mean it. By framing forgiveness in performative terms, Haber raised a series of important questions about the conditions that must be met for forgiveness expressions to be true or false (Merolla, 2014). For instance, when John says "I forgive you" to an offender, must John have completely overcome his resentment for his utterance to be true? Or is it sufficient that he sincerely promises to eliminate his resentment? Haber concluded that "forgiveness is more like promising than we would otherwise suspect" (p55). From a speech act perspective, "I forgive you" (and similar types of utterances) functions as a promise of future behavior, rather than merely as an external and definitive manifestation of one's transformation of motivation and emotion.

Haber's (1991) work helps to frame questions about the effects that forgiveness expressions have on offenders. Haber reasoned that when someone expresses forgiveness to an offender, "in addition to performing the illocutionary act of expressing forgiveness, he is also performing the perlocutionary act of inviting the listener to believe that he is forgiven" (p52). Haber's perspective identifies the complex ways that forgiveness is partly *undetermined* in any given moment.

Forgiveness can be viewed as the result of how victims and offenders treat one another over time, as well as how they construe their past, present, and future behavior and responsibilities to one another.

Forgiveness-Granting Styles

Joining Haber (1991) in his interest in the communicative elements of the forgiveness process are various communication researchers. Kelley (1998) reviewed existing models of forgiveness and concluded that, despite the existence of important research programs on forgiveness, there was a lack of work on "how forgiveness is *communicated* in daily interactions" (p258, italics in original). To examine communication aspects of forgiveness, Kelley collected narrative accounts from people who have been hurt by friends and family members. His analysis identified several key forgiveness motivations, forgiveness communication styles, and forgiveness outcomes. In terms of forgiveness communication, three general styles emerged: direct, indirect, and conditional. Direct forgiveness involves the victims discussing the transgression with the offender and clearly expressing forgiveness. Indirect forgiveness involves nonverbal displays of forgiveness, implicit understandings between partners, and the resumption of "normal" behavior. Conditional forgiveness involves victims forgiving with stipulations that must be met by the offender.

Kelley's (1998) forgiveness communication typology prompted several additional studies of forgiveness communication (see Table 13.1 for a complete listing of the forgiveness styles in the literature). Waldron and Kelley (2005), for instance, built on Kelley's (1998) initial work by analyzing the frequency and correlates of forgiveness-granting communication styles. They created a self-report index of forgiveness communication and surveyed college students in romantic relationships about forgiveness episodes they had experienced. Waldron and Kelley's factor analytic work yielded a five-factor measure of forgiveness communication. The five factors were *nonverbal display, conditional, minimizing, discussion,* and *explicit forgiveness* (see Table 13.1). Results indicated that forgiveness communication is related to the nature of the reported transgression and relationship outcomes. Conditional forgiveness, for example, was positively related to transgression severity, whereas nonverbal displays and minimization were negatively related to severity. Moreover, the forgiveness styles of discussion and explicit forgiveness were related to relationship strengthening following transgressions, while conditional forgiveness was related to relationship weakening. This set of findings showed that analyzing *how* people communicate forgiveness might be a reliable way to parse differing types, degrees, and phases of forgiveness.

Spotlight on One Research Line on Forgiveness Styles

My own work on forgiveness communication, which was very much influenced by the social and clinical psychological as well as communication research on

TABLE 13.1 Types of Forgiveness Communication Identified in the Literature (Alphabetical Order)

Forgiveness-granting styles	Definition
Conditional	Telling someone that he or she is forgiven only if he or she meets some stated standard.
Discussion	Initiated dialogue about the offense as well as partners' relational norms and values.
Explicit	Clearly telling another person that he or she is forgiven (e.g., "I forgive you").
Habits of forgiveness	Signaling forgiveness through habituated conflict management and relational maintenance behaviors.
Interaction sequences	Using previously effective conflict management patterns that show that forgiveness has commenced.
Kind gesture★	Doing something kind, such as gift giving, to show that resentment has diminished and forgiveness has occurred/begun.
Minimizing	Telling the other person that the offense is no longer a serious issue in the relationship.
Non-expression	Choosing not to communicate forgiveness, even though it has occurred and the relationship has continued.
Nonverbal display	Showing forgiveness through facial expressions or behaviors such as hugs.
Reinitiating contact★	Communicating forgiveness by contacting an offender after a long period of avoidance.
Relational rituals	Understanding forgiveness has occurred by partners' joint engagement in a cultural or relational ritual or tradition.
Returning to normal	When partners intuit forgiveness based on the fact that communication has normalized.
Third-party/requesting intervention	When an intervener helps the discordant partners work through their differences.
Unsaid-yet-understood/natural occurrence★	When forgiveness naturally emerges. Although not stated, the partners are clearly aware that forgiveness occurred.
Using time	Allowing time to pass in a manner that opens up space for eventual dialogue and relational renegotiation.

Note: These styles and definitions are drawn from Kelley (1998) and Waldron and Kelley (2005, 2008). Styles denoted with asterisk were drawn from the pretest reported in Merolla et al. (2013).

forgiveness reviewed in this chapter, has focused primarily on understanding the commonness of forgiveness style usage and determining the extent to which different forgiveness styles shape personal and relational well-being. A central theme in my research is that forgiveness communication matters in relationships. That is, how individuals recall communicating forgiveness following interpersonal conflicts seems to offer unique insight into the forgiveness process, thus complementing existing work on forgiveness that focuses primarily on cognitive and motivation correlates of forgiveness. In this section, I review some of the work my colleagues and I have conducted on forgiveness communication. I also discuss some of our emerging ideas about how forgiveness communication can be conceptualized and investigated to promote future research and facilitate cross-study comparison of results.

In the first study I conducted on forgiveness, I attempted to build upon Kelley's (1998) typological work by examining the predictors and relational consequences of forgiveness-granting styles (Merolla, 2008). Based on content analysis of retrospective reports of forgiveness episodes in friendships and dating relationships, results indicated that transgression severity and offender blameworthiness (i.e., perception of responsibility and intentionality) influenced how forgiveness was communicated. Participants reported using conditional and indirect styles more often than direct styles following offenses of increasing severity and blameworthiness. Findings also revealed that conditional forgivers were more likely than direct or indirect forgivers to harbor ongoing negative emotions related to the transgression. This finding helped explain some of the results of Waldron and Kelley (2005). In particular, it seemed plausible that conditional forgiveness contributed to relational weakening because partners who used conditional forgiveness remained hurt and angry about the offense. I speculated that conditional forgiveness in ongoing relationships could be reflective of *pseudoforgiveness* (Enright & Fitzgibbons, 2000), experienced when partners lack trust, yet still want to maintain the relationship.

Additional evidence regarding the effects of forgiveness communication came from research I conducted with Shuangye Zhang (Merolla & Zhang, 2011). Results based on structural equation modeling indicated that, across romantic, friend, and family relationships, use of direct forgiveness reduced self-reported relational damage and increased relational satisfaction. Conditional forgiveness, by contrast, positively predicted relational damage. Based on these findings, we suggested that direct forgiveness (involving both verbal and nonverbal features) could be a key element of successful relational maintenance. Conditional forgiveness, however, though not without utility, might signify that a relationship is still in a state of repair (see also Merolla et al, 2013).

To try to make sense of conditional forgiveness, we offered three reasons that its use might be linked to negative emotion, relational damage, and weakening across studies. First, it could be that the relational damage linked to the use of conditional forgiveness results from the fact that conditional forgiveness is most common following especially hurtful offenses. Second, it could be that partners on the receiving end of conditional forgiveness are left feeling uncertain (or even manipulated) about whether or not they have been truly forgiven. Third, because conditional forgiveness is face threatening, it potentially instigates further conflict in relationships. The causes and effects of conditional forgiveness are worthy of much additional research. Conditional forgiveness indeed presents a series of conundrums for researchers to make sense of (Merolla, 2014). In particular, research is needed that determines the factors and contexts differentiating productive and problematic uses of conditional forgiving. It would seem that there are times when conditions are appropriate (e.g., following especially severe offenses). Research, however, has not yet clearly delineated these conditions. Moreover, research has not identified the precise tradeoffs involved in conditional forgiveness. It is plausible, for instance, that conditional forgiveness promotes behavior change by offenders, while also negatively affecting, at least temporarily, the overall quality of communication in a relationship.

Because existing work on forgiveness communication has primarily been conducted with respondents from the United States, Shuangyue Zhang, Shaojing Sun, and I examined forgiveness communication in both the United States and China (Merolla et al, 2013). Utilizing the earlier-described theoretical model of collectivistic forgiveness (Hook et al, 2009), as well as existing work on culture and conflict management, we explored similarities and differences in the predictors, consequences, and communication propensities of American and Chinese students in their close relationships. Although slight communication differences emerged, there was also remarkable similarity in the results. For example, in both samples, offenders' use of sincere apologies was a good predictor of direct, conditional and indirect (i.e., in the form of *non-expression*; see Table 13.1) forgiveness communication. Further, in both studies, direct forgiveness was negatively linked to perceptions of relational damage, whereas conditional forgiveness was positively associated with ongoing negative emotion. It is also interesting to note that, in both samples, unexpressed forgiveness was associated with increased perceptions of relational damage.

In addition to exploring forgiveness communication in multiple cultural contexts, several others issues need to be addressed. One such issue is the lack of coherence amongst the forgiveness communication styles examined by researchers. As shown in Table 13.1, a wide range of styles has been examined. The fact that multiple communication styles have emerged in the research literature is not surprising given that this is a relatively new and growing area of research. In efforts to begin addressing this issue, though, my colleagues (Shuangyue Zhang and Jennifer McCullough) and I recently conducted research that categories forgiveness communication styles in a straightforward yet adaptable model (Merolla et al, 2016). Influenced by Rusbult and colleagues' (1991) work on the accommodation model, which is a 2 x 2 matrix of relational conflict responses along the dimensions of *active-passive* and *constructive-destructive*, we have proposed a 2 x 2 forgiveness communication model, along the dimensions of *direct-indirect* and *healing-threatening*.

To construct this simple model, we relied on the existing research on forgiveness communication. We proposed four overarching forms of forgiveness communication that we termed *engaging* (direct-healing), *de-emphasizing* (indirect-healing), *conditioning* (direct-threatening), and *suppressing* (indirect-threatening).

At this point, our goals are more descriptive than prescriptive in scope. That is to say, we believe each forgiveness style has important functions in social and personal relationships. Moreover, the effectiveness of the style is determined in part by the goal of the forgiver. For example, when individuals wish to clearly communicate forgiveness to an offender in a manner that will promote discussion of an offense (and what it means for the future of a relationship), engaging forgiveness communication would seem especially functional. In contrast, when individuals' goals are to not only clearly express forgiveness, but also to draw a line in the sand about intolerance for repeat behavior, conditioning forgiveness might be an appropriate choice. Alternatively, suppression is an important option because, although it might not be as promotive of relational maintenance as engaging or de-emphasizing forgiveness communication, it might be a viable option when reconciliation with an offender is untenable. These ideas are speculative, but reflect some of the topics that we hope the model will help us explore.

Our initial research using the four-style model has yielded some interesting results. Using quantitative and qualitative methods, we examined how people respond to receiving different forms of forgiveness communication. Results suggest that, in the context of ongoing relationships (friendships, in particular), engaging forgiveness communication is the most preferred style, followed in order by de-emphasizing, conditioning, and suppressing. Based on qualitative analysis (i.e., coding of open-ended responses), it appears that people prefer engaging forgiveness communication because it offers a sense of completeness to the forgiveness process and opens up the possibility of relationship strengthening via dialogue about the offense. Results also raise the possibility that people have schematic representations of forgiveness communication. In regards to conditioning forgiveness communication, for instance, several participants reported that the presence of conditions run counter to how they believe genuine forgiveness should be expressed in relationships. We also conducted follow-up experimental analysis and found that conditioning forgiveness leads to greater negative and less positive emotion compared to engaging or de-emphasizing forgiveness communication. This result is consistent with some of our earlier speculation about the effects of conditional forgiveness in relationships (Merolla & Zhang, 2011).

Overall, our initial work with this four-category conceptualization of forgiveness is promising yet preliminary. We hope that the model can provide an overarching set of categories that will eventually capture a more refined set of forgiveness communication sub-categories. For example, within, say, the engaging forgiveness communication category, sub-styles could identify forms of communication that are deemed more or less preferable by receivers and more or less appropriate in certain relational contexts (e.g., romantic relationships versus family relationships). It is also possible that the styles of forgiveness communication are relevant to contexts beyond interpersonal conflict management. When groups or institutions need to communicate forgiveness for misconduct (e.g., financial mismanagement, data breaches, product recalls), they might also find themselves selecting among different styles of forgiveness. Their style selection, moreover, could be consequential to how they are perceived by their various constituencies and the general public.

Forgiveness as Negotiated Morality

The aforementioned work on forgiveness performance and forgiveness-granting styles has helped to shift attention toward communication aspects of the forgiveness process. But this work has several limitations. With its focus on communication styles – collected through cross-sectional methods, typically with one partner in a relationship – this research cannot account for processual features of forgiveness. Moreover, it is difficult to address the fact that forgiveness styles might have unique meanings and effects in relationships depending on the partners' relational history, as well as their individual personalities and moral codes.

Fortunately, scholars have built upon previous work and offered more sophisticated models of how partners, through both communication and cognition, negotiate meaning to foster forgiveness. Chief amongst this work is Waldron and Kelley's (2008) Negotiated Morality Theory (NMT). With NMT, Waldron and Kelley highlight how people express forgiveness – with a given style, at a given moment in time – as well as how they communicate *about* forgiveness, *frame* transgressions, and *make sense of* harm to construct a relational future.

Central to NMT are partners' socially-constructed values. The theory proposes that relationships are fundamentally organized around values, and that violations of values result in relational trauma. Partners have the opportunity to both restore and reconstruct their values following trauma through communication (i.e., "moral discourse"). NMT guides research of the specific types of verbal and nonverbal communication "by which moral standards are expressed, questioned, reinforced, and reevaluated as forgiveness is negotiated" (p79). NMT represents the newest and most forward-thinking scholarship on the communication of forgiveness and promises to promote new research that integrates communication, sociological, and psychological perspectives (see, e.g., Gerlach et al, 2012).

Forgiveness As a Communication- and Meaning-Centered Process

A third way to examine forgiveness communication is to conceptualize it as a form of everyday talk. As noted earlier, forgiveness may be far more common than we think (McCullough, 2008). As a result, our day-to-day discourse should be explored to contextualize how forgiveness promotes relational repair following conflict. Even more basic, studying everyday talk can reveal what forgiveness actually looks and sounds like in relationships. To promote a communication and meaning-centered approach to forgiveness, I will utilize Duck's (1994) theorizing on everyday talk and meaning creation in relationships. The foundation of Duck's work is the argument that talk is the primary means by which partners create and sustain meaning in relationships. It is through talk that individuals reveal themselves to one another and create a relational identity. Duck (1994) noted, however, that scholars often reduce talk to a vehicle through which cognition is expressed. Scholars assume the heavy lifting of relational life is processed in our minds, with talk functioning as the mere output of our mental labor. Later, I offer some tentative theoretical propositions for how this perspective can guide research on forgiveness. First, though, I briefly summarize elements of Duck's theorizing, particularly his conceptualizations of talk and meaning in relationships.

Conceptualizing Talk

Duck (1994) argues that talk might be the most important part of relational life. Talk plays at least three roles. First, talk functions as a *source of information*. Partners express and display themselves – directly and indirectly – through talk. This includes their inner-most thoughts and their fleeting ideas. Second, talk functions as a *persuasive tool*. It offers a glimpse of one's viewpoints and thoughts about how the world operates; these views are shaped by many factors, including culture and "folk logic". Speech, Duck said, "argues for a view of things, it uses the metaphors and terms that a person finds helpful, it preaches the speaker's viewpoint, it is 'sermonic' (Hauser, 1986)" (p12). Third, talk functions as a *vantage point*. It informs partners of what each other thinks is true, false, and undetermined in their relationship.

Conceptualizing Meaning

Above all else, talk matters because it is through talking with one another that partners create meaning. Talk provides the basis for expressing individual identities, constructing a joint relational identity, and sustaining the relationship as a unique social entity that has a symbolic past, present and future (that can be recounted in narrative form). Based on Duck's work, at least three critical forms of meaning must be considered as emergent in everyday talk. First, everyday talk conveys *individual meaning*. Talk reveals our ideas and emotions and indicates how we feel about the persons with whom we interact.

Second, everyday talk involves *joint meaning*. Duck said that "persons symbolize their relationships with other people in many ways through talking (p149). For example, partners' similarity or dissimilarity to one another does not come just from direct discussion about overlap in interests and hobbies. It also comes from observing each other and listening to the ways they *talk about* their likes and dislikes. Third, talk between partners involves *temporal meaning*. As relationships progress, partners come to share mutual understanding of themselves, their relationship, and the world around them. Although meanings are created in moment-by-moment interactions (and are thus located in a particular time and space), meaning unfolds over time. Meaning, moreover, can change as partners experience new things together and apart.

Theoretical and Methodological Challenges and Opportunities

At this point, the study of forgiveness communication has contributed new insights into the interpersonal forgiveness process. To move forward, several issues must be addressed, particularly with regard to theoretical and methodological advancement. The remainder of this chapter focuses on these issues. In the following sections I first offer some tentative propositions for meaning-centered perspective on forgiveness. Second, I make some recommendations on methodological approaches that researchers can take to extend the study of forgiveness communication.

Theoretical Advancement: A Meaning-Centered Perspective on Forgiveness

Based on Duck's (1994) theorizing on talk and meaning construction I outlined earlier, I offer the following eight tentative propositions regarding the interpersonal forgiveness process:

1. Forgiveness is a meaning-making process – for victims and offenders – guided by their intrapersonal and interpersonal communication.
2. Forgiveness is a narrative process. Partners create and revise explanations for why offenses occurred. Such narratives shape partners' beliefs about how forgiveness should proceed (if at all). And such narratives factor into long-term relational maintenance.
3. Forgiveness is shaped by "folk logic." As Duck (1994) explained, the metaphors and common-sense wisdom we use to interpret our relational experience "are already available in the culture to elucidate our experience" (p25).
4. Forgiveness may or may not be communicated in a relationship, but the choice to express or withhold forgiveness is important for the trajectory of the relationship and its repair.
5. Forgiveness and unforgiveness enable and constrain certain forms of relational communication, and shape patterns of relational interaction over time.
6. Forgiveness is punctuated and time-bound, such that the ways in which partners make sense of, and talk about, transgressions, are subject to attributional processes. Attributions, moreover, color partners' (re)interpretations of past, present, and future behavior in the relationship.

7. Forgiveness is a "reflective meta construction" (Duck, 1994, p65), such that people have the ability to consciously think about how they are making sense of a transgression, and such thinking influences if and how their forgiveness is communicated.
8. Forgiveness is a *persuasive act* – how partners communicate about forgiveness reveals their implicit meaning systems about themselves, their partners, and their relationships.

Adopting a perspective rooted in these propositions can offer new insight on issues discussed throughout this chapter. Consider, for instance, the earlier-described research on the "darkside" of forgiveness (McNulty, 2008, 2010b). As McNulty and his associates have shown, forgiveness does not always lead to positive outcomes. To understand these effects, it would be helpful to know how people in this research understand forgiveness. In McNulty's line of research, partners are often asked to self-report whether or not they forgave their partner. Yet, it is plausible that such a question means different things to different people. Some individuals might believe that forgiveness can occur despite feelings of great pain, fear, and sadness. Thus, knowing whether or not someone says they have forgiven a partner does not tell us much about their personal meaning system. Examining how partners talk about their understandings of forgiveness might help cast light on why forgiveness leads to both positive and negative relational outcomes. Moreover, if it appears that forgiveness can, at times, invite partner misbehavior (McNulty, 2010a), it would be interesting to understand how partners' interaction styles and patterns change on days before and after forgiveness (and unforgiveness) transpires.

A communication and meaning-centered perspective can also be used to examine the role of culture in the forgiveness process. Earlier it was described how people from collectivistic and individualistic cultures differentially conceptualize forgiveness and reconciliation. Whereas, for instance, collectivists tend to understand forgiveness in terms of its harmony enhancement functions, individualists tend to view forgiveness as a means of self-healing (Hook et al, 2009). These differing conceptualizations would seem most important when they shape partners' communication with one another. We can thus analyze talk in relationships to better understand the effects of cultural norms on forgiveness. People's use of language (e.g., "we language", metaphors, idioms) might indicate when and how culture is salient.

As a final example, consider how we might apply this perspective to the study of conditional forgiveness. As was discussed, research shows that use of conditional forgiveness predicts higher levels of ongoing negative emotion (Merolla et al, 2013) and relationship weakening (Waldron & Kelley, 2005). It would seem, though, that not all uses of conditional forgiveness are problematic (Waldron & Kelley, 2008). Thus, future work might parse the personal meanings that people have for use of conditional forgiveness and show how partners differentially perceive its use and reception. If partners construe the use of conditional forgiveness in similar ways (e.g., as a justified and appropriate warning about future behavior), it might be beneficial in relationships. But if partners differentially construe the use of conditional forgiveness, it could cause conflict.

Methodological Advancement

Regardless of the theoretical lens researchers apply to study forgiveness, they will confront significant challenges in collecting rich data on the everyday expression of forgiveness. As noted throughout this chapter, forgiveness appears to be shaped by various factors at the offense, individual, and relational levels (e.g., transgression severity, relationship type, and time). Perhaps the most fundamental methodological challenge facing researchers of forgiveness communication, though, is the difficulty of capturing actual interaction between offenders and victims, or at least accurate recollections of that interaction. These are, of course, issues facing nearly all researchers of conflict and communication. To address these challenges, we can turn to established, as well as emerging, methodologies.

To date, studies of forgiveness communication have relied mostly on retrospective self-reports of how forgiveness transpired in current or past personal relationships. There is much value to this approach because it enables researchers to learn from people's personal experiences (Metts et al, 1991). The drawbacks to this approach, however, is that it often yields the perspective of one partner in a relationship, and is susceptible to distortion of memory given that a reported offense can occur weeks, months, or years ago (Merolla & Zhang, 2011). Rather than eliminating the use of self-report methodologies, we should complement them with alternative methodologies (Metts et al, 1991).

Relying solely on retrospective self-report to study forgiveness communication can be problematic because it might lead us to oversample severe and memorable interpersonal transgressions and under-sample subtler moments of forgiveness. One way to increase access to day-to-day forgiveness experiences would be to utilize experience sampling approaches and diaries (Bolger & Laurenceau, 2013). This could be done with traditional written diaries, text message reminders, or smartphone apps (see, e.g., Miller, 2012). With these approaches, people can report on their own experiences of forgiveness (both as the forgiver and forgiven) as well as their observations of forgiveness in their families, workplaces, or communities. Data collected in this manner can still be limited by issues of reporting accuracy, but it offers the distinct advantage of being collected in close temporal proximity of people's forgiveness experiences. Furthermore, if relational dyads are included in the participant pool then researchers could potentially gain near real-time insight from multiple individuals involved in an interpersonal conflict.

Moving beyond self-report data, researchers have also demonstrated ways to capture recordings of actual interaction as it naturally occurs in relationships. Alberts, Yoshimura, Rabby, and Loschiavo (2005), for example, showed how routine relational maintenance communication could be studied by collecting and analyzing at-home audio recordings of couples' daily interaction. Although this data can be challenging to collect and analyze, it offers especially rich transcripts of interaction. Duck (2002), in calling for additional theory and research on everyday talk in relationships, commented that most of our everyday conversation in relationships is "populated with the thousand unimportant revelations and involuntary interpretations, pointless conversations, and routine interactions that are, in a Sartrean way, the nauseating commonalities of life as we live it" (p54). Yet if forgiveness is embedded within such interaction (and accomplished in rather unremarkable turns of talk), it is all the more reason for researchers to work towards collecting and analyzing everyday talk in their research; otherwise, we run the risk of greatly mischaracterizing what forgiveness actually looks and sounds like in people's day-to-day relational lives.

Collecting actual interaction might also be accomplished in more novel ways. Emerging methodologies, such as the use of avatars (e.g., Pinto et al, 2013), could be used to re-create forgiveness situations. Participants could, for instance, interact with on-screen avatars, and that interaction could be recorded and analyzed for communication features. Experimental design features could also be included in such research (e.g., by manipulating avatar behavior). This type of research also reflects ways that interpersonal and human-computer interaction researchers can collaborate to extend theory in both areas of scholarship (see, e.g., Nass & Yen, 2010).

Forgiveness researchers can also consider exploring various forms of media. I referred earlier to Duck's (1994) insight that our communication is heavily influenced by the folk logic present in popular media narratives. Thus, it makes sense for us to study how relational communication concepts and theories play out in the primary sources of these narratives, namely popular film, theatre, and literature (Anderegg et al, 2014, Conville, 1997; Merolla, 2009). Narratives of conflict and forgiveness, whether they come from one-on-one interviews, focus groups, or media portrayals can provide us insight regarding how people make sense of conflict and forgiveness (Cloke & Goldsmith, 2000; Duck, 1994; Waldron & Kelley, 2008). Research has shown, moreover, that powerful media narratives and portrayals of conflict behavior have the potential to feed back into people's communication as well as their expectations for relational interaction (Aubrey et al, 2013; Segrin & Nabi, 2002).

By combining self-report methodologies, experimental designs, experience sampling, human–computer interaction approaches, and narrative analysis, researchers can gain a comprehensive understanding of the interpersonal forgiveness process, communicative elements, in particular. This includes issues such as how forgiveness is discussed by victims, offenders, and third parties; why people decide to offer or withhold expressions of forgiveness; what factors shape successful and unsuccessful reconciliation; and where forgiveness is best situated with the larger process of relationship maintenance in romantic relationships, families, groups, and organizations.

Conclusion

Forgiveness resides at the intersections of failure and strength, pain and healing, conflict and closeness. This chapter attempted to review what existing social scientific research on forgiveness suggests about what forgiveness is, when it occurs, and why it can be an essential feature of the relational repair process. At the outset of this chapter, I referenced the story of Samuel and Connie. Their story reminds us that conflict and forgiveness are central to our lives and can be important sources of strength in personal relationships. And as we learn more about forgiveness, including such fundamental issues as its evolutionary roots and neurological basis, we must also remember that there is much insight to be garnered by studying people's talk, and listening to their stories.

References

Alberts, J. K., Yoshimura, C. G., Rabby, M., & Loschiavo, R. (2005). Mapping the topography of couples' daily conversation. *Journal of Social and Personal Relationships, 22,* 299–322. doi: 10.1177/0265407505050941

Anderegg, C., Dale, K., & Fox, J. (2014). Media portrayals of romantic relationship maintenance: A content analysis of relational maintenance behaviors on prime time television. *Mass Communication and Society*. doi: 10.1080/15205436.2013.846383

Aubrey, J. S., Rhea, D. M., Olson, L. N., & Fine, M. (2013). Conflict and control: Examining the association between exposure to television portraying interpersonal conflict and the use of controlling behavior in romantic relationships. *Communication Studies, 64,* 106–124. doi: 10.1080/10510974.2012.731465

Austin, J. L. (1962). *How to do things with words*. Cambridge, MA: Harvard University Press.

Belcher, J. (Producer). (2013, June). *"You feel like being gay is like a virus"*. Retrieved from storycorprs.org.

Bolger, N., & Laurenceau, J.-P. (2013). *Intensive longitudinal methods: An introduction to diary and experience sampling research*. New York, NY: Guilford.

Caughlin, J. P., & Vangelisti, A. L. (2006). Conflict in dating and marital relationships. In J. G. Oetzel & S. Ting-Toomey (Eds.), *The Sage handbook of conflict communication: Integrating theory, research, and practice* (pp129–157). Thousand Oak, CA: Sage.

Cloke, K., & Goldsmith, J. (2000). *Resolving personal and organizational conflict: Stories of transformation and forgiveness*. San Francisco, CA: Jossey-Bass.

Conville, R. L. (1997). Between spearheads: Bricolage and relationships. *Journal of Social and Personal Relationships, 14,* 373–386. doi: 10.1177/0265407597143006

Duck, S. (1994). *Meaningful relationships: Talking, sense, and relating*. Thousand Oaks, CA: Sage.

Duck, S. (2002). Hypertext in the key of G: Three types of "history" as influences on conversational structure and flow. *Communication Theory, 12,* 41–62. doi: 10.1111/j.1468-2885.2002.tb00258.x

Enright, R. D., & Fitzgibbons, R. P. (2000). *Helping clients forgive: An empirical guide for resolving anger and restoring hope*. Washington, DC: APA.

Feeney, J. A., & Hill, A. (2006). Victim-perpetrator differences in reports of hurtful events. *Journal of Social and Personal Relationships, 23,* 587–608. doi: 10.1177/0265407506065985

Fehr, R., Gelfand, M. J., & Nag, M. (2010). The road to forgiveness: A meta-analytic synthesis of its situational and dispositional correlates. *Psychological Bulletin, 136,* 894–914. doi: 10.1037/a0019993

Friesen, M. D., & Fletcher, G. J. O. (2007). Exploring the lay representation of forgiveness: Convergent and discriminant validity. *Personal Relationships, 14,* 209–223. doi: 10.1111/j.1475-6811.2007.00151.x

Gerlach, T. M., Agroskin, D., & Denissen, J. J. A. (2012). Forgiveness in close interpersonal relationships: A negotiation approach. In E. Kals & J. Maes (Eds.), *Justice and conflicts: Theoretical and empirical contributions* (pp377–390). London, United Kingdom: Springer.

Haber, J. G. (1991). *Forgiveness.* Savage, MD: Rowman & Littlefield.

Holmgren, M. R. (2012). *Forgiveness and retribution: Responding to wrongdoing.* New York, NY: Cambridge University Press.

Hook, J. N., Worthington, Jr., E. L., & Utsey, S. O. (2009). Collectivism, forgiveness, and social harmony. *The Counseling Psychologist, 37,* 821–847. doi: 10.1177/0011000008326546

Hook, J. N., Worthington, E. L., Utsey, S. O., Davis, D. E., Gartner, A. L., Jennings, D. J., Tongeren, D. R. V., & Duecek, A. (2012). Does forgiveness require interpersonal interactions?: Individual differences in conceptualization of forgiveness. *Personality and Individual Differences, 53,* 687–692. doi: 10.1016/j.paid.2012.05.026

Karremans, J. C., & Aarts, H. (2007). The role of automaticity in determining the inclination to forgive close others. *Journal of Experimental Social Psychology, 43,* 902–917. doi: 10.1016/j.jesp.2006.10.012

Karremans, J. C., Regalia, C., Paleari, G., Fincham, F. D., Cui, M., Takada, N., Uskul, A. K. (2011). Maintaining harmony across the globe: The cross-cultural association between closeness and interpersonal forgiveness. *Social Psychological and Personality Science, 2,* 443–451. doi: 10.1177/1948550610396957

Kelley, D. (1998). The communication of forgiveness. *Communication Studies, 49,* 255–271. doi: 10.1080/10510979809368535

Lawler, K. A., Younger, J. W., Piferi, R. L., Billington, E., Jobe, R., Edmondson, K., & Jones, W. H. (2003). A change of heart: Cardiovascular correlates of forgiveness in response to interpersonal conflict. *Journal of Behavioral Medicine, 26,* 373–393. doi: 10.1023/A:1025771716686

Lin, W.-F., Mack, D., Enright, R. D., Krahn, D., & Baskin, T. W. (2004). Effects of forgiveness therapy on anger, mood, and vulnerability to substance use among inpatient substance-dependent clients. *Journal of Counseling and Clinical Psychology, 72,* 1114–1121. doi: 10.1037/0022-006X.72.6.1114

Luchies, L. B., Finkel, E. J., McNulty, J. K., & Kumashiro, M. (2010). The doormat effect: When forgiving erodes self-respect and self-concept clarity. *Journal of Personality and Social Psychology, 98,* 734–749. doi: 10.1037/a0017838

McCullough, M. E. (2008). *Beyond revenge: The evolution of the forgiveness instinct.* San Francisco, CA: Jossey-Bass.

McCullough, M. E., Rachal, K. C., Sandage, S. J., Worthington, E. L., Jr., Brown, S. W., & Hight, T. L. (1998). Interpersonal forgiving in close relationships: II. Theoretical elaboration and measurement. *Journal of Personality and Social Psychology, 75,* 1586–1603. doi: 10.1037/0022-3514.75.6.1586

McCullough, M. E., Fincham, F. D., & Tsang, J.-A. (2003). Forgiveness, forbearance, and time. The temporal unfolding of transgression-related interpersonal motivations. *Journal of Personality and Social Psychology, 84,* 540–557. doi: 10.1037/0022-3514.84.3.540

McCullough, M. E., Kurzban, R., & Tabak, B. A. (2013). Cognitive systems for revenge and forgiveness. *Behavioral and Brain Sciences, 36*, 1–15. doi: 10.1017/S0140525X11002160

McNulty, J. K. (2008). Forgiveness in marriage: Putting the benefits into context. *Journal of Family Psychology, 22*, 171–175. doi: 10.1037/0893-3200.22.1.171

McNulty, J. K. (2010a). Forgiveness increases the likelihood of subsequent partner transgressions in marriage. *Journal of Family Psychology, 24*, 787–790. doi: 10.1037/a0021678

McNulty, J. K. (2010b). When positive processes hurt relationships. *Current Directions in Psychological Science, 19*, 167–171. doi: 10.1177/0963721410370298

Merolla, A. J. (2008). Communicating forgiveness is friendships and dating relationships. *Communication Studies, 59*, 114–141. doi:10.1080/10510970802062428

Merolla, A. J. (2009). Utilizing contemporary short fiction in the interpersonal communication classroom. *Communication Teacher, 23*, 7–10. doi: 10.1080/17404620802581869

Merolla, A. J. (2014). Forgive like you mean it: Sincerity of forgiveness and the experience of negative affect. *Communication Quarterly, 62*, 36–56. doi: 10.1080/01463373.2013.860903

Merolla, A. J., & Zhang, S. (2011). In the wake of transgressions: Examining forgiveness communication in personal relationships. *Personal Relationships, 18*, 79–95. doi: 10.1111/j.1475-6811.2010.01323.x

Merolla, A. J., Zhang, S., & Sun, S. (2013). Forgiveness in the United States and China: Antecedents, consequences, and communication style comparisons. *Communication Research, 40*, 595–622. doi: 10.1177/0093650212446960

Merolla, A. J., Zhang, S., & McCullough, J. L. (2016). *How do you like your forgiveness?: Communication style preferences and effects.* Manuscript submitted for publication.

Metts, S., Sprecher, S., & Cupach, W. R. (1991). Retrospective self-reports. In B. M. Montgomery & S. Duck (Eds.), *Studying interpersonal interaction* (pp162–178). New York, NY: Guilford.

Miller, G. (2012). The smartphone psychology manifesto. *Perspectives on Psychological Science, 7*, 221–237. doi: 10.1177/1745691612441215

Murphy, J. G. (2005). Forgiveness, self-respect, and the value of resentment. In E. L. Worthington (Ed.), *Handbook of forgiveness* (pp33–40). New York, NY: Sage.

Nass, C., & Yen, C. (2010). *The man who lied to his laptop: What machines teach us about human relationships.* New York, NY: Current.

Paz, R., Neto, F., & Mullet, E. (2008). Forgiveness: A China-Western Europe comparison. *Journal of Psychology, 142*, 147–157. doi: 10.3200/JRLP.142.2

Pinto, M. D., Hickman, R. L., Clochesy, J., and Buchner, M. (2012). Avatar-based depression self-management technology: Promising approach to improve depressive symptoms among young adults. *Applied Nursing Research, 26(1)*, 45–48. doi: 10.1016/j.apnr.2012.08.003

Riek, B. M., & Mania, E. W. (2011). The antecedents and consequences of interpersonal forgiveness: A meta-analytic review. *Personal Relationships, 19*, 304–325. doi: 10.1111/j.1475-6811.2011.01363.x

Rusbult, C. E., Verette, J., Whitney, G. A., Slovik, L. F., & Lipkus, I. (1991). Accommodation processes in close relationships: Theory and preliminary empirical evidence. *Journal of Personality and Social Psychology, 60*, 53–78. doi: 10.1037/0022-3514.60.1.53

Sandage, S. J., & Williamson, I. (2005). Forgiveness in cultural context. In E. L. Worthington, Jr.(Ed.), *Handbook of forgiveness* (pp41–56). New York, NY: Brunner-Routledge.

Scobie, E. D., & Scobie, G. E. W. (1998). Damaging events: The perceived need for forgiveness. *Journal for the Theory of Social Behaviour, 28*, 373–401. doi: 10.1111/1468-5914.00081

Segrin, C., & Nabi, R. L. (2002). Does television viewing cultivate unrealistic expectations about marriage? *Journal of Communication, 52*, 247–263. doi: 10.1111/j.1460-2466.2002.tb02543.x

Waldron, V. R., & Kelley, D. L. (2005). Forgiving communication as a response to relational transgressions. *Journal of Social and Personal Relationships, 22*, 723–742. doi: 10.1177/0265407505056445

Waldron, V. R., & Kelley, D. L. (2008). *Communicating forgiveness*. Los Angeles, CA: Sage.

Worthington, E. L. (2005). Initial questions about the art and science of forgiving. In E. L. Worthington (Ed.), *The handbook of forgiveness* (pp1–13). New York, NY: Sage.

Worthington, E. L., Jr., Witvliet, C. V. O., Pietrini, P., & Miller, A. J. (2007). Forgiveness, health, and well-being: A review of evidence for emotional versus decisional forgiveness, dispositional forgiveness, and reduced unforgiveness. *Journal of Behavioral Medicine, 30*, 292–302. doi: 10.1007/s10865-10007-9105-9108

14
EXPRESSING AND SUPPRESSING CONDITIONAL FORGIVENESS IN SERIOUS ROMANTIC RELATIONSHIPS

Dayna N. Kloeber and Vincent R. Waldron

Forgiveness is considered a healthy reaction to the inevitable hardships that befall most relationships at one time or another (e.g. Enright, 2001; Hargrave, 1994a, 1994b; Waldron & Kelley, 2008; Worthington, 2005). Few debate its association with individual peace of mind and feeling connected to others (Bono et al, 2008) and, according to one study, 88 percent of mental health professionals consider it an important topic for their clients (Konstam et al, 2000). In addition to being associated with mental health, forgiveness is positively linked with physical health (e.g. Coker et al, 2000; Lawler et al, 2005; Whited et al, 2010), sleep quality (Stoia-Caraballo et al, 2008) and happiness (Macaskill, 2012). Parents who practice forgiveness have stronger parental alliances (Gordon et al, 2009). The findings have motivated researchers to more clearly define forgiveness and the ways in which it is enacted.

Explicating Forgiveness as Conditional

Researchers typically define forgiveness as an internal transformation from negative to positive feelings toward the offender along with a decision to forego revenge or seek retribution (e.g. Enright, 2001; Worthington, 2005) Yet, clinicians and lay people define it differently (Anderson, 2007), often focusing on behavioral aspects, such as expressions of remorse and the ways in which forgiveness can facilitate reconciliation. Consequently, scholars have been urged to develop definitions that are more firmly grounded in lived experience (Cosgrove & Konstam, 2008). Based on their interviews with long-term romantic couples, Waldron & Kelley (2008) defined forgiveness as a relational process negotiated through the communicative acts of the partners:

Forgiveness is a relational process whereby harmful conduct is acknowledged by one or both partners; the harmed partner extends undeserved mercy to the perceived transgressor; one or both partners experience a transformation from negative to positive psychological states, and the meaning of the relationship is renegotiated, with the possibility of reconciliation

(Waldron & Kelley, 2008, p19).

Reconciliation is a related but distinct process of relationship repair (Hawk, 2007). The desire for reconciliation often motivates partners to forgive (Kelley, 1998; Strelan et al, 2013). Roloff, Soule, and Carey (2001) found that the fear of losing a relationship positively influences partners to move past transgressions. Likewise, partners with a "high mate value" are more likely to be forgiven (Sidelinger & Booth-Butterfield, 2007). The desire to preserve relational bonds can foster an obligation to forgive, particularly in non-voluntary (i.e. parent/child) relationships (Carr & Wang, 2012). Nonetheless, it is quite possible to forgive without reconciling with the offender or to reconcile without forgiving. Due to these complicated dynamics, researchers have become increasingly interested in how partners negotiate forgiveness and reconciliation in response to conflict in close relationships. For some, forgiving creates prerequisites for restoring the relationship to its original state – a resumption of intimacy and interdependence. For others, the process appears to redefine the relationship, with new moral commitments, levels of intimacy, and rules of communication (Kloeber, 2011; Waldron & Kelley, 2008).

Communication scholars have made a significant contribution to what is known about forgiveness and reconciliation (i.e. Guerrero & Bachmann, 2010; Kelley, 1998; Kelley & Waldron, 2006; Merolla, 2008; Merolla & Zhang, 2011; Waldron & Kelley, 2005, 2008). Early investigations determined that some partners communicate forgiveness explicitly whereas others use an implicit style that sometimes includes nonverbal cues (such as renewed touching or eye contact). Others impose conditions as part of the forgiveness process (Kelley, 1998). Subsequent research identified five categories of forgiveness granting: explicit, discussion, conditional, nonverbal, and minimization (Waldron & Kelley, 2005). Direct communicative approaches are preferred by partners (Morse & Metts, 2011; Kingsley Westerman, 2013), and yet, Merolla (2008) reported that indirect approaches were most common in friendships and dating relationships. Conditional forgiveness ("I will forgive you if you do/don't do X") is also common in close, romantic relationships (Waldron & Kelley, 2005). Scholars posit that conditional forgiveness (CF) asserts control in relationships (Waldron & Kelley, 2008), but for some writers (Enright, 2001), the use of stipulations repudiates the inherently unconditional nature of true forgiveness. Understanding why and how conditional forgiveness is communicated is the topic of the current investigation.

CF has been investigated by a relatively small group of scholars thus far (Guerrero & Bachmann, 2010; Kloeber, 2008, 2011; Merolla, 2008, Merolla &

Zhang, 2011; Waldron & Kelley, 2005). A number of interesting findings have resulted. CF is quite common, having been reported by nearly a third of romantic partners (Waldron & Kelley, 2005) often in response to severe transgressions (Merolla & Zhang, 2011, Waldron & Kelley, 2005), such as substance and physical abuse (Kloeber, 2011). CF is more frequent in serious romantic relationships than among friends or dating partners (Merolla & Zhang, 2011) and more prevalent when a partner is highly invested in the relationship (Guerrero & Bachmann, 2010). CF could be a means of delaying "true" forgiveness until the partner expresses genuine remorse. However, at least one study found that CF was used after the offending partner offered a sincere apology (Merolla & Zhang, 2011). Taken together, these studies suggest that CF is a preferred approach, but they reveal little about the motives for its use.

Existing research suggests that the use of CF has relational consequences. Its use has been associated with a decrease in relational satisfaction above and beyond the effects of transgression severity (Waldron & Kelley, 2005). A subsequent secondary analysis revealed that CF was sometimes offered in a constructive spirit, with support for the partner and concern for the future of the relationship (Kloeber, 2008). At other times the conditions were expressed as a warning or even a punishment (i.e. "I told her I still love her, but hope she's learned her lesson and would promise never to do it again."; "I told them that I would (forgive). But understand that once you screw up, admit it and don't let it happen again.") An unexpected discovery was the use of implicit (unexpressed) conditions. In such cases, a wounded partner formulated clear behavioral expectations but chose not to discuss them. Kloeber observed that each instance of implicit CF was a response to physical or substance abuse. She speculated that users of implicit CF may internalize feelings to avoid provoking additional abuse. In this way, implicit CF may be protective. Another possibility is that conditions such as the cessation of abuse are so self-evident that stating them is unnecessary. Finally, implicit CF may be a "secret test" by which the partner's commitment to improved behavior is assessed (cf. Baxter & Wilmot, 1984).

It appears that CF is a nuanced and complicated response to conflict in personal relationships. A qualitative analysis of CF narratives found that serious romantic partners gave voice to a complex knot of seven dialectical tensions: reconcilable-irreconcilable, individual identity-couple identity, risk-safety, certainty-uncertainty, mercy-justice, heart-mind, expression-suppression (Kloeber, 2011). An overarching dialectic concerned whether the partners should reconcile, and if so, under what circumstances. Kloeber's participants appeared to use CF as a way to work through the complexities of this decision. For example, one spouse seemed to favor a forgiving response to her partner's infidelity but wanted to prevent a reoccurrence. She stipulated monitoring of his behavior – knowing his whereabouts and having access to passwords. She was simultaneously merciful and self-protective. Interestingly, the husband's new reporting regimen could be viewed as a negative consequence (punishment) of his unfaithfulness. In that sense CF allowed her to experience a measure of justice even as she acted mercifully. Building on Kloeber's work, researchers should look more closely at the motives for using CF, even if they are often mixed. Doing so would help us understand how this form of forgiveness shapes the quality of relationships in the wake of serious transgressions.

Research Expectations

Previous work suggests that CF leads to relationship deterioration (Merolla, 2008; Merolla & Zhang, 2011; Waldron & Kelley, 2005). Our data afforded an opportunity to confirm this finding with a larger sample, as noted by H1: Partners who use CF should also report a decline in relationship quality. Several antecedent perceptions may account for differences in the outcomes of forgiveness episodes (Waldron & Kelley, 2008). One of these is perceived quality of the relationship. Partners are more invested in high quality relationships (Guerrero & Bachman, 2010) and thus antecedent relationship quality should be positively associated with improvements after the CF episode (H2). Another factor is the perceived severity of the transgression (Merolla & Zhang, 2011). With the most serious transgressions, forgiveness (of any kind) may be considered impossible, or simply a secondary concern, as suggested by H3: Transgression severity will be negatively associated with improvement in relationship quality after a CF episode. When transgressors apologize, relationship quality tends to improve after a forgiveness episode (Merolla & Zhang, 2011; Kelley & Waldron, 2005). We expected this finding to extend to CF episodes, as noted by H4: Expressions of remorse should be positively associated with improvement in relationship quality.

Partners sometimes choose not to articulate verbally their intention to seek or give forgiveness (Kelly, 1999). Instead, they make a private commitment to do so, use nonverbal signals, or simply allow the relationship to "return to normal" (Waldron & Kelley, 2005). Researchers have yet to examine the degree to which users of CF employ explicit approaches, so this matter is addressed by RQ1: What percentage of CF users explicitly communicate the conditions to their partners? We expected the positive outcomes associated with explicit forgiveness to hold when partners use explicit CF (H5): Explicit communication of conditions will be positively associated with relational improvement. Finally, partners' motives for using CF are not well understood. Kloeber proposed several motives, such as minimizing risk of repeated transgressions, facilitating relational justice, and reducing uncertainty about the future. RQ2 guided our efforts to analyze qualitatively motives for using explicit CF: Why do partners communicate conditions during forgiveness episodes?

A Spotlight Study of Conditional Forgiveness

Mixed methods were used to gain a more complex understanding of this communicative phenomenon. Quantitative data was best suited to seek answers about associative relationships (H1-H5); simple quantitative data were used to answer RQ1, which concerned the relative frequency of explicit/implicit CF. Alternately, a qualitative analysis was necessary to answer RQ2, which addressed the motives of conditional forgiveness. To answer this question we needed to analyze participants' experiences with CF, as revealed in their open-ended responses to survey questions. In order to glean a complete understanding of phenomenon, human inquiry often requires both quantitative and qualitative techniques (Tracy, 2013).

Participants

After elimination of 26 of 226 surveys, the sample size was 200. Participants were 66.7 percent female and 33.3 percent male with a mean age of 24.6 years. At the time of the forgiveness episode participants averaged 21.7 years of age. In terms of marital status, 18 percent were married at the time of the survey, 2 percent were divorced or separated, and 78 percent were unmarried. Roughly two thirds of the sample identified themselves as Caucasian or White, while the remainder identified a wide variety of ethnic backgrounds.

Measures

When asked to rate how clearly they remembered the forgiveness episode using a five-point Likert-type scale (5 = extremely well), the mean response was 4.3 with all respondents remembering at least "moderately well". Respondents answered open-ended items asking them to explain the context of the transgression and how they communicated CF.

Relationship quality, the key dependent variable, was estimated at three points in time (before episode, after the transgression, and at the present time) by having partners rate the quality (e.g., "We had a high quality relationship before the offense"), stability, and intimacy of the relationship on a seven-point Likert-type scale (see Waldron & Kelley, 2005). As Cronbach's α statistics were relatively high (.74, .84, and .93), summative measures were created for each point in time. Transgression severity was assessed using a summative measure (α = . 84) based on three items (e.g., "at the time this occurred, how threatening to your relationship was this action?") reported in previous research (Waldron & Kelley, 2005). Following Merolla and Zhang (2011), partner remorse was measured with a scale (α = .93) comprised of three items (e.g., "My partner acknowledged that he/she hurt me"). Finally, the explicitness of CF was assessed with two questions: "Did you communicate the conditional forgiveness to your partner?" and "Did you communicate to your partner the reasons why you offered conditional forgiveness?" Participants who answered at least one of these questions affirmatively were considered to have used explicit CF.

Qualitative Data Coding

A qualitative methodology was used to examine RQ2. Informed by Lindlof and Taylor (2002), the first step of data coding for RQ2 consisted of researcher one reading through the participant responses to the question "Why did you use conditional forgiveness?" Next, as is customary with the constant comparative method, a rough category system began to emerge as each response was analyzed for novelty and placed in existing or new categories (Lindlof & Taylor, 2002). This "open-coding" phase produced a plethora of categories with accompanying exemplars. Next, both researchers began the process of axial coding or collapsing categories (Lindlof & Taylor, 2002). They reached consensus on points of disagreement through discussion, referring to the exemplars, and returning to the raw data for context when necessary. There were two phases of axial coding. The perpetual goal was cogent categories that preserved authenticity and uniqueness. Finally, exemplars were extracted to help illustrate the interpretation.

Results

Preliminary statistical analyses addressed RQ1 and H1, both of which could be evaluated using simple statistical tests. A frequency count answered RQ1, which concerned whether participants voiced their conditions or not. Results indicated that 56 percent used explicit CF.

H1 predicted that those involved in CF episodes would report reductions in relationship quality. Within-subjects t-tests were used to compare mean scores before and after the CF episode. Results indicated that mean relationship quality dropped precipitously, from 17.4 to 11.6, t (185) = 9.6, $p <. 0001$. We also examined the difference between the initial quality score and relationship quality "immediately after the offense" (mean = 12.1). Results confirmed that relationship quality was significantly lower after the offense, t (190) = 12.7, $p < .0001$. However, the change from immediately after the offense to the current time was insignificant, t (186) = .68, $p < .49$. These results partially support H1. CF episodes were associated with relationship decline. However, the insignificant result pertains to the time period in which participants most likely communicated CF (during the post-transgression period). Although we see no evidence that CF improved relationship quality, this finding leaves open the possibility that the use of CF slowed the rate of post-transgression decline.

To address H2 through H5, we used linear regression procedures to predict relationship quality from four blocks of variables: relationship quality before the episode, transgression severity, partner remorse, and explicit communication of CF. This last block included dummy coded responses to the two questions measuring explicitness of CF. Relationship quality, the dependent variable in each analysis, was operationalized in three ways: as relationship quality "now" (after the episode; at the time of the report); as the change in relationship quality from before the transgression (Time 1) to the present (Time 3); and as the change in relationship quality from immediately after the transgression (Time 2) to the present (Time 3).

A forced entry approach was used first because the Waldron & Kelly (2008) forgiveness model suggests a temporal ordering of the variables. In particular, we expected the independent variables to contribute in a temporal sequence, with pre-exisiting relationship quality first, the severity of the offense second, partner remorse third, and the quality of CF fourth. Variables were entered in that order. Subsequently, stepwise regression was used to identify a more parsimonious set of predictors. Statistics are reported in Table 14.1.

In predicting the quality of the relationship at the present time, the entry of prior relationship quality significantly improved model fit (R^2 change = .03). The addition of event severity at step 2 yielded an insignificant improvement (R^2 change = .02). The addition of partner remorse also improved model fit (R^2 change = .06) as did the fourth variable block, explicit communication (R^2 change = .05). Adjusted R^2 for the resulting model was .12. The stepwise procedure yielded a model that included partner remorse (Beta = .29), explicit communication (Beta = .19), and event severity (Beta = − .17).

In predicting change in relationship quality from before the transgression (Time 1) until the present (Time 3), a similar pattern emerged from the forced entry procedure, with the resulting model yielding an adjusted R^2 of .21. However, the stepwise procedure yielded a model that included all four variable blocks: relationship quality prior to the episode (Beta = − .32), partner remorse (Beta = .21), explicit communication (Beta = .20), and event severity (Beta = − .17). Finally, only

TABLE 14.1 Hierarchical regression table predicting relationship quality measures from prior relationship quality, transgression severity, partner remorse, and explicit conditional forgiveness

| | | Relationship Quality Outcomes ||||||
| | | Current Quality (T3) || Change (T1 to T3) || Change (T2 to T3)[a] ||
Predictor		R^2 change	B	R^2 change	B	R^2 change	B
Step 1	Prior Quality	.03**	.16**	.11***	−.32***	.00	−.03
Step 2	Severity	.02*	−.13*	.02	−.14*	.00	.04
Step 3	Remorse	.06***	.26***	.06***	.25***	.01	.12
Step 4	Explicit CF	.05**	.16**	.06***	16**	.07**	.24**
Total R^2			.12**		.21***		.05**
n			185		182		183

Note: [a] T1 is relationship quality prior to the forgiveness episode; T2 is quality of the relationship immediately after the transition occurred. T3 is quality of the relationship currently (after the episode).
* $p <.10$, ** $p <.01$, *** $p <.001$

the explicit communication variable (R^2 change = .07; Beta = .24) significantly improved model fit in the analysis when the dependent variable was change in quality from Time 2 (immediately after the transgression) to Time 3 (the present time).

To summarize, the quantitative results generally support H2–H5. Prior relationship quality was positively associated with current relationship quality as expected (H2), but results also indicate that high quality relationships experienced greater declines during these CF episodes. Transgression severity had negative effects as predicted by H3, but these were modest. Partner remorse, a measure of forgiveness seeking communication, was a substantive predictor of CF (supporting H4). Perhaps most unequivocal were the results of H5. As expected, explicit communication of conditions was associated with relational improvement on all three measures of relationship quality. Thus, it appears that any deleterious effects of CF may be due to implicit or uncommunicated conditions.

We pursued RQ2 to understand why partners use this approach to forgiveness. Qualitative analysis yielded several predominant motives.

Weighing Relational History

Investment, relational satisfaction, the prospect of a positive outcome, or the concern that a negative trend had begun, all motivated the use of CF. For example, "I used conditional forgiveness because of what we had, the history we had, the way our relationship was and how happy I was, and the fact that she was someone I could see myself with" (010). Participants also noted "out of character" behavior. For example, someone responded, "Because the incident was out of character and I felt as though it was a one-time occurrence and truly would not happen again" (048). Someone else shared, "I used conditional forgiveness because it was the first time that such an incident had happened and because of the length of our relationship" (216). Alternately, an impending trend motivated CF. "Because it had happened previously and I was not willing to tolerate this type of behavior anymore" (207) and "I had already been hurt once before in (a) similar manner and I had not set a condition then" (061).

Restoring/Enacting Moral Standards

CF sometimes defined conduct that was considered to be right or wrong, acceptable and unacceptable. For instance, "I used conditional forgiveness because I don't want to date a drug user" (040). Someone else stated, "I would not tolerate someone who lied to me" (152). Another shared, "Because I loved this woman and did not want to leave her, but I knew I could not tolerate living with an abusive partner again" (121). Severe moral violations were considered "deal breaking" (i.e., "Affairs are not acceptable in any situation" (132)) and in the words of this respondent, intolerable:

> I used conditional forgiveness because the transgression was not something that could be tolerated in my mind and according to my standards. Also, I felt taken advantage of, and did not want to give him the impression that it was something that I would allow myself to go through again
>
> *(122).*

Comments of this kind suggested that through the imposition (or re-imposition) of moral codes, the offended partner regained self-respect and made the relationship itself respectable.

Others felt a moral duty to forgive; CF was an enactment of their commitment to do what seemed right or good. For instance, one empathetic respondent framed the episode as an opportunity to be merciful. "Because I think that everyone makes mistakes, we are only human. If it had been me, I would want someone to give me a second chance" (063).

Clarifying Needs or Expectations

The desire to be explicit, open, and honest motivated CF. For instance, "I felt I should be honest about my feelings in order to allow her to make a decision on a committed relationship" (078). Another shared, "Because she lives in her own world and if I am not explicit in my needs she may well not notice them, and unintentionally do more damage than otherwise intended" (077). A third sounded compelled: "Because I needed to show him how serious I was. I do not want him drinking and driving" (178). As a group, these participants wanted to eliminate ambiguity.

Self/Partner-Protecting

Moving in a different direction, stipulations were sometimes used to protect a victimized partner from future hurt. Someone plainly said, "To protect myself" (163). Another elaborated retrospectively, "Now that I look back I used conditional forgiveness to help myself feel more secure about forgiving him and going back" (023). Some forgivers felt pressured or rushed to forgive or reconcile; consequently, CF provided a way to "slow down" the process. One reported feeling "trapped in the relationship" and another felt uncertain about the future of the relationship, and used conditions during the interim:

> ... it took me by such surprise that I had not had time to let it sink in fully (about what just) happened. I was introduced to the situation and then immediately was asked to (forgive). So I gave forgiveness with a disclaimer attached
>
> *(134).*

Some reported that they used conditions until trust was reestablished. For example, "Because I felt that she was hiding something and I couldn't prove it.

Otherwise I would not have ever talked to her. I consider that forgiveness for now" (135). One person invoked a maxim, "I always have believed the saying 'actions speak louder than words' so saying sorry isn't enough and I have to see that change will/has occurred" (105).

Others were motivated out of concern for a partner's safety. In particular, one person reported, "I didn't want my partner to hurt herself by doing the action she had done. (i.e., drunk driving)" (046).

Enacting Justice/Exerting Control

CF was sometimes offered in the spirit of justice – an effort to even the scales, gain vindication or administer punishment. Often the wounded partner used CF to wrest control of the relationship and the partner. One participant proclaimed, "It's leverage especially if the person knows they screwed up" (190). Another admitted, "It's a way for me to leverage the pain and control the situation" (188). One respondent said, "I was upset and was trying to manipulate her into facing me and owning up to what she did, rather than hiding behind a phone" (209). Some motives were rooted in anger and spite: "Because I was still angry and I didn't trust him any longer. Plus I wanted control ..." (the ellipses are the participant's) (064). Another participant realized she was exerting control. ("I didn't think about it at the time but I used it to control his actions") (198).

CF was also magnanimous, apparently motivated by the partner's efforts to do the right thing. "He seemed to be telling the truth and was very sincere" (181). Another shared, "Because I ... believed he was truly sorry and would never do it again" (131). In these cases, the partners appeared to be atoning for acts of wrongdoing.

Best Alternative to Unconditional or Genuine Forgiveness

Interestingly, some participants conceptualized CF as a "best alternative" to unconditional or what some referred to as "genuine" or "complete" forgiveness. A woman who was trying to forgive her husband for an affair during her third pregnancy said, "It was the start of saving my marriage. It was what was best for me and my children at the time" (203). Another used CF, "Because it is something that is realistic" (215). Others admitted, "I don't know enough about complete forgiveness" (148) and "Because it is the only way for me to even begin to forgive" (091). Two other representative comments: "I think that it was the best form of forgiveness just short of not forgiving my girlfriend" (038) and "I used conditional forgiveness because I did not want to worsen the situation and often fear conflict. I have found that I have a problem with actual forgiveness and often use conditional forgiveness" (026).

Hoping for an Improved Future

The next motive of CF was closely related to the former, best alternative. However, there were two distinct contrasts. First, the overall tone was more hopeful; second, the optimism was focused on the partner's improved behavior. One participant explained, "Because I want to believe that people can change and that people are good people at heart" (169). Another said, "Because I loved her and wanted to believe she could be better" (194).

Metatheme: Facilitating Reconciliation

The desire to fully reconcile with a partner (or not) was an overarching theme that pervaded nearly every account. In fact, reconciliation has been previously conceptualized as *the* underlying concern of conditional forgivers (Kloeber, 2008). When asked why she used CF, one respondent stated flatly, "I wanted my marriage to work" (220). For some, cultural commitments to marriage motivated CF, "it was how I was raised. I am religious, my parents have the mentality that when you marry (you're) in it for life" (208). This participant's commitment to the institution of marriage illustrates the paradox many face when confronting a relationship-threatening transgression – the deeply rooted obligation to stay married in tension with the need for a mutually satisfying, respectful and safe relationship. CF provided the space, "To fix the problem" (168).

Others expressed the desire to reconcile in terms of love, care, or passion. One person explained, "Because I care about her and felt it was necessary, but also that it wasn't a problem to break up over" (206). An impassioned respondent exclaimed, "Because I loved her! Nothing else mattered. Opinions of friends or family didn't matter. She was my world and a person I thought I wanted to be with forever" (226).

Discussion

These results support previous work suggesting that the use of CF is associated with relational decline, over and above other considerations such as the severity of the offense or the remorse expressed by the partner. They also yield new insights. Among them are the distinctions between implicit and explicit CF, the functions of both approaches, the possibility that explicit CF may have facilitating effects, and better understanding of the communication practices and motives associated with this unique form of forgiveness.

Consistent with past research, we observed a precipitous drop in self-reported relationship quality over the course of CF episodes. CF tends to be used after extremely serious episodes (Kloeber, 2008; Waldron & Kelley, 2008), so relationship decline, at least in the short term, is likely. However, it does appear that a wounded partner's approach to CF accounted for as much, perhaps more, of the relational decline than did transgression severity and other elements of the forgiveness model proposed by Waldron and Kelley (2008). In other words, communication matters. Our results pertaining to RQ1 confirm Kloeber's observation: many of those claiming to use CF do not communicate those conditions. Consistent with previous work (Merolla & Zang, 2011; Waldron & Kelley, 2008) it appears that these implicit forgivers are more likely to report negative relational outcomes compared to those who voiced their expectations.

Our results question the prevailing assumption that conditional approaches to forgiveness inevitably lead to negative relational outcomes. Instead, explicitly stating conditions may have facilitated relationship recovery after the transgression. This result is consistent with previous studies suggesting that explicit communication can help ameliorate negativity and repair relationships, even in the face of serious transgressions (Morse & Metts, 2011). Perhaps the use of explicit CF signals relational commitment, a willingness to remain engaged, or hopefulness about the future. Our qualitative analyses reveal that participants' motives for using explicit CF often appeared constructive. They hoped to clarify expectations, reestablish a moral framework, to slow down a conflict that may have been careening out of control. The conditions often seemed to balance the wounded partner's need to protect the self while leaving open the possibility of reconciliation.

Whereas explicit CF may be a constructive response, in the sense that it creates possibilities for reconciliation, the implicit form may serve different purposes. One of these may be retribution. In at least a few cases, the silent setting of conditions denied the offending partner the relief that might accompany forgiveness. Perhaps a kind of quiet justice is extracted in these cases. Another purpose for implicit CF seems to be self-protection. Some partners simply could not verbalize their expectations out of fear that it would escalate conflict, antagonize the partner, or simply prolong a painful relational episode. Finally, implicit CF may be an information seeking strategy, a secret test (Baxter & Wilmot, 1984) to see if the partner "gets it" without being told.

The possibility that explicit CF may benefit relationships is consistent with recent theorizing. Waldron and Kelley (2008) have argued that forgiveness is sometimes a prerequisite for satisfying reconciliation. Their negotiated morality theory (NMT) suggests that forgiving communication can function to clarify and renew the partners' moral commitments. By using CF, some of our participants seemed to be reestablishing common moral ground, a renewed understanding of the commitments that define the relationship. They did so by asserting moral standards, reestablishing relational justice, and acknowledging efforts to atone for misdeeds. Explicit CF may clear the moral undergrowth, making it possible to imagine a relational future defined by shared values and renewed mutual respect.

Kloeber's (2011) dialectic theorizing imagines CF as a way to manage tensions between three competing forces – a cultural/religious mandate to forgive unconditionally, the pressure to reconcile (or terminate) a relationship that has been hurtful, and the need to create the conditions that honor and protect the self. Implicit approaches to CF may resolve these tensions in the direction of self-protection and relationship termination. Silence may be more self-protective than an explicit offer of forgiveness, at least in the short term. Indeed, a five year longitudinal study of married couples found that self-esteem is reduced in partners who continue to forgive recurrent offenses (Luchies et al, 2010). Persistent silence may be harmful as well, as it further disempowers those who are undervalued or abused in relationships (Montalbano-Phelps, 2003). But it may be that users of implicit CF also see the practice as a step toward termination of a relationship that has been persistently hurtful and unsafe. These partners might worry that the act of offering explicit stipulations would convey falsely a sense of commitment to the relationship that they simply do not feel. In this way, implicit CF could be a silent sign of resignation about the future.

In proposing NMT, Waldron and Kelley (2008) suggested that the forgiveness literature is largely psychological, with relatively few studies of forgiveness discourse. The current study identifies concrete communication practices partners use to enact CF. In our surveys, participants described a rich assortment of explicit approaches to CF. For example, some invoked conditions to slow down relational time. They asked for time to decide, claimed the right to take time, or slowed the process to let feelings and intentions become clearer. Another approach was predicated on the communication of emotion in the partner. Did he or she seem remorseful enough? Some conditions were intended to cultivate humility in the partner – to make him or her "beg for forgiveness". Still another approach involved what Waldron and Kelley described as forecasting the relational future. Here the conditions were sometimes cast as confidence building steps. The partner was required to behave in a manner that offered some assurance about what the relationship would be like if forgiveness was granted. These and other forms of explicit CF should be the subject of additional study by discourse analysts.

In his early study of forgiving communication, Kelley (1998) identified a variety of motives for forgiveness, including a desire to reconcile with the offender and the need to regain one's mental health. Our qualitative analysis builds on this early work by exploring why people use conditional forms of forgiveness. Certainly, the goal of reconciliation was prominent in the minds of many of our participants. Consistent with previous research (Guerrero & Bachman, 2010) this theme seemed most prominent when the forgiver was highly invested in the relationship. However, other motives were less reminiscent of Kelley's early work. For some respondents, CF was motivated by a need to exact justice. These forgivers may have been less concerned about the long-term prospects of the relationship. Instead, they were focused on "evening the scales" or the partner learning a lesson. These cases make obvious that justice is often integral to forgiveness, not something distinct. They also remind us that forgiveness needn't always lead to reconciliation. It can stand on its own. Finally, we note that some respondents chose CF as the only feasible option. For these individuals unconditional forgiveness was an unrealistic ideal or simply a naive response to relational wrongdoing.

Methodological Challenges and Areas for Examining Forgiveness in the Future

Our study lends itself to several practical applications for couples, educators, and therapists. First, the "communication part" of forgiveness contributed significantly to partner's self-reported relational outcomes, over and above such factors as relationship quality and offense severity. For that reason, communication educators and therapists may find it useful to help students and clients expand their repertoire of forgiving responses during relational conflicts. Second, romantic partners should know that implicit CF may be an ineffective approach, particularly if relationship reconciliation is a valued goal. Third, our results suggest that CF is used for varied reasons, relationship reconciliation certainly in some cases, but also self-protection, moral commitments, or relational justice. These are worthy goals in and of themselves and CF (rather than unconditional forgiveness) may be preferable during times of relational crisis. Finally, contrary to previous studies, we find evidence that CF is associated with improvements in the quality of some damaged relationships. As some of our participants suggested, it may be the only realistic alternative under some circumstances.

These conclusions are offered with some, well, *conditions*. In particular, we point to the limitations of our research methods, some of which are challenges to the study of forgiveness generally. We chose to collect anonymous survey data in the hope of collecting unvarnished accounts of private and hurtful relational episodes. The descriptions are indeed vivid and seemingly honest, but we are left with limited means of verifying veracity. Participants did report remembering the events clearly. Moreover, the data present only one participant's perspective. Responsibility for transgressions is sometimes shared and forgiveness is a collaborative activity. Future forgiveness researchers should consider collecting data from both parties, perhaps by interviewing the parties separately and then together (see Waldron & Kelley, 2008). Because it is often an intensely private matter, forgiveness is difficult to observe in an ecologically valid manner. However, some couples may be willing to make recordings of their discussions available to researchers, perhaps in conjunction with therapy sessions.

Another caveat comes from the preliminary nature of research on the communication of forgiveness generally, and CF particularly. In our own work we hope to learn more about the circumstances that give rise to the use of CF. We suspect that it is more common after repeated transgressions and when the offending partner is unpredictable, lacking in empathy, or even abusive (Kloeber, 2008). This speaks to a larger concern about the dark side of forgiveness (Waldon & Kelley, 2008). A person who has been victimized should not be compelled to forgive. Indeed, coerced forgiveness is a kind of double victimization. Abusers may be particularly adept at seeking forgiveness as a step toward reconciliation with their victims. CF may offer a defense against such manipulations. Future research is needed on the dynamics of these dark-side interactions.

CF research should be extended to additional relationship contexts. In familial relationships, forgiveness is sometimes perceived as obligatory (Carr & Wang, 2012). In friendships or work relationships that might not be the case. Perhaps CF is more common in such circumstances. We note further that interpersonal acts of forgiveness expose, contest, and enforce the moral standards that partners acquire from cultural and religious sources. Most studies of forgiveness involve samples of people shaped by Western cultures and Judeo-Christian beliefs. Diverse religious and cultural forgiveness practices should be the subject of future research.

There are many obvious methodological challenges to studying forgiveness. Privacy. Capturing organic interactions. Gathering multiple perspectives. These are real and need to be addressed by ethical and creative scholars. But there is another deep human reality of studying forgiveness: People get emotional about it. Forgiveness scholars, especially when we present our work to audiences, need to be prepared for what gets agitated in people. When we conduct community-based forgiveness education, our local group of forgiveness colleagues that includes both authors of this article (Waldron, Kloeber) and Doug Kelley provides a list of resources that includes therapists, forgiveness readings, and our contact information. We also usually devote a large amount of time for group discussion and stay behind talking with community members, sometimes long after events end. We aren't therapists. However, we should be sensitive and thoughtful listeners so that we can connect people with the proper resources. By being fully prepared for the emotional audience member both interpersonally and with adequate resources, we make our work relevant to those who experience conflicts in their close relationships.

Forgiveness can be a constructive and hopeful response to conflict in close relationships. Our participants convince us that it needn't be an unconditional response. But we do find evidence that forgiveness should not be a silent response to relational hurt. Indeed, it appears to us that explicit communication of conditions sets in motion a process that may heal the self and, in some cases, the relationship. Of course, as communication researchers we might be expected to embrace that claim. Forgive us.

References

Anderson, J. (2007). Forgiveness – a relational process: Research and reflections. *European Journal of Psychotherapy, Counseling & Health, 9*(1), 63–76. doi: 10.1080/13642530601164380

Bachman, G. F., & Guerrero, L. K. (2006). Forgiveness, apology, and communicative responses to hurtful events. *Communication Reports, 19*(1), 45–56. doi.org/10.1080/08934210600586357

Baxter, L. A., & Wilmot W. (1984). Secret tests: Social strategies for acquiring information about the state of the relationship. *Human Communication Research, 11*, 171–202.

Bono, G., McCullough, M. E., & Root, L. M. (2008). Forgiveness, feeling connected to others and well-being: Two longitudinal studies. *Personality and Social Psychology Bulletin, 34*, 1406–1419. doi.org/10.1177/0146167207310025

Carr, K., & Wang, T. R. (2012). "Forgiveness isn't a simple process: It's a vast undertaking": Negotiating and communicating forgiveness in nonvoluntary family relationships. *Journal of Family Communication, 12*(1), 40–56. doi.org/10.1080/15267431.2011.629970

Coker, A. L., Smith, P. H., Bethea, L., King, M. R., & McKeown, R. E. (2000). Physical health consequences of physical and psychological intimate partner violence. *Archives of Family Medicine, 9*(5), 451–457. doi.org/10.1001/archfami.9.5.451

Cosgrove, L., & Konstam, V. (2008). Forgiveness and forgetting: Clinical implications for mental health counselors. *Journal of Mental Health Counseling, 30*(1), 1–13.

Enright, R. D. (2001). *Forgiveness is a choice.* Washington, DC: American Psychological Association.

Gordon, K. C., Hughes, F. M., Tomcik, N. D., Dixon, L. J., and Litzinger, S. C. (2009). Widening spheres of impact: The role of forgiveness in marital and family functioning. *Journal of Family Psychology, 23,* 1–13.

Guerrero, L. K., & Bachman, G. F. (2010). Forgiveness and forgiving communication in dating relationships: An expectancy-investment explanation. *Journal of Social & Personal Relationships, 27*(6), 801–823. doi: 10.1177/0265407510373258

Hargrave, T. D. (1994a). Families and forgiveness: A theoretical and therapeutic framework. *The Family Journal: Counseling and Therapy for Couples and Families, 2*(4), 339–348. doi.org/10.1177/1066480794024007

Hargrave, T. D. (1994b). *Families and forgiveness: Healing wounds in the intergenerational family.* New York: Brunner/Mazel Publishers.

Hawk, G. W. (2007). Mending the broken branch: Forgiveness and reconciliation. In W. W. Wilmot, & J. L. Hocker (Eds.), *Interpersonal Conflict* (pp297–325). New York: McGraw Hill.

Kelley, D. (1998). The communication of forgiveness. *Communication Studies, 49,* 255–271. doi.org/10.1080/10510979809368535

Kelley, D. L., & Waldron, V. R. (2005). An investigation of forgiveness-seeking communication and relational outcomes. *Communication Quarterly, 53*(3), 339–358. doi.org/10.1080/01463370500101097

Kelley, D. L., & Waldron, V. R. (2006). Forgiveness: Communicative implications for social relationships. In C. S. Beck (Ed.), *Communication yearbook* (pp303–341). Mahwah, NJ: Lawrence Erlbaum Associates. doi.org/10.1207/s15567419cy3001_7

Kingsley Westerman, C. Y. (2013). How people restore equity at work and play: Forgiveness, derogation, and communication. *Communication Studies, 64*(3), 296–314. doi.org/10.1080/10510974.2012.755641

Kloeber, D. N. (2008, February). The language of conditional forgiveness. Paper presented at the Annual Conference of the Western States Communication Association, Denver/Boulder, CO.

Kloeber, D. N. (2011, November). Voicing the knot of conditional forgiveness. Paper presented at the Annual Conference of the National Communication Association, New Orleans, LA.

Konstam, V., Marx, F., Schurer, J., Harrington, A., Lombardo, N. E., & Deveney, S. (2000). Forgiving: What mental health counselors are telling us. *Journal of Mental Health Counseling, 22*(3), 253–267.

Lawler, K. A., Younger, J. W., Piferi, R. L., Jobe, R. L., Edmondson, K. A., & Jones, W. H. (2005). The unique effects of forgiveness on health: An exploration of pathways. *Journal of Behavioral Medicine, 28*(2), 157–167. doi.org/10.1007/s10865–10005–3665–3662

Lindlof, T. R., Taylor, B. C. (2002). *Qualitative communication research methods* (2nd ed.). Thousand Oaks, CA: Sage Publishers.

Luchies, L. B., Finkel, E. J., McNulty, J. K., & Kumashiro, M. (2010). The doormat effect: When forgiving erodes self-respect and self-concept clarity. *Journal of Personality & Social Psychology, 98*(5), 734–749. doi.org/10.1037/a0017838

Macaskill, A. (2012). A feasibility study of psychological strengths and well-being assessment in individuals living with recurrent depression. *Journal of Positive Psychology, 7*(5), 372–386. doi.org/10.1080/17439760.2012.702783

Merolla, A. J. (2008). Communicating forgiveness in friendships and dating relationships. *Communication Studies, 59*(2), 114–131. doi.org/10.1080/10510970802062428

Merolla, A. J., & Zhang, S. (2011). In the wake of transgressions: Examining forgiveness communication in personal relationships. *Personal Relationships, 18*(1), 79–85. doi.org/10.1111/j.1475-6811.2010.01323.x

Montalbano-Phelps, L. (2003). Discourse of survival: Building families free of unhealthy relationships. *Journal of Family Communication, 3*(3), 149–177. doi.org/10.1207/s15327698jfc0303_02

Morse, C. R., Metts, S. (2011). Situational and communicative predictors of forgiveness following a relational transgression. *Western Journal of Communication. 75*(3), 239–258. doi.org/10.1080/10570314.2011.571652

Roloff, M. E. & Soloman, D. (2002). Conditions under which relational commitment leads to expressing or suppressing relational complaints. *International Journal of Conflict Management, 13*(3), 276. doi.org/10.1108/eb022877

Roloff, M. E., Soule, K. P., & Carey, C. M. (2001). Reasons for remaining in a relationship and responses to relational transgressions. *Journal of Social & Personal Relationships, 18*(3), 362. doi.org/10.1177/0265407501183004

Sidelinger, R. J., & Booth-Butterfield, M. (2007). Mate value discrepancy as predictor of forgiveness and jealousy in romantic relationships. *Communication Quarterly, 55*(2), 207–223. doi.org/10.1080/01463370701290426

Stoia-Caraballo, R., Rye, M. S., Pan, W., Brown Kirschman, K. J., Lutz-Zois, C., & Lyons, A. M. (2008). Negative affect and anger rumination as mediators between forgiveness and sleep quality. *Journal of Behavioral Medicine, 31*(6), 478–488. doi: 10.1007/s10865-10008-9172-9175

Strelan, P. (2006). The prosocial, adaptive qualities of just world beliefs: Implications for the relationship between justice and forgiveness. *Personality and Individual Differences, 43*(4), 881–890. doi.org/10.1016/j.paid.2007.02.015

Strelan, P., McKee, I., Calic, D., Cook, L., & Shaw, L. (2013). For whom do we forgive? A functional analysis of forgiveness. *Personal Relationships, 20*(1), 124–139. doi.org/10.1111/j.1475-6811.2012.01400.x

Tracy, S. J. (2013). *Qualitative research methods: Collecting evidence, crafting analysis, communicating impact.* Hoboken, NJ: Wiley-Blackwell.

Waldron, V. R., & Kelley, D. L. (2005). Forgiving communication as a response to relational transgressions. *Journal of Social and Personal Relationships, 22*(6), 723–742. doi.org/10.1177/0265407505056445

Waldron, V. R., & Kelley, D. L. (2008). *Communicating forgiveness.* Newberry Park, CA: Sage Publishers.

Whited, M., Wheat, A., & Larkin, K. (2010). The influence of forgiveness and apology on cardiovascular reactivity and recovery in response to mental stress. *Journal of Behavioral Medicine, 33*(4), 293–304. doi.org/10.1007/s10865-10010-9259-9257

Worthington, E. L. (Ed.). (2005). *Handbook of forgiveness.* New York: Routledge.

Worthington, E. L. (2006). *Forgiveness and reconciliation: Theory and application.* New York: Routledge.

INDEX

Bold page numbers indicate figures, *italic* numbers indicate tables.

Abbott, L. 96
Abra, G. 76, 81, 84
abusive relationships 96
accommodation of problem behavior 95–6
actor effects 98
actor-partner-interdependence-model 19, **20**, 32–3, **33**, 98, 100, **100**, 152
adolescent-parent conflict: as characteristic of developmental stage 166; coding of behavior 172–3; demand/withdraw pattern 166–7, 172–3, 174–9; emotion experience 167–70; future research 179–80; importance of 166; limitation of research 179; methodology for research 171–2; negative emotion experience 168–70, 173, 174, 175–8; perceived resolvability 170–1, 173, 174–5, 178–9
adulthood: and childhood experiences of verbal aggression 11–12. *See also* domestic labor conflict; marital conflict; parent-child conflict; parental conflict
affective style 215–16
Afifi, T. 59, 97, 149, 155–6, 188, 191
aggression: and alcoholism 216–17. *See also* verbal aggression
Agostinelli, J. 147
Alberts, J. K. 146, 244–5
alcoholism 216–17
allostatic load 212–13
argumentative skills deficiency model 11–12

arguments: types of 113. *See also* serial arguments
Arroyo, A. 216
authority and power 77–8
avatar, interaction with 245
avoidance: children in divorced/non-divorced families 186–8; and communication skills of parents 195–8; conflict-related cognitions 149–54, **154**; dependence power 96–7, 99; domestic labor conflict 147–50, 149–54, **154**; forms of 147–8; negative outcomes of 148; parental conflict 195–8, 201; reasons for 148–50; serial arguments 130–1, 137; sexual discrepancies 49, 50–1; surveying perceptions of 156; tactics 155–6; technology-mediated communication 59, 63–4, 65, *66*, 67
avoidance-distributive-integrative conflict strategy typology 129

Bacharach, S. B. 97
Beauchaine, T. P. 15
Becker, P. E. 147
behavior: accommodation of problem behavior 95–6; directed 13; verbal aggression as 13
behavioral activation system (BAS) 15, 22
behavioral inhibition system (BIS) 15–16, 22

beliefs: about power 82; domestic labor conflict 149–54, **154**
Benin, M. H. 147
Bevan, J. L. 81, 113, 130, 133
biological mediators 208
blood pressure 210
bolstering effect 231
borderline personality disorders (BPD) 218–19
Branje, S. J. T. 167
Burgoon, J. K. 76, 82, 83

cardiovascular functioning 210
Carey, C. M. 251
Carr, K. 117
Cate, R. M. 40, 49
Caughlin, J. P. 61, 67, 166–7
cell phones. *See* technology-mediated communication
Chen, E. 212
child-parent conflict: as characteristic of developmental stage 166; coding of behavior 172–3; demand/withdraw pattern 166–7, 172–3, 174–9; emotion experience 167–70; future research 179–80; importance of 166; limitation of research 179; methodology for research 171–2; negative emotion experience 168–70, 173, 174, 175–8; perceived resolvability 170–1, 173, 174–5, 178–9
childhood experiences: behavioral activation system (BAS) 15; behavioral inhibition system (BIS) 15–16; methodological challenges 24; social learning theory 21–2; verbal aggression 11–12, 15–21, **20**
children: avoidance of parental conflict 195–8, 201; as caught in the middle of parental conflict 187–8, 194–5, 201; communication skills of parents 189, 193, 195–8; compromised parenting 213; conflict patterns in divorced/non-divorced families 188–9; in divorced/non-divorced families 186–8; health outcomes 211–14; inappropriate disclosures to 190–1; mental health 214–19; parental conflict, impact of on 185, 188; perceptions of parental conflict 189–91; physiology of 212–13; static/erratic emotional reactions in parental conflict discussion 199–201; underestimation of knowledge of parental conflict 198–9

chilling effect 96–7
Cho, V. 59
clinical endpoints 208
cognition/cognitive processes: behavioral activation system (BAS) 15, 22; behavioral inhibition system (BIS) 15–16, 22; conflict-related cognitions 149–54, **154**; and dependence power 94–5; schemas 14. *See also* desensitization to conflict
cognitive-contextual framework 188
collectivistic forgiveness 233, 243
communication: constructive 114–15; distributive 130, 137; domestic labor conflict 145–6; forgiveness styles 235–40, *236*; integrative 129–30, 137, 145–6; multiple goals theories of 59–60; patterns 129; skills of parents with children 189, 193, 195–8, 203; styles 58–9, 69
communication interdependence perspective 60–1, 67–8
communication technologies. *See* technology-mediated communication
complaint expression. *See* dependence power
Comstock, J. 42
conditional forgiveness: as alternative to complete forgiveness 259; antecedent perceptions of 253; clarification of expectations through 258; complexity of 252–3; control gained through 259; and culture 264; definitions of forgiveness 250–1; explicit/implicit 252, 253, 261–2; frequency of 252; future research 243–4; history, relational 257; hope and improvement 259–60; implicit/explicit 252, 253, 261–2; justice gained through 259; methodology/methodological challenges 253–5, 262–4; negative side to 263; negotiated morality theory (NMT) 261; protection of self/partner through 258–9; quality, relationship 255–7, *256*; quality of relationship 253, 260–1; reasons for using 251, 257–60, 262; and reconciliation 260; relational consequences 252; restoring/enacting moral standards through 257–8, 261; results of study 255–60, *256*; severity of transgression 253; as style of forgiveness 235, 237–8, 251; variety of conditions 262
conflict: cultures of 1; desensitization to 13–14; persistent interest in 2; as a tide 1–2

conflict strategies typology 129–31, 134–5, 137–8
Constantine, M. G. 218
constructive communication 114–15
control attempts 78–9, 80
Coontz, S. 156
coping strategies: constructive communication 114–15; desensitization to conflict 24–5; destructive/constructive 114–15; resigned stance 114; serial arguments 114–15; soulmate theory 36
cortisol 14, 19–21, **20,** 209
Creasey, G. 169
cross-citing 2
culture(s): and conditional forgiveness 263–4; of conflict 1; Dyadic Power Theory 87–8; and forgiveness 233, 238, 243; marriage, commitment to 260
Cummings, E. M. 188, 190
Cupach, W. R. 40, 42

Davies, P. T. 170, 188
deescalation of conflict 47, *48,* 50–1
demand/withdraw pattern: domestic labor conflict 148; future research 36; goals-based approach 176; health impacts 29; limitations of study 36; negative emotion experience 168–70, 174, 176–8; parent-child conflict 166–7, 172–3, 174–9; partner-demand/self-withdraw 29; perceived resolvability 170–1, 178–9; resolution 112, 116; self-demand/partner-withdraw 29; serial arguments 112, 116, 131–2, 139; in serial arguments 28–9; and soulmate theory 30, 31–6, *32,* **33,** *34;* topic ownership 166
dependence power: abusive relationships 96; accommodation of problem behavior 95–6; actor effects 98; actor-partner-interdependence-model 98, 100, **100;** avoidance during conflicts 96–7, 99; as cause **and** effect of communication 103–4; chilling effect 96–7; and cognition in relationships 94–5; concept of 93–4; as formative index 98, 99; future research 102, 103; males/females 99–102; measures 99; method for study 98–9; operationalization of 98, 99; partner effects 98; relationship-specific, dependence as 102; resource-specific, dependence as 102; self and partner power 97; theoretical implications of study 100–2; uncertainty in relationships 95; verbal aggression 101–2
depression 217–18
desensitization to conflict: childhood experiences of verbal aggression 15–21, **20;** as form of coping 24–5; methodology/methodological challenges 24–5; stress response system 17–21, **20;** verbal aggression 13–14, 22–3
destiny theory 30
Deutsch, F. M. 146
direct/indirect forgiveness 235, 237
directed behavior 13
disrupted attachment 218
distributive communication 130, 137
divorced/non-divorced families: caught in the middle, children as 187–8, 194–5; children in 186–8; co-parenting 186; conflict patterns 188–9; parental conflict 186–8; stressors 187
domains, relational 85–7
domestic labor conflict 78; avoidance 147–50; belief structures 149–54, **154;** 'capturing' avoidance 155–6; cognitions, conflict-related 149–54, **154;** demand/withdraw pattern 148; between different residencies 145; dyadic analyses 155; emotional costs 150; forms of avoidance 147–8; and health 146; heterosexual couples 145–6; hidden disagreement 147; historical context 157; implicit agreement 146–7, 157; incompatibility of negotiating 150, 157; integrative communication 145–6; management of conflicts 145; methodology/methodological challenges 151–2, 155–8; perceived resolvability 149–50; precedent, adherence to 146–7; public/private spheres of work 157; reasons for avoiding 148–50; research on 144–5; results of study 152–4, **154;** silent agreement 146–7, 157; socio-cultural contexts 156–8; sources of 144; voice effect 145; women and 145; worth of engaging in 156–7
dominance: Dyadic Power Theory **79,** 79–80; perceptions of 82
doormat effect 231
Duck, S. 241–2, 245
Dunbar, N. E. 76, 77, 78–9, 80–1, 82, 83, 84
Duran, R. L. 59

dyadic data 18–19, 32, **33**
Dyadic Power Theory: aims of 76; authority 77–8; beliefs about power 82; control attempts 78–9, 80; cultural differences 87–8; domains, relational 85–7; dominance **79**, 79–80; future expansion of 85–8; household labor conflict 78; inequalities and relational satisfaction 81–2; interactional factors 78–80, **79**; methodological challenges in testing 82–4; naturally-occurring relationships 83–4; organizational actors 88; perceived power and control relationship 78–80; perceptions of dominance 82; post-interactional factors 80–2; pre-interactional factors 77–8; relational satisfaction 80–1; resources and power 77–8, 88; self-report data 82–3; stigma of low power 83; studies of 76, 77; types of relationships 84; unequal couples, difficulties researching 83

eating disorders 215–16
emotion: domestic labor conflict 150; emotion experience in parent-child conflict 167–70; emotional security hypothesis 188; experience during parent-child conflict 167–70; expressed emotion 215–16; negative emotion experience 168–70, 173, 174, 175–8; in research situations 264; static/erratic reactions in parental conflict discussion 199–201
endocrine system 208–9
escalated conflicts in sexual communication 47
ethical conduct in research 25
expressed emotion 215–16

family relationships. *See* childhood experiences; children; domestic labor conflict; marital conflict; parent-child conflict; parental conflict; physiology/physiological systems/health
family-wide effect of conflict 213–14
Faulkner, S. 41
Feeney, J. A. 218
Fehr, R. 229, 232
Fincham, F. D. 188
Folger, R. 145
forgiveness: antecedent variables 231–2; benefits of 230, 250; bolstering effect 231; categories of granting 251; as communication- and meaning-centered process 240–4; communication of 233–40, *236*; as critical to relationship repair 228; and culture 233, 238, 243; definitions 228–9, 250–1; direct/indirect 235, 237, 238; doormat effect 231; everyday acts of 229, 240–1; evolutionary perspective 230–1; forms of 229–30; frequency of 229–30; individualism/collectivism 233, 243; meaning-centered perspective 242–4; methodological challenges 244–5; model, communication 238–40; negative effects of 230–1, 243; negotiated morality theory (NMT) 240; reasons for 231–3; and reconciliation 228–9, 251; relational damage/satisfaction 237–8; and resentment 230; and revenge 231; stories of 227–8; styles of 235–40, *236*; talk and meaning in relationships 241–4; and time 232–3; transgressions, levels of 230; value-neutral stance 230–1; verbal/nonverbal 234; virtuist stance 230. *See also* conditional forgiveness
Franiuk, R. 31, 35–6
Frazier, P. 167–8
Frisby, B. N. 58

gender roles: and alcoholism 216–17; dependence power 99–102; domestic labor conflict 145, 148–9
Gerlach, T. M. 229
goals: in communication 59–61, 67, 81; demand/withdraw pattern 176; serial arguments 81, 130, 134
Gottman, J. M. 29, 145
Gouin, J. P. 209–10
Graham, J. E. 209–10
Gray, J. A. 15
Greene, K. 41
ground theory approach 46
Grych, J. H. 188

Haber, J. G. 234–5
Hample, D. 133
Hansell, S. 212
harm due to serial arguments 113–15, 116–17, 122
health. *See* physiology/physiological systems/health
Heavey, C. L. 171
Heffner, K. L. 209
Hesson-McInnis, M. 169

heterosexual couples, domestic labor conflict between 145–6
Hoff, N. 111–12
Holmgren, M. 230
Hook, J. N. 229, 233
household labor conflict. *See* domestic labor conflict
Huggins, C. E. 168
Hung, H. 59
hypothalmic pituitary adrenal axis 14

illness. *See* physiology/physiological systems/health
immune functioning 209–10, 212
implicit decision-making: conditional forgiveness 252, 253, 261–2; domestic labor conflict 146–7, 157; theories of relationships 30–1
individualistic forgiveness 233, 243
inflammation 209–10, 212
information communication technologies (ICTs). *See* technology-mediated communication
initiator/resistor roles 139; in serial arguments 28–9, 30–1, 115–17, 118–19, 122–3; and soulmate theory 31–6, *32*, **33**, *34*
integrative communication 129–30, 137, 145–6
interdependence 60–1, 67–8; arguments as continuing, likelihood of 117–18; future research 124; longitudinal studies 123; measurement of role in serial arguments 123; methodological challenges 123; methodology for research 119–20; partner's views, consideration of 117–18; results of research 120, *121*, 122; roles in serial arguments 118–19, 122–3; serial arguments 117–25, *121*; voicing of concerns, tendency to 118
interparental conflict. *See* parental conflict
interviews 44–5
involvement 125

Johnson, K. L. 112, 113, 115–16, 117, 128

Kanter, M. 59
Keck, L. K. 69
Kelley, D. L. 235, 240, 250–1, 261, 262
Kelly, L. 59
Kiecolt-Glaser, J. K. 29, 209
Kloeber, D. N. 252, 261
Knobloch, L. K. 95
Komter, A. 149

La France, B. H. 41
Lawler, E. J. 97
Lindlof, T. R. 255
loneliness 218
Loschiavo, R. 244–5
Luchies, L. B. 231
Lundberg, O. 212

Malis, R. S. 112–13, 113–14, 116, 119, 166–7
Mania, E. W. 232
Margolin, G. 188
marital conflict: and adult physical health 208–11; compromised parenting due to 213. *See also* domestic labor conflict; parental conflict; serial arguments; sexual communication; sexual discrepancies
McCullough, M. E. 228, 230–1, 231–2, 232–3
McGinn, M. M. 208
McNaughton, N. 15
McNulty, J. 231, 243
meaning in relationships 241–4
Mechanic, D. 212
Mejia, R. 80
men: and alcoholism 216–17; domestic labor conflict 148
mental health: alcoholism 216–17; children 214–19; depression 217–18; disrupted attachment 218; eating disorders 215–16; expressed emotion 215–16; and family conflict 214–19; intrusiveness from parents 215; loneliness 218; mood disorders 217–18; personality disorders 218–19; sensitization hypothesis 214; serial arguments 113–15, 116–17, 122; social anxiety 218. *See also* desensitization to conflict; physiology/physiological systems/health
Merolla, A. J. 237–40, 251
messages: aggressive 11, 17–18, 21, 23, 24, 25; carried between conflicted parents 187; compliance-gaining 81; control attempts 79; and goals 60; serial arguments 129, 130, 137, 138, 139, 140; technology-mediated 58–9, 63, *64, 66,* 67, 68, 81
metabolic syndrome 210
methodology/methodological challenges: assessment of conflict 219–20; audio recordings 245; avatar, interaction with 245; capturing avoidance 155–6; capturing interaction 244–5; coding of

behavior 172–3; conditional forgiveness 253–5, 262–4; demand/withdraw 36; dependence power 98–9; desensitization to conflict 24–5; diversity of research methods 138–9; domestic labor conflict 151–2, 155–8; dyadic analyses 155; Dyadic Power Theory 82–4; emotion in research situations 264; ethical conduct 25; experience sampling approaches 244; forgiveness 244–5; health and conflict 219–20; measurement bias 23; measurement of role in serial arguments 123; media narratives 245; mother-adolescent conflict 171–2, 179; naturally-occurring relationships 83–4; operationalization of childhood experiences 24; parental conflict 191–3, 201–2; self-report data 51, 52, 82–3, 244; serial arguments 119–20, 123, 133–5, 138–9; sexual communication 43–5, 51–2; socio-cultural contexts 156–8; suppression of indicators in laboratory setting 83–4; technology-mediated communication 62–3, 68; thematic analysis 46; as theme 2; unequal power couples, difficulties researching 83; veracity of accounts, verifying 263; video recall 186, 192, 193–201, 201–3

Metts, S. 40, 42
Miller, C. W. 114, 117
Miller, G. E. 212
mobile phones. *See* technology-mediated communication
Moen, P. 147
mood disorders 217–18
mortality 211
mother-adolescent conflict: as characteristic of developmental stage 166; coding of behavior 172–3; demand/withdraw pattern 172–3, 174–9; emotion experience 168; future research 179–80; importance of 166; limitation of research 179; methodology for research 171–2; negative emotion experience 173, 174, 175–8; perceived resolvability 170–1, 173, 174–5, 178–9
motivational systems 15–16, 22
multiple goals theories of communication 59–60, 67
Murray, S. L. 30

negative affective style 215–16
negotiated morality theory (NMT) 240, 261
nervous system 212–13
neuroendocrine functioning 208–9
nonverbal communication 12–13, 234

organizational dyads 88

parent-child conflict: acculturation 218; as characteristic of developmental stage 166; coding of behavior 172–3; demand/withdraw pattern 166–7, 172–3, 174–9; emotion experience 167–70; future research 179–80; importance of 166; limitation of research 179; methodology for research 171–2; negative emotion experience 168–70, 173, 174, 175–8; perceived resolvability 170–1, 173, 174–5, 178–9
parental conflict: avoidance 195–8, 201; caught in the middle, children as 187–8, 194–5, 201; children, impact on 185; co-parenting 186; cognitive-contextual framework 188; communication skills of parents with children 189, 193, 195–8, 203; compromised parenting due to 213; conflict patterns 188–9; data analysis 192; differing reactions to videos 202; divorced/non-divorced families 186–8, 188–9; emotional security hypothesis 188; escalation of negativity 193; future research 202; inappropriate disclosures to children 190–1; methodology for research 191–3; mood disorders 217–18; perceptions of, parents' and children's 189–91, 193–201; positive conversations 193–4; static/erratic emotional reactions 199–201; theoretical frameworks 188; underestimation of child's knowledge of 198–9; video recall 186, 192, 193–201, 201–3
parenting: compromised 213; intrusiveness from parents 215. *See also* parent-child conflict
partner-demand/self-withdraw 29
partner effects 98
perceived power and control, relationship between 78–9
perceived resolvability 120, 123, 130, 131, 132, 134, 149–50; parent-child conflict 170–1, 173, 174–5, 178–9
perception(s): antecedent, of conditional forgiveness 253; of avoidance 156; of dominance 82; of parental conflict 189–91, 193–201; self 13

personal harm. *See* mental health; physiology/physiological systems
personality disorders 218–19
physical violence in relationships 96
physiology/physiological systems/health: alcoholism 216–17; allostatic load 212–13; biological mediators 208; blood pressure 210; cardiovascular functioning 210; child health outcomes 211–14; children's 212–13; clinical endpoints 208; compromised parenting 213; demand/withdraw, impact of 29; desensitization to conflict 14; domestic labor conflict 146; endocrine system 208–9; family-wide effect of conflict 213–14; forgiveness 230; hypothalmic pituitary adrenal axis 14; immune functioning 209–10, 212; inflammation 209–10, 212; marital conflict and adult health 208–11; metabolic syndrome 210; methodology/methodological challenges 219–20; mortality 211; nervous system 212–13; neuroendocrine functioning 208–9; serial arguments, harm caused by 113–15, 116–17, 122; soulmate theory 36; stress response system 17–21, **20**; surrogate endpoints 208. *See also* mental health
power in dyadic relationships: theories 75. *See also* Dyadic Power Theory
privacy 51–2, *64*, 65, 83, 155, 158, 263, 264
private/public spheres of work 157

qualitative coding 255

Rabby, M. 244–5
Rahim, M. E. 50
Ramey, M. E. 166
reconciliation: and conditional forgiveness 260; and forgiveness 228–9, 251
relational communication. *See* marital conflict; parent-child conflict; parental conflict; serial arguments; sexual communication; technology-mediated communication
relational domains 85–7
relational satisfaction 80–2; demand/withdraw pattern 131; forgiveness 237–8; resolution 112–13; serial arguments 112–13
resentment and forgiveness 230
resistor/initiator roles 139; in serial arguments 30, 115–17, 118–19, 122–3; and soulmate theory 31–6, *32*, **33**, *34*

resolution: demand/withdraw 112, 116; domestic labor conflict 149–50; parents' conflict resolution skills 189; perceived resolvability 112–13, 114, 120, 123, 130, 132, 134; relational satisfaction 112–13; serial arguments 112–13, 114, 115, 116, 123, 130, 132
resources: dependence as resource-specific 102; and power 77–8, 88
revenge and forgiveness 231
Reznik, R. M. 114
Rick, B. M. 232
Roaru, T. 59
Robbins, S. 59
Robles, T. F. 208
roles in serial arguments 28–9, 30–1, 115–17, 118–19, 122–3, 139
Roloff, M. E. 94, 112–13, 113–15, 115–16, 117, 119, 128, 251
romantic relationships: negative emotion experience 169; verbal aggression in 15–17, 23. *See also* forgiveness; parental conflict; sexual communication; sexual discrepancies
rumination: and conflict strategies 130–1; measurement of 135; and serial arguments 133–8
Rusbult, C. E. 117–18, 238

Sagrestano, L. M. 101
Samp, J. A. 69, 96, 97, 168
Sandage, S. J. 233
satisfaction, relational 80–2; demand/withdraw pattern 131; forgiveness 237–8; resolution 112–13; serial arguments 112–13
schemas 14
Schrodt, P. 188
Scobie, E. D. 230
Scobie, G. E. W. 230
Scott, A. M. 67
Segrin, C. 216
self-concept 13
self-demand/partner-withdraw 29
self-perception 13
self-report data 51, 52, 82–3, 244
sensitization hypothesis 214
serial arguments: avoidance 130–1, 137; communication patterns 129; conflict strategies 129–31, 134–5, 137–8; as continuing, likelihood of 117–18, 137–8; coping strategies 114–15; cyclical nature of 112; defined 128; demand/

withdraw 112, 116, 131–2, 139; demand/withdraw in 28–9; descriptive model of 111–12; distributive communication 130, 137; diversity of research methods 138–9; future research 124–5, 139–40; goal orientation 81; goals 130, 134; harm caused by 113–15, 116–17, 122; initiator/resistor roles 28–9, 30–1, 115–17; integrative communication 129–30; interdependence in 117–25, *121*; involvement 125; longitudinal studies 123, 132–3; measurement of role in 123; messages, observing 138, 139; methodology/methodological challenges 119–20, 123, 133–5, 138–9; origin of concept 111, 128; partner's views, consideration of 117–18; perceived resolvability 112–13, 114, 116, 120, 123, 130, 132, 134; process model 130, 131, 133; research attention 128; resigned stance 114; resolution 120, 123, 132; resolvability 112–13, 114, 115, 116; results of research 120, *121,* 122, 135, *136,* 137; role in 28–9, 30–1, 115–17, 118–19, 122–3, 139; and rumination 133–8; same-sex relationships 139–40; satisfaction, relational 112–13, 120, 122; and soulmate theory 30–1, 31–6, *32,* **33,** *34*; stress 122; stress caused by 113–15, 116–17; theoretical implications 124–5; types of arguments 113; voicing of concerns, tendency to 118

sexual communication: amount of discussion 47, 49; avoidance strategies 49, 50–1; deescalation of conflict 47, *48,* 50–1; depth of discussion 47; escalated conflicts 47; future research 51–2; importance of 41–2; interview protocol 44–5; methodological challenges 51–2; methodology 43–5; no conflict reported 49; purpose of study 42–3; romantic relationships 41–2; self-report data 51, 52; and sexual discrepancies 42–51, *45, 48*; studies on 41–2; thematic analysis 46; triggers for conflict 50

sexual discrepancies: amount of discussion 47, 49; avoidance strategies 49, 50–1; communication around 42–51, *45, 48*; deescalation of conflict *48,* 50–1; defined 40; depth of discussion 47; escalated conflicts 47; future research 51–2; interview protocol 44–5;

methodological challenges 51–2; methodology 43–5; no conflict reported 49; potential for conflict 40; purpose of study 42–3; self-report data 51, 52; thematic analysis 46; triggers for conflict 50

Sharabi, L. L. 61
Siegel, R. B. 157
Sillar, A. L. 129
Singer, M. I. 23, 125
Slatcher, R. B. 208
smart phones. *See* technology-mediated communication
Smith, J. C. S. 78
Smith, T. W. 210
social anxiety 218
social learning theory 21–2
social media. *See* technology-mediated communication
socio-cultural contexts 156–8. *See also* culture(s)
Solomon, D. H. 94–5, 97, 102
Soule, K. P. 251
soulmate theory: as coping strategy 36; and serial arguments 30–1, 31–6, *32,* **33,** *34*
Sprecher, S. 40, 49
Stern, M. I. 219
strategies. *See* coping strategies
stress: childhood experiences of 17–21, **20,** 22; demand/withdraw pattern 131; desensitization to conflict 14; divorced/non-divorced families 187; hormones 209; serial arguments 113–15, 116–17, 122
Sun, S. 238
surrogate endpoints 208
surveys: perceptions of avoidance 156. *See also* individual topics

talk and meaning in relationships 241–4
Tashiro, T. 167–8
Taylor, B. C. 255
technology-mediated communication: analysis of results 63; avoidance of face-to-face conflict through 65, *66,* 67; as avoidance strategy 59; communication interdependence perspective 60–1, 67–8; communication styles 58–9; disinterest shown by use of 67; in existing conflicts 58–9; during face-to-face conflicts 63, *64,* 65; future research 68–9; goals in communication 59–61; integration with face-to-face 61, 67–8; interference/

facilitation distinction 61; lack of research on 57, 58–9; limitations of study 68–9; method for study 62–3; methodological challenges 68; multiple goals theories of communication 59–60, 67; overall results 66–7; potential benefits of using 58; as source of contention 59; understanding of, need for 57

tide, conflict as a 1–2

time and forgiveness 232–3

Trapp, R. 111–12, 128

Trombello, J. M. 208

uncertainty in relationships 95

verbal aggression: action/reaction distinction 23–4; argumentative skills deficiency model 11–12; as attack on self-concept 13; as behavior 13; behavioral activation system (BAS) 15, 22; behavioral inhibition system (BIS) 15–16, 22; childhood experiences 11–12, 15–21, **20**; defined 11, 12–13; dependence power 101–2; desensitization to conflict 13–14, 22–3; as directed 13; as directed behavior 13; ethical conduct in research 25; hypothalmic pituitary adrenal axis 14; measurement bias 23; methodological challenges 24; and nonverbal communication 12–13; in romantic relationships 15–17, 23; social learning theory 21–2; stress response system 17–21, **20**, 22

Verhofstadt, L. L. 167

video recall 186, 192, 193–201, 201–3

voice effect 145

Waldron, V. R. 235, 240, 250–1, 261, 262

Westerman, D. 58

Wheeless, L. 41–2

Whisman, M. A. 210

Wiesmann, S. 146, 147, 149, 150

Williamson, I. 233

Winsper, C. 219

women: and alcoholism 216–17; domestic labor conflict 145, 148–9

Worthington, E. L. 228, 230

Yela, C. 41

Yelsma, P. 42

Yoshimura, C. G. 244–5

Zhang, S. 237, 238

Taylor & Francis eBooks

Helping you to choose the right eBooks for your Library

Add Routledge titles to your library's digital collection today. Taylor and Francis ebooks contains over 50,000 titles in the Humanities, Social Sciences, Behavioural Sciences, Built Environment and Law.

Choose from a range of subject packages or create your own!

Benefits for you
- Free MARC records
- COUNTER-compliant usage statistics
- Flexible purchase and pricing options
- All titles DRM-free.

Benefits for your user
- Off-site, anytime access via Athens or referring URL
- Print or copy pages or chapters
- Full content search
- Bookmark, highlight and annotate text
- Access to thousands of pages of quality research at the click of a button.

REQUEST YOUR FREE INSTITUTIONAL TRIAL TODAY

Free Trials Available
We offer free trials to qualifying academic, corporate and government customers.

eCollections – Choose from over 30 subject eCollections, including:

Archaeology	Language Learning
Architecture	Law
Asian Studies	Literature
Business & Management	Media & Communication
Classical Studies	Middle East Studies
Construction	Music
Creative & Media Arts	Philosophy
Criminology & Criminal Justice	Planning
Economics	Politics
Education	Psychology & Mental Health
Energy	Religion
Engineering	Security
English Language & Linguistics	Social Work
Environment & Sustainability	Sociology
Geography	Sport
Health Studies	Theatre & Performance
History	Tourism, Hospitality & Events

For more information, pricing enquiries or to order a free trial, please contact your local sales team:
www.tandfebooks.com/page/sales

Routledge
Taylor & Francis Group

The home of
Routledge books

www.tandfebooks.com